FROM THE MINERS' DOUBLEHOUSE

FROM THE MINERS' DOUBLEHOUSE

Archaeology and Landscape in a
Pennsylvania Coal Company Town

Karen Bescherer Metheny

University of Tennessee Presss / Knoxville

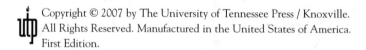
LIBRARY OF CONGRESS CATALOGING-IN-PUBLICATION DATA

Metheny, Karen Bescherer, 1960–
From the miners' doublehouse : archaeology and landscape in a Pennsylvania coal
company town / Karen Bescherer Metheny. — 1st ed.
    p. cm.
Includes bibliographical references.
ISBN-13: 978-1-57233-495-3 (hardcover : alk. paper)
ISBN-10: 1-57233-495-9 (hardcover : alk. paper)

1. Helvetia (Pa.)—Antiquities. 2. Helvetia (Pa.)—Social life and customs. 3. Coal
miners—Pennsylvania—Helvetia—Social life and customs. 4. Community life—Pennsylvania—Helvetia—History. 5. Coal mines and mining—Social aspects—Pennsylvania—
Helvetia—History. 6. Landscape—Social aspects—Pennsylvania—Helvetia—History.
7. Helvetia (Pa.)—Buildings, structures, etc. 8. Company towns—Pennsylvania—Case
studies. 9. Helvetia (Pa.)—Biography. 10. Oral history. I. Title.

F159.H475M37 2007
974.8'61—dc22   2006011487

To Rookie, whose footsteps led me here.

CONTENTS

ILLUSTRATIONS

FIGURES

TABLES

ACKNOWLEDGMENTS

I owe a debt of gratitude to many individuals who assisted in the preparation of this volume. I must surely begin with those people who are the subject of this study, the former residents of Helvetia, Pennsylvania, and the former employees of Helvetia Mine. I would like to thank in particular the individuals who consented to participate in oral history interviews for this project: Veronica McKee, Thomas Crop, William and Sara Crop, Lloyd Gray, and William "Rookie" Brown. I must also thank Tom Bukousky of the *DuBois Courier-Express*, Ray Yusnukis, Samuel King, Raymond Kriner, Betty Haddow Hamilton, Marlin Deitch, Doris Andrulonis, Ron and Gary Chollock, James Haag, and the many other individuals who helped to shepherd me through this process, loaning materials for this study and sharing with me photographs, videotapes, news clippings, and other remembrances of this community. Though they are too numerous to mention here, I wish to acknowledge the dozens of individuals who formerly made their home in Helvetia and gave up their time to talk to me at the Helvetia reunion or stopped by the excavation site to add what they could to the oral history of this community. It is with regret that I note the passing of several of these individuals in the years since our collaborative study of Helvetia's coal mining history: Raymond Kriner, Sara Haag Crop, "Bunny" Lloyd Gray, James Haag, and William Brown, my husband's grandfather and a sorely missed friend and companion.

I wish to acknowledge Eileen Cooper, Phillip Zorich, and staff members working in the Special Collections Department at Stapleton Library, Indiana University of Pennsylvania. Eileen helped me to find my way through the vast archive of official papers belonging to the Rochester and Pittsburgh Coal Company, while her staff members willingly responded to my many inquiries and carried endless boxes of company papers back and forth for my use. Eileen regularly brought me copies of documents that she thought might be of interest to me—

from correspondence between members of the local branch of the United Mine Workers of America to documents concerning benefits and compensation for Helvetia's miners. I am grateful for her interest and for the assistance that she extended to me from our first meeting. Thanks also to Pamela Seighman of the Coal and Coke Heritage Center at Penn State Fayette, Diane Reed of the Pennsylvania Historical and Museum Commission, Mary Louise de Sarran of the Maryland Historical Trust, and especially Paula Zitzler of the Westsylvania Heritage Corporation for their assistance in tracking down the originals of several elusive photographs.

I extend my deepest thanks to Andrew Kovalchick of the Kovalchick Salvage Company, Sykesville, Pennsylvania, for granting me permission to access the town and mine site and to conduct excavations at the doublehouse. I also wish to recognize the Rochester and Pittsburgh Coal Company of Indiana, Pennsylvania. Mr. Dave Davis, manager of human resources; Neil Kok, land manager; and Al Miller, real estate manager, provided invaluable assistance, making arrangements for me to conduct an architectural survey of the engineer's house that still stands in Helvetia, procuring a copy of Eileen Cooper's history of the R&P Coal Company for my use, and searching the home office for maps, blueprints, and documents that might be of interest. I was saddened to learn that the R&P no longer exists. A merger with Consol Energy in 1998 brought to a close a chapter of our industrial past spanning 117 years. I do thank Marshall W. Hunt of Consol Energy for his help in locating materials originally obtained from the R&P's main office and for authorizing the use of those materials in the present study.

The research presented in this volume was funded by a predoctoral grant from the Wenner-Gren Foundation for Anthropological Research. The grant was used to hire and house a crew for a six-week excavation of a miners' doublehouse and to conduct several weeks of oral history interviews and documentary research in Pennsylvania. Without the foundation's generous support, the original study could not have taken place and the present volume, based on my doctoral dissertation, could not have been written.

I wish also to express my deepest appreciation to Mary Beaudry of the Department of Archaeology at Boston University, as well as Richard Candee of the Department of American and New England Studies at Boston University, Rick Elia of the Department of Archaeology at Boston University, and Anne Yentsch, associate professor of Historical Archaeology at Armstrong Atlantic State University, for ensuring that the present study was truly contextual and interdisciplinary in its scope. I am especially grateful to Mary for her continued support, her insight, and her friendship. I hope that both Mary and Anne, my former master's advisor, can find a little bit of themselves in the story of this coal mining community, for I am grateful for the many years of mentoring I have received.

Finally, I must thank the members of my family—my husband, Andrew; my parents; my mother-in-law, Judy Metheny, who gave us a home while my crew was in the field during the summer of 1995; and especially my three children, Hannah, Aaron, and Abigail—for their support and encouragement. My children have grown up with this project, and in a way this story is for them, because it tells of the experiences of their great-grandfather. I wish they had been given more time to know him, so if I can bring them closer to Rookie in telling this story of Helvetia, that is all to the better.

INTRODUCTION

Throughout America in the nineteenth and twentieth centuries, small company-built towns dotted the landscape. Many were "single-enterprise towns" (Garner 1992:3), built at the site of a particular resource or raw material associated with extractive industries such as mining, oil, and timber. Structures were erected to house those who labored for the company and to provide basic services for workers and their families—schools, stores, and churches—in what was often a physically remote location. In this setting, workers were subject to a corporate/industrial regimen that would penetrate and often dominate nearly every aspect of their daily lives. Owned and controlled by a company or individual, rather than by the workers themselves, the company town had many feudalistic qualities, with employment and tenancy in company housing contingent upon whatever regulations or conditions the owner might set. The company town of memory, preserved in the recollections and songs of coal miners and in the works of Long (1989), Sheppard (1947), Korson (1943), and others, evokes powerful, uncompromising images of worker exploitation and owner domination. These images permeate much of today's scholarship on industrial capitalism and corporate paternalism of the nineteenth and early twentieth centuries. But do they convey the full experience of the working classes within the industrial landscape during this period? What is the nature of that experience?

A review of current scholarship reveals that workers and their families are often cast as helpless, even hapless, victims of economic processes and dominant elites. In other studies, members of the working classes are overshadowed by the effects of market forces, by the history of unionization and labor leaders, by the technological and architectural aspects of industrialization, even by a kind of ecological determinism. The company town, a hallmark of industrial capitalism, is often studied as an example of model architectural design and social engineering, or as a case study in town planning and urban development, while descriptions of worker housing are built upon brick and mortar but give little thought to their former tenants. The experience of the worker is largely obscured in such studies.

This critique may be applied broadly within the social sciences. Despite recent paradigmatic shifts, there is still a tendency among scholars from many different fields—anthropology, archaeology, history, sociology, economics—to emphasize the power of industrialists and capitalists and institutions at the expense of the working classes (for a critique, see Wolf 1982:354–355; see also Gutman 1977 and Metheny 2002).[1] This institutional bias has had the unfortunate effect of skewing our understanding of the working-class experience. When events are framed only in terms of domination, conflict, and coercion, the oppressed can only be reactive, resistant, in conflict, or passively submissive. Those who are without power—whether in the broader context of industrial relations or within the hierarchy of organized labor—can only be subordinate to political, social, and economic elites. The net result is that workers are seen as powerless to contest their situation or to shape their own existence. Further, the many diverse and often divergent interests of workers are masked because workers are treated as an undifferentiated mass.

In the end, we are no closer to understanding the full spectrum of worker experiences, for large segments of the working-class population, and the ways they coped with industrialism on a day-to-day basis, are left out of these histories. It is this aspect of industrial relations that is the subject of the current volume. Behind the brick and mortar of the industrial plant and the company town, behind the company agents and the union, are individuals who daily made decisions about their welfare, who not only responded to but also acted upon various aspects of the industrial regimen as it related to living and working conditions and to the well-being of their families, who daily negotiated identity and place within the industrial landscape.

WORKER AGENCY IN THE INDUSTRIAL LANDSCAPE

The purpose of this volume is to examine issues of worker agency and working-class behavior within the setting of the company town, with particular emphasis on the role of landscape, material culture, and social action in the creation of a living environment and in the negotiation of place within the corporate landscape. Multiple lines of evidence, including oral histories, documentary sources, and architectural, material, and archaeological evidence, are used to reconstruct living and working conditions in the company town of Helvetia, Pennsylvania (1891–1947), and the practices of its parent company, the Rochester and Pittsburgh Coal Company.[2] The R&P was one of the largest producers in the Pennsylvania bituminous coal fields for much of the late nineteenth and early twentieth centuries, and Helvetia Mine was for many years among the largest and most productive mines in the region, employing upwards of 1,200 men at the height of production in the 1930s and 1940s. The town itself may have supported as many as 1,000 residents during its heyday. Its population was made up of the hundreds of coal miners and laborers who were employed at Helvetia Mine, their families, and company officials who managed operations in the mine and in town. Some of the town's residents were second- and third-generation Americans, but most were recent immigrants to the United States. The admixture of so many individuals resulted in an ethnically and socially diverse community bounded by company hierarchy and corporate policy.

In this respect, the town of Helvetia represents industrial society in microcosm and thus serves as a case study through which the issues of industrial relations, working-class behavior, working-class culture, and human agency may be explored. Unquestionably, the working lives of Helvetia's residents were centered around the operation of the coal mine and their daily lives were structured by company policies and company-sponsored institutions. The company's needs and schedules set the rhythm of daily life. Nonetheless, Helvetia's residents brought to this community their own sets of cultural practices, traditions, and beliefs. It is in the intersection of these two vastly different and competing lifeways, private and corporate/industrial, that evidence of working-class behavior and worker agency is revealed.

At the heart of this study are a series of questions that are relevant to other working-class communities: How did miners and their families cope with the industrial regimen established by the coal company? In what ways, if any, did they shape or alter the cultural and physical landscape in order to improve their own lives, and what effects did these actions have, in turn, on the policies of the company? How did they perceive themselves within the landscape of corporate paternalism? Did they see themselves as victims of exploitation, powerless to change their situation, or did they perhaps see themselves as actors with the ability to influence the course of their daily lives?

The evidence presented in this volume suggests that Helvetia's residents, like those in many other working-class communities, actively shaped and negotiated their entry into the industrial landscape as well as their physical, social, and economic well-being within the company town. This evidence, found in the physical remains at the site of Helvetia and in the written and oral records of the community, shows that Helvetia's residents used landscape, material culture, and social discourse, often in ways that differed from company expectations, to construct and solidify their identities. The data suggest that the "creation" of environment, both physical and cultural, was a key strategy through which Helvetia's residents were able to mediate between traditional lifeways and the corporate/

industrial landscape, and to direct the course of their daily lives despite the restrictive, controlling atmosphere of the company town and the exploitative practices of industrial capitalism and corporate paternalism.

CONCEPTUALIZING THE INDUSTRIAL LANDSCAPE

Archaeology has the potential to move us toward a better understanding of working-class lives through the recovery of the evidence of day-to-day living. There are now a number of studies that focus on industrial and working-class communities and domestic sites ranging from the physical remains of worker camps and settlements associated with extractive industries and the production of materials for industrial purposes (Brashler 1991; Colorado Coalfield War Archaeology Project [CCWAP] 2000, 2002; Franzen 1992; Schmitt and Zeier 1993; Van Bueren 2002; Zeier 1987) to worker housing, urban working-class neighborhoods, and company towns (Baugher 1982; Balicki, O'Brien, and Yamin 1999; Cotz 1975; De Cunzo 1982, 1983, 1987; Gradwohl and Osborn 1984; Richner 1992; Shackel 1993a, 1994; Warfel 1993; Yamin 1998, 1999, 2001). Each study has the potential to provide insight into working-class behavior and the issue of worker agency.

The treatment of the worker has been problematic, however. Historical archaeology has gone through its paradigmatic shifts like many other disciplines, and reports on industrial sites have ranged from the strictly technical and descriptive to basic functional analyses to pattern recognition (for a review, see Metheny 2002). Missing from these studies, however, is the social or symbolic context in which material culture, landscape, and behavior are situated; we are therefore limited in what we can learn about worker behavior and working-class culture. Anthropology has much to say about social interaction and social relations, agency, and meaning in the landscape and in material culture, but such concepts have been largely absent from archaeological studies of working-class communities and industrial workers.

Recently there has been an emergence of archaeological studies of the worker that are informed by social theory. This trend is driven in part by a number of historical archaeologists who use a Marxist-materialist perspective to look at the social relations of production (Mrozowski 1991; Mullins 1992, 1996; Paynter 1988; Paynter and McGuire 1991). While important for recognizing issues of class, power, and inequality, many of these studies are ultimately dissatisfying because working-class behavior is so often reduced to fit within a framework of domination (be it economic, social, or political) and resistance (McGuire 1991; Orser 1996: 159–182; Paynter and McGuire 1991; Shackel 1993b, 1996), or it is subsumed under the framework of the dominant ideology thesis (Leone 1988; Leone, Potter, and Shackel 1987).

In this conceptualization of industrial relations, workers are still largely portrayed as victims of economic processes who are resistant to or passive recipients of corporate ideology. In this context, their only recourse is resistance, their role is reactive, not active, and their efforts to change their situation are portrayed as ineffective and even meaningless. McGuire, for instance, has argued in a study of industrial workers in Broome County, New York, that because the workers had "no power to alter the company's position in a world economy," their power of negotiation had little meaning (1991:123). Orser's formulation of a global historical archaeology actually goes so far as to devalue efforts to document the active creation of working-class culture because, in his view, to focus on such examples of worker agency is to downplay the power of elites (1996:179).

Implicit in many of these studies is the premise of "culture loss"—that is, the traditions and values of the weaker (working-class) culture are replaced by those of the dominant (capitalist, paternalistic, exploitative) culture (Leone, Potter, and Shackel 1987; Shackel 1993b, 1996; cf. Mullins 1992, 1996).[3] The process of establishing a dominant ideology and achieving hegemony is typically seen as a unidirectional process, often coercive in nature, wherein the traditions, beliefs, and behavioral patterns of the weaker culture are lost as they are replaced by those of the dominant culture. Further, the weaker culture ultimately has no power to alter the situation.

Domination and resistance studies and the dominant ideology thesis in particular have been criticized elsewhere (Abercrombie, Hill, and Turner 1980; Beaudry, Cook and Mrozowski 1991; Comaroff and Comaroff 1992; Hall 1992a; Hodder 1991:27, 68–70; Miller and Tilley 1984:143; Trigger 1989:339; but see also Orser 1996). The premise of "culture loss" also has been heavily criticized within archaeology and anthropology for its failure to recognize the multidirectional exchange of cultural traditions and beliefs, as well as variability in the process of culture change (Beaudry 1990, 1993; Beaudry, Cook, and Mrozowski 1991; Hall 1992a; Rogers and Wilson 1993; Rosaldo 1989; Spector 1993). Comaroff and Comaroff (1992:21) argue that this is a weakness of Marxist scholars who are too often focused on the *reproduction* of systems of domination while ignoring the possibility of *transformation*. This model has been challenged outside the fields of archaeology and anthropology as well. In a social history of the working classes, Gutman argues that "the very rapidity of [economic changes] meant that many [working people] lacked the time, historically, culturally, and psychologically, to be separated or alienated from settled ways of work and life and from relatively fixed beliefs. Continuity not consensus counted for much" (1977:40). The importance of cultural traditions to immigrant working-class communities has been demonstrated clearly. Miller and Sharpless (1985), for example, have shown the essential link between individual, family, and community stability and the perpetuation of Old World traditions among the Irish and Slavic communities in the anthracite coalfields of Pennsylvania. The survival of strongly heterogeneous industrial communities today is a reflection of that continuity and the strength of tradition.

CONSTRUCTING AN ALTERNATIVE VIEW

The problem of how to treat the working classes seems to center on issues of agency—who has power, who is active or passive—and context. Whether implicitly or openly stated in models of domination and resistance, many scholars assign power and agency almost exclusively to owners except in the context of group resistance in the form of labor movements and unionization. The worker has no power and no recourse outside of the union. Alternately, worker actions are depicted as a knee-jerk reflex—mechanical, almost involuntary responses that have no meaning outside the context of the ongoing class struggle. In reducing the spectrum of human behavior to such narrow dimensions, this model of industrial relations effectively obscures and even denies the existence of worker agency, the localization of power, the existence of competing interests within the industrial landscape, and variation within working-class communities.

An alternative view of the industrial landscape is suggested by scholars who begin with the worker and move outward, from "the bottom up" and from "the inside out" (Beaudry, Cook, and Mrozowski 1991:156).[4] A growing number of archaeologists use an interpretive, contextual approach to examine working-class behavior and identity and to reconstruct the social and symbolic context in which material culture, landscape, and behavior are situated (Beaudry 1989, 1993; Beaudry and Mrozowski 1987a, 1987b, 1988, 1989; Beaudry, Cook, and Mrozowski 1991; Brashler 1991; De Cunzo 1996; Landon 1997; Metheny 1992, 1994; Wegars 1991; see also Cohen 1986; Gutman 1977; Hareven and Langenbach 1978).

The wealth of data conveyed by this research indicates that there is far more to a social history of the working classes than "detailing their subjugation" by the forces of capitalism. Indeed, these studies reveal that workers were able to creatively shape, alter, adjust to, and reject working and living conditions in the emerging industrial landscape in a variety of ways, even under a system of corporate paternalism. The data demonstrate too that members of the working classes not only had the power to act and negotiate as individuals and as members of diverse interest groups (subcultures), but responses and actions, as well as their assigned meaning, may have varied within the community by race, ethnicity, age, or sex (Beaudry 1993; Bell 1994; Bond 1989; Cohen 1986; Cook 1989; Landon 1989, 1997).[5]

Existing oral histories of industrial workers and communities also demonstrate the complexity of industrial relations and the importance of studying worker responses to and perceptions of the workplace. An excellent example is a study by Hareven and Langenbach (1978), who recorded the recollections and oral traditions of former workers at the Amoskeag Manufacturing Company in Manchester, New Hampshire. In so doing, the authors have documented a past that differs from the one found in company records. The Amoskeag was a standard of corporate paternalism during the nineteenth and twentieth centuries, and its history has been written many times over. The oral narratives reveal another side of the Amoskeag's industrial past that is less well known. They show how employees crafted their individual and group identities in relation to the company and the industrial workplace, and how they viewed their past (and present) lives, both in the workplace and in the home, as Amoskeag workers. The oral histories also call our attention to the considerable cultural, ethnic, and social diversity among workers.

Hareven and Langenbach's work has strongly influenced the present study, as have several exceptional works by historical archaeologists who have utilized oral sources to tell the stories of individuals and communities in the past (Beaudry and Mrozowski 1987a, 1989; Brashler 1991; Costello 1998; Purser 1992; Spector 1993; Yentsch 1988; Yamin and Bridges 1996). It is clear that oral history can be an especially valuable part of a contextual historical archaeology of the industrial landscape, contributing the worker's perspective to the growing body of archaeological and documentary evidence. Oral narratives give voice to those not previously heard in traditional histories. This quality has particular relevance for those constructing a social history of the working classes. Oral histories draw our attention to the biases of different pasts and different voices and may help to redress the inequities within our own perceptions of what constitutes the past. It is for these reasons that oral narratives from Helvetia are an important part of this study.

A QUESTION OF AGENCY

Hareven and Langenbach's analysis of oral narratives from the Amoskeag touches on a central point of contention among scholars—the question of worker agency. The authors argue convincingly that the working classes "had a realistic view of industrial life, with all its difficulties and exploitation, and they accepted the modern world into which they had been swept. In adapting themselves to it, they also modified it, wherever possible, to fit their own needs and traditions" (1978:12).

The issue of agency is of central importance to the present study since the focus of research is a company town, one of the most potent symbols of corporate power in America in the nineteenth and twentieth centuries. To properly address this issue, we need to construct an alternate framework of industrial relations that acknowledges the possibility of worker agency and multiple centers of power within the context of industrial capitalism and corporate paternalism (Beaudry, Cook, and Mrozowski 1991; Comaroff and Comaroff 1992:17, 28–30; Cook 1989, 1995). This framework should recognize, as Foucault has stated, that power may be productive, not merely repressive; that the exercise of power is based on social relations and acts of intentionality, not economic processes; that power or agency may be localized at many levels, be it institutional, within the community, or within the family; but also that power may be exercised by individuals and is not limited to dominant social groups (see Tilley 1990:285–286).

It should also acknowledge the potential for negotiation among competing interests and ideologies. When social and economic relationships between Helvetia's residents and owners are examined within this alternate framework, it is possible to look at *how* members of the community might have exercised power and negotiated with others to shape both living and working conditions outside of organized labor movements.[6]

In reconceptualizing the worker experience, then, several approaches are suggested. First, to glimpse the depth and complexity of working-class behavior, it is necessary to examine the full range of social and economic relationships within the industrial landscape. Second, to understand the place of the worker within industrial society, it is necessary to contextualize worker behavior from the perspective of those we study. This requires the use of multiple independent lines of evidence—archaeological, historical, and oral. Following, then, is a brief description of the framework of analysis and interpretation that is used to examine the community at Helvetia. This framework draws from anthropological and archaeological method and theory to construct an alternate view of industrial relations. Having acknowledged the role of worker agency and the complexity of industrial relations, we may begin to identify examples of agency among Helvetia's workers and to explore these actions for their meaning and significance.

CULTURE AS DISCOURSE

Anthropologists have long interpreted social action and social interaction as meaningful practice (e.g., Comaroff and Comaroff 1992:32; Geertz 1973, 1983; Hodder 1991), even if they have not always been in agreement as to what that practice signifies. In recent years, a number of anthropologists have begun to define social action as text and discourse (Ricoeur in Moore 1990:97–99; see also Geertz 1973:18–20, 1983:30–33); these models are most frequently used by those working in a hermeneutic or interpretive tradition.

As characterized by Brink (1992:125), Ricoeur's definition of discourse is that "someone says something to someone about something." The paradigm of culture as discourse has influenced the work of many anthropologists and archaeologists in the postmodernist or postprocessual traditions (e.g., Beaudry, Cook, and Mrozowski 1991; Brink 1992; Geertz 1973, 1983; Hall 1991, 1992a; Markell 1992), and discourse analysis has been expanded to include material objects (Tilley 1990) as well as social action. In this broader model of culture as discourse, discourse may take the form of action or words, preserved in text and oral narrative, or it may be objectified or fixated as material culture. With the latter, the transition from language event to language-as-act takes place through the inscription or fixation of meaning in material form, as text or material artifact.

Because of the focus upon material remains in historical archaeology, many archaeologists have embraced a model of material culture as text and as an ele-

meaning of
social action + ...
nonverbal discourse (+ ...)
work

ment of discourse. Hall, for instance, has described material culture as "text without words" (1992b:373), as a "non-verbal language through which people define themselves" (1992a:24). Both Hall and Brink (1992) have emphasized the symbolic role of architecture in discourse concerning social, economic, and gender relations in colonial South Africa, though architecture is intricately interwoven with landscape and material culture as elements of nonverbal discourse. Brink (1992) has also argued that part of this discourse or dialogic exchange took the form of social action as symbolic, nonverbal language, and she uses the example of social visiting, and the associated display of material goods, to demonstrate the role of discourse between producer and reader, between the free Burghers and "others."

The trend in discourse analysis has been to think about social action or practice as well as cultural artifacts as elements of discourse. For archaeologists looking at historical communities, that practice may be objectified and its meaning encoded in the material residues of the past—ceramics, glass, food remains, household furnishings, tools, architecture, historical landscapes—or it may be expressed as written text or oral narrative. Social action may be seen as social discourse as well—thus, for example, we may usefully look at an archaeology of manners, ritual, social visiting, or social display in relation to discourse (Goodwin 1999). The two languages—verbal and nonverbal—are often interwoven as part of social discourse, and that practice—be it verbal or fixed in material culture—may take on multiple meanings for its readers. Since discourse is active and ongoing, material culture and social action may become multi- or polyvocal, assuming meaning beyond that intended by the producer. Hodder cautions us to distinguish between meaning and intention as we grapple with our interpretations (1995:12–16); he argues, nonetheless, that meaning is situated in a historical and cultural context and therefore may be recovered through an interpretive or hermeneutic approach. Geertz rightly asserts, however, that the point of analysis is not just to determine what meanings may best fit the action of discourse, but also to understand how and why this discourse takes place (1983:31).

Material Culture

Archaeologists and anthropologists have previously identified a number of ways in which material culture has been used in social discourse to communicate meaning within or outside a group; material objects may also be used to construct a sense of identity, to develop and express group values, to construct social and cultural boundaries, and to reify those constructions (Cook 1989; Douglas 1982; Douglas and Isherwood 1979; Ferguson 1991; Miller 1987; Praetzellis, Praetzellis, and Brown 1988; Yentsch 1991; see also Beaudry 1996). It follows, then, that material culture as social discourse may be used in the negotiation of group or individual interests and in the exercise of power.

Beaudry, Cook, and Mrozowski (1991) have concluded, for example, that archaeological remains from the boardinghouses in Lowell, Massachusetts, embody the beliefs and values of nineteenth-century mill workers, aspects of working-class identity that are generally omitted from company records and often from social and labor histories of the working classes. The authors argue that different forms of material culture, such as tobacco pipes, tablewares, and alcoholic beverage containers, reflect some of the leisure-time activities of boardinghouse residents that were used to construct individual and group identities and to construct and reinforce cultural boundaries.

Beaudry has stated elsewhere the relevance of "active voice" analysis (after Douglas 1982, in Beaudry 1996:477, 485–486) to an understanding of how material culture is used in various forms of "communication, negotiation, and manipulation." This approach to material culture is used in the present study. Material remains from Helvetia are interpreted as multivocal elements of discourse that were used in the processes of constructing and expressing group and individual identity, community formation, boundary maintenance, and negotiation.

It is important to note that among the textile workers at Lowell, the meanings expressed through material culture were often at odds with corporate ideology (Beaudry 1993; Beaudry, Cook and Mrozowski 1991).[7] Cohen's study (1986) of material culture in working-class homes of the late nineteenth and early twentieth centuries demonstrates a similar opposition between working-class values and the ideology of the domestic reform movement. In surveying the material culture of working-class homes dating from 1885 to 1915, Cohen found that worker choices were often made in opposition to the prescriptions of domestic reformers, most notably in the selection and use of furnishing and decorations, and in the use of domestic space. The present study will show that there is a similar disjunction—what Firth calls "a gap between the overt superficial statement of action and its underlying meaning" (1975:26; see also Yentsch 1996)—between material culture and corporate ideology within the company town of Helvetia.

Landscape

It is also argued here that the landscape was used by the community at Helvetia, in both a physical and symbolic sense, in the process of negotiating, shaping, and adjusting to the industrial regimen established by the Rochester and Pittsburgh Coal Company. This aspect of my study is influenced by the work of Rodman (1992) and recent studies of the historical landscape. Building from the concepts of multivocality and discourse in anthropology and the work of cultural geographers such as Tuan, Rodman has used the term "multilocality" to emphasize that "place"—the meaning of a landscape—is socially constructed at many levels by many individuals and groups: "a single physical landscape can be multilocal in the sense that it shapes and expresses polysemic meanings of place for different users. Multilocality conveys the idea that a single place may be experienced quite differently [by others]" (1992:647). Thus landscapes may encompass multiple expressions of cultural tradition and identity, aspects of community and kin relations, history, mythic history, and other associations. Rodman also notes that "the social landscape is both context and content, enacted and material" (1992:650); thus, landscape, like material culture, may be used by different individuals to actively construct, signify, and reify the identity, values, and beliefs of a group, and to exert power in a positive or productive context.

The interpretation of historical landscapes has paralleled and often built upon the ideas expressed by Rodman. Since landscape archaeology emerged in the mid-1980s as a distinct subfield of North American historical archaeology, archaeologists have sought to define, in increasingly sophisticated ways, the multiplicity of meanings to be found in historical landscapes for the wealthy and the poor, for the social elite and the underclasses, for slaves and free persons, for men and women (see, for example, Joyce 1997; Kelso and Most 1990; Yamin and Metheny 1996; Yentsch 1996). These studies suggest that the meaning of the landscape, like material culture, is culturally constructed, symbolic, and reflexive.

I have found a number of landscape studies to be useful in the present project. Dell Upton's analysis of the landscape of seventeenth- and eighteenth-century Virginia (1990) is of interest, for example, because he attempts to visualize the landscape as it might have been interpreted by nonwhite members of this society. He suggests that slaves viewed the landscape in terms of free versus controlled spaces. Did workers and residents of Helvetia view the controlled landscape of the company town in a similar fashion? Upton's study of the smells, sounds, and sights of the city speaks to the different experiences of individuals in an urban environment (1992). This same approach may be usefully applied to a study of a mining landscape. How did the smoke and the dust and the noise from the coal plant affect life in the company town?

Yentsch (1988, 1996) has shown that landscapes often incorporate elements of mythic history and cultural ideology, and they may therefore serve in a transfigurative role (see also King 1996; McKee 1996; Sahlins 1981, 1985). Do industrial landscapes likewise incorporate elements of corporate ideology and the transformation of the corporate landscape by Helvetia's mining families? Or do they show the transformation of family structures and kin networks as families encountered the industrial regimen of the company?

Hall (1991, 1992b, 1994), Brink (1992), and Markell (1992) have examined South African material culture, architecture, and landscape using a discursive framework to reveal a dialogue of power, domination, and resistance during the colonial period. Economic, social, gender, class, and racial relations are also signified within the landscape. We will see that the corporate landscape of Helvetia likewise carries multiple meanings and signifies a variety of social, cultural, and economic practices.

Discourse and Negotiation

In this volume, then, material culture, landscape, and social action are treated as culturally meaningful phenomena, reflecting the beliefs, values, preferences, agendas, needs, and traditions of different parties. Further, they are recognized as media through which Helvetia's residents engaged in discourse and the negotiation of identity and place within the setting of the company town. The concepts of discourse, multivocality, and multilocality are well suited to a study of the industrial landscape, particularly landscapes of corporate paternalism, since these programs created an opposition between owners and workers, between corporate ideology and working-class values. Through this conceptualization of the industrial landscape, it is possible to see how Helvetia's residents established, negotiated, and expressed a set of relationships with the coal company and within the community. A discursive framework also allows us to recognize variation within the actions and responses of community members, according to ethnicity, cultural background, gender, or other subgroup, and to view those actions and responses as part of an ongoing dialogue. The resulting study provides an alternative view of social and economic relations within the setting of the company town and reveals the active, agentive role of the miners and their families in the shaping of their daily lives.

RECONSTRUCTING CONTEXT

To reconstruct the community that lived and worked in the company town of Helvetia and to address issues of worker agency, this study relies upon two key methodological approaches. First, the analytical techniques of historical ethnography (Comaroff and Comaroff 1992) are used here as applied by historical archaeologists and anthropologists to a variety of documentary sources (Beaudry 1988; Wallace 1988; Worrell, Simmons, and Stachiw 1996; Yentsch 1975, 1980, 1988), ethnohistorical sources (Bragdon 1988, 1997; Spector 1993; Wallace 1972), and, more recently, oral sources (Lamphere 1987; Purser 1992; Spector 1993) in order to conduct highly contextualized, interpretive studies of households, families, and communities (Beaudry 1984; De Cunzo 1996). Comaroff and Comaroff (1992:32) urge ethnographers to approach their subject "as meaningful practice, produced in the interplay of subject and object, of the contingent and the contextual." But historical anthropology, they write, is more than the creation of "a mosaic of narratives, images, and signifying practices" (1992:30). In their view, the purpose of historical ethnography is to establish "*how* collective identities are constructed and take on their particular cultural content" (1992:44).

This study begins, then, with—and works outward from—individual oral accounts, primary documents, and excavations at the household or family level to address larger questions about working-class culture and behavior. The strength of this approach lies in the construction of an emic perspective—the local (internal) social, cultural, and physical contexts for action and meaning—that can be juxtaposed against the larger (external/etic) social and economic context of industrial capitalism and corporate paternalism of the late nineteenth and early twentieth centuries. This allows us to contextualize questions about the past—to address issues of working-class behavior and culture without losing sight of the individual or the community in which action was situated and meaning assigned.

The methodological framework for this study draws from Alison Wylie's conceptualization of historical archaeology as the construction of "cables of inference" through an interactive, dynamic approach to archaeological, written, and oral sources of evidence (1993:14). Wylie has argued that it is the process of weaving multiple, independent sources of data together in a "dynamic of mutual constraint" that gives strength to observations, hypotheses, and interpretations of the archaeological record and, ultimately, allows us to link the data to the larger historical and cultural questions about "unobservable causes and structures" (1993:7). Wylie's methodological approach is used here to reconstruct and compare life in the company town of Helvetia as intended by its owners (documentary sources), as remembered by its inhabitants (oral histories), and as lived (the archaeological record).

Oral histories provide an emic perspective of life in a company town—that is, working and living conditions as perceived and remembered by Helvetia's residents, the coal miners and their families. This perspective is compared to an alternate view of Helvetia's community, one that is derived from the records of the Rochester and Pittsburgh Coal Company and therefore reflects the intentions and goals of the owners. Primary and secondary written sources provide yet another perspective on the history of the town. Archaeology comprises the fourth line of evidence. Included here are the physical remains of the town and mine, both above and below ground. The use of multiple, independent lines of evidence is crucial to site interpretation, revealing disjunctions between company practices, owner intentions, worker responses (actual and perceived), and the realities of daily life in the town of Helvetia. The results speak, as well, to the larger issue of working-class behavior within the industrial landscape.

RECONSTRUCTING ENVIRONMENT

The processes of archaeological inference and explanation are critical to this study, particularly in the reconstruction of "environment," for living environments are as much a creation of individual perceptions and needs as they are a function of interacting "physical, climatological, and biological" variables (Dincauze 1997:1). Dincauze recently defined environment as "the context within which lives are lived" in a discussion of how archaeologists may reconstruct and interpret past environments (1997:1–5), and it is a useful definition for the present study. This is not a particularly new concept in historical archaeology; though reversing the key words, Hodder earlier defined "context" as "the totality of the relevant environment" (1991:143; 1995:14). But Dincauze's definition, though directed primarily toward the analyses of prehistoric landscapes, has relevance to the present study for a number of reasons. In defining environment as "the context within which lives are lived," Dincauze asks us to expand the boundaries of physical space to include the cultural landscape and also to acknowledge the role of individual perceptions in the creation of a living environment.

The thoughts and perceptions of individuals from the past are mostly lost to us through the passage of time. In this study, however, Helvetia's past is still part of living memory. Oral histories are an especially rich source of ethnographic and "environmental" data for Helvetia and other industrial communities, providing details of daily life in a coal mining community, of living and working conditions, of hardships and pleasures, of social gatherings and social conflict—details that are often absent from the written record. The value of oral history to social and labor historians who study working-class, industrial communities of the late nineteenth and early twentieth centuries is clear and compelling (Blewett 1990; Brestensky, Hovanec, and Skomra 1991; Hareven and Langenbach 1978; Lamphere 1987; Michrina 1993). In the present study, interviews with former residents of Helvetia provide an emic perspective of life in a company town; that is, working and living conditions—"environment"—as perceived and remembered by the coal miners and their families. Such perceptions are as important to our understanding of how environments are created as actual physical conditions, and they are essential to the reconstruction of Helvetia's past.

ARCHAEOLOGY AND LANDSCAPE IN A COAL COMPANY TOWN

This volume is a study in historical archaeology. It is contextual in its orientation; it is interdisciplinary in its scope and its implementation. The importance of this approach will become apparent as the story of Helvetia's miners and families unfolds.

The volume begins with a brief history of the company town in America. The concept of the company town as it developed in the late nineteenth and early twentieth centuries was a phenomenon of industrial capitalism. This term refers to a period beginning in the second quarter of the nineteenth century when, inspired by rapid advances in technology, investors amassed large amounts of capital to form corporate-owned factories and industries. The period was characterized by the introduction of the factory system, increasing mechanization, and mass production. It was also marked by the introduction of paternalism in the workplace. The reader is therefore provided with a discussion of the ideology of corporate paternalism and a review of paternalism in its various forms, from its emergence in the mills in the early nineteenth century to its fullest definition and ideological realization in that hallmark of social and economic control, the company town. This places the study of this particular industrial community within a broader historical and socioeconomic context. Corporate paternalism and the coal company town are then placed within a regional context before the scope of study is narrowed to a discussion of local conditions.

The chapters that follow comprise the historical, oral, and archaeological evidence that is used to examine the issue of worker agency in the town of Helvetia. The reader is provided with a history of the Rochester and Pittsburgh Coal Company and its corporate ideology. The origins of Helvetia's mining community are explored using census data and other primary sources. Oral histories are then used to construct a view of the company town and the R&P's program of corporate paternalism from the perspective of the miners and their families. The narratives tell the story of work and daily life in Helvetia as perceived by the town's inhabitants and nonresident employees of the R&P.

Yet another view of the company town is constructed from archaeological evidence recovered during excavations of a company house in Helvetia. The last four chapters explore the role of material culture, the physical landscape, and social action in the negotiation of place and the creation of a living environment within the company town by the miners and their families. The oral testimony of residents and employees and the evidence of owner intentions, as reconstructed from company documents, are set against and contrasted with the view of daily life that emerges from the archaeological evidence. The data are used to construct "cables of inference" about working-class behavior and agency, and to construct an alternate view of industrial relations in the company town—one that recognizes members of the working classes as social actors who had the ability to act with intentionality, to negotiate as individuals and as members of diverse interest groups in order to shape the course of their daily lives despite the practices of industrial capitalism, and to respond to exploitation through positive social action and not just through resistance.

John and Jean Comaroff have written that "improperly contextualized, the stories of ordinary people past stand in danger of remaining just that: stories. To become something more, these partial, 'hidden histories' have to be situated in the wider worlds of power and meaning that gave them life" (1992:17). What follows, then, is the creation of a historical ethnography, wherein the details of everyday life in Helvetia are reconstructed and examined in the context of the larger questions concerning worker agency and industrial relations. This is done so that the stories of these ordinary people, the miners and families of Helvetia, may be told.

 CHAPTER 1

CORPORATE PATERNALISM
AND THE COMPANY TOWN

The company town is an enduring symbol of industrial capitalism, and its form dominated the industrial landscape for more than a century. By 1930, when use of this type of settlement peaked, nearly 2,000,000 Americans resided in company towns.[1] Yet at that date many company towns still did not provide electricity or running water to their residents, and fewer still had any regulations regarding sewer and sanitation. The company town subsequently went into a decline in the 1930s and 1940s and is now a form rarely seen in this country.

The history of the company town in this country is marked by controversy. Since the appearance of the earliest company-built and company-controlled settlements in the United States, the owners of company towns have alternately been reviled and praised for their treatment of industrial workers. Though its origins are uncertain, the term "company town" is thought to have first appeared in late-nineteenth-century America. Garner's research suggests that from the outset, the term had a pejorative connotation from an early association with poor-quality, short-lived settlements, particularly those related to extractive industries (Garner 1992:3–4). These sites were remotely placed and often hastily built of log, canvas, or clay; they frequently operated with technology that was as primitive as the amenities for workers (Brashler 1991; Elston and Hardesty 1981; Franzen 1992; Hardesty 1988; Rogers 1995:32–33, 49–50; Roth 1992:176, 179; Van Bueren 2002).

Such camps stood in sharp contrast to the comparatively stable mill towns and industrial villages of early- to mid-nineteenth-century rural New England (Garner 1984; Prude 1983). Yet even the more permanent, planned company towns and settlements came to have negative associations that stemmed from chronic labor disputes, sporadic violence, and the nightmarish struggles of many laborers to survive harsh, oppressive living and working conditions (Corbin 1981; Long 1989; Miller and Sharpless 1985; Sheppard 1947; Walkowitz 1978). By the early decades of the twentieth century, however, many company towns were viewed as models of social engineering, enlightened management practices, and owner benevolence, not just by planners and reformers, but by many employees as well (Crawford 1995:67–77; Hareven and Langenbach 1978; Metheny 1992; Wright 1981:177–192). The company town is thus a symbol of contradictory and controversial meanings and images.

Because the form, function, and underlying ideology of the company town have been in continuous evolution over time, some background on the history and development of company towns in the United States is provided in this chapter. While Garner's definition (1992:3) of a company town as "a settlement built and operated by a single business enterprise" was used in the introduction to this study, other scholars have found it useful to define this entity in narrower terms to distinguish it from the working-class neighborhoods and industrial communities that most often developed in urban environments. Thus Crawford's study of American company towns takes from the *Encyclopedia of Social Sciences* a definition of the company town as "a community inhabited chiefly by the employees of a single company or group of companies *which also owns a substantial part of the real estate and houses*" (1995:1, emphasis added). It is the ownership of the real estate by the company or industrial concern that gives the company much of its power to influence and control. Helvetia was established in this manner: all town lands and all facilities, including all forms of housing, were owned and managed by the coal company. This distinction is important, and we will return to Crawford's more narrowly defined industrial settlement later in this discussion.

DEFINING THE COMPANY TOWN

To chart the evolution of the company town, we need to look first at the interrelated variables of location, form, and function. Location, for most industries, was shaped by the physical needs of the industrial process. The constitution of a company town as part of an urban community, as an adjunct to a rural village, or as an isolated work camp or settlement was, until the twentieth century, determined by geological, environmental, and geographic factors—the presence of natural and mineral resources, the need for a power source, and access to transportation networks. Company mining camps in the western United States, for example, were established on the industrial frontier at the sites of key natural resources; as noted earlier, the camps were built in isolated settings and were often very temporary in nature, as the drive for profit meant that operators employed any means necessary to extract the resource as rapidly as possible before moving on (Gillespie and Farrell 2002; Hardesty 1988; Markley 1992; Roth 1992; cf. Franzen 1992; Richner 1992). Mills and factories in nineteenth-century New England, by contrast, were often established in densely populated areas because of existing transportation networks and markets, ease of access to machinery and technology, and the presence of a large workforce. Many mill complexes were closely integrated with the region's larger urban centers. Other mills, such as those built at Lowell, Massachusetts, were the first structures to be built on site. These areas were quickly urbanized, however, as the workforce expanded and other industries and businesses were drawn to the area. Still others were established along rivers and streams throughout rural New England. In each case, the prime consideration for site selection was the presence of a suitable power source. With the abundance of water sources to power the mills, however, investors had considerable flexibility in choosing a site. As a consequence, such factors as the type and availability of labor or access to existing markets could be given greater weight in the decision-making process.

The presence of transportation networks was also integral to the site-selection process for all company towns and was perhaps the single most influential factor to shape the course and speed of industrial expansion across the country. There is a direct link, for instance, between the flow of technology and machinery into the country's eastern seaports and the establishment and expansion of New England industries in the first half of the nineteenth century. Similarly, the movement of industrial capital into the interior lands of the United States was contingent upon the existence of viable links to market.[2] There is also a relationship between the expansion of transportation routes, particularly the railroad, and the establishment of company towns in the West.

The industrial process itself—that is, the extraction and/or production process—shaped the landscape of the company town, determining the form and arrangement of the industrial plant and its ancillary structures, the type and quantity of worker housing, and the types of facilities and services provided to company employees. Technological advances, the discovery and depletion of resources, and changing consumer demands made the landscape of the company town dynamic over time and space.

Crawford (1995:2) has noted too the role of expediency and precedent in shaping the earliest company towns. Owners relied on the experience of others and were quick to adopt "tried and true" designs of industrial plants and company towns. An example of this was the swift replication of what came to be known as the Waltham system by textile manufacturers in nineteenth-century New England (Candee 1985:17–19). The mill complex first created in Waltham, Massachusetts, in 1814 by the Boston Manufacturing Company was duplicated by the same group of investors at the sites of Lowell, Massachusetts, and Dover, New Hampshire. Plans for the machinery and mill layout were patented and then carefully distributed to others. In the succeeding decades of the 1820s–1830s, this arrangement of machinery and buildings was repeated at many sites throughout New England, creating a distinctive architectural style and plan among mill buildings and worker housing (Candee 1985:28–29; 1992). The role of precedent in shaping the landscape and architecture of company towns, and especially housing forms, will be particularly evident in the coal company town.

There is some correlation between the form of worker housing and the types of employees hired by owners as well. In southern Massachusetts and Rhode Island in the early nineteenth century, owners like Samuel Slater who relied upon the English family labor system to staff their mills most often built housing to accommodate families—duplexes or small cottages, for example. Mills patterned after the Waltham system contained a mix of family housing and dormitory-style boarding-houses for single men and women (cf. Prude 1983:50, 96–97; Candee 1985:26–29). By contrast, company towns that relied upon temporary, seasonal workers spent very little on housing compared to those that supported year-round, permanent employees (Elston and Hardesty 1981; Paterlini de Koch 1992).

Economic considerations—the accumulation of a surplus and the realization of a profit—were of course uppermost in the minds of the corporations and industrial concerns that fashioned company towns out of the wilderness or wove them into the fabric of the city. The profit motive guided decision making at all levels of the corporate hierarchy, from the architects and engineers who built the company town, to the superintendents and agents who directed the industrial process, to those with responsibility for worker housing and services. Despite professions of concern for the welfare of employees, the cost for each service for workers and their families was weighed carefully against the need to generate a profit. Ideals of benevolence and reform rarely survived strong economic challenge. Employee benefits and wage agreements were the first expenses to be reduced or jettisoned when demanded by company losses or external economic pressures.

Company towns were generally small in size. Garner's study shows that the populations of company towns rarely exceeded a few thousand residents, while most had no more than a few hundred (1992:4). Only the large model company towns created in the late nineteenth and early twentieth century, such as Pullman, Illinois, Goodyear Heights, Ohio, and Tyrone, New Mexico, were designed to house populations numbering in the thousands (Crawford 1995:39, 95–96, 137–145; Roth 1992:184–187; Wright 1981:183–185). Size, however, was not always the overriding factor in deciding how many and what types of structures to build on a given site. In more densely populated areas and urban environments, owners might limit company-built facilities to worker housing or build no housing at all—for example, Gary, Indiana, or Homestead, Pennsylvania (Crawford 1995:43–44, 68–69; Serrin 1993). Yet other corporations constructed both company store and commercial buildings, boardinghouses and hotels, band stands and public libraries (cf. Candee 1985:29–33, 39; Crawford 1995:11–98; Hareven and Langenbach 1978:14–16, 22). In more isolated regions, company towns typically built housing, school, church, and a company store to provide basic services for employees, while temporary camps and settlements often contained only a bunkhouse and cookhouse for workers (Franzen 1992).

With the growth of Progressive and reform ideologies in the late nineteenth century, many corporations began to change and expand the forms of paternalism found in company towns. Under a program of welfare capitalism, company towns increasingly contained parks and garden landscapes, libraries, swimming pools, band halls, recreation centers, hospitals, and educational centers. Such amenities became regular features of the industrial landscape with the advent of the model company town in the twentieth century (Crawford 1995:61–77; Wright 1981:177–192).

Variation in the form of the company town also reveals the changing ideology of corporate paternalism that shaped the landscape of industry. As Crawford has noted, company towns "invariably became sites of struggle" (1995:12), so we must examine the physical conditions that shaped conflict in these places in the context of the competing ideologies, practices, and values of worker and owner.[3] The conflict between the corporate/industrial regimen and traditional lifeways clearly marked the industrial process and the cultural landscape. But the struggle between worker and owner was not limited to the clash between the new industrial regimen and the older, traditional rhythms of rural life, because many workers adjusted to and even accepted the new industrial order with little difficulty (Bodnar 1985; Hareven and Langenbach 1978). Rather than view this conflict as one arising solely from the efforts of industrial capitalists to dominate and subordinate the working classes—a fairly static, narrow representation of industrial relations—we may usefully examine worker behavior in terms of action and negotiation, not just reaction and resistance. From this perspective, working-class behavior may be seen as part of an ongoing dialogue between competing interests within the industrial landscape. To do so, however, we must define the ideology of corporate paternalism and examine its role in the conception and operation of the company town.

DEFINING CORPORATE PATERNALISM

The practice of corporate paternalism was integral to the design and operation of the company town throughout the nineteenth and twentieth centuries. Though its form and the scope of its influence have changed through time, the practice of paternalism in American industry extends back to the first quarter of the nineteenth century. A useful definition of the term appears in an article by Philip Scranton (1984), in which paternalism is characterized as a style of management associated with industrial capitalism in which social relations between employer and employee are constructed upon the notion of patriarchal authority and/or mutual obligation. Scranton notes further that paternalism developed as a bridging form between rural agrarian lifeways and artisan traditions, and an emerging industrial economy.[4] Scranton's review of the forms of paternalism is specific to the American textile industry, but as corporate practices in the textile mills in many ways served as the model for paternalism used by other industries, it is clearly relevant to this study. He makes the salient point too that past attempts to generalize and classify types of paternalism by geographic region and time period have helped to obscure the variation that more truly characterized paternalistic forms in all American industries.

Scranton's survey demonstrates that the social relations of production in a paternalistic setting (i.e., the context of production) were contingent upon what he has described as "constellations of material and cultural conditions" (1984:236); in other words, the style of factory paternalism was fitted to existing economic, technological or material, and cultural conditions in order to accumulate a surplus and attain a profit. He has characterized these forms as formal, familiar, and fraternal styles of paternalism, and each varied "in logic and character of obligation" between employer and employee (1984:235) and in terms of "provision, protection, and control" (1984:237). Each form differed, then, in its set of material, economic, and cultural traits, be it housing forms or company services, the extent of supervision or moral policing by the owner, or the types of relationships established between owner and laborer. The latter, Scranton notes, were at times based on historical relationships and networks within the existing community; at other times, relations of paternalism had a mythic quality, creating a hierarchy using idealized forms of obligation and duty.

While the formal style is most relevant to the present study of the company town at Helvetia, it is nonetheless useful to consider all three forms, thus laying the contextual background for the form of paternalism that evolved in the coalfields of western Pennsylvania and, more specifically, under the Rochester and Pittsburgh Coal Company. The formal style, of which the Lowell mills and, more generally, all of the Waltham-style textile manufactories are a preeminent example (Scranton 1984:239–240; see also Candee 1985:18), was highly structured (i.e., a corporate hierarchy and formal corporate structure were in place), heavily capitalized, and characterized by impersonal relations between employer and employee. Working and living environments were highly controlled. Owners and their agents assumed moral guardianship over all of their workers while acting *in loco parentis* to the single young women who tended the looms. In this setting, owners hoped to engender a sense of obligation from their workers through the claim of moral guardianship and the replication of paternalistic ties.

Familiar forms of paternalism first emerged in the mill villages that dotted the New England landscape in the early to mid-nineteenth century (Scranton 1984:240–241; for an extended discussion, see Prude 1983). These concerns were characterized by moderate to small capitalization. Mill owners attempted to reproduce or replicate rural social and community networks and to create an affective quality in the mill that encouraged familial or paternal bonds between owner and laborer, thus promoting loyalty and a sense of duty among their workers.

A fraternal style of paternalism emerged only in highly specialized areas of textile production, most notably in Philadelphia (Scranton 1984:241–242).

These types of firms were noncorporate, low capital, and characterized by a reliance upon skilled craftsmen who, linked by bonds of mutuality, had the opportunity for vertical movement within their craft. The potential for advancement within the company stands in strong contrast to the lack of movement within a formal corporate hierarchy. In the latter context of production, employees could only move horizontally—that is, out of the mill—and this is one of the reasons that worker transience was so high under a formal style of paternalism. In the specific settings where it emerged, then, the fraternal form of paternalism contributed greatly to the stability of the workforce, marked as it was by bonds of mutuality rather than obligation and dependency.

THE COMPANY TOWN AND THE LANDSCAPE OF CORPORATE PATERNALISM

Crawford (1995:2) cites a 1645 iron works as the first company town in America, and numerous examples of industrial settlements have been documented that date to the seventeenth and eighteenth centuries. These earliest settlements and plantations were not financed with large amounts of capital, however. Nor could they be characterized as one of the new industrial concerns that fueled the engine of the Industrial Revolution in America, for they did not rely upon mechanized production to achieve their purpose. If these criteria are used to define the type of company town built under industrial capitalism, then Alexander Hamilton may be credited with having conceived and built the first model company town in this country during the last decade of the eighteenth century.

The town of Paterson, New Jersey, established in 1791, was laid out and constructed under the direction of a holding company, the Society for Establishing Useful Manufactures, which Hamilton created expressly for this purpose (Crawford 1995:13–15; Yamin 1999). The site was marked by most of the traits of later company towns—the project was heavily capitalized, the land was under the direct control of the holding company, and the town was carefully designed with factories at the core. Adjacent areas, containing standardized worker housing, were divided by orderly streets and linked to the industrial center, thus imposing efficiency and order upon the landscape. It is interesting to note that plans for the town were shaped by two conflicting ideologies, that of the designer, Pierre L'Enfant, and that of the members of the Society for Establishing Useful Manufactures. Though both parties were motivated by a desire to demonstrate to the nation the benefits of industrialization under careful, controlled planning, their ideologies were fundamentally different. L'Enfant's conceptualization of an industrial center that glorified the possibilities of industry—in a style and scale comparable to that of the newly built capital in Washington, D.C.—was ultimately passed over in favor of an ideology of efficiency and functionalism held by investors.

While this project failed after only a few years, it marks the first use of the company town by industrial capitalists in America, and the first use of a planned industrial settlement or company town to formulate and express a new relationship between owner and worker in the context of emerging industrial production. Succeeding ventures that incorporated a company town in their design were dominated initially by textile manufacturers who were the first industrialists to successfully achieve mechanized factory production. Company towns began to proliferate in the 1810s–1820s as a result of this achievement. Wright notes that there were but 250 textile mills in New England in 1810, yet an estimated 12,000 existed by 1820 and five times that number only 10 years later (1981:66).

Corporate Paternalism in the Workplace

It was through the textile mills of New England that the company town came to be integrally linked with the philosophy and practice of corporate paternalism. If paternalism is defined as a form of social relations between capital and labor, we can look at the earliest examples of paternalism in the mills as attempts by owners and investors to create a successful, productive working relationship with their employees in the context of emerging factory production. In developing these new social relations, mill owners found it most useful to frame their new relationship with labor in terms of a benevolent, fatherly interest or moral guardianship. This claim to a familial or paternal authority—to a "protective" role—allowed them to ease the suspicions and fears of industrialization held by a largely agrarian society. At the same time it provided mill owners with the justification for introducing an "overly intrusive style of management" (Prude 1983:116) and for imposing social and economic controls over employees both in and out of the workplace.[5]

Two forms of paternalism developed in the mills of New England: those based on formal relations between owner and employee and those based on familiar relations (Scranton 1984). Variations arose from technological differences in the mills, from different hiring practices and the availability of capital, and from the willingness of local communities to accommodate changes brought about by industrialization or, conversely, resistance to the new order. Nonetheless, early forms of paternalism in the mills shared a similar purpose. These practices were designed to supervise the conduct of employees in the workplace; to mold them into an orderly, disciplined, efficient, and moral workforce; to foster contentment and stability among workers through the establishment of a healthy, safe working and living environment; and to attract new labor.

Paternalism and the Rural Mill Villages of New England

The earliest textile mill villages in rural New England were small operations, only moderately capitalized, that generally focused on a single process in textile manufacture—for example, the spinning of cotton (Candee 1981; 1985:112; 1992:17–18; Prude 1983). Owners of these early mills evolved a set of relationships with their operatives and weavers based on the English family labor system, finding that system to be most suited to the type of labor present in these rural agricultural communities and best suited to address or ease concerns and fears about industrialization that were so prevalent at this time. To demonstrate that the introduction of a new industrial economy did not mean the disruption of traditional agricultural practices and could in fact be beneficial to all, owners set about recruiting women and children in addition to male employees. The former group was, in fact, the most readily available source of labor in rural communities and as such would likely be most receptive to the arrival of industrial manufacture, viewing it as a welcome means of supplementing the family income. While some owners were willing to take orphans and the indigent into their mills, most elected to recruit families and single, male, free-wage laborers and artisans (Crawford 1995:15–18; Prude 1983:43, 46; 1987:91, 100–101). In this context of production, mill owners developed a familiar, hands-on style of management characterized by direct personal contact with their employees and a family-type atmosphere of concern.

Further, mill owners found it beneficial, both as a means to attract laborers and as a matter of efficiency in the workplace, to frame their new relationship with their employees in the form of a paternal authority or moral guardianship, with its attendant and reciprocal bonds of obligation and duty. Prude's research indicates that mill owners themselves quickly coined the term "paternalistic" to describe the personal style of management in the mills, where members of this industrial "family" found themselves under the direction of a "fatherly proprietor" (Prude 1983:115–116).[6] It was as fatherly proprietors that owners began the practice of constructing housing and company stores for employees, serving as both landlord and manager; similarly, they established Sunday schools and day schools for employees and their families. Claiming a familial interest and, at times, a Christian responsibility, owners took a direct interest in the health and welfare of their employees, developing a series of benevolent practices suited to the context of mill production in these rural communities.

But it was also this claim of paternal interest that was used to justify the "overly intrusive managerial presence" of owners and agents in the lives of mill workers—acts that included the physical separation of children from their parents in the mills and, later, the exclusion of fathers of mill workers from employment in the complex as well as strictures against the employment of married women. Owners also imposed restrictions upon tenants who resided in mill housing and instituted work contracts to reduce or eliminate worker transience (e.g., Prude 1983:117–118; 1987:113–114).

The policies and practices that developed under the Slater or Rhode Island system in the 1810s and 1820s served as a prototype for paternalism in the American workplace, yet the relationship between owner and employee began to change almost immediately. Examples of these transformations included reduced rates for piecework, tighter discipline over outworkers and the eventual elimination of outwork from family-style mills, the replacement of hand weavers with power looms, work contracts, and layoffs (Prude 1983:122–123; 1987:113–114). In a dialectic between economic modes of production and the social relations of production, the forms of paternalism employed by owners in existing mills and factories, as well as in newly organized ventures, were altered to fit fluctuating economic conditions, advances in technology, and changes in the workforce. The trend in the industrial workplace was increasingly toward what Crawford has described as relationships of "structured dependency" and, later, "enforced benevolence" between worker and owner (1995:12).

Formal Paternalism under the Waltham System

The Waltham-style mills and corporations that were introduced in the 1820s and 1830s were quite unlike the mill villages scattered throughout rural Massachusetts and Rhode Island, and their owners embraced a formal style of paternalism from the outset. The two classes of mills—Rhode Island and Waltham—had notable differences in mill technologies, in the planning and architecture of the factory complex and company housing, in hiring practices and wage guidelines, and in the amount of capitalization, management style, and structure of the company hierarchy (Candee 1985:17–19, 26–27).[7] The Waltham system, which emerged under the direction of the Boston Manufacturing Company and, later, the Boston Associates, was characterized by the use of a fully integrated manufacturing process (e.g., carding, spinning, and weaving) under unified management. Mills of this type were heavily capitalized and most were incorporated. Employees operated within a formally structured corporate hierarchy. Mill owners gradually shifted their hiring practices, placing less emphasis on or even replacing family and child labor, and turning instead to the recruitment of single men and women. The payment of cash wages also set Waltham-style mills apart from Rhode Island or family-style mills (Candee 1985:19; 1992:27; cf. Prude 1983:89–91).

Given the context of production in these mills, owners evolved a very different set of relationships with their employees. Under the Rhode Island system, mill owners claimed to improve the lives of their operatives by making a neat, orderly, productive, and moral class of workers. The analogy of family and father was used to create bonds of obligation with workers. By contrast, the corporations to the north made the claim of maintaining and preserving moral character, particularly for single young women, under the protective mantle of the corporation and its agents (Prude 1983:113–116). Paternalistic practices were still intended to provide an attractive, safe working and living environment and to promote a moral, orderly workforce. Under the Waltham system, however, social relations were now formalized and highly structured, and the controls exerted by companies over their employees were substantially increased, both in and out of the workplace.

As with familiar styles of paternalism, owners cast themselves in the role of moral guardians. By assuming parental authority over their employees and particularly their young women, owners sought to reassure parents, provide workers with a sense of well-being, attract new labor, and justify the close supervision of employee conduct in and out of the workplace. Asserting that worker productivity was greatly benefited by the use of an "industrious, sober, orderly, and moral class of operatives" (cited in Dublin 1979:77), employees were supervised, ostensibly on a 24-hour-a-day basis, through restrictions on public and private behavior in the mills and in factory-owned housing. In Lowell, for example, where the daughters of Yankee farmers comprised the most desirable type of labor from the 1820s to the 1840s, boardinghouses for the mill girls were designed as instruments of social control. Residence in company housing was mandatory for all unmarried female employees, and boardinghouse keepers were expected to supervise their behavior and to enforce company rules and regulations. Corporations imposed curfews, required mandatory attendance of Sunday school or church services, and issued prohibitions against the use of spirits and other immoral behaviors (Beaudry 1989; Beaudry, Cook, and Mrozowski 1991; Candee 1992; Dublin 1979:77–79; Eisler 1977; Zonderman 1992:144–162). To these social controls were wedded economic controls in the form of hiring practices, one-year contracts, wage schedules, and, later, wage reductions, blacklisting, eviction from company housing, and termination of employment.

Company Towns and Industrial Settlements, 1820–1880
A formal or corporate style of paternalism, in which social relations between owner and worker were established under the guise of moral concern and familial or paternal interests, was used successfully to conceive, implement, and justify the often extreme measures of social and economic control exerted over company employees in New England's textile factories. This form of paternalism became the model for social relations in other industries as mechanization and the factory system spread quickly into other areas of manufacture—for example, weapons, agricultural tools and machinery, industrial machinery, clocks, garments, and shoes—in the second quarter of the nineteenth century (e.g., Blewett 1988; Gordon and Malone 1994; Hindle and Lubar 1986; Shackel 1996; Zonderman 1992). The rapidity of industrial expansion was made possible by a combination of factors: advances in technology, the adoption of the steam engine, the development of alternative fuel sources such as anthracite and, later, bituminous coal and coke in place of charcoal or wood, and improvements in transportation.

At the same time, the intensification and acceleration of the factory process for all types of manufacture fueled and sustained the development of other industries such as coal, oil, iron, and steel. The interrelationship of these processes is readily apparent. After 1810, for example, investors began to buy up mineral rights throughout the anthracite fields in eastern Pennsylvania following the introduction of anthracite-burning grates and stoves for the home and the successful conversion of furnaces for the iron industry. The ensuing rush to create a viable link to those eastern markets led to the rapid construction of canals in the 1820s. Not only did supply and labor camps for the canal builders appear in the landscape beginning in the 1820s, but these settlements were followed in the 1830s and 1840s by the work camps of competitors who hoped to create an alternative transportation network based on the railroad (Gordon and Malone 1994; Miller and Sharpless 1985). Competition for markets and superior transportation systems stimulated developments in the iron and steel industries, as well, spurring the construction of locomotive works, furnaces, and rolling mills (Bomberger and Sisson 1991; Brown 1989). The close relationship between the coal, iron, and steel industries and emerging transportation concerns was crucial to industrial development in many areas of the country.

As owners, investors, entrepreneurs, and adventurers sought new opportunities in other spheres of production, they turned to the examples of those who had proceeded them, relying in large part, as Crawford (1995:2) notes, upon historical precedent and expediency to guide their decisions. During the second quarter of the nineteenth century, the ideologies and practices of corporate paternalism were introduced into other areas of manufacture and into burgeoning industries as a means of increasing worker productivity; of introducing the factory system and the concepts of industrial time, work discipline, and the division of labor; and of managing worker-owner tensions that resulted from increased mechanization and technological advances.

Similarly, after 1830 there was a notable increase in the use of company-owned settlements and towns to house and supervise company workers, particularly among the extractive industries. The company mine patch first appeared in the Pennsylvania anthracite fields in the 1830s and 1840s; during the same period, the first company towns were erected in the bituminous fields of western Maryland and West Virginia (Cohen 1984; Harvey 1969; Miller and Sharpless 1985). In western Pennsylvania, industrial capital financed the first company towns for the iron industry in the 1840s and 1850s, for steel manufacture by the 1870s, and for the production of bituminous coal and coke—materials that were needed to fuel the iron and steel industries—by the 1850s but especially after 1870 (America's Industrial Heritage Project [AIHP] 1992; Bennett 1990; Bodnar 1977; Brown 1989; DiCiccio 1996:89; Mulrooney 1989). Similar development occurred in the iron, steel, and coal mining industries in Ohio, Indiana, and Illinois, while commercial copper mining began along Lake Superior in the 1840s

(Lankton 1991). In the Pacific Northwest, the first company-built and company-owned lumber towns and logging camps were erected beginning in the 1850s (Roth 1992), while company mining camps and towns appeared after 1850 in the various mining regions of the American West (Hardesty 1988; Lalande 1985; Roth 1992). Most of the latter types of settlements were intended to be temporary camps, offering only the most primitive living conditions (tents, dugouts, adobe, log cabins, and movable boxcars) with few, if any, amenities for the miners and loggers who took up residence at these sites. Few permanent, planned company towns were built in the West before 1900, simply because transportation systems were insufficient for the needs of large-scale commercial mining in most regions until the 1870s or later (Roth 1992).

CREATING AN ENFORCED DEPENDENCY

The introduction of the company town into established communities and into the industrial frontier led to the replication of formal types of paternalism within many of these settlements. Though modeled to some extent upon the management practices that emerged in the textile mills of New England, specific forms and practices were adapted to the location and type of resource to be mined or manufactured by the company. Other considerations were the type of labor (e.g., skilled vs. unskilled) required by technological systems, the available source of labor, the amount of capitalization and the size of the industrial concern, and economic pressures (e.g., marketing and competition) within the industry. The ideologies and management philosophies of the corporation or company were shaped by these conditions and directly impacted the nature of housing, employee services, and social relations at each company town, settlement, or camp.

Location was particularly important in determining the structure of industrial relations and the forms of corporate paternalism at these sites. Those settlements that were most isolated evolved as closed social systems, with a rigid hierarchy and stringent forms of economic and social controls over employees. It is under such conditions that some of the most notorious company towns were established, particularly in the anthracite and bituminous coal industries (cf. Kenny 1998; Long 1989; Miller and Sharpless 1985:142–143, 176–178, 230–239; Sheppard 1947; Wallace 1988), and these companies made few claims to a paternalistic concern for their workers.[8]

The autocratic rule of the closed company town, though prevalent, cannot be said to be the measure of all company-owned settlements and towns of the period; nonetheless, all companies and corporations that extended some form of paternalism into worker housing and company settlements held substantial power over employees and their families, though the degree to which they asserted this control varied from place to place. In physically remote locations, employees were often completely dependent upon the company for housing, food, and supplies.

Many companies used this situation to create an "enforced dependency." Employees who were indebted to the company for stores and equipment found it difficult to end their employment. Owners also used the threat of eviction from company housing, termination, and blacklisting to exact complete obedience to their policies, to dispel labor unrest, and to blunt or suppress calls for unionization. Through a combination of social and economic controls and coercive measures, companies were able to exert complete, summary control over workers and their families. The expansion of company-owned settlements and towns under these circumstances led to some of the most repressive and hazardous living and working conditions that members of the working classes would face in the nineteenth century (Corbin 1981; Demarest 1992; Kenny 1998; Miller and Sharpless 1985; Sheppard 1947).

The company towns of this period were also characterized by overt expressions of ethnic prejudice, much of it directed at immigrants by the companies themselves in the form of discriminatory hiring practices, rock-bottom wages, and assignment to the most hazardous jobs or to the lowest paid tasks. This is again a retreat from or a reversal of the paternalistic practices seen in the textile mills in the early part of the century, when companies and corporations carefully cultivated an idealized set of relationships with their native-born workers. As will be seen in the next chapter, housing was also used to express ethnic preferences and prejudices. Companies typically provided inferior housing for immigrants and in many instances refused to provide any housing at all for their temporary laborers—for the Irishmen who built the canals in Lowell, for example, or the many immigrants who worked as day laborers to construct the mills, the towns, and the industrial plants that spread across the landscape. Immigrants were often left to fend for themselves, such that tent cities and shanty towns were common sites along the margins and peripheries of company towns (Dublin 1979:145–146; Miller and Sharpless 1985:142–144, 176–180).[9]

The transformation of industrial relations during this period reflects a shift in the ideology of corporate paternalism from a management style and philosophy that originally had been framed in terms of a paternal concern to one that, although still occasionally couched in terms of benevolence, was marked by the complete ascendancy of corporate control and corporate domination. The transition to "structured dependency" (Crawford 1995:12) came at the expense of the reciprocal bonds of obligation that had characterized relations in many early New England textile mills. This shift may be attributed in part to changes in the material conditions of production—increased mechanization, advances in technology, economic pressures, and especially the vast supply of cheap immigrant labor—but also to what Scranton has termed the accumulation matrix or profit motive (1984:236), now enhanced by the increased capitalization, incorporation, and consolidation of industrial concerns. Increasingly, companies created and relied upon forms of structured dependency within the corporate landscape to obtain and maintain leverage over employees, and to force acceptance of or compliance with a particular factory system or industrial regimen that many would otherwise reject or seek to alter as the pace of industrial labor accelerated, as hazards increased, as wages were reduced, and as working and living conditions deteriorated.

Few of the company towns built during this period practiced paternalism as defined earlier in this chapter; indeed, the living and working conditions that characterized these settlements represent a retrenchment from the policies, standards, and ideals of the textile corporations and mill owners of nineteenth-century New England. Rather, the companies in question borrowed some of the practices of paternalism (providing worker housing and services, for example) and reworked them to fit a new industrial regimen, but in a form divested of the morals and ideals that had originally shaped early styles of paternalism. The apparent stability and tranquility of nineteenth-century New England textile mills and factories stands in sharp contrast, then, to the autocratic and often oppressive conditions encountered in many company towns that followed in their wake. Yet all such workplaces and company towns were subject to increasing levels of owner control and domination, and the seeds of discontent, anger, and conflict were present in each of these settings.

CONFLICT AND RESPONSE IN THE WORKPLACE

Prude argues that tension and conflict are intrinsic to the industrial workplace, indeed that they are and have always been part of the industrial process (1983:xii, 263) and, further, that friction and discord between employer and employee stem from issues of control and freedom, power and class. In his study of New England mill villages in the early industrial era (1810–1860), Prude documents numerous examples of conflict between mill owners and employees. Responses of the workers varied, and many of these behaviors may be interpreted as acts of resistance. Such acts included theft, arson and sabotage, absenteeism and tardiness, transience, and, more rarely, work stoppages or strikes (Prude 1983:44–45, 133–157; 1987).[10]

As Prude notes, however, many of these same acts can be viewed as forms of negotiation—as part of a dialogue between worker and owner (Prude 1983:133–157; 1987:92, 106–107). From this perspective, the actions of workers may be seen as attempts by a new class of laborers to modify both industrial time and industrial discipline to meet their own needs, and to negotiate a sense of place in the mills. There is evidence that responses and actions varied by age, sex, class, and level of skill. The high level of transience among adult male employees may represent a gender-based strategy of negotiation (1983:146–150). Contemporary records indicate too that children regularly presented overseers with disciplinary problems and high rates of absenteeism (1983:137–138). Other examples include frequent disputes between supervisors and parents over the control of children in the mills; negotiations over the volume of and price for work "put out" to handworkers such as pickers and weavers; and the quickness of employees to distinguish between the workweek as set by owners (a standard 12-hour day, six days a week) and anything in excess of that amount—in other words, the negotiation of overtime (1983:140; 1987:104). Negotiation over the payment of employee wages in some mills resulted in the retention of some elements of a more traditional barter system, with labor provided in exchange for a mix of cash, credit, or goods (1983:76–77).

Transience, absenteeism, and slackness on the job were the most common responses to the new industrial regimen. The departure of employees was particularly evident at harvest time during the early years of industrialization (Crawford 1995:21; Prude 1987:103–104). Other conflicts ensued over the disruption of the more traditional rhythms of rural life, particularly with the institution of a year-round, 12-hour workday by factory owners (Prude 1987:103–104).

As noted, too, under formal and familiar types of paternalism, workers had few opportunities to advance vertically within the company hierarchy; for most, movement was possible only by taking up employment in another mill, thus, the new industrial worker quickly became a member of an increasingly mobile workforce. In contradistinction, then, to the claims of employers that industrial labor created a steady, reliable workforce, employees were continually pulling up stakes and shifting to other mills. Indeed, many used this freedom of movement as leverage to improve working conditions, to increase wages, to modify work discipline, or to cope with their participation in the industrial economy (Prude 1983:148).

In the larger mills to the north, where relations between employer and employee were formalized, the system of rules and regulations more stringent and inflexible, and the control of the company more pervasive, it was much more difficult for workers to negotiate change within the workplace, particularly as the size of industrial interests increased. Absenteeism and transience were not options open to female operatives who were dissatisfied with their wages or with living and working conditions, particularly if these behaviors resulted in a dishonorable discharge from the mill and blacklisting by their employer. Acts of resistance and negotiation, in the form of petitions and lists of grievances, meetings, worker protests, strikes or turnouts by women operatives, and incipient labor movements, usually were met with an aggressive counterresponse. These included intimidation and the physical removal of public demonstrators, the blocking of legislative initiatives to decrease the workday, and the discharge and blacklisting of malcontents (e.g., Dublin 1979:86–107; Zonderman 1992:225–228, 234–254).

Many employees, particularly the mill girls, also found the management practices of these corporations to be not only intrusive but oppressive and objectionable, particularly the moral policing of workers by agents and boardinghouse keepers (Eisler 1977). A small number of operatives responded by relocating to a more amenable living situation, by evading curfews, or by exerting pressure as a group upon boardinghouse keepers to ease their enforcement of company policies. Restrictions on drinking, curfews, visitors to the boardinghouse, and mandatory attendance of Sunday worship services were behaviors most subject to negotiation in this setting.

Some of the more subtle responses of workers to the industrial regimen imposed by the corporations are visible archaeologically. Excavations in the backlots of a Lowell boardinghouse recovered evidence of a mill worker subculture that was expressed through a mix of public and private behaviors. Working-class preferences and attitudes were apparent in articles of dress and personal adornment, and through a number of leisure-time activities, including the consumption of alcohol at the boardinghouses—the evidence suggests that some of this was done in secret, but it is not clear that boarders always engaged in this activity in private—and the smoking of clay tobacco pipes (Beaudry, Cook, and Mrozowski 1991: 168–169; see also Beaudry 1993; Beaudry and Mrozowski 1987a; 1987b; 1989).

While acts of negotiation and resistance were most often carried out in a private, rather than public, sphere, the discontent of some operatives did find limited public expression in publications such as the *Lowell Offering* (1840–1845). Other mill girls found an outlet for their frustrations in the growing number of self-improvement clubs and organized, after-hours activities that were established through their own initiative, not through corporate sponsorship (Crawford 1995:25; Eisler 1977:33).

In the end, however, negotiations for reduced hours and better wages were unsuccessful, and mill girls responded with the ultimate act of resistance to the industrial regimen. Faced with wage cuts and threats to their independence, with deteriorating conditions in the workplace and in worker housing, these native-born women began to desert the mills in such large numbers that by the 1850s the corporations were forced to find a new source of labor. The famed mill girls of Lowell were replaced from the vast pool of immigrant labor, and the face of industry was permanently changed.

CHANGING FORMS OF PATERNALISM

In Marxist interpretations, there is a direct relationship—a dialectic—between economic structures (the modes of production) and industrial relations (the social relations of production); a change in the former results in tension, conflict, and then resolution in the other (Scranton 1984:236, 238; see also Crawford 1995:5–6). While this model is somewhat formulaic, it nonetheless captures the essential relationship between the material conditions of industry and changing forms of paternalism in the workplace during the nineteenth century. Throughout the nineteenth century, owners and corporations responded to a changing context of production—fluctuating economic pressures, technological advances, changing demographics of the workforce, and increasing labor unrest—by altering the ideology and the practice of paternalism (Scranton 1984:248). The responses and actions of workers would change accordingly.

Companies that increasingly relied upon unskilled and, for the most part, uneducated immigrant labor no longer attempted to re-create the affective qualities that had proved so attractive to their earlier recruits. Owners no longer claimed or exploited the ties of home, family, and community, with their reciprocal bonds of obligation, nor did they continue to offer the benefits of moral protection and economic security in exchange for hard work and obedience from their new employees. Many corporations moved away from the use of housing and real estate as a form of economic and social control; still others found it practical in urban settings to abandon the company store. Faced with a decrease in wages and with deteriorating conditions in the mills, textile workers increasingly turned toward organized labor movements, a trend that was paralleled in other types of manufacture; examples of militancy among some workers also increased dramatically (e.g., Blewett 1988; Dublin 1979; Walkowitz 1978; Zonderman 1992; cf. Corbin 1981; Demarest 1992; Miller and Sharpless 1985). In some industries, particularly those that exerted heavy control over employees within a closed company town, workers found it difficult to break the rule of the corporation or to negotiate directly with their companies and so would turn to the same forms of action, response, and confrontation in their efforts to shape the industrial landscape (Corbin 1981; Miller and Sharpless 1985; Zonderman 1992). It was in response to the threat of labor unrest and unionization in the third quarter of the nineteenth century that corporations again began to alter the shape of paternalism, leading to the creation of a new type of company town that would dominate the industrial landscape for the next 70 years.

WELFARE CAPITALISM AND THE MODEL COMPANY TOWN

Company towns built after 1880 were shaped by an increased commitment to the welfare of employees and to the improvement of living and working conditions, largely in response to worker protest and the threat of organized labor. The forms and practices associated with this changing corporate ideology have been collectively termed welfare capitalism. Crawford argues that Pullman, Illinois, constructed in 1883, represents the first of the model company towns founded under this new corporate ideology and therefore marks the beginning of this new stage of development (1995:6).

Welfare capitalism of the late nineteenth and twentieth centuries was characterized by a variety of enlightened social and economic programs that were intended to improve employee living and working conditions, promote company loyalty, and create a contented workforce—most notably through the creation of planned industrial communities (Crawford 1995; Garner 1992:3–14; Wright 1981:177–192) and the introduction of "controlled leisure time" (Seymour 1990:215; see also Hareven and Langenbach 1978). By the turn of the century, a social or cognitive ideal was as important, if not more important, to the design of many company towns as the economic, geographic, and material constraints that had previously dictated form and location (Crawford 1995:2; Scranton 1984). Indeed, by 1910, model towns were created by architects, landscape architects, designers, social theorists, and city planners, independent of their industrial roots and in isolation from the technological and environmental factors that had shaped earlier landscapes. The design was based on social theory and progressive ideologies; its form was strictly a matter of architectural design and town planning. Many businesses and industries turned to planned industrial communities for their workers, often hiring professionals from outside the company for the purpose of designing a town that emphasized the ideals of community, civic pride, education, physical and mental health, moral rectitude, and religious values (Crawford 1995; Metheny 1992; Roth 1992; Wright 1981).

Contemporary business leaders argued that planned communities and displays of increased company concern for the welfare of their workers were a matter of business, a pragmatic response to the current conditions of industry, and "a sound business investment," rather than acts of philanthropy or paternalism, since "every feature . . . is designed to have some constructive influence for specifically benefiting the workman for his work, and he gets nothing he does not pay for" (Wright 1981:182). Many owners turned to welfare capitalism after coercive measures failed to stem the threat of unionization and labor strikes. Others invested in such programs to be more competitive with their business rivals. A measure of their success can be seen in the negative response of organized labor. Indeed, the unions objected to this form of paternalism precisely because of its appeal to workers; such programs, they argued, permitted the companies to take power and control away from the unions and their constituents. For all of its attractiveness, the outward show of concern for employees, and the real gains experienced by the workers in the quality of living and working conditions, welfare capitalism was just a more subtle, "more diffuse but nonetheless controlling form of paternalism" than that seen in the early textile mills of New England (Beaudry and Mrozowski 1988:2), for it allowed the corporations to once again extend their influence, under a claim of benevolence, to worker behavior outside of the workplace.

Some scholars have argued that this form of paternalism was merely a facade to mask growing inequalities in the distribution of wealth and resources (McGuire 1991; Seymour 1990). The motivations behind the practice of twentieth-century welfare capitalism are complex, however, for its roots are to be found not only in nineteenth-century paternalistic practices, but also in urban and social reform movements of the late nineteenth and early twentieth centuries. There are many parallels between the social programs of the Progressive Movement and those of industrial capitalism. In their efforts to counteract the increasingly evil influences of city life, urban reformers sought to instill social mores in city dwellers, to strengthen the values associated with communities, and to create a binding "social cement" (Boyer 1978:222) within the city. Their program sought "through consciously planned and organized efforts to influence that range of social behavior outside the purview of criminal law, yet not entirely private and personal" (1978:viii).

In the early twentieth century, urban reformers turned to a "more subtle and complex process of influencing behavior and molding character through a transformed, consciously planned urban environment" that included dance pavilions, parks and playgrounds, and organized recreational activities as well as tenement reforms and city planning (1978:221–222). Parks, for example, were designed as "social artifacts expressing the class realities of urban-industrial society and inculcating the social values and outlook of the dominant group," such that "every detail should reflect in a literal and explicit way the social values of its planners" (1978:241).

The parallels are evident. Like urban reformers, many companies created planned industrial communities that emphasized the values of community, productivity, stability, and morality as a way to structure and influence the behavior of their employees inside and outside of the workplace. Business leaders saw that coercive and repressive measures had failed to end labor disputes, had failed to bust the union, had failed to avert strikes in the workplace. Thus, owners were led to try alternate forms of social control that were in many ways more encompassing and more persuasive than earlier forms of paternalism.

The Failure of Pullman

The effectiveness of the new company town and its associated welfare programs varied. Pullman is an interesting study because as the first planned model town associated with this new ideology, it seemed to offer unheralded benefits and opportunities to its employees, yet it failed abysmally (Crawford 1995:37–45; Wright 1981:183–184). This city of over 12,000 residents was carefully engineered, incorporating progressive management practices and the latest theories on social reform with urban landscaping and a full range of welfare programs and employee services. Yet George Pullman's excessively restrictive and rigid governance of all aspects of the city—from worker behavior to the maintenance of buildings—and his intransigence over high rents, high costs of living, and other worker grievances created tensions that erupted in rioting and the largest labor strike up to that time. Investigators looking into the causes of the 1894 Pullman strike concluded that Pullman himself was to blame and the State of Illinois ruled that Pullman's ownership of the town was in violation of state law; by 1898 he was forced to sell off all holdings in Pullman that were extraneous to the production of the Pullman sleeping-car.

Standard Oil: Creating Social Cement

By contrast, the Standard Oil Corporation, which was notorious for unfair business practices and its ruthless strong-arm tactics (Tarbell [1904] 1969), successfully created and cultivated its image as a model employer and a benefactor of the community (Metheny 1992). This exemplar of industrial capitalism was founded in 1870 by John D. Rockefeller and quickly became the largest industrial monopoly of the period, controlling some 90 percent of refining and transportation interests before its dissolution in 1911 under the Sherman Anti-Trust Act. It was perhaps this legacy—the desire for efficiency and control of the market during this period—that influenced the company's treatment of and investment in its employees in the early twentieth century. The welfare program at Standard Oil was a model of enlightened self-interest and indicates that the company owners found greater efficiency in a satisfied, contented workforce than a dissatisfied one. Standard Oil built houses for its workers. The company offered health benefits and a hospitalization plan to its employees, as well as a pension and retirement plan. In later years, the company sponsored a continuing education program and paid tuition costs for its employees to continue their schooling. Standard also sponsored competitive, organized baseball teams for its employees for many years.

But Standard also looked outward to the surrounding community. Headquartered in Whiting, Indiana, the company made many contributions to the city, even as it expanded to include other businesses and neighborhoods that were unrelated to the refinery and its employees. The company built a community center with a swimming pool, a 700-seat auditorium, and a bowling alley. Standard paid for the center's upkeep and eventually deeded it to the city of Whiting. The company also fluoridated the community water supply and held charity drives for various causes. Among the many recreational activities sponsored by the company were dances in the park pavilion, picnics, and holiday festivities, including yearly parades on the Fourth of July and Christmas parties at the community center for the children of Standard employees. The company also sponsored plays at the community center and a big band for its employees, directed by Morgan L. Eastman. The band played concerts for KYW radio and performed in the park band shell on the Fourth of July and at the community center.

The image of Standard Oil that emerged from oral history interviews with former employees and family members was of a benevolent employer and a very active, generous force in the Whiting community (Metheny 1992). In this sense, Whiting was truly a company town; employees spoke of Standard Oil's contributions to the community with personal pride, thus affirming that the Standard Oil Company provided, as did many other corporations during this period, "the social cement of a cohesive urban community" (Boyer 1978:222).

Amoskeag Men and Women

Perhaps the best illustration of the adaptability of industrial corporations and the changing face of corporate paternalism is found in the history of the Amoskeag Manufacturing Company. The Amoskeag, established in 1838 in Manchester, New Hampshire, carried the traditions of nineteenth-century paternalism into the twentieth century and thus provides a useful benchmark for measuring the shifts in corporate ideology. Hareven and Langenbach note that "from its inception, the Amoskeag was a paternalistic corporation, similar to . . . other planned New England industrial communities" (1978:25). The Amoskeag incorporated its social program into the design of its mill yard, its company housing, and its industrial regimen for workers. Company policies changed over time, reflecting both the different types of labor employed at the mills and the different needs of company management. Some of the boardinghouses built for mill girls in the 1830s were remodeled into family-style housing as the workforce changed in the 1850s and 1860s. Later, the constant stream of immigrants into Manchester led to further changes in policy; as more workers lived outside of company housing, greater effort was made to control the social environment within the city. Since the Amoskeag had established and essentially built Manchester, the company was able to exert considerable economic, political, and social control over city residents and businesses through zoning and property sales, deed restrictions, endowments for various institutions, and close ties with the city aldermen and police force.

By 1910, the changing composition of the workforce meant that a new form of corporate paternalism was required to "attract additional immigrants to the city, to socialize them to industrial work, to instill loyalty to the company, and to curb labor unrest and thus prevent unionization" (1978:26). Only 15 percent of worker housing was company owned by this time; most employees lived in the growing ethnic neighborhoods of Manchester. The company turned to other forms of paternalism to exert influence over its workers. Seymour has noted that the idea of "controlled leisure time" was well established by the 1880s (1990:215), and it is one that the Amoskeag incorporated into its program of welfare capitalism in the early twentieth century. The Amoskeag Textile Club, for instance, sponsored organized social and recreational activities for mill employees, including sewing and cooking classes, theater, athletics, and group outings. That this paternalistic program was only partially successful is clear from a series of strikes (1918 and 1922) that shook the Amoskeag community. Yet throughout its long history, until the textile manufacturer closed its doors permanently in 1936, both workers and management identified with an "Amoskeag spirit," and in many ways they constructed their sense of self around their association with the company. They thought of themselves as "Amoskeag Men and Women."

IDEOLOGY IN A COMPANY TOWN

The variation that has characterized both the physical form of the company town, the social structure of the community therein, and the cultural landscape in which it was placed is paralleled by variations in the social relations of industry, specifically the form and underlying ideology of corporate paternalism. As this discussion moves toward an examination of the coal towns of western Pennsylvania, it will be important to recognize both patterned behavior and variation, and to compare the corporate/industrial regimen with the beliefs and traditions of the working classes. To understand the context of work and daily life in the company town of Helvetia, it is necessary to identify and understand the underlying ideologies that shaped social relations in this community and the dialogue that ensued between the corporation and its employees, the miners of Helvetia and their families. Those data will be outlined in the chapter that follows.

 Chapter 2

Building the
Coal Company Town

> If a person suddenly found himself in the middle of a company-owned town, he
> would have little difficulty identifying it as such, for certain general features usu-
> ally stood out. First to be noted would be the standard, uniform architecture of
> the company-owned houses. In a prominent location, however, would stand a
> larger, more imposing structure: the home of the company manager or superin-
> tendent. It would be observed that the town seemed to center around a focal
> point where a store, community hall, school, and other public buildings were
> located. The company store usually dominated the group. It would be noted that
> the settlement had no "suburbs," or no gradual building up from a few scattered
> homes to a center of population. Rather, one would note the complete isolation
> of the community and the definiteness of its boundaries. Finally, it would be
> apparent that the existence of the community was completely dependent upon
> a single enterprise, because a mine, mill, or smelter would seem to dominate the
> entire scene [Allen 1966:79–80].

James Allen captured the essence of western company towns in a single paragraph,
but this passage could just as easily describe the company towns of West Virginia
or Iowa or western Pennsylvania. Most company towns across the United States
were characterized by a uniformity and repetition in town plan and worker housing. Perhaps nowhere is this patterning more evident than in the company towns
built by the coal industry in the late nineteenth and early twentieth centuries.

    The similarity in form and layout may be partly explained by considering the
historical antecedents for worker housing in America. Just as forms of corporate
paternalism in the late nineteenth and early twentieth centuries had their origins in the textile mills of early nineteenth-century New England, so too were the
arrangement and types of corporate housing of the later company towns derived

from earlier forms of mill-worker housing in Rhode Island and Massachusetts (Crawford 1995; Mulrooney 1989:10–11; Prude 1983:50, 96–97; Wright 1981).[1] Family housing types that were common in the early New England mill village were reproduced both conceptually and in physical form in a variety of industrial settings, but the coal industry in particular was characterized by its reliance upon such forms.

As described by Allen, there were other features that made the coal company town distinctive, and those features were repeated in coal towns across the country. Following, then, is a discussion of the factors that shaped the landscape of the coal company town, and, more specifically, the bituminous fields of western Pennsylvania. The latter is necessary to place Helvetia within a regional context of architectural design and town planning. It is also necessary to examine the first mining communities to emerge in Pennsylvania. The anthracite mining town first appeared in the late 1830s, preceding its sister coal towns in the western part of the state by 30 to 40 years. The conditions and techniques of mining in the two regions were vastly different, as were labor relations (cf. DiCiccio 1996; Dix 1988; Miller and Sharpless 1985; Wallace 1988), and the two industries were separated not only geographically and geologically but also in a temporal sense. There are nonetheless certain parallels between the bituminous and anthracite industries that merit a closer look, particularly with reference to the development of company towns and worker housing. Indeed, the standard form of miners' housing and the spatial organization of the bituminous coal company town appear to be derivatives of forms developed in the anthracite region.

THE LANDSCAPE OF
THE COAL COMPANY TOWN

As noted by James Allen, coal companies characteristically built or set aside land for company stores, housing, churches, schools, and a few additional structures that served a variety of corporate and community needs in the company town (AIHP 1992; Allen 1966; Corbin 1981; DiCiccio 1996:89–91; Francaviglia 1991:117–118; Gardner and Flores 1989; Gradwohl and Osborn 1984; Miller and Sharpless 1985:143; Mulrooney 1989). An overwhelming proportion of corporate housing was built for families. It has also been observed that the housing forms in these towns were typically built to re-create and reify in lumber, mortar, and brick the corporate structure of the company (AIHP 1992:47–49; DiCiccio 1996:92; Gardner and Flores 1989:80, 104–110; Mulrooney 1989:16; for examples outside of the coal industry, see Beaudry and Mrozowski 1987b:2, 7–9; Crawford 1995:26, 86, 129, 139–142; McGuire 1991:104; Wright 1981). Rank within the hierarchy of management and labor was evident through the use of specific housing types for each group, and through size, material, design, and location. Finally, housing and company facilities were carefully laid out on gridded streets in hierarchical fashion, but all in close proximity to the mine.

Scholars who have examined the institution of the coal company town or studied specific examples of this form of settlement have argued that the uniformity and sameness that pervaded the coal mining landscape were a result of economic and geographic conditions that shaped the industry as a whole. First, "[each] town was financed, built, owned and operated by only one company. Unlike other single-enterprise towns, the primary employer was also the primary landholder" (Mulrooney 1989:1). Coal companies became both landowner and landlord because operators needed to own both surface and mineral rights. Here Crawford's narrower definition of a company town (1995:1) becomes important in explaining the developing economic and social character of these mining communities and the creation of a "mining culture" (Mulrooney 1989:27; see also Francaviglia 1991:117–118). Companies alone determined the physical form and the economic and social structure of their company towns.

Second, the physical isolation of the mines, whether in mountainous terrain or on the open plains, was itself a cause for the similarity in form and function among coal company towns. Geographically, most bituminous mine sites were remote and relatively inaccessible when first developed. Thus, of necessity, companies provided housing and services for their employees.

Third, because of the economic structure of the bituminous coal industry and the trend toward consolidation, incorporation, and increased capitalization during this period, the mines in a particular region were often dominated by a few large corporations and companies, though production was shared with numerous small, independent coal operators (e.g., AIHP 1992:34–37; DiCiccio 1996:101–103; Gardner and Flores 1989:79). Corporations like the Rochester and Pittsburgh Coal Company, the Berwind-White Company, or the Union Pacific Railroad, which mined its own coal in Wyoming, might operate dozens of company towns and were likely to replicate the same town plan and building forms in each, with some variation for site topography, for the size of the proposed operation, and for the types of ancillary industrial processes, such as coke production and power generation, to be conducted on site.

Finally, coal operators did not see real estate and worker housing as a long-term investment (Mulrooney 1989:14–16), and indeed by the 1870s to 1890s, many industries no longer built housing with the intent of profit, a trend that coincided with changes in the composition of the workforce and the increased reliance upon immigrant labor (DiCiccio 1996:85–90; Gardner and Flores 1989:79; cf. Hareven and Langenbach 1978:25). Coal operators always viewed camps and even planned towns as temporary expedients; the towns would function only until the coal supply was exhausted.

COLD IN THE WINTER, HOT IN THE SUMMER

With few exceptions, then, worker housing was built at minimum cost and as quickly as possible. This expediency is reflected in the use of low-cost building materials, and it led generally to the construction of low-quality housing and minimal investment in the infrastructure of the town (AIHP 1992:48–49; Corbin 1981:67–68; DiCiccio 1996:88–95; Gardner and Flores 1989:78–82, 105–106; Mulrooney 1989:1, 14–16; cf. Slickville, Pennsylvania, and other model coal company towns, in Mulrooney 1989:19; DiCiccio 1996:95–100).[2] The U.S. Coal Commission, investigating the causes of a protracted strike in 1922–1923, surveyed 713 company-owned and operated communities and some 71,000 units of company housing for the purpose of documenting the living conditions of the miners (Hunt, Tryon, and Willits 1925:143–144). The commission's report confirms the prevalence of low-cost and often substandard construction methods in these communities. The report noted that two-thirds of the family dwellings surveyed had weatherboard exteriors, some of which were sheathed only with a layer of tar paper and some of which had no additional finish at all. A small percentage had clapboard siding. Twenty-five percent had board-and-batten exteriors, described by the commission as the cheapest type of construction.[3] Just over a third of the houses had a plaster interior finish, while more than half had wood sheathing to finish the interior. The commission reported that these communities frequently suffered from inadequate sewage disposal and that most houses lacked running water. Less than 3 percent had indoor baths, 3 percent had indoor toilets, and only 14 percent had running water even though nearly 61 percent of these company towns had a water system. The commission graded each community based on the quality of the town's infrastructure and the services provided by the operators, including housing, water supply and distribution, sewage and waste disposal, community layout, food and merchandise supply, medical and health provisions, and provisions for recreation, religious worship, and education (Hunt, Tryon, and Willits 1925:145–146). The results of this evaluation indicate that most company towns were substandard in construction, maintenance, and services. Only 9 percent scored 75 or more points out of 100, 11 percent fell under 50 points, and 80 percent were rated somewhere in between 50 and 75 points.

The quality of housing was a problem throughout the industry. In Pennsylvania, the worst examples of miners' housing were found in the settlements that collected at the collieries or mines run by small, independent operators who often could not or would not invest in facilities or services for the miners. A contemporary report noted that "living conditions in this district [DuBois region] are in general very poor. The majority of companies are small with insufficient capital to install modern improvements at their mines, and the workmen must provide for their own welfare. The houses are cheap, cold in the winter time, and tin roofs make them almost unbearably hot in the summer. Nine out of ten mining towns or camps have no sewerage regulations" (Sisler 1924:138). Such conditions were not confined to the smaller operations, however. Many of the larger mining corporations, run by absentee owners, were also guilty of providing inferior housing for their workers—for example, the Union Pacific Railroad (Gardner and Flores 1989) and John D. Rockefeller Jr., owner of Colorado Fuel and Iron (Crawford 1995:81). This was particularly so in West Virginia, where the coalfields were dominated by out-of-state investors and a small number of coal operators who were closely allied with the state's political machine (Corbin 1992; Eller 1982).

REGIONAL VARIATION AND THE EMERGENCE OF THE PENNSYLVANIA MINERS' DWELLING

Mulrooney (1989:139–141) has compared company towns and housing forms in several coal-producing regions, including those in the eastern coalfield (Pennsylvania, Maryland, Virginia, West Virginia, Alabama, Kentucky, and Tennessee), as well as those found in the midwestern or central United States. The survey suggests that distinct regional variations existed within the bituminous industry, and these differences were most visible in the types of dwellings built for the miners. Mulrooney attributes these variations (e.g., layout, number of stories, construction materials, the presence of a cellar) to differences in climate, the date of construction, the composition of the workforce, and the preexistence of a strong vernacular architectural style in certain regions.

Mulrooney's survey of the eastern or Appalachian field records four basic housing forms: the shotgun, a one- or two-family dwelling found throughout the southern portion of the eastern coalfield (Alabama and portions of Kentucky); a one-story, detached or semidetached cottage built on post foundations with a hipped or pyramidal roof, found in the southern Appalachian region (Kentucky, Tennessee, Alabama); a one-story, single-family, gable-roof "bungalow" with or without an attached ell that was common in the southern Appalachian region after 1910; and the Pennsylvania miners' dwelling, a two-story, semidetached, gable-end, wood-frame structure found throughout the northern Appalachian region (Pennsylvania, Maryland, Virginia, West Virginia, and, to a lesser degree, Kentucky) (1989:1, 126–141).

It is the latter form that is of interest here. The Pennsylvania miners' dwelling was the standard corporate house form built for miners and laborers in southwestern Pennsylvania (Figure 1). This structure provided two families with an identical four-room unit in the main block; an additional one to two rooms was often added using an attached rear ell. For many years, these structures had no insulation, no running water, and no indoor plumbing, yet most were lighted by electricity from the power plant. Each doublehouse was constructed close to the front of the lot, leaving little or no setback from the unpaved street. Residents of the two units shared a long, narrow backlot in which were situated numerous outbuildings, including outdoor privies and coal sheds, as well as family vegetable gardens. Mulrooney's survey and other AIHP studies document the widespread use of this housing form throughout southwestern Pennsylvania, not only across the main bituminous field but also in the Broad Top and Georges Creek fields (e.g., AIHP 1988; 1990; 1991; 1993; Bennett 1990) (Figure 2). Similar workers' housing is found in Maryland and West Virginia coal company towns as well (AIHP 1992; Harvey 1969:83; Mulrooney 1989:125–132).

This typological study of bituminous coal towns in southwestern Pennsylvania also documents a similarity in town planning and layout within these communities.[4] Five physical traits in particular were consistently identified in the survey: the town lands were owned by a single company; the corporate hierarchy of the coal company was expressed through architecture; low-cost building materials were used to construct company housing; the housing forms replicated a regional style; and the town plan expressed both the corporate hierarchy and efficiency in its spatial arrangement (Mulrooney 1989:1–2, 33). Other unifying elements include the use of a gridded street layout, clustering of houses along the street, and minimal investment in infrastructure.

Mulrooney's analysis is helpful in understanding why this type of construction and town planning was consistently used by Pennsylvania's bituminous operators. She concludes that western Pennsylvania's coal company towns were shaped by the same factors that affected the coal industry as a whole, but she also points to an existing regional housing type that strongly influenced the shape of coal towns in this area. It is here that Mulrooney draws a link between the bituminous coal towns of the 1870s to 1890s and the mining communities that developed several decades earlier in Pennsylvania's anthracite region. There has been no systematic study of the state's anthracite mining towns thus far. It is apparent nonetheless

FIG. 1. Rows of miners' doublehouses in Phillips, Pennsylvania. Pennsylvania State Archives.

BUILDING THE COAL COMPANY TOWN

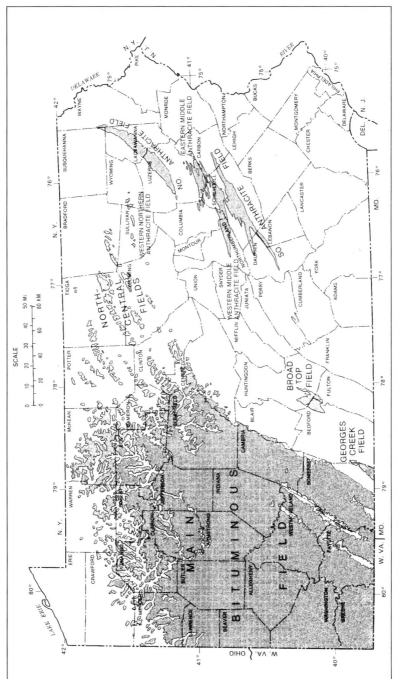

FIG. 2. Bituminous and anthracite coalfields of Pennsylvania. Commonwealth of Pennsylvania.

that in both types of communities company engineers replicated clustered family housing, with gridded streets, long and narrow lots, and standardized housing forms that were efficiently laid out in close proximity to the mine and its associated industrial plant (Gordon and Malone 1994:126; Miller and Sharpless 1985; Mulrooney 1989; Wallace 1988:144–145). Let us take a closer look, then, at these anthracite communities.

ANTHRACITE LANDSCAPES

The earliest anthracite company towns, known as mining patches, were built by the area's coal operators beginning in the late 1830s to early 1840s (Miller and Sharpless 1985:142–144; Wallace 1988:144–145; Warfel 1993). Patch towns were constructed in isolated valleys, separated from each other by the hills and mountains that dominate the landscape of eastern Pennsylvania. Unlike the larger urban settlements and boomtowns where members of the new coal and railroad aristocracies lived, patch towns were characterized by extremely primitive living conditions and an unhealthy living environment from their proximity to the colliery. The coal mining process and its waste by-products marred the landscape. While miners alone faced the dangers of working in the deep underground mines, miners and village residents alike were confronted daily with health hazards: coal dust, pollutants released into the water and the surrounding environment, and inadequate sanitation (Gordon and Malone 1994:124–126; Miller and Sharpless 1985:176–181, 323–324). Miners' dwellings were overcrowded and poorly built.

Described by Miller and Sharpless as "total communities" (1985:142–144), everything in the mining patches—from worker housing, stores, and community services to the land itself—was under company ownership. Coal operators imposed rigid and harsh controls over their workers in these settlements. Companies regularly resorted to the summary termination, eviction, and blacklisting of their employees. The Coal and Iron Police, a private security force authorized by the state legislature in 1865–1866, used intimidation and physical coercion to enforce company controls and to repress worker unrest and militancy in the region (DiCiccio 1996:166; Kenny 1998; Miller and Sharpless 1985:142–143).

Unlike the bituminous region in western Pennsylvania, there are few published architectural or archaeological surveys of the anthracite region that may be used for comparative purposes. Mulrooney (1989), for instance, relies largely upon labor statistics and government-sponsored reports on worker housing that were compiled in the 1920s. There is, however, a published archaeological study (Warfel 1993) of an anthracite miners' dwelling that allows a preliminary comparison of housing in the anthracite and bituminous regions. A surviving two-and-one-half-story, wood-frame miners' doublehouse in Eckley, Pennsylvania, was investigated by the Pennsylvania Historical and Museum Commission (PHMC) in 1991. Research included historical, oral, and archaeological components, with excavations focused on delineating landscape and construction sequences prior to restoration of the structure.

The Eckley patch, laid out in 1854 in an area adjacent to the coal breaker, contained a company store, a hotel, churches, a school, and worker housing—201 housing units during its heyday—arranged in linear fashion on a single main street and two parallel side streets (Figure 3). The town was further divided by two back alleys and three cross streets (Warfel 1993:6–9). Architecturally, the town's domestic structures are typical for the region. Company officials were provided with single-family detached houses. Miners and laborers were assigned housing in gable-end, semidetached wooden doublehouses of varying size and quality. The doublehouse examined by the PHMC comprises a main block and attached rear ell (Figure 4). A scale plan of houselot no. 117/119 depicts a front block that is 30 ft wide x 25 ft deep (9.14 x 7.62 m); the rear ell measures 40 ft wide x 10 ft deep (12.19 x 3.05 m) (Warfel 1993:230). As will be seen, this dwelling is roughly comparable in size and shape to the doublehouses constructed in Helvetia and indeed is largely representative of what has been termed the Pennsylvania miners' dwelling in the western part of the state (DiCiccio 1996:100; Mulrooney 1989:125–127).[5]

The miners' houses in Eckley and other patch towns were built without running water and indoor plumbing. Domestic structures were clustered, and each was located at the front of the lot, abutting the road. The lots, as shown on the 1873 map of Eckley, were long and narrow. Oral testimony and landscape features indicate that the lot for no. 117/119 measured some 90–100 x 160 ft (27.43–30.48 x 48.77 m) (Warfel 1993:230). Architectural and oral evidence also shows that each houselot in Eckley had associated outbuildings located in the rear portion of the yard. Shanties or summer kitchens, coal sheds, outdoor privies, pigeon coops, and multipurpose sheds were common.

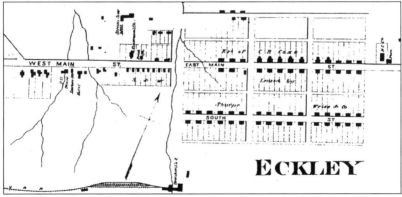

FIG. 3. An 1873 map of Eckley, Pennsylvania. From *A Patch of Land Owned by the Company* (Warfel 1993:8). Pennsylvania Historical and Museum Commission.

FIG. 4. House no. 117/119 in Eckley Miners' Village, site of archaeological excavations. From *A Patch of Land Owned by the Company* (Warfel 1993:2). Pennsylvania Historical and Museum Commission.

THE MINERS' DOUBLEHOUSE IN WESTERN MARYLAND

The miners' doublehouse also became a standard housing type in western Maryland's bituminous coalfields in the late 1830s–1840s (Harvey 1969:82–83; Mulrooney 1989:127–128, 142 n. 4). Mulrooney speculates that there is a relationship between the doublehouse as it developed in Pennsylvania's anthracite communities and Maryland's bituminous company towns, since both coalfields developed simultaneously, though there is not yet sufficient evidence to determine the exact nature of the relationship (Mulrooney 1989:142 n. 2). What is clear is that the earliest coal companies in Maryland built corporate, family-style housing similar to that seen in Pennsylvania's coalfields.

In Lonaconing (est. 1838), one of Maryland's earliest coal company towns, the George's Creek Coal and Iron Company built an industrial plant, worker housing, a company store, a church, and a school on company-owned lands (Balicki, O'Brien, and Yamin 1999:97–98; Harvey 1969:29, 75–77). While several housing forms, including log cabins, single-family cottages, and boardinghouses, were used as both temporary and permanent accommodations for company workers, the doublehouse was the predominant and preferred form built by the coal company (Figure 5). Original plans called for the construction of some 400 units of family housing. Company correspondence from 1845 describes one-and-one-half-story, wood-frame, cellarless, gable-end doublehouses, 32 x 32 ft (9.75 x 9.75 m) in size, with three rooms on the first floor, a fourth room on the upper floor, a shared central chimney, and shared porch across the front of the house (Harvey 1969:82–83).

FIG. 5. Semidetached vertical plank miners' dwelling in Lonaconing, Maryland, built circa 1840. Photograph by Mark R. Edwards, 1982. Lonaconing Historic District, Allegany County. On file at the Maryland Historical Trust.

Examples from other communities show that two-story duplexes or "blocks" with four rooms and an attached kitchen ell or shed were also common. Double-houses were constructed both of wood and stone during this period, as both materials were readily available in the region. Insurance maps of company towns like Lonaconing suggest that the homes were clustered along the street on narrow, deep lots, and that a majority of houses had little or no yard space in the front (Balicki, O'Brien, and Yamin 1999; Cheek, Yamin, and Heck 1994; Harvey 1969:83; O'Brien et al. 1997).

BITUMINOUS LANDSCAPES AND THE COAL COMPANY TOWN

The commercial exploitation of bituminous coal in western Pennsylvania began several decades later than in western Maryland, spurred by the rise of the iron and steel industries and the demand for coke. The country's new railroads also became heavy consumers of coal, and many of Pennsylvania's coal companies were created as subsidiaries of the railroad interests that dominated the region (Cooper 1982; DiCiccio 1996:37–38).[6] The increased demand for bituminous coal coincided with a search for additional resources. The second state-sponsored Geological Survey of 1874–1884, which documented the presence of coal beds lying just below the surface, spurred the development of commercial coal interests in western Pennsylvania (Cooper 1982:11; DiCiccio 1996:63). The growth of company towns mirrors the expansion of coal and coke interests in this region.

The mining of bituminous coal generally occurred in physically isolated locations where transportation was difficult and services were few (Cooper 1982:61–68; DiCiccio 1996:88–100, 127–131; Mulrooney 1989). As with the anthracite region, the company town was a key feature of this remote industrial landscape, and its presence was crucial to the success of coal mining companies in western Pennsylvania for a number of reasons. First, the establishment of company-built and company-owned worker housing on site was seen as a way to attract a large and therefore cheap immigrant labor force and to overcome the difficulties of physical access to the mines. The offer of housing was enticing to many and, together with a variety of other company-sponsored services, was more likely to attract married men, who were seen as more stable employees, and their families. For newly arrived immigrants, especially, the promise of a long-term arrangement for housing and services was particularly appealing. The construction of miners' dwellings could also give the owners of company towns a competitive edge over other mining interests in the region, especially those operators with insufficient capital to invest in amenities for the miners.

While the quality of corporate worker housing varied from town to town, most company houses of the period were constructed in neat, orderly rows, giving at least the outward appearance of spaciousness, stability, and comfort. The standard house form for miners and laborers, the Pennsylvania miners' dwelling, resembled the structure documented at Eckley, as noted. The landscape of the bituminous coal company town was spatially ordered in the manner of anthracite patch towns like Eckley as well. Each dwelling, located near the front of the parcel, was provided with a sizable backlot for the use of the mining families. In Eckley, the two families shared a lot that was approximately 90–100 ft x 160 ft (27.43–30.48 x 48.77 m) (Warfel 1993:230). Mulrooney states that the typical backlot in the bituminous company towns of Star Junction, Windber, and Colver measured 50 x 150 ft (15.24 x 45.72 m) per unit, or 100 x 150 ft (30.48 x 45.72 m) for each doublehouse (1989:33) (Figure 6). The backlots contained the outhouse, a variety of sheds, and other outbuildings. The lots were typically enclosed by painted fences. All the miners' dwellings, laid out on gridded or linear streets, were located within short walking distance of the mine entrance. Company towns in the bituminous fields also provided schools, churches, and the company store. The physical resemblance between the company towns of the two coal regions is considerable, from the street plan and the placement of worker housing to the actual form of miners' housing.

In other respects, however, the company towns of western Pennsylvania took on a form and appearance that set them apart from their predecessors.[7] As has been noted, Pennsylvania's anthracite communities had their origins in particular economic and geological circumstances that were not replicated in the western portion of the state.[8] The planning of anthracite towns also seems to have been less programmatic, less systematic, even haphazard compared to the towns

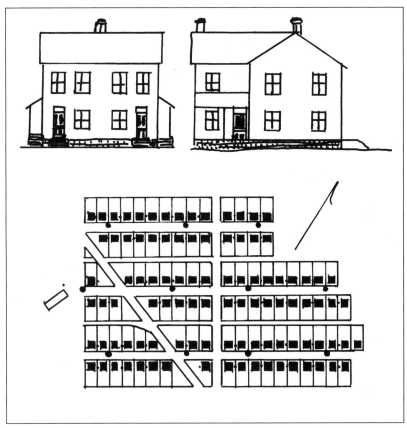

FIG. 6. Map of Eureka No. 40, a satellite of Windber, Pennsylvania, built by the Berwind-White Coal Mining Company. The plan shows the standardized appearance of the houses and the regularity of the street grid and backlots (drawing after U.S. Immigration Commission Report [1911] as printed in Mulrooney [1989:76]).

that emerged in Pennsylvania's bituminous region. The most important distinction that may be drawn, however, between the anthracite miners' patch and the bituminous company town of western Pennsylvania arises from the creation of a new style of paternalism that was incorporated into the very fabric of the coal company town.

CORPORATE PATERNALISM AND THE NEW COAL COMPANY TOWN

It is the corporate regimen, with its paternalistic bent, that set bituminous company towns apart from mining communities in the anthracite region of Pennsylvania and the bituminous fields of western Maryland. Indeed, industrial relations were redefined within Pennsylvania's bituminous region. Operators implemented a series of paternalistic policies and programs for the miners and their families that would distinguish the new company town from its predecessors. Workers were drawn to these towns not only by the offer of housing but also by the schools and churches provided or subsidized by the company, by corporate-sponsored recreational activities, and a variety of other services, including the company doctor. The presence of so many coal communities in the bituminous fields with uniform housing, standardized town plans, and paternalistic programs suggests that this type of town succeeded in attracting the workers most desired by coal operators.

Further, it suggests that most companies found this combination ideally suited to their purpose, for with this realignment or redefinition of paternalism there was an accompanying change in the extent of supervision or moral policing by the owner—in short, in the "logic and character of obligation" between employer and employee and in terms of "provision, protection, and control" (Scranton 1984:235, 237). Companies did not relinquish the feudalistic control achieved earlier in the century; rather, that control was broadened and strengthened by a new benevolence or corporate paternalism. Notwithstanding the many attractions of the new company town and the real gains in quality of life that such communities often represented for the miner and his family, this realignment created a program of "structured dependency" between employer and employee (Crawford 1995:12). Residents were subject to the authority of the coal company as never before, and the new corporate ideology would permeate nearly every aspect of work and daily life.

Indeed, the new company town served as a highly effective mechanism by which companies and operators exerted social and economic control over the miner and his family. It is clear from the historical record that such paternalistic programs, though mutually advantageous, were intended chiefly for the benefit of the company, promoting stability and complacency among the miners while muting the calls for unionization. Even company-sponsored recreational activities and competitions, which were extremely popular in the mining communities, were intended to win the loyalty of employees and to promote group solidarity and a sense of pride among families, at the same time defusing their sense of alienation from the company and deflecting their criticism of its practices (Brestensky, Hovanec, and Skomra 1991; Dix 1988; Metheny 1992; Miller and Sharpless 1985). Though subtle, even innocuous, these programs were in many ways more binding upon the miner than earlier forms of paternalism.

Many companies still relied upon coercive measures to stifle unrest. The threat of eviction from company housing was still the most direct form of control over the miner and his family. Other tactics included mine closings, and the firing of strikers and union sympathizers, followed by the rehiring of nonunion labor. Like coal operators in the anthracite region, many companies relied upon private police to enforce company regulations and evictions, and to intimidate or coerce workers and family members (DiCiccio 1996:127–128; Dix 1988:168–169; Miller and Sharpless 1985:142). But in the company towns that emerged in western Pennsylvania after 1870, owners increasingly relied upon alternate forms of social and economic control to extend their authority over the worker both in and out of the workplace. Families who were attracted to the services provided in a company town often became financially dependent upon or in debt to the company for the use of those services, for example. Deductions for rent, doctor's fees, mining equipment, or for purchases made at the company store often exceeded the miner's earnings. In many towns, residents were expected to purchase goods at the company store and nowhere else. Such programs, together with intimidation and coercive measures, led to the curtailment of personal liberties and fostered a repressive atmosphere in many coal company towns of the period (AIHP 1992:45, 49–52; DiCiccio 1996:127–131; Mulrooney 1989:9, 25–27). Other programs, designed to foster stability and contentment among workers and their families, were equally effective in muting calls for improved living and working conditions, and for unionization.

The practices of the bituminous coal companies of this period must be considered in the context of social and economic currents of the time. The construction of bituminous towns in western Pennsylvania coincided with the growth of labor movements after 1870, thus the paternalistic programs offered by companies may be seen as a response to worker unrest and to the increasingly successful attempts by miners to organize a national union.[9] These practices must also be considered in the context of industrial capitalism and the trend toward welfare capitalism as it emerged in the late nineteenth century. Formulated in response to both the pressures for social reform, the changing composition of the workforce, and growing labor unrest, paternalistic programs that were instituted during the last quarter of the nineteenth century were more encompassing than anything previously attempted by industry, offering an increasingly broad range of programs and practices to bring stability to the nation's industrial workforce. In this sense, the paternalistic offerings of the coal company towns—from housing and access to medical care to educational programs and organized recreation— were consistent with those tendered by other industries. Although settlements that were isolated still evolved as closed social systems, with a rigid hierarchy and stringent forms of economic and social controls over employees, many owners turned away from coercion to alternate forms of persuasion.

The paternalistic practices of the coal companies, whether offered under the guise of benevolence or pragmatism (cf. Crawford 1995; Hareven and Langenbach 1978; Metheny 1992; Wright 1981), were clearly used to manipulate and control the behavior of company employees and their families. Some scholars have debated whether the practices that were institutionalized in the coal company towns truly represented a continuation of early forms of benevolence and paternalism, and they have questioned the motivations of the corporations and companies that promoted such practices. Others, however—including contemporary observers—have nonetheless declared the corporate program of the coal mining town to be a form of paternalism, because "it is done for the miners, not by them, given in abnegation of the ordinary privileges of workmen" (cited in Mulrooney 1989:26; see also Crawford 1995:28, 31–33). In this sense, the use of the term "paternalism" is consistent with the historical practice of "benevolence" by industrialists (Scranton 1984).

Finally, these programs must also be understood in the context of national events and economic conditions within the coal industry itself. Bituminous operators as a whole flourished for some 50 years—from the 1870s when intensive commercial development of the mines began until the Depression years of the 1920s–1930s. Yet the industry was marked by fierce competition, overproduction, fluctuating markets, and unstable prices (AIHP 1992:iv; see also DiCiccio 1996; Dix 1988; Fishback 1992). The miner, as a result of these conditions, was frequently unemployed and, as a result of advances in mechanization, increasingly marginalized.

Conflict invariably arose over working and living conditions and the miner's wage, and was manifested in labor unrest, in attempts by miners to unionize, and in work stoppages and strikes. The corporate regimen that evolved in the coal company town was dynamic, then, as companies responded to changing economic conditions and labor issues. Since company towns were privately owned, few changes could be forced upon the coal companies from without until after World War II. In fact, programs of paternalism developed by the nation's coal operators were largely effective in keeping the unions out until the 1930s. It was left to the worker, through protest and unionization, through action and negotiation, as well as through resistance, to effect substantial changes in wages and in working and living conditions.

 CHAPTER 3

IN THE COALFIELDS OF WESTERN PENNSYLVANIA: THE ROCHESTER AND PITTSBURGH COAL COMPANY

Having set out the historical and social context that shaped industrial relations within the coal company town, we will now look more closely at the company town of Helvetia and at the philosophies and practices of its parent company, the Rochester and Pittsburgh Coal Company. The historical background that is presented here has been reconstructed from a variety of primary and secondary sources as well as from the official papers of the Rochester and Pittsburgh Coal Company.[1] The history of Helvetia that has been reconstructed from these records creates a baseline for this study, providing a detailed account of the paternalistic practices of the R&P, including its policies regarding the provision of housing and services, its attitudes toward its employees and its stance on corporate welfare, and company policy for behavior in and out of the workplace. To some extent, these records also preserve details on the construction and maintenance of company houses, rent levels, regulations regarding worker and tenant behavior, sanitation, land-use practices, and goods and services provided by the company store.

It is important to establish the intentions of the coal company in this study, since these data offer a view of daily life in the town of Helvetia that often diverges from the archaeological and oral evidence. Company policies were not always observed by those for whom they were intended, and corporations were rarely successful in uniformly imposing their ideologies upon their subordinates, as studies of the working classes repeatedly show (e.g., Beaudry 1993; Beaudry, Cook, and Mrozowski 1991; Cohen 1986). Indeed, it is the disjunction between the R&P's corporate ideology, as expressed through its policies and regulations in the company town, and the actions and perceptions of Helvetia's residents that will be most revealing of the negotiation of place and the agentive role of workers in shaping this community.

THE FINEST MINES IN THE COUNTRY

An early and dominant presence in the coalfields of western Pennsylvania, the Rochester and Pittsburgh Coal Company became one of the largest bituminous coal producers in the state and indeed the country for some 50 years. The company supplied coal and coke to the burgeoning iron and steel industries in the Great Lakes region and Canada, as well as to a variety of manufactories and industries in New York and New England (Cooper 1982:32–33, 46; DiCiccio 1996:102). The R&P was heavily capitalized at the outset by financial and banking interests from Wall Street. These investors, who initially subscribed $4,000,000 dollars to the company, were also involved in the creation of a regional rail system, the Buffalo, Rochester, and Pittsburgh Railway (Cooper 1982:14–16).[2] Together, the BR&P and its subsidiary, the R&P, monopolized production and transport of coal and coke out of the region for many years.

During its peak years of production, the R&P owned and operated some two dozen mines or groups of mines in a four-county area (see Cooper 1982). To house its employees, the R&P also built or purchased 22 company towns for its principal operations between 1882 and 1947. The company town of Helvetia, located in Brady Township in Clearfield County, was purchased by the R&P in 1896, just five years after operations began on the site (Figure 7). Helvetia Mine quickly became one of the largest producers in the region, dominating the Reynoldsville coalfield for many years (McCreighton 1938:25).

What drew investors to this portion of Brady Township was a vast, six-foot coal seam lying just beneath the surface of cultivated fields and timber stands. Though coal had been mined in the county during the first half of the nineteenth century, largely from surface outcrops, significant commercial mining activity did not commence until after the Pennsylvania Geological Survey of 1874–1884. Lands and mineral rights in this portion of Brady Township—some 7,000 to 8,000 acres—were secretly purchased and consolidated in the late 1880s and early 1890s by Adrian Iselin, a New York investment banker. Although the firm of A. Iselin and Company was the major holder of stock in the R&P through its purchase of the BR&P in 1885, Helvetia Mine was owned exclusively by Iselin and operated independently of the R&P until 1896, when it was joined to other R&P holdings (Cooper 1982:23–25, 40). Thus it was Adrian Iselin who first put his stamp on the company town, not the R&P. While Cooper (1982:40) suggests that the mine was opened through a cooperative arrangement with the R&P, it seems more likely that Iselin's purchase was a surprise.[3] Iselin's correspondence does indicate that these parties at least shared a mutual interest in having the control of such lands in the hands of a friendly agent, rather than a competitor, and after Helvetia opened, Iselin and the R&P seem to have acted cooperatively in a number of matters regarding wages, transportation rates, and the mining and coking operations at Helvetia between 1891 and 1896 (e.g., Rochester and Pittsburgh Coal Company [R&PCC] 1890a, 1890b, 1894a).

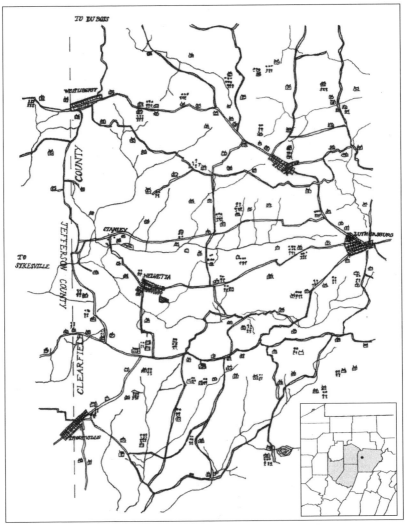

FIG. 7. The primary holdings of the Rochester and Pittsburgh Coal Company were located in a four-county area in the western portion of the state (see inset). Helvetia is located in Clearfield County. When first constructed, the villages of Luthersburg, Salem, West Liberty, and Troutville were closest to the new company town. The city of DuBois was some six miles distant. Drawing based on an area map in Caldwell's Atlas (1878:128–129) and an early twentieth-century topographic map (USGS 1924).

Three periods of ownership are documented for the company town at Helvetia. Iselin built the town and started commercial operations at the mine around 1890–1891. Early correspondence from Helvetia shows that Adrian Iselin Jr. often served as his father's representative during this period and that after 1894 he increasingly managed operations in the new town and mine. In 1896, as noted, the mine and town were merged with the R&P's other holdings. During this second period of ownership, from 1896 to 1947, management and operations at Helvetia were under the direct control of the R&P. Company records show that operations at Helvetia were brought into line as much as possible with those in the R&P's other company towns, though Helvetia retained several unique characteristics in its management and operation; having been built separately from the other towns, it never fully conformed to the R&P's own prototype or design for its company towns. There was some continuity in overall management, however, as members of the Iselin family continued their father's association with the R&P. As business manager for A. Iselin and Company and eventually as a major stockholder of the R&P, Adrian Iselin Jr. continued to influence the R&P's corporate policies in Helvetia and its other company towns for nearly four decades, albeit indirectly through the company president and the mine superintendents. The mine operation at Helvetia flourished under the R&P and eventually became one of the company's most productive, employing upwards of 1,200 men at the peak of operations in the 1940s.

In 1947, with the coal industry in decline, the R&P sold all of its company towns, including Helvetia, to the Kovalchick Salvage Company (Cooper 1982:100). Helvetia's miners continued to rent their houses from the new landlord, but the coal company ceded all responsibility for and control of operations in the town. The mine was permanently closed in 1954. Though some families continued to live in Helvetia, most of the town's residents left in search of employment. The impact of the salvage company's operations on the town site after 1947 will be discussed in a later chapter; in this section, the focus will be on the first two periods of ownership, when Helvetia was a company town in the strictest sense of the term—that is, when the two coal companies had direct control over tenancy, land ownership, and worker behavior in the town.

A TOWN AND COMMUNITY EMERGE, 1890–1919

The town that Adrian Iselin built to support the mining operation at Helvetia provided housing and essential services to hundreds of miners, laborers, and their families throughout its years as a company town (1891–1947) (Figures 8 and 9). This type of provisioning was necessary to attract and support the mine's employees. Though located in close proximity to several communities, Helvetia was nonetheless isolated from its neighbors for many years, as access to the mine site was time consuming and often expensive (see Figure 7). The mine was roughly six miles distant from the city of DuBois, the largest community and provider of services in the area. The nearby villages of Stanley, Luthersburg, and Troutville were small agricultural communities at the time of Helvetia's founding and offered few amenities for the miners and their families. Sykesville, some three miles distant, later supported several mining operations, brick manufacture, and other industries, but it too was a small community in the early 1890s.

FIG. 8. Early views of Helvetia. The first photograph, taken in the mid- to late 1930s, provides a close look at the doublehouses on First Street; the double and single houses on Second Street are visible just behind them. The second photo, also of Helvetia's downtown, dates to circa 1963. Bethel Union Church appears on the left in both images. Photographs courtesy of Lloyd Gray and Doris Andrulonis.

FIG. 9. Undated postcard of Helvetia Mine and the company town. The view is of Helvetia's uptown. The schoolhouse is visible in the upper left corner near the top of the hill. Photograph courtesy of Tom Bukousky.

The mine was serviced via the Mahoning Valley Railroad, a one-and-three-quarter-mile-long rail spur built by Adrian Iselin to connect with the BR&P rail network at Stanley. The R&P often used the BR&P line to run special cars for company officials traveling to Helvetia, but it is not likely that the BR&P transported miners, except for newly recruited hands who were conveyed to the mine by rail from cities on the eastern seaboard (Cooper 1982:20–22). *Caldwell's Atlas* shows a well-established network of roads in this corner of Brady Township in 1878, including the roads that eventually formed the main axes of Helvetia's gridded street plan (1878:128–129). But travel to Helvetia was difficult for the common miner until first Stanley and then Helvetia were linked to the street-car system connecting DuBois and Sykesville around 1906 (Albert 1980:21). The trolley companies offered a "working man's special," selling blocks of tickets at a discount; the DuBois Traction Passenger Railway Company also ran special cars, called "Black Hand Cars," to some of the area's outlying mines (Albert 1980:7; Nichols 1994:214). The trolley and, later, the bus provided Helvetia's workers with the option of living and shopping outside of the company town. The advent of the motorcar made little difference to Helvetia families until the 1920s, when automobiles became more affordable. Helvetia's residents, then, were largely dependent on their employers for services during the mine's earliest years of operation.

The Industrial Plant

The surviving Helvetia ledger, local tax records, and several pieces of correspondence make it clear that Adrian Iselin began construction of the coal plant, offices, worker housing, the company store, and other town facilities in late 1890.[4] The May 1891 tax assessment for Brady Township documents the presence of five dwelling houses, a store, and a tipple. Iselin was eager to begin production, and his correspondence shows that the mine was operating by early 1891, while tonnage records indicate the mine was producing well by 1892. Construction of the power plant began in March of 1891 and the town waterworks in September of that year. By 1892, the industrial plant for the mine had grown considerably to include a blacksmith shop, a general office building, a steam saw and shingle mill, the powerhouse and its related machinery, and the tipple. A weigh office and scale were added in 1895.

Coke ovens were apparently built as part of the coal plant in 1892, though no mention of the ovens can be found in the tax records until 1895 when the assessor noted that 28 ovens were located on site. The local DuBois paper stated, however, that construction was scheduled to begin in the late spring or summer of 1892 (*DuBois Express*, Jan. 29, 1892, p. 5). In June of that same year, the newspaper noted that work on the coke ovens was progressing and that "Helvetia will soon be sending her light heavenward to mark her location as well as her sister mining towns" (*DuBois Express*, June 10, 1892, p. 8). Adrian Iselin's correspondence from November 1892 instructed the superintendent to shut down the coking operation at Helvetia because a high sulfur content made the coke unsalable. This process resumed at some point, for an 1895 letter was found indicating that Iselin wished to increase the total number of ovens at Helvetia to 100, while a second letter specifically ordered the construction of 10 additional ovens. From the tax records, however, it appears that Iselin himself did not build any additional coke ovens at Helvetia, nor was his vision realized, most likely because the R&P's company officials, who assumed control of operations at Helvetia the following year, had already begun to recognize that the future of the company's coking operations was limited. The R&P did increase the number of ovens at Helvetia to 40 in 1898, but, significantly, when the company opened its new operation at Florence the next year, the industrial plant did not include coke ovens. This decision reflects the company's awareness of its disadvantage in head-to-head competition with the Connellsville coke region, and the company's recognition that the recent introduction of byproduct ovens made the beehive oven all but obsolete (Cooper 1982:48).[5] It is no surprise, then, that Helvetia's ovens were all reported as abandoned by 1918. Cooper notes that the R&P gradually curtailed its coking operations at all of its mines, producing only what it needed for two area blast furnaces in which the company had a financial interest (1982:48–51).

The Company Town

Iselin did not neglect provisions for his employees as the coal mining operation got under way at Helvetia. Construction of the company town seems to have begun almost immediately. Iselin's ledger book shows rental income for the first time on February 28, 1891, for a modest $52.07 for the month, while Helvetia Supply Co. store sales reached $351.64 for the same period. Indeed, records indicate that the bulk of Helvetia's housing and many of the town's facilities were built between 1890–1896 under the direction of Adrian Iselin.[6] Sixty-two miners' doublehouses and 10 single houses, or 134 total units, were built for the company town under Iselin's tenure, beginning in November 1890. Assessment records show that 41 double-block houses and 10 single houses were complete by May of 1892. Listed separately from all of these structures in 1892 and in subsequent tax rolls are two dwelling houses, one for the engineer and one for the superintendent of the mine. Finally, Iselin's correspondence indicates that a brick house, known as the Haskell Mansion, was built for the manager of the mines. Fifteen new doublehouses were assessed in 1893, bringing the number of miners' dwellings to 56. Instructions for the construction of additional housing appear in the Helvetia ledger in 1895: "Mr. Iselin has no objection to your putting up four more [blocks of housing or doublehouses], making six in all, to cost about $4000" (R&PCC 1895c). Tax records for 1895 and 1896 confirm that these block houses were built, bringing to 62 the total number of miners' doublehouses erected within the company town.

Construction of a new company store for Helvetia also began in 1892. Although the original store building was but a year old, Iselin decided on a visit to the town in August that the latter structure was too small and inconveniently located for the miners (*DuBois Express*, Aug. 26, 1892, p. 2).[7] A column in the *DuBois Express*

(Dec. 2, 1892, p. 8) offered the opinion that the new building, 80 x 45 ft (24.38 x 13.72 m) in size, would be "a magnificent structure" when complete. The column also noted that the Mahoning Valley Railroad spur was being graded up to the building. The original store building was converted into a dwelling.

A schoolhouse, under construction in September 1892, opened for classes the following month (Figure 10). The school received a 600-pound bell in December of that year, paid for by subscriptions from town residents and by a contribution from the mine superintendent, John McLeavy. A doctor's office was constructed in the same year.

FIG. 10. Helvetia's seventh- and eighth-grade football players sit in front of Helvetia's three school-houses in 1934. Lloyd Gray, an oral informant for this project, is seated in the first row on the far left. Photograph courtesy of Lloyd Gray.

Additional entries from the Helvetia ledger make reference to a boarding-house, a "Club House," and a farm. The boardinghouse would have been used by bachelor employees and by laborers involved with the town's construction. To date there is no evidence for such a structure within the confines of the company town per se, but the R&P did operate a boardinghouse in Stanley (Kriner 1992).[8] The farm may refer to a stable located on the hill above the mine. This seems likely as the company used both horses and mules for many years.[9] But many companies including the R&P set aside land for agricultural uses, and there are references to rye, oats, clover, corn, and potatoes grown at Helvetia and several of the R&P company farms. We can only speculate on the clubhouse. It is possible that this latter facility was an amenity for mining officials, similar to the hotel and dining room that were constructed by the R&P in its company town of Walston in 1883. Cooper writes that "these establishments filled an important function in the early days when Company officials and construction personnel often journeyed out by horse and wagon and needed a place to spend the night" (1982:28).

From the above evidence, it is clear that between 1890 and 1896 Helvetia assumed an appearance and arrangement that would have been recognizable even to those residents who lived in the town after the mine closed in 1954. From the physical layout of its streets to the quantity and architectural style of its housing, the template of the company town at Helvetia was fashioned under the direction of Adrian Iselin and would survive essentially unaltered until the town's sale in 1947 (Figure 11). A newspaper column featuring news items from the various mining communities noted in 1892 that "a good size mining town [now stood] over in the woods [with] about 200 buildings completed or in the course of construction" (*DuBois Express*, Aug. 26, 1892, p. 2).[10] The buildings were described as "good mining houses, built on stone foundations." An engineer's report from 1896, the year of Helvetia's acquisition by the R&P, stated that the houses were "substantially built—and located on streets well laid out and kept in good condition" (Cooper 1982:40, 42). According to Cooper, a map accompanying this report indicates that the gridded street plan recorded on the 1924 U.S. Geological Survey map of Helvetia and the Kovalchick Realty Plat of 1947 was already in place in 1896; the sequence of maps confirms that the basic street layout was unchanged over a 50-year interval.

The R&P was responsible for the construction of other town facilities and significant community institutions. Documentary sources suggest that Bethel Union Church was built between 1896 and 1898; St. Anthony's Roman Catholic Church was apparently built just a few years later (Figures 12 and 13).[11] The R&P contributed land for these churches, along with building funds and, later, monies for repairs and upgrades to some church facilities. Today the Bethel Union Church is the still the first structure a visitor sees when entering Helvetia from the west. St. Anthony's was destroyed by fire in 1955 and was not rebuilt.

Under the R&P's tenure, the town of Helvetia was also given a third company store, erected after the second building was destroyed by fire in 1921, and a fourth, built after another fire in 1939. Two additional schoolhouses were built at the top of the hill above Helvetia to accommodate the growing number of children in town. Perhaps the most important contribution made by the R&P, at least in the eyes of the town's residents, was the construction of cement sidewalks in the 1930s along the western half of Helvetia's main street and along First Street.

A Paying Investment

In addition to these major construction projects, the R&P was responsible for the upkeep, renovation, and replacement of various structures as the town aged.

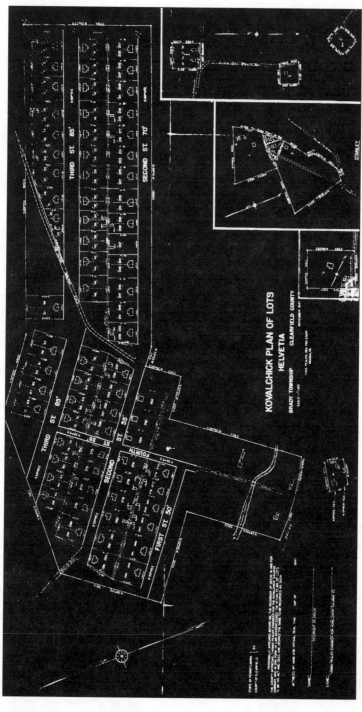

FIG. 11. A 1947 plat of Helvetia, made for the Kovalchick Salvage Company upon the sale of the town by the R&P Coal Company. Doublehouses are indicated by a T-shaped block. Single houses, represented by a square block or an L-shaped block, are congregated at the center of town. Only three company houses are extant today: no. 262, the engineer's house; no. 278, the store manager's house; and no. 74/76, a doublehouse. The former company store, located at the turn in the main road, also survives. Courtesy of Indiana University of Pennsylvania, Special Collections and Archives, and Consol Energy, Inc.

FIG. 12. Bethel Union Church of Helvetia, located at the western end of town. The church was in active use until just a few years ago.

FIG. 13. St. Anthony's Catholic Church of Helvetia was located at the eastern end of the company town. Courtesy of Doris Andrulonis.

Tax rolls and various company documents show that some houses were disman-
tled or replaced, and other structures were lost to fire over the years, though the
total number of housing units varied only slightly during the R&P's 51 years of
ownership. Most had an extended lifespan through regular maintenance by the
company. In 1916–1917, however, a decision was made by company officials to
renovate and upgrade the town facilities. The houses, "while of excellent character from the standard of the time they were built," had deteriorated greatly but
were, officials felt, "well worthy of rebuilding, in that we will have use for them
for at least 12 or 15 years yet" (R&PCC 1916a). Lucius W. Robinson, president
of the R&P, ordered re-roofing, foundation and sill repairs, re-siding, new plaster, painting, and the renewal of floors, porches, and windows for each of Helvetia's houses. Robinson estimated the cost would average $300 per house and
$20,000–$24,000 for the entire site, exclusive of painting. The amount for all
labor, including painting, was revised upward to $65,000 in August 1917 (R&PCC
1917). In describing these improvements, Robinson made it clear that the R&P
viewed its corporate housing as a "paying investment" as well as a necessity. This
policy stands in contrast, then, to the actions of other coal operators of the period,
many of whom treated miners' housing as a temporary expedient worthy of only
minimal investment.

CORPORATE IDEOLOGY AND
PATERNALISM UNDER ADRIAN ISELIN

Something of the guiding philosophy behind Helvetia's inception and early years
of operation (1891–1896) may be gleaned from the correspondence of Adrian
Iselin Sr. and his son, Adrian Iselin Jr., who served as his father's business partner and as manager of A. Iselin and Company. In a letter dated April 23, 1890,
Iselin Sr. wrote of his intent to "put up the very best plant that can be got" and
to use his considerable experience to best his competitors (R&PCC 1890c). To
establish the "finest mines in the country," Iselin planned to invest in superior
materials, from machinery in the mines to the electric plant to housing for skilled
workers. The latter would be single houses, of better quality than the housing for
ordinary laborers, as an incentive to employees (R&PCC 1890d). Furthermore,
Iselin was very active in planning the construction and operation of the coal
plant and town. From the outset, he maintained a heavy correspondence with
his superintendent and requested weekly reports. He also toured the site in person on several occasions. Iselin himself devised managerial plans by which the
mine's various departments were organized. Company records indicate that he
sought efficiency, productivity, and quality in all aspects of the mine's operation.

By all accounts, Iselin was a generous man, and he invested heavily in the
mining operation and in the town itself. He also invested in the welfare of the
men who worked for him. Iselin instructed his superintendent at Helvetia to

drain the swamp along Stump Creek in the second year of the town's operation, "for otherwise sickness may arise from it" (R&PCC 1892c). Over the years, he and his wife built or donated land for churches in several R&P towns and for a miners' hospital in the company town of Adrian. There are other examples of Iselin's philanthropy, both locally and in New York (Cooper 1982:24, 34–36). Iselin and his son, Adrian Jr., shared this paternalistic view toward the miners with L. W. Robinson, a president of the R&P.

But it is also clear that Iselin's philanthropic tendencies were tempered by a clear-eyed, hard-edged business sense. Much of the surviving correspondence from this period shows that to remain competitive and to keep Helvetia Mine productive, Iselin was unwilling to pay more to his employees than was paid by his competitors, and he was willing to fix wage rates in cooperation with other coal companies, including the R&P. In dealing with work stoppages and demands for wage increases, both Iselin and his son were quite willing to have striking miners and their families evicted and to bring in new labor in order to effect a wage settlement in their favor (R&PCC 1894a, 1894c, 1894d, 1894e).[12]

CORPORATE IDEOLOGY UNDER THE R&P

As yet, little else has been discovered in the historical record that contributes to a more explicit understanding of Adrian Iselin's operations within Helvetia. There are, however, several sources that provide a clear sense of the R&P's corporate philosophy, one that prevailed through much of Helvetia's tenure under the R&P (1896–1947), as well as the nature of the R&P's corporate presence within the town itself. An overall statement of company goals and intentions with respect to its company towns can be found in a series of letters and a memorandum written by Lucius W. Robinson, president of the R&P Coal Company from 1899–1919 (R&PCC 1916e; 1916f; 1916g) (Appendix A).

The two letters, written to Adrian Iselin Jr., suggest that the paternalistic practices of the corporation were influenced to some extent by the model company town movement and by current trends in welfare capitalism, social engineering, and urban reform. Robinson noted that "there is very wisely a growing tendency, not only in mining towns, but in connection with all industrial affairs, to furnish labor employed better accommodations. This has grown out of the desire on the part of employers to do all possible for their workers, and somewhat of a necessity also to attract the most desirable labor" (R&PCC 1916f). The discussion, initiated by Adrian Iselin Jr., indicates that company officials were desirous of maintaining attractive, clean towns that offered a variety of services and activities for the miners and their families. Indeed, Robinson argued the necessity of "look[ing] after the interests of the families in that I find the men appreciate this even more than for their own special amusement." Unfortunately, none of the younger Iselin's letters to Robinson (there were at least two) have been located, for the exchange of letters must have been quite revealing of his own views toward the responsibilities of the industrial capitalist. Robinson's letters suggest nonetheless that Iselin's personal views were in concert with his own. They also outline a range of paternalistic programs that the two men considered for the R&P's towns, as well as the motivations for trying them.

In response to Iselin's first letter stating his desire to make "our mining towns the most attractive of any in the country," Robinson informed Iselin that much had already been done in the last two years to spruce up the appearance of the R&P's mining towns, particularly the older ones like Helvetia, through painting and general beautification (R&PCC 1916e). He cited the examples of laying walks and building fences for the miners' gardens as further improvements the company could make. Additionally, he planned to offer prizes for "the best kept up yards and house surroundings, and in the spring the same feature for the best gardens and yards and surroundings" (R&PCC 1916f). Competitions like these were fostered by other coal companies as well (e.g., Brestensky, Hovanec, and Skomra 1991; DiCiccio 1996:97).

A glance at early photos of these communities reveals that mining landscapes of the period were typically barren of trees and vegetation, with only the miners' gardens to provide a touch of green (see Figure 8). Indeed, a 1916 review of worker housing in American company towns was critical of employers for their common "disregard of the advantages of vegetation, planting of trees, grass, and shrubbery" (Magnusson 1917:871). The author rebuked owners and operators for the unsightliness of bare lots and for creating a "menace to health as the dust and dirt that collect are prolific carriers of disease." The implication of the R&P's desire to relieve an otherwise bleak landscape and to improve the physical appearance of that company's mining towns is that both gentlemen saw improvements to the living environment as a key to enhancing the miner's sense of well-being and contentment. It is also important to recognize that the streets were unpaved, choked with dust when dry, and thick with mud in the wet weather. The construction of a sidewalk would have been seen by residents as a tremendous benefit. Some of the R&P's towns, such as Adrian, were originally built with wooden sidewalks for pedestrians. It is not known if walkways were constructed in Helvetia or in the other towns as part of the R&P's improvements of 1916–1917. Helvetia received cement walks in the 1930s, a feature that made the little mining town unique among its sister communities, but this occurred many years after Robinson initiated improvements in the coal towns.

Robinson and Iselin also discussed the merits of building facilities for "the amusement and recreation of the women and children," such as amusement halls where the community could hold a dance, church activities, sports, concerts, and band practice, go roller skating, or show motion pictures (R&PCC 1916f). Nickelodeons were also suggested for winter amusement, and outside parties were given permission to establish these entertainments in several R&P towns. Robinson twice mentioned the importance of encouraging town bands, suggesting that the company should erect a bandstand in each town, like the one recently built in Yatesboro. The two men also discussed the possibilities of building community swimming pools or bathhouses for the miners, but agreed that these facilities had not always been successful when tried in other company towns and model towns. A final suggestion was for the installation of "a few inexpensive facilities" for children's playgrounds in a nearby grove or "shady spot"; Robinson noted that "this has been very successfully worked in some of the cities and would be we think very much appreciated by the women and children" (R&PCC 1916g).

Iselin must have stated in his first letter that he thought these types of improvements would attract a better class of men, in response, no doubt, to chronic labor unrest, worker transience, and the difficulty the R&P was having that summer in holding the miners to the terms of their contracts (R&PCC 1916h). Robinson agreed, saying "they will want to work at places where they have schools, churches and some amusements for their families and they will be more contented as workmen if their families are thus provided for in some way at least" (R&PCC 1916g).

Robinson's letters make it clear, however, that whatever their concerns for the welfare of the miners and their families, company efforts to carry out these programs were continually hampered by financial constraints. While other industries and companies had a surplus of funds and could "move along these lines without any embarrassment," Robinson stated that the R&P's current finances would prevent them from making substantial outlays for these programs (R&PCC 1916f). Robinson felt that the company should do all it could, starting with the most practical and least costly improvements, and beginning with the most remote communities, as "relief from the ordinary monotony, it being isolated and impossible to get out of the town without great inconvenience." He noted too that the same type of investment would not be required in those towns more conveniently situated. Finally, Robinson assured Iselin that "the character of houses is . . . certainly at least equal to the best in the country and superior to the average," and though "we have done less than some people in the way of amusement and furnishing amusement features, the character of our towns built the last year years [sic] has certainly been strictly up to date"—most likely a reference to the higher standards of model towns built under the influence of the Progressive and reform movements. Robinson promised to keep Iselin apprised of their progress and to "report what we think can be accomplished along practical lines."

The exchange of letters resulted in a memorandum issued by Robinson to various R&P managers and superintendents inviting them to "express their views of what seems to be the best for your particular surroundings" (R&PCC 1916g). He stated that the company would institute a competition for best kept yard or garden during the following spring, offering cash prizes or perhaps a garden fence as incentive to the families. He reviewed the list of improvements under consideration and suggested that these officials install a bandstand and a playground at the first opportunity, these items being of fairly low cost to the company. He also recommended the planting of Lombardy poplars, "which are very rapid growers and which would soon make a considerable showing planted either in the yards or along the streets. They are very cheap and the expense would not be large for setting out a considerable number of these in many of our mining towns."

The letters evince a genuine concern for the welfare of the R&P's employees and their families. The R&P did institute a number of the improvements in its company towns as a result of the discussion between Iselin and Robinson. All of the older mining towns were retrofitted, the appearance of each town enhanced. Certainly some towns received new sidewalks, and possibly trees as well. Helvetia's residents began to participate in a series of competitions sponsored by the R&P for the best-kept yard or best garden at this time.

There is insufficient documentation on when other features were constructed in Helvetia and whether they were part of the improvements made by Robinson in 1916–1917, but the town did have its own playground and park, a ballfield, and an election hall/band hall that may have served as a community center. Any of these spaces might be used for community gatherings or entertainments.[13] The churches were also available, and several individuals recalled activities in the basement of Bethel Union Church, including roller skating (William Brown, Nov. 16, 1991; Thomas Crop, Mar. 10, 1994; Jack Hilliard, personal communication, 1995). While former residents did not say whether the company spon-

FIG. 14. Helvetia's baseball team, circa 1932, photographed on the ballfield at the western end of town. Bethel Union Church is visible in the background. William Brown, an informant for this project, is kneeling in the front row, fourth from the left. Papers of William Brown.

sored dances or movies or some of the other events described in Robinson's letters, three activities—the town band, the gardening competitions, and the very popular R&P baseball league—can be categorized with certainty as company-sponsored entertainments that were initiated or received continued corporate sponsorship during this period of improvements to coal-town life (Figure 14).[14]

POLICY AND JUDGMENT

As the above review of Lucius W. Robinson's correspondence indicates, after the R&P's purchase of Helvetia and for the next two decades under Robinson's tenure, the coal company was willing to invest in decent housing and other services and programs within its company towns in order to facilitate the creation and maintenance of a stable, contented, compliant, nonunion workforce. Ultimately, however, the above investments were tied to the cost of production and the price of coal (R&PCC 1908). Company records clearly show that cost and profit were the operative concerns for the company, affecting all decisions regarding employees, wages, and benefits. On one occasion, Robinson refused to idle the mines at Walston on the day of a church picnic, though he was willing to have the superintendent spare as many of his men as possible "without seriously crippling him in operating the mines" (R&PCC 1902a). On other occasions, however, Robinson did just that: "I have decided to shut your mine down Thursday of this week to enable your men to attend the Fair, but will expect them to work all other days this week" (R&PCC 1900a). In the latter instance, Robinson recognized that the quality of work would suffer so much and absenteeism would be so high that the company would gain little in trying to maintain its regular work schedule.

Though the company occasionally made minor concessions to its workers in response to daily conditions in its towns, as in the above example, at various times in its history the R&P made more significant concessions to the miners regarding wages, benefits, and working conditions. These concessions were in part a response to heightened pressure from organized labor movements and from the R&P's own employees. Whether large or small, all such concessions may be seen as part of a process of negotiation between employer and employee that began as early as 1894 when Helvetia's miners staged a strike. The strike ended unsuccessfully when workers were ordered to return to work at the old wage level or face eviction from Iselin's company housing, yet Helvetia's miners were back the next year, alongside men from the surrounding communities, to present their demands to the general managers of the area's mines (*DuBois Express*, Reynoldsville edition, June 29, 1894, p. 8; April 5, 1895, p. 6). Indeed, miners' meetings in Helvetia were a common occurrence in the first 10 years of the mine's operation. Reports from Leis Hall, a privately owned structure just outside of Helvetia proper, were regularly featured in the local papers. The effectiveness of such meetings may be questioned because labor was still relatively disorganized during this period, but the efforts of Helvetia's miners to collectively negotiate with Iselin, and later the R&P, must be seen in the context of a growing labor movement at both regional and national levels of organization. Taken in concert with similar efforts in the area, then, the effectiveness of Helvetia's miners increases.

The concessions made by the company to its workforce must also be considered in the context of economic conditions within the coal mining industry, however. It appears that most concessions were made by the R&P only under extreme economic pressures, and that prior to unionization, chronic labor shortages were perhaps more beneficial to the miners' cause than any efforts to negotiate with the company. In a letter written July 7, 1902, the president of the R&P, Lucius W. Robinson, wrote to Adrian Iselin Jr. stating that it was time for the company to recognize some level of organization among the miners to avoid conflict and loss of production, particularly given the difficulty of finding outside labor in the event of a strike (R&PCC 1902b). In 1916, Robinson addressed the same problem in a letter to Iselin, once again arguing the need to accommodate the miners because of a severe labor shortage:

> There is not only a great shortage of labor, but those working are thoroughly dissatisfied although they are not only enjoying steady work but the highest wages ever paid with conditions better than ever known . . . it is absolutely useless and out of the question to try to get them [the miners' organization] to keep it [a contract], and instead use the best of policy and judgment in making such concessions as necessary to keep them at work regardless of the terms of the contract [R&PCC 1916h].

To some extent, the history of the R&P charts a change in attitude within the official hierarchy, from its earliest days when the company held firm against miners' demands for wage increases or for improved living and working conditions, to a later time, prior to the Depression, when the company demonstrated a willingness to negotiate with company employees to prevent a loss of production (e.g., R&PCC 1902b; 1942; see also DiCiccio 1996; Dix 1988; Fishback 1992). This is an obvious example of both the power of negotiation and resistance by organized labor and individual miners, as well as the power of external economic forces. It is also true, however, that at times of low coal prices, poor markets, or excessive production by its competitors, and before its mines were unionized, the R&P's workers regularly suffered from reduced hours or layoffs, a loss of wages, and evictions from company housing, and there was nothing to be done about it.

NOT A DESIRABLE MAN

The company did not often need to make concessions to its workers and was able to balance any concessions with other forms of social and economic control. A review of its official papers indicates that the R&P did not rely exclusively on

forms of paternalism to influence the miners and their families but routinely
resorted to other practices that, though common to the period, seem today to be
vastly unfair. The R&P used these social and economic controls both in and out
of the workplace to select and control the men they employed and to keep the
union out of its mines. These policies were implemented through formal programs
and institutions as well as through unofficially sanctioned practices.

Company papers and oral histories indicate that the R&P had several methods for keeping only "desirable" men on the job and for creating a rigid social and
economic hierarchy within its mines. First, the company actively recruited immigrant labor, primarily from eastern and southern Europe, for its low-wage jobs
(Cooper 1982:20–22; R&PCC 1902c; 1902d; 1902e; 1902f). The company hired
firms to distribute flyers; representatives set up booths and advertised the need
for workers by word of mouth as well. The R&P enticed many of its recruits by
offering to pay their travel fare, though the cost was to be deducted from their
wages. Contemporary observers noted that many immigrants who were so recruited
arrived at the mines with nothing more than the clothes on their back and their
name and the name of the mine or company pinned to their shirts (AIHP
1992:46). The R&P's supervisory positions were to be awarded to the English,
Welsh, and Scotch. Blacks and Irishmen were to be excluded from the mine altogether. In general, the R&P steered away from hiring English-speaking laborers,
"for [they are] too apt to be strikers and cast-off labor from other mines" (R&PCC
1902c; 1902g). That this was a long-enduring and common practice in the coal
industry is indicated in a letter published by the *DuBois Express* describing the
deplorable condition of the miner:

> One cannot help but think surely the mining craft has shouldered all the impo-
> sitions that it is possible for corporate power to heap upon them. But no, although
> the miners are in a semi-starving condition our oppressors are not satisfied but
> are resorting to the very meanest tactics to still further reduce their humble
> slaves. It is heart rending to see the many half-starved and half-clad miners going
> about from place to place seeking employment only to be refused and more espe-
> cially if they are English speaking men. But it is foreigners who get the prefer-
> ence [Reynoldsville edition, Feb. 15, 1895, p. 3].

Company papers also show that the R&P regularly blacklisted labor agitators
and unionizers, and company officials used the ever-present threat of eviction
and mine closures to stamp out unrest. The general correspondence of L. W.
Robinson is filled with examples that reveal the perceived dangers of organized
labor to the company:

> Robert Hughes, treasurer of the Local union at Eleanora and employed by us at
> that mine, has resigned, please see that he is not employed at any of our mines
> under any circumstances [R&PCC 1900b].

I understand there is a man somewhere in this region by the name of John, or Jack, O'Connell, representing himself as a correspondent of the Pittsburgh Dispatch, who I have reason to believe is here for another purpose detrimental to our interests. I wish you to keep a lookout for this man if he calls at your mine and see that he does not get admission to the mine or any information about our business if it can be prevented [R&PCC 1901e].

The following men have been discharged from Florence mines:

> Jos. Formick, Loader, Italian.
> Anthony or Louis Campseny, Loader, Italian.
> Thomas Geneo, Loader, Italian.
> Robert English, Miner, English speaking.
> William Ruhl, Driver, English speaking.

Please be careful that none of these men get employment at your mines as they are very undesirable men [R&PCC 1901f].

Though Robinson and other company officials vehemently opposed efforts to organize the mines, it is clear that labor supporters had their own difficulties in unifying area miners for many years (see also Corbin 1981). Robinson wrote of the failure of union organizers during a work suspension in 1914. Though "the organization tried to flood the Indiana mines with organizers, they have had very poor success and up to date have accomplished nothing," he noted (R&PCC 1914a). Miners in the region, including those working for the R&P, voted to accept a contract between the United Mine Workers and area operators and supported a return to work by more than a two-thirds majority of those voting.[15] The R&P's mines were not permanently unionized until 1933 (Cooper 1982:93–94).

There is little doubt that prior to unionization the R&P had tremendous leverage over its employees in the mines. The company dictated where and when people worked. The length of the workweek was shaped by the demand for coal and the price per ton. Slowdowns and work stoppages often occurred as the demand for coal decreased nationwide. Miners complained of abuses by the company and of the difficulty in earning a living wage: "short weighing" (short-weighting or fixing the scales) by management; docking a man's car for sending up dirty coal (coal mixed with unacceptable levels of clay or shale) or for unacceptable behavior; low wages or no pay for dead work (working through shale and clay to reach the coal seam); unfair hiring and arbitrary firing practices; and favoritism in assigning rooms were common before the mines were unionized (William N. Brown, Nov. 16, 1991; Jan. 3, 1992; Thomas Crop, July 29, 1994; see chap. 5). As noted, such practices were typical of the industry during this period (AIHP 1992; Brestensky, Hovanec, and Skomra 1991; DiCiccio 1996; Dix 1988; Miller and Sharpless 1985).

Enforcement of company policies on the job was problematic, however, as evidenced by numerous memoranda and official correspondence detailing problems with employee slackness, negligence on the job, drunkenness, and absenteeism (e.g., R&PCC 1902e; 1902h; 1902i; 1916a; 1916i; Appendix A). These documents indicate that worker behavior did not always coincide with company ideals and standards, and they clearly express the frustration of managers and superintendents who were daily faced with undesirable behavior on the part of their employees—particularly in the mines, where supervisors might only see their workers once or twice a day. Dirty coal, a problem that affected not only the price per ton but the company's reputation, was a common complaint, and managers were urged to take action to prevent such carelessness on the part of the loaders (e.g., R&PCC 1902i). Penalties were enforced against miners caught smoking or carrying combustible materials (e.g., Kriner 1992:100). The R&P's superintendents regularly complained of inebriated miners, indifferent work, and carelessness on the part of their employees.

Unlike many coal companies of the period that hired a private police force to threaten or coerce their workers, the R&P did not have coal and iron police. On rare occasions, the company hired a detective or "Special Officer" to protect its property, to handle "obnoxious characters," or to clamp down on activities that were detrimental to the R&P's operations, such as coal stealing (e.g., R&PCC 1900a; 1902j; 1902k). The company used its influence to get a State Constabulary Troop detailed in the Punxsutawney area in 1906 during an extended period of strikes and heightened criminal activity—bootlegging, theft, and a string of murders—in Florence, Whiskey Run, and the general Punxsutawney area by members of the "Black Hand Society" (Cooper 1982:29, 70–71). Robinson argued that the presence of this troop was more useful, even in times of peace, reducing the number of drunken and disorderly acts in the town. He wrote that "it was not an uncommon daily sight to see 40 or 50 of our employees attending hearings before Justices of the Peace and court hearings" (R&PCC 1910).

Coal towns had the reputation for violence and a wild, frontierlike atmosphere, but former residents recall that Helvetia had but a single constable in town who maintained order for the company and escorted intoxicated miners or rowdy youngsters home (Thomas Crop, March 10, 1994; Lloyd Gray, Sept. 11, 1995). Helvetia is remembered as a calm, quiet little town, but newspapers indicate that for the first two decades of the town's existence, Helvetia had a reputation for being a lawless community, the scene of murder and mayhem (e.g., *DuBois Express*, Reynoldsville edition, Feb. 9, 1894, p. 1; March 2, 1894, p. 1; Nov. 15, 1895, p. 1). With headlines like "Nihilists at Helvetia," "Dynamiters at Large," and "Riot at Helvetia," it is not hard to understand the comments of a contemporary, who declared that murders were so common around Helvetia and DuBois as to be ordinary occurrences (*Jefferson Democrat*, 1902). Much of the trouble, including the "riot," was attributable to excessive alcohol consumption. While such examples of lawlessness at the turn of the century are at odds with Helvetia's later reputation as a quiet little mining community, it does not appear that Adrian Iselin or the R&P used coal and iron police to control their workers or town residents.

UPTOWN AND DOWNTOWN: LIVING UNDER THE COMPANY

Outside of the workplace, the R&P's corporate ideology impacted nearly every aspect of town life. The imposition, application, enforcement, and effectiveness of each program or policy was enhanced by the physical isolation of the community at Helvetia. Because the mine site was remote, Helvetia was from the outset physically isolated from neighboring communities, and for most of its residents, this isolation continued until the advent of trolley service or until such time as families could afford to purchase a car. This isolation impacted the coal company and the miners in two important ways. First, it meant that from the day construction began on the mine at Helvetia, the operator of the coal mine had to provide housing and on-site services for its employees. This need lessened over the years as transportation services improved throughout the region. Second, the physical isolation of the site meant that miners had little choice but to live in Helvetia and to rely upon the coal company for the supplies and services they needed. With no other options available to them, these individuals found themselves living under the powerful arm of the company on a day-to-day basis. An effect of the town's diminishing isolation, particularly after 1920, was increased freedom for the miner, who no longer had to live in company housing, while those who continued to live in the company town now had an affordable means of travel, allowing them to seek out goods and services at more competitive prices.

Families who lived within the confines of the company town were subject to the influence of the R&P's corporate ideology in a number of ways. This ideology is most obvious, perhaps, in the spatial layout of the town and in its company housing. The economic and social hierarchy within the mines was reflected in housing assignments made by the company. Under the R&P, a section of the "downtown" was reserved for men of western European descent—English, Welsh, and Scottish miners—who also occupied a higher rank within the company hierarchy as foremen, managers, engineers, and so on. Twelve of the houses in this section were single houses. The 1947 town plat shows that residents of Helvetia's downtown were closer to the mine entrance and to the company store than their more distant counterparts uptown (see Figure 11). Most miners and unskilled workers were housed in the large "uptown" and in the upper and lowermost rows of houses downtown.

The history of the coal company town in western Pennsylvania is replete with examples of preferential treatment and ethnic and/or religious bias or prejudice, often through housing assignments. That this was a common practice is evident from surveys by Mulrooney (1989) and others who have studied spatial relationships in company towns as well as housing typologies (DiCiccio 1996; Eller 1982; Harvey 1969; Shifflett 1991). Certainly Helvetia's former residents and employees felt there was a division in their community that was based on religion—the uptown was for the Catholics, the downtown for Protestants—as well as ethnicity. To some extent, this division, or polarization, of people and cultures must have been deliberate and purposeful on the part of R&P officials, given the geographical separation of the community's two churches, which were located at opposite ends of the town on land owned by the company. As shown in the next chapter, however, the composition of the workforce was probably the stronger influence in determining housing assignments.

Company Housing

As was true in many company towns, the corporate hierarchy was clearly evident in housing forms, with rank indicated through size, shape, material, and location (Figures 15 and 16). The company hierarchy was also extended beyond the workplace through housing assignments. Management received superior accommodations to those of skilled workers; they in turn had better quarters than unskilled laborers.[16] Since members of the upper levels of the company hierarchy were almost exclusively English, Scottish, and American, this division shows the same ethnic preferences or biases of the company that we saw previously in the documentary record. The oral histories that are presented in this volume indicate that these divisions and biases permeated many aspects of community life and that self-imposed social boundaries also existed between the two "communities." Interaction between these groups was generally limited to the company store, the schoolhouse, and the ballfield.

If housing told the miner where he stood in the eyes of the corporation, the lease for the house, or lack thereof, told the miner in no uncertain terms that his status and continued employment were contingent upon his adherence to company rules. Although the company archives contain rent rolls for some of the R&P's company towns, Helvetia's ledgers were not found, nor has a documentary search of the company's official records indicated whether the company had its workers sign a lease or what the conditions of that lease might have been. As oral histories conducted for this project were with nonresident employees or else with former residents who grew up as children in Helvetia but were not heads of households in the town during its years under company management, the interviews did not clarify the question of lease agreements in Helvetia.

FIG. 15. No. 278, a single house built for managers and company officials living in Helvetia. For many years, this dwelling was occupied by the manager of the company store. It has been the home of Veronica McKee for more than 50 years.

FIG. 16. A miners' doublehouse in Helvetia's uptown in the 1970s. Courtesy of Doris Andrulonis.

It can be stated that many companies did not offer leases, which could be considered legally binding documents. Some companies offered leases with a clause stating that the operator was obligated to give little or no warning prior to eviction. In so doing, companies retained the right to summarily evict men who were perceived as "undesirable," and their families, without any notice (AIHP 1992:50–

51; Corbin 1981:9, 67; Magnusson 1917:879; Mulrooney 1989:25–26).[17] The relationship of landlord and tenant gave coal companies the power to evict men who were laid off from the mines, men who had been fired, strikers (who were technically not working for the companies while on strike), suspected union organizers, or even men suspected of holding sympathies with organized labor of any kind. Some leases extended the relationship of landlord-tenant to all company property, from the houses and the mine to the roads accessing the site; thus companies could legally exclude anyone they desired from entering a company town. As Magnusson noted in his survey of worker housing, "a housed labor supply is a controlled labor supply" (1917:879). Mulrooney concurred, arguing that the employer, "by holding the leases on an employee's house . . . secured a total control not possible in a normal management-labor relationship" (1989:25).

Housing assignments and rental agreements were perhaps the most obvious demonstrations of the company's influence outside of the workplace, but the R&P exerted its corporate regimen by other means as well. Other visible displays of company policy center on the use of company land and property. A variety of directives were issued by the company president and by the mine superintendents regarding the upkeep of company houses and yards, the maintenance of livestock in each town, sanitation practices, and general living conditions. The R&P also had policies for painting and whitewashing the houses and fences in town. No directives for Helvetia were found in the company's papers, but every person interviewed for this project who lived in Helvetia under the company's control stated clearly that the R&P set certain regulations and enforced its standards of cleanliness and order in the town, particularly in terms of the appearance and upkeep of its houses. At some point, rubbish was regularly collected and disposed of by the company. Outhouses in Helvetia were dipped annually. Fees were assessed for roving livestock after a grazing area was fenced off.

THE COMPANY STORE

The company store was the most notorious institution of the coal industry and has become one of the most lasting and potent symbols of company domination and oppression. As George Korson (1943) wrote, miners thought of this institution as the "pluck-me" store. In many company towns, particularly those that were closed, miners and their families were obligated to purchase their groceries, supplies, and mining equipment from the company store. Miners, union officials, and government investigators complained of abuses by the company store, citing monopolistic practices, inflated prices, payment of miners' wages in company scrip (paper or metal tokens) that could only be redeemed in goods at the company store, and price increases that coincided with and negated the effects of wage increases. Such complaints had little effect, however, since company towns were privately owned and were rarely incorporated. While many families were able to manage their spending and bring home cash wages or at the least maintain a credit balance with the company, others fell into debt. The burden was doubled then, because not only were these families given no choice about where to buy their supplies, but frequent purchases on credit from the company store often left the miner too greatly in debt to leave the mine at all.

In Helvetia, the company store was located at the center of town as a convenience to its residents (Figure 17). The R&P ran its company stores through a subsidiary, the Mahoning Supply Company. While there was evidently some competition from the Leis General Store, a privately owned business located but a short distance from the eastern end of Helvetia, the R&P company store was for most families the only source of groceries and dry goods until transportation to neighboring communities was possible (for most, this was not until the 1920s or later). The company store ledgers for Helvetia were not located during a search of the R&P archives; it was hoped that these might have shown what each Helvetia miner or family purchased on credit or in cash. Oral histories with former residents and surviving ledgers from the R&P's other company stores indicate that the Mahoning Supply Company stocked its aisles and counters with a wide variety of merchandise, including groceries and green goods, dry goods (clothing and shoes), sporting goods, hardware, furniture and appliances, and miners' supplies such as explosives and tools (see also Cooper 1982; Fello 1969:42–44).

FIG. 17. The Helvetia company store in the post-company era. The Mahoning Supply Company, a subsidiary of the R&P, operated a company store in Helvetia beginning in 1896. This store building, the fourth structure built for this purpose, was constructed in 1939 and was converted to a residence some time after this photograph was taken. It is one of only four company structures still standing in Helvetia. Courtesy of Ron Chollock.

The company store at Helvetia does not seem to have evoked the same level of bitterness or claims of unfairness among its patrons as the more extreme examples described above. In his study of the Mahoning Supply Company, Fello (1969) notes that payment was generally made to the R&P's company stores by one of three methods: cash, installment basis, or passbook. Miners purchasing on credit could sign a card authorizing a deduction from their weekly pay. Scrip was apparently not used in Helvetia. While one informant, perhaps speaking of her own experiences in another Pennsylvania mining town, recalled that those whose spending had exceeded their earnings would receive a "snake"—a slip of paper with a line drawn through it—to indicate that the miner had no credit (Veronica McKee, March 10, 1994), others stated that the company always found a way to get the miner what he needed (William and Sara Haag Crop, Sept. 11, 1995; Lloyd Gray, Sept. 11, 1995).

While many admired the quality and selection of goods offered by the company, almost all stated their conviction that prices were deliberately inflated (e.g., William Brown, Jan. 3, 1992; Lloyd Gray, Sept. 11, 1995). Every coal miner in the industry had heard of unethical practices by the coal companies, no matter if they lived in West Virginia, Illinois, Pennsylvania, or Colorado. Every miner or resident of Helvetia contacted during this project spoke in a general sense of the company store's reputation in the coalfields for unfairness and corruption. They had even heard of some of the abuses that are still shocking today, even if they did not experience that unfairness firsthand in Helvetia. They did not specifically charge the R&P and its subsidiary, the Mahoning Supply Company, with similar abuses; rather, they knew of the unequal relationship fostered between the company and the miner through this institution generally, and all felt that the R&P held the upper hand through its monopoly of the company store.

BEHAVIOR OUTSIDE THE WORKPLACE

Other forms of social and economic control that were exerted over the miner outside the workplace were more subtle in design and were contrived through company-sponsored institutions and programs. While miners and families harbored mixed feelings about the company store, company-sponsored recreational activities—including gardening competitions, the town band, and organized sports—were very popular among residents. The R&P Baseball League, in particular, fostered lively competitions and fierce rivalries between area mining towns for many years. Baseball was a particular favorite in mining communities, but also among company officials, for the organized competitions drew the miners together, created a spirit of loyalty—if not to the company, then at least to the particular community or patch—and served to redirect or even dispel the emotions and frustrations of employees and their families (Metheny 1992; Seymour 1990).

Gardening was especially encouraged by the company as a means to keep families busy during leisure hours, to tie them more closely to their homes, and to create the semblance of stability. Gardening competitions sponsored by the R&P also created a sense of pride in home and community. These activities, together with the company-sponsored band, a community school and church, a playground and park, and a company doctor, were certainly benefits to the town of Helvetia and meant a substantial improvement in living conditions for many; but they were also a subtle means by which the R&P hoped to bind the miner and his family to the company and to control their behavior outside of the workplace.

A STRUCTURED LIVING

This is the industrial regimen that operated within Helvetia. The working lives of Helvetia's residents were centered around the operation of the coal mine, and the company determined where and when they worked, at what task, and at what pay rate. The company set rules for their behavior in the mines and relied upon its supervisors and a series of practices, not all of them ethical, to enforce discipline. Outside the mine, the daily lives of Helvetia's residents were also structured by company policies, and their behavior was shaped and even controlled or manipulated through company-sponsored institutions. Officials of the R&P decided who was allowed to live in company housing, where, and for how long. They determined the quality of housing and, to a great extent, the quality of life in the town. Corporate policy set the rates for rent; the cost for mining equipment, food, and supplies at the company store; the fee for medical services and recreational activities; and fines assessed for improper or unacceptable behavior in the eyes of the company. The industrial operation shaped the landscape and impacted the surrounding environment, often to the detriment of the town's residents. And every aspect of life in this company town was subject to change at the will of its owners.

CHAPTER 4

WE LIVE IN THIS PLACE

Miss Lizzie Brown is visiting friends at Woodland.

Rev. Hougle of Punxsutawney, preached to a large audience in Leis' hall Sunday night.

The work on the new school building is being pushed on rapidly. When finished it will present a beautiful and striking appearance.

The Mountain City band of Eleanora came over to Helvetia Friday and after furnishing the town with music, and serenading the newly married couple at the Eldorado, marched to the Helvetia platform where a social dance took place in the evening.

Davie, infant son of Mr. and Mrs. John Harrison, died Saturday, September 3d, aged 5 months. The remains were taken to Beechtree for interment on Monday.

The baseball team of this place went to Coal Glen Monday and played a game of ball with the team at that place. The game stood 16 to 8 in favor of the latter.

Mrs. James Patterson is very low at this writing with cancer of the stomach. She cannot recover.

Peter Lynn and Anthony McDevitt spent Sunday with friends in DuBois.

Isaac Johns moved his family on Saturday to Walston.

[Excerpts from the *DuBois Express* and the *DuBois Express*, Reynoldsville edition, 1892–1898]

Who were the men and women who joined their lives to the company and came to live in the town of Helvetia? Where did they come from? What were their ethnic backgrounds? Their cultural traditions? How long did they stay in Helvetia? What strategies did they use to cope with the corporate industrial regimen established by Adrian Iselin and the R&P?

Several primary sources—census records, tax assessments, and contemporary newspapers—help to reconstruct the community that lived and worked in

Helvetia during the first three decades of the mine's operation. Most useful are the U.S. population schedules from 1900, 1910, and 1920.[1] The 1910 and 1920 population schedules are particularly helpful because the census takers recorded the assigned number for each unit of corporate-owned worker housing in Helvetia, and the numbers are consistent with those recorded on the 1947 Kovalchick plat (see Figure 11). Looking at the latter document, it is possible to follow the path of the census taker as he walked through the town in 1910 and 1920. More important, it is also possible to look at the distribution of housing assignments among various ethnic groups.

The three schedules contain a wealth of data that are pertinent to this study. The population schedules do not provide a comprehensive listing of the R&P's resident employees in Helvetia, however. There are no census data for the period in which the mine and town were under Adrian Iselin's ownership, 1891–1896, nor do they exist for 1896–1899, the first few years of the R&P's tenure. Regrettably, Helvetia's rent ledgers do not appear to have survived, nor are there any employment records for Helvetia in the R&P archives.[2] Tax rolls for Brady Township serve as a supplement to the census records but provide only a partial listing of those who lived in the company town between 1892 and 1899, along with their occupation and a list of their taxable property. In addition, there are innumerable inaccuracies in these documents. Names are often illegible. House numbers are missing. Ages and dates often do not coincide from one census to the next. Foreign names were spelled phonetically in many instances and vary from one census to the next, and often from one page to the next, making it difficult to follow families and individuals from decade to decade.

This analysis is therefore limited in its scope, narrowed by deficiencies in the extant documentary record and the absence of certain types of company papers. At its broadest level, the documentary analysis covers the period between 1892 and 1920. The time frame narrows, however, when addressing certain questions. In the absence of company ledgers, for instance, the sequence of tenants living in company housing cannot be fully reconstructed. The population schedules are of limited use in this respect, because there seems to have been considerable movement by individuals during the 10-year interval between each census. In addition, the 1900 census does not use house numbers. Any study of tenancy is therefore limited to the years between 1910 and 1920, although in rare instances tenancy can be traced for certain individuals back as far as 1892. The analysis of housing assignments by ethnic background is similarly constrained.

Despite these inadequacies, the population schedules, tax assessments, and extant company papers do provide sufficient information to address many of the questions outlined at the beginning of this chapter. These materials are supplemented by other primary and secondary sources. Helvetia did not have its own newspaper, but news from this mining community was often carried in other area papers. A search of several contemporary DuBois publications produced a small number of news columns that describe local events in Helvetia between 1892 and 1920. Area and regional histories were also consulted, along with materials collected by former residents of the town.

There are several issues that may be addressed once the data have been woven together to reconstruct this portrait of Helvetia's residents. First, certain characteristics of the town may be examined both in the context of other mining communities and in the context of the R&P's corporate practices. For example, coal operators were known to recruit specific types of labor to work in the mine, offering low wages and the worst jobs to recent immigrants from eastern and southern Europe. Conversely, skilled and supervisory positions were given almost exclusively to English-speaking, Protestant miners from America and Great Britain, and these men received preferential treatment from coal operators. The analysis of census materials allows the comparison of the R&P's hiring policies, as expressed in official company correspondence, with a partial list of their employees.

Having determined the ethnic composition of the community in Helvetia, it is also possible to consider how ethnic background influenced housing assignments in this company town. Oral history interviews presented in the next chapter show that many former residents perceived a social division within the town of Helvetia that was based on ethnicity, with the town's many eastern European families living uptown and its American, English, Scotch, Welsh, and German families living downtown. Religion may have also been a basis for the division seen by residents since the Catholic church was situated at the top of the hill and the Protestant church at the other end of the town. Some relevant questions, then, concern when these social divisions emerged and whether they were the product of company rental policies and the R&P's corporate ideology, or whether they were constructed by community members in an effort to establish and maintain their cultural or group identities. This documentary analysis also permits the creation of a second baseline—the cultural background of the miners—that stands in contrast to the corporate regime established by Iselin and the R&P Coal Company. It is through the juxtaposition of the two sets of data that the effects of industrialization upon individuals, families, and groups within the town may be measured.

HELVETIA IN THE 1890S

A newspaper column, published in 1894, noted that "the large mine at Helvetia under the general management of Mr. John McLeavy is running about two-thirds time, employing 350 men, putting out about 1,400 tons per day" (*DuBois Express*, Reynoldsville edition, Nov. 16, 1894). In the absence of employment rolls or employment records for this period, we must turn to other documentary sources for additional information on Helvetia's first miners. Tax rolls from Brady Township do provide a record of all taxable property—land, houses, mills and places of manufacture (e.g., furnaces, forges), subsurface coal or mineral rights, livestock, horses, mules, and dogs—owned by male residents over the age of 21. The tax lists also provide a record of each man's occupation (Table 1). Unfortunately, the names of Helvetia's earliest residents are discernible only when accompanied by a house number because the township's tax rolls are listed alphabetically, not geographically. The use of house numbers by the assessor was irregular, even haphazard, between 1892 and 1899 and nonexistent after 1899.[3] Only the 1898 assessment contains a substantial number of individuals—92 individuals representing 92 households—who are specifically identified as residents of the mining town. Since it has been established that the housing stock in town remained more or less steady at 134 double- and single-family housing units from 1895 onward, this figure represents at best only 70 percent of Helvetia's housing units. Other problems arise because the house numbers used between 1892 and 1894 are not consistent with those that appear in the 1910 and 1920 population schedules or those printed on the 1947 Kovalchick plat.[4]

TABLE 1.
Occupation of Helvetia residents listed in the
Brady Township tax rolls, 1892–1899

	1892	1893	1894	1895	1896	1897	1898	1899	Total
Miner	23	35	4	10	–	11	88	–	171
Carpenter	1	1	–	–	–	–	–	–	2
Barber	1	–	–	–	–	–	–	–	1
Stonemason	1	–	–	–	–	–	–	–	1
Butcher	–	1	–	–	–	–	–	–	1
Laborer	–	1	–	–	–	–	–	–	1
Engineer	–	1	–	–	–	–	1	–	2
Bookkeeper	–	1	–	–	–	–	–	–	1
Clerk	–	–	–	1	–	–	1	–	2
Foreman	–	–	–	–	–	–	1	–	1
Machinist	–	–	–	–	–	–	1	–	1
Weigh boss	–	–	–	–	–	–	–	1	1
Stable boss	–	–	–	–	–	–	–	1	1
Total	26	40	4	11	0	11	92	2	186

Despite these difficulties, some general observations can be made regarding this sample of the town's early residents. First, it is plain that these individuals owned very little taxable property. There were 159 individuals identified as residents of Helvetia from the 186 entries found in the tax rolls. Not surprisingly, none of these workers—miners, laborers, machinists, bosses—had any taxable land. During this eight-year period, only 25 cows, 41 dogs, and a single horse were listed as taxable property held by members of this group (Table 2).[5] Approximately 16 percent of these individuals owned cows. Of the 25 men who were assessed for ownership of a cow between 1892 and 1899, only 4 owned their cows for more than a single year. No individual owned more than one cow. Cows were assessed at a value of $12.00 to $15.00. The single horse, valued at $40.00, belonged to a machinist. Nearly one-fourth of the individuals in this group owned dogs, however, and each was assessed at a value of 50¢ per canine. No other taxable property or income was recorded.

TABLE 2.
TAXABLE PROPERTY OWNED BY HELVETIA RESIDENTS, 1892–1899,
FROM BRADY TOWNSHIP TAX ROLLS

	1892	1893	1894	1895	1896	1897	1898	1899	Total
Cow	2	5	3	2	–	–	16	–	28
Horse	–	–	–	–	–	–	1	–	1
Dog	6	16	2	1	–	3	17	–	45

Another question that can be examined using the tax rolls is length of employment at the mines and length of residence in Helvetia. The assessment lists themselves do not provide this information per se, but questions regarding mobility versus longevity in terms of employment and residence can be addressed through a comparison of the tax rolls with the U.S. population schedules of 1900, 1910, and 1920. Of the 159 individuals identified as Helvetia residents and workers between 1892 and 1899, 133 (84%) appear only once on these rolls. Twenty-six men (16%) appear on the tax rolls for a second year. Only one of these individuals appeared on the tax rolls for a third year. To the 26 who appeared more than once on the rolls, however, must be added 17 individuals who, though listed only once in the tax rolls from 1892 through 1899, appear in one or more of the population schedules from 1900, 1910, and 1920. Approximately one-fourth (n=43 or 27%), then, of the men identified from the tax rolls worked and resided in Helvetia for more than one year. Recognizing the incompleteness of the list of residents, these figures suggest nonetheless that it was not at all uncommon for miners to pick up their tools and move their families to another location.

Given the fluctuation in employment conditions and productivity levels within the coal industry during this period, such mobility is understandable.

These data can be broken down further. Twenty-four individuals (15%) appearing on the tax rolls between 1892 and 1899 also appear in a later census or are known to have had family members present in Helvetia beyond the record for their own employment or residence in town, many as late as the 1920 census (Table 3). An additional 19 individuals (12%) are listed more than once in the tax rolls, indicating a stay of at least one year, but do not appear in later population schedules. The two sets of documents indicate that for those who stayed in the town for more than a year—approximately one-fourth of those identified as early Helvetia residents—the length of employment and residency was either comparatively short, from 2 to 5 years (n=28 or 65%), or exceeded 11 years (n=13 or 30%) (Table 4). The numbers shift slightly when looking at the length of res-

TABLE 3.

HELVETIA RESIDENTS, 1892–1899, WHO APPEAR IN A LATER U.S. POPULATION SCHEDULE OR HAVE FAMILY MEMBERS WHO APPEAR IN A LATER POPULATION SCHEDULE.

Census	Individuals	% of Helvetia residents	Family	% of Helvetia residents
1900	10	6.2	8	5.0
1910	8	5.0	7	4.4
1920	6	3.8	9	5.6
Total	24	15.0	24	15.0

Sources: Brady Township, 1892–1899; U.S. Population Schedules, 1900, 1910, 1920.

TABLE 4.

LENGTH OF EMPLOYMENT AND/OR RESIDENCE BY INDIVIDUALS IDENTIFIED AS HELVETIA RESIDENTS, 1892–1899, OR THEIR FAMILY MEMBERS

# of years	Individuals	%	Family	%
2–5	28	65	17	40
6–10	2	5	0	0
11–15	6	14	4	9
16–20	1	2	1	2
21–25	4	9	7	16
25+	2	5	2	5
Unknown	–	–	12	28
Total	43	100	43	100

Sources: Brady Township, 1892–1899; DuBois Express; U.S. Population Schedules, 1900, 1910, 1920.

WE LIVE IN THIS PLACE

idency by the individual's family members. Thirty-one of those 43 individuals (72%) are known to have had family living in town during their employment at the mine (at least 2 to 5 years) and in some cases after their retirement or death. Seventeen of these early miners had family members in town for a span of 2 to 5 years (40%). Fourteen still had family members living and working in Helvetia after more than 10 years (32%).

This comparison of the tax rolls with later census schedules suggests that Helvetia's workforce remained largely mobile during the first decade of the mine's operation. The development of a mobile workforce in the coalfields was in part a response to work stoppages, slowdowns, and the continued struggle for better wages. Columns in the *DuBois Express* indicate that the mine had periods of high productivity or at least steady work in 1892 and 1893 (e.g., Reynoldsville edition, July 8, 1892, p. 5; Aug. 25, 1893, p. 8). This period of relative stability was followed by several miners' meetings and conventions that culminated in a strike by Helvetia's miners in 1894. The strike ended in June when the miners were informed they could return to work at the old wage rate or face eviction (May 25, 1894, p. 8; June 29, 1894, p. 1; see also R&PCC 1894a, 1894c, 1894d). Subsequent reports indicate that the mine was operating at two-thirds time or less after the miners returned to work. Continued "slackness" at Helvetia Mine was cited as the cause for poor attendance at school the following spring, and Helvetia's miners voted to suspend work later that year following a miners' convention in Clearfield County (*DuBois Express*, Reynoldsville edition, Nov. 16, 1894, p. 3; May 31, 1895, p. 1; Oct. 18, 1895, p. 6). Most interestingly, the 1900 census shows that of the 121 individuals identified both as employees in Helvetia Mine and as residents of the company town, more than 80 percent had experienced anywhere from one to six months of unemployment prior to the start of the census in June.

These reports suggest that the mobility of Helvetia's bituminous miners was in part a deliberate strategy, pursued in the hope of obtaining more work and better wages. This strategy was not uncommon in other coalfields.[6] It is perhaps more surprising that many families often moved only as far as the next coal mine. Local news columns made note of many individuals who moved their families to other towns in Clearfield, Indiana, and Jefferson counties, often to other company towns owned by the R&P.[7] It was also not uncommon for these miners to move back to Helvetia the next year. It is likely that many families did so in search of better wages, or better working conditions, but perhaps they also sought better living conditions or ties to a stronger, more closely knit community or family network. Perhaps there was some service provided by the coal company—church, school, doctor—or other benefit, tangible or intangible, that the miner or his family sought in another town or in another mine. Perhaps they moved to be with kin. There is ample evidence, to be discussed in the next section, that suggests it was quite common for families of certain ethnic backgrounds to share their house with members of their extended families, including fathers, mothers, in-laws, nieces and nephews, and stepchildren. The presence of such extended households indicates not only the importance of family support networks but also the existence of an economic strategy that allowed these immigrant families to pool their income and their resources and thereby improve their standard of living or supplement their savings. For all of these reasons, the evidence suggests that in contrast to the popular image of the coal miner living under the thumb of the coal company, crushed by the burden of debt or cowed by the threat of blacklisting or physical violence, Helvetia's miners had a great deal of freedom, which they exercised quite often as a means of negotiating their place within the industrial landscape.

It is difficult to know more about these early residents. Given the incompleteness of the documentary record, there are few quantitative observations possible regarding the ethnic background of this workforce, for example. At least 40 percent of the names extracted from the tax rolls appear to be eastern or southern European in origin, but it is impossible to say more without additional information. The assessments do not indicate who spoke English. There is no information on country of origin or the length of residence in the United States. Nor is it possible to determine the distribution of housing assignments or jobs within the mines based on ethnic origin. There are other sources, however, from which we begin to sense the impact of the arrival of a large immigrant labor pool in the area.

For example, a search of contemporary area newspapers produced some 60 columns or news items from Helvetia between 1892 and 1899, yet the activities reported in the newspapers were almost exclusively those of local residents, including area farmers, who lived in this corner of the township but outside of Helvetia proper, or those of the English-speaking, Anglo-Saxon Protestant members of Helvetia's workforce. The activities of Helvetia's foreign-born workers were largely absent from the newspaper. Indeed, only a handful of references from this period provide any hint of the large number of immigrants streaming into the area. There were announcements for Catholic church services at Leis' Hall, located on the outskirts of Helvetia. The Helvetia Primary School Report for the month ending December 3, 1894, noted that 10 nationalities were represented in the school community (*DuBois Express*, Reynoldsville edition, Dec. 7, 1894, p. 1), though the report failed to list those nationalities. Several marriage licenses were announced that suggest the presence of an ethnically diverse community within Helvetia. And several editorials blamed foreigners en masse for excessive alcohol consumption and for contributing to, if not creating, the lawless atmosphere and criminal behavior that characterized the town during much of this period. Foreigners were also blamed (along with the coal companies) for unsatisfactory working conditions in the mines.

What is perhaps most telling about the mining columns, which reported accidents, deaths, and other news from this community, is that their writers rarely provided the name of an individual of eastern European origin, unless that person was considered an exemplary member of the community—"a prominent citizen"—or the tragedy that befell the individual or family was so terrible as to be truly sensational. The anonymous victims of roof falls, runaway cars, and explosions in the mine were most often identified only by their ethnic background, and even then with such terms as Liths, Huns, Poles or Polanders, and Slavs. The same was generally true for incidents outside of the workplace, where only the most notorious crimes and most sensational events merited the use of the person's name. In this sense, the newspapers seem to have captured local attitudes and prejudices of the period, and it is likely that many of the immigrant men, women, and children who came to Helvetia in the 1890s were treated as second-class citizens, certainly by the coal company, but also by their neighbors.

HELVETIA AFTER 1900

That Helvetia became an ethnically and socially diverse community after 1900 is evident from the 1900, 1910, and 1920 U.S. population schedules. Population counts extracted from the census schedules vary, however, partly as a result of recording errors and incomplete surveys (Table 5). The figures from 1910 appear to be most representative of the full population within town, listing individuals from 97 percent of the town's 134 housing units. The count from this schedule fixes Helvetia's population at 790. The 1920 census produced a slightly smaller population count, but 11 houses were omitted from that census, thus only 91.8 percent of the town's housing stock was accounted for by the enumerator. An adjusted population count was calculated by multiplying the number of missing units by the average household size in 1920 (5.52 members where n=696÷126 households), raising the count to an estimated 757 residents, a figure more consistent with that extracted from the 1910 census. The figures from the 1900 census are more difficult to interpret: the schedule lists the residents of only 63 housing

TABLE 5.
POPULATION ESTIMATES FOR HELVETIA, 1900–1920,
AS INDICATED BY U.S. CENSUS SCHEDULES

Census	Actual population count	# of housing units	# households	Average size of household	% of known housing units (n=134)	Adjusted population count
1900	381	63	67	5.69	47.0	785
1910	790	130	143	5.52	97.0	812
1920	696	123	126	5.52	91.8	757

Sources: Brady Township, 1892–1899; DuBois Express; U.S. Population Schedules, 1900, 1910, 1920.

units—less than 50 percent of the 134 housing units known to have been built within the company town by 1895. Were many of the houses empty? That is certainly a possibility. The census does show that more than 80 percent of the 121 individuals identified both as company employees and residents of the town were unemployed from one to six months prior to the start of the June census. Tonnage records provide a measure of the mine's level of productivity but could not be located for 1900. There was nothing in company papers, local newspapers, local histories, or oral interviews, however, to suggest that the mine was closed, that the miners were on strike, or that levels of employment were severely reduced during the summer of 1900, conditions that might lead to a high number of vacancies.[8]

Other possible explanations were considered, including a gap in the census districts. Until a separate precinct for Helvetia was created in 1920, federal returns from this mining town were alternately recorded in the Luthersburg (1900) and Troutville (1910) voting precincts. The fluctuation in precinct boundaries is also visible in the tax records for Brady Township, so it is a real possibility that confusion over the district boundaries may have led to a very substantial undercount in the 1900 enumeration for Helvetia. The 1900 count is further complicated by the absence of house numbers. Helvetia's residents and other township residents can be differentiated only through the clustering of coal miners and members of the R&P's corporate hierarchy in a large block of names and by following the geographic progression of the census taker. With these two concerns in mind, the 1900 returns from both the Troutville and Luthersburg precincts were searched to see if any of the missing households could be located. While several individuals in the Troutville district are identified as Helvetia residents in later census schedules, there was no definitive evidence for the other 71 housing units. The 1900 schedule may therefore provide only half of the total population for the town. For this reason, the count was adjusted by multiplying the average size of the household in 1900 (5.69 individuals) by the number of missing housing units (n=71), to produce a revised population estimate of 785, a figure that is more consistent with the adjusted counts for 1910 and 1920. The revised population estimates for all three decades also provide an average of 785 residents during the first quarter of the twentieth century.

The number of males who worked for the R&P Coal Company and were resident in Helvetia ranged from 121 in 1900 to 248 in 1910 and 197 in 1920. Again, if the 1900 census is treated as a sample of slightly less than 50 percent of the population, the resident workforce may have been much closer in size to that of 1910 or 1920. In the absence of company records, estimates of the size of the total workforce, both resident and nonresident, have been culled from other sources. These sources indicate that the number of men employed by the R&P varied substantially as a result of fluctuating levels of production and economic conditions, but also in tandem with labor struggles, and it is difficult to get a sense of the size of Helvetia's workforce under typical operating conditions. Figures range from 428 miners in 1918 and 288 in 1923 to less than two dozen for most of 1924–1926 when the mines were idled (Commonwealth of Pennsylvania 1927:108, 259, 520, 657; Kriner 1992:138). Other reports suggest that employment was steady in the early 1930s, with some 700 to 800 men at work (William Brown, Nov. 16, 1991; Cathie Hughes, personal communication, April 13, 2001). Another source states that employment levels peaked at upwards of 1,200 men at the height of production in the 1940s. At that time, the mine was running three shifts to meet the demand for coal (*Clearfield Progress* 1993:75, 129; Kriner 1992:188). The numbers suggest that after 1900, as the size of the workforce increased, perhaps only one-third or even one-quarter of the R&P's employees lived directly under the rule of the company in Helvetia between 1900 and 1920, a comparatively small percentage compared to other mining communities in Pennsylvania or to other coal-mining regions, and something to be considered when evaluating the impact of the company store or the impact of the R&P's program of corporate paternalism upon the town's residents.[9]

The census schedules also provide a partial answer to the question of who these workers were. All three census schedules record in some manner the place of birth for each individual and his or her parents, although the fluctuation of political boundaries during this period means that caution must be observed in assigning ethnicity. The physical boundaries of Austria-Hungary and Russia varied from census to census according to the declining fortunes of these empires, and distinctive regions with their own cultural traditions were generally subsumed within these larger political units. Thus, in 1900 Helvetia's enumerator grouped most immigrants of eastern European origin under the countries of Austria, Hungary, or Russia, thereby concealing the diverse ethnic origins of these individuals. By contrast, the census enumerator for 1920 listed many smaller nationalities such as Galicia (Austrian Poland), Lithuania, and Slovenia as country of origin, although many immigrants were still lumped together under the heading of Austria or Hungary, and it is only by looking at the native language of these individuals that it becomes apparent that there were in fact both Polish- and Slavish-speaking Austrians and Magyar- or Slavish-speaking Hungarians. The most revealing census is the 1910 schedule, which recorded both the country of origin, using contemporary political boundaries, and the cultural affiliation or ethnic background of each immigrant. These data are summarized in Tables 6 and 7.

The census schedules show that Helvetia's residents were exclusively white. While more than a dozen nationalities were represented in the census, Helvetia's residents were predominantly of eastern European or American birth. Western Europeans were in the minority throughout this period. In 1900, some 82 percent of Helvetia's resident workers were immigrants from eastern Europe. Only 7 percent

TABLE 6.

NATIVITY, R&P RESIDENT EMPLOYEES, 1900–1920,
AS INDICATED BY U.S. CENSUS SCHEDULES

Country of origin	1900	%	1910	%	1920	%
Austria	62	51.24	56	22.58	46	23.35
England	1	0.83	7	2.82	6	3.04
Galicia	–	–	–	–	4	2.03
Germany	–	–	2	0.81	–	–
Hungary	16	13.22	18	7.26	8	4.06
Italy	–	–	5	2.02	–	–
Lithuania	–	–	–	–	5	2.54
Poland	1	0.83	–	–	28	14.21
Russia	20	16.52	72	29.03	2	1.02
Scotland	8	6.61	20	8.06	7	3.55
Slovakia	–	–	–	–	3	1.52
Slovenia	–	–	–	–	1	0.51
Slovinka	–	–	–	–	1	0.51
United States	–	–	1	0.40	–	–
Maryland	–	–	–	–	1	0.51
New York	–	–	2	0.81	–	–
Ohio	1	0.83	1	0.40	1	0.51
Pennsylvania	12	9.92	60	24.19	82	41.62
Wales	–	–	2	0.81	–	–
Unknown	–	–	2	0.81	2	1.02
Total	121	100.00	248	100.00	197	100.00

were of English or Scottish extraction. There were but a handful of Italians and no Irish immigrant laborers at all. Just 11 percent of these men were native-born Americans. The percentage of eastern European immigrants declined to 59 percent in 1910 as the number of native-born Pennsylvanians climbed to 24 percent of the resident workforce in that year. Approximately 12 percent came from England, Scotland, and Wales; 3 percent from central and western Europe; and another 2 percent from other parts of the United States. The trend toward an increased number of native-born workers continued in 1920. Approximately 50 percent of Helvetia's resident workers declared an eastern European nation as their coun-

TABLE 7.
CULTURAL OR ETHNIC AFFILIATION OF RESIDENT EMPLOYEES, 1900–1920,
AS INDICATED BY U.S. CENSUS SCHEDULES

Cultural affiliation	1900	%	1910	%	1920	%
American	–	–	1	0.40	–	–
Maryland	–	–	–	–	1	0.51
New York	–	–	2	0.81	–	–
Ohio	1	0.83	1	0.40	1	0.51
Pennsylvania	12	9.92	60	24.20	82	41.62
Austrian	62	51.23	–	–	–	–
English	1	0.83	9	3.63	6	3.04
German	–	–	1	0.40	–	–
Hungarian	16	13.22	–	–	4	2.03
Italian	–	–	5	2.01	–	–
Lithuanian	–	–	2	0.81	5	2.54
Magyar	–	–	13	5.24	4	2.03
Polish	1	0.83	73	29.44	35	17.77
Russian	20	16.53	–	–	–	–
Scottish/English	8	6.61	20	8.06	7	3.55
Slavish	–	–	–	–	52	26.40
Slovak	–	–	13	5.24	–	–
Slovenian	–	–	46	18.55	–	–
Welsh/English	–	–	2	0.81	–	–
Total	121	100.00	248	100.00	197	100.00

Note: The 1900 census lists only the country of origin, which has been included here for comparative purposes and as a very general indicator of cultural affiliation. The 1910 census contains both political unit and cultural affiliation. The 1920 census lists only the country of origin but also records the native tongue of each individual, suggesting general cultural affiliation.

try of origin, 42 percent came from Pennsylvania, 7 percent from England and Scotland, and 1 percent from other areas in the United States.

The census schedules indicate that the bulk of Helvetia's eastern European immigrants came from Austria, Hungary, or Russia, but when country of origin is compared with cultural affiliation or ethnic background, as recorded by the enumerator in 1910, or with the native language of these workers, as recorded in 1920, it is evident that most of these people thought of themselves as something other than Austrian, Hungarian, or Russian. Table 7 shows that they were in fact

Poles, Slovaks, Slovenes, Lithuanians, and Magyar. Of all the immigrants who came to Helvetia, Poles and Slavs were predominant.

Both Tables 6 and 7 suggest that by 1920 the R&P was hiring nearly equal amounts of immigrant and native-born labor. These figures are somewhat deceptive, however, for while some 41 percent of Helvetia's resident workers were born in the United States in 1920, only nineteen of Helvetia's native-born workers (23%) had one or more parents who were themselves born in the United States. More than three-fourths of these native-born miners (n=65 or 77%) were first-generation Americans, and of these most were the sons of eastern European immigrants (n=52 or 80%) (Table 8). Though American citizens by birth, they were probably still regarded as "foreigners" by many people, including the coal company. More than half of this group still lived at home with their immigrant parents and relatives (Table 9) and would have retained close cultural ties with their parents' countries of origin. Yet all were able to speak English, and one-half to three-fourths had kinsmen who had worked or still worked in the mine; thus, unlike their parents who were largely untrained as miners, at least half of these immigrant sons were second-generation miners. There are no such statistics available for Helvetia, but during the nineteenth and early twentieth centuries, the father-son relationship was very important, not only for securing a job in the mine but also in terms of training. Family members worked together, and a young man often served an informal apprenticeship under his father or kinsman (e.g., Brestensky, Hovanec, and Skomra 1992; see also oral interviews with William Brown, Nov. 16, 1991, and Jan. 3, 1992).

To summarize, the available data on Helvetia's resident workers show that the R&P initially drew the bulk of its workforce from a growing pool of immigrant labor, predominantly Poles and Slavs, but as the flow of immigrants ebbed with the onset of World War I and a new generation of American-born workers matured, the proportion of immigrant labor to native-born labor became more balanced. Despite an increase in native-born labor during this period, however, only a small percentage of Helvetia's resident miners were second- or third-generation Americans. This is likely to be true for Helvetia's nonresident miners as well. While there are no figures on the R&P's nonresident employees, the census schedules from surrounding communities suggest that between 1900 and 1920 quite a few of the area's miners were drawn from local farms. Many of these native-born individuals turned to mining to supplement their income, returning to their farms at the start of each growing season.[10] Yet given the lateness of settlement in western Pennsylvania, it is reasonable to assume that a substantial number, if not a majority, of the R&P's nonresident employees were also first-generation Americans or recent immigrants.[11]

Overall, the figures compiled from the census records on the community's ethnic composition are consistent with the hiring policies expressed by the R&P

TABLE 8.

PERCENTAGE OF NATIVE-BORN AND FOREIGN-BORN RESIDENT EMPLOYEES
IN HELVETIA, 1900–1920, AS INDICATED BY THE U.S. CENSUS SCHEDULES

Census	Native-born of one or more native-born parents	Native-born of immigrant parents	Foreign-born	Total
1900	6 (4.96%)	7 (5.79%)	108 (89.25%)	121
1910	23 (9.27%)	41 (16.53%)	184 (74.20%)	248
1920	19 (9.64%)	65 (33.0%)	113 (57.36%)	197

TABLE 9.

KINSHIP AND RESIDENCE PATTERNS AMONG NATIVE-BORN EMPLOYEES LIVING IN
THE COMPANY TOWN, 1900–1920, AS INDICATED BY THE U.S. CENSUS SCHEDULES

	1900	1910	1920
Native-born with father or kin in mines	7 (53.8%)	46 (71.9%)	59 (70.2%)
Native-born, no kin in mines	6 (46.2%)	18 (28.1%)	25 (29.8%)
Total	13	64	84
Native-born living with parents	6 (46.2%)	36 (56.3%)	49 (58.3%)
Native-born, head of household	7 (53.8%)	22 (34.4%)	30 (35.7%)
Native-born, living with kin	–	4 (6.2%)	5 (6.0%)
Native-born, boarder	–	2 (3.1%)	–
Total	13	64	84

in official company correspondence. As stated in the previous chapter, the R&P actively recruited immigrant labor, primarily of eastern European origin, from the major cities along the eastern seaboard, particularly in the first decade of the twentieth century. Company documents also show that R&P officials wished to avoid hiring English-speaking laborers, Irishmen, and blacks while reserving skilled and supervisory positions for white, English-speaking, Protestant immigrants—men from England, Wales, Scotland, and Germany who for many years had provided the skilled labor necessary for mining in this country. As the previous tables demonstrate, the R&P was quite successful in recruiting its desired workforce. Table 10 indicates further that the coal company successfully implemented its policies regarding the establishment of a hierarchy within the mine.

The distribution of skilled, unskilled, and management positions is consistent with the company's goals, with divisions occurring largely on the basis of nationality or ethnic background. This is not surprising, since few of the eastern Europeans recruited by the R&P were miners by trade.

The proportion of immigrant to native-born labor seen in the Helvetia schedules is also consistent with that found in other mining communities in western

TABLE 10.

OCCUPATIONS BY NATIONALITY FOR HELVETIA'S RESIDENT WORKFORCE, 1900–1920, AS INDICATED BY THE U.S. POPULATION SCHEDULES

	American			English/Scottish/ Welsh/German			Eastern European/ Southern European		
	1900	1910	1920	1900	1910	1920	1900	1910	1920
Underground									
Laborer/ day laborer	2	5	4	–	4	–	–	12	4
Miner	10	45	59	8	17	7	91	140	88
Cutter	–	–	–	–	–	–	–	–	1
Driver	–	–	3	–	–	–	–	–	–
Mule driver	–	–	–	1	–	–	–	–	–
Rope rider	–	–	–	–	–	1	–	–	–
Fireman	1	2	1	–	–	2	–	–	–
Motorman	–	5	6	–	3	–	–	–	2
Surface									
Coke drawer	–	–	–	–	–	–	6	–	–
Coke loader	–	–	–	–	–	–	1	–	–
Construction/ maintenance									
Blacksmith	–	–	1	–	–	–	1	–	–
Builder, supply store	–	1	–	–	–	–	–	–	–
Electrical engineer	–	1	–	–	–	–	–	–	–
Engineer	–	1	–	–	–	–	–	–	–
Motor repairman	–	–	1	–	–	1	–	–	–
Timberman	–	–	1	–	–	–	–	–	2
Tracklayer	–	–	–	–	–	–	–	–	1
Watchman	–	–	–	–	–	–	–	–	1

TABLE 10. (CONTINUED)								
	American			English/Scottish/ Welsh/German			Eastern European/ Southern European		
	1900	1910	1920	1900	1910	1920	1900	1910	1920
Management									
Mine foreman	–	–	2	–	–	–	–	–	–
Fire boss	–	–	–	–	2	1	–	–	–
Foreman	–	–	–	–	2	–	–	–	–
Assistant foreman	–	–	–	–	1	–	–	–	–
Check weighman	–	1	–	–	–	–	–	–	–
Weigh master	–	–	1	–	–	–	–	–	–
Machine boss	–	–	–	–	1	–	–	–	–
Motor boss	–	–	–	–	–	1	–	–	–
Mule barn boss	–	–	–	–	1	–	–	–	–
Company store									
Manager, co. store	–	1	1	–	–	–	–	–	–
Butcher, co. store	–	–	1	–	–	–	–	–	–
Clerk, co. store	–	–	2	–	–	–	–	–	–
Salesman, co. store	–	1	–	–	–	–	–	–	–
Other									
Minister	–	–	–	–	1	–	–	–	–
Physician	–	1	1	–	–	–	–	–	–
Bookkeeper	–	–	–	–	–	–	–	–	1
Total (566)	13	64	84	9	32	13	99	152	100

Pennsylvania's bituminous coalfields, and the R&P's hiring practices are consonant with general practice in the bituminous industry and indeed with those of other major industries in the region, including steel manufacture and the railroads, between 1890 and 1914 (AIHP 1992; DiCiccio 1996:85–88; cf. Bodnar 1977, 1985; Brown 1989). Anthracite operators in eastern Pennsylvania also followed this trend (Miller and Sharpless 1985). The practice of recruiting cheap immigrant labor waxed and waned with the flow of people into the country.[12]

The arrival of large numbers of eastern Europeans in Helvetia is also a reflection of broader population movements in the late nineteenth and early twentieth centuries. The amalgamation of agricultural lands in eastern European countries precipitated much of this movement. The displacement of millions from the empires of Austria-Hungary and Czarist Russia resulted in the immigration of Slovenes, Slovaks, Poles, Magyars, and Lithuanians to Helvetia, though other ethnic groups from Eastern and southern Europe also immigrated to Pennsylvania. Mining communities in southwestern Pennsylvania drew large numbers of Italians and Greeks, for instance, while steel-producing centers such as Pittsburgh, Steelton, and Johnstown attracted Italians, Poles, Serbs, and Croats. The variation that is evident in the composition of these industrial communities is in part the product of movement into areas already populated with members of the same ethnic group. Bodnar has noted that immigration was often stimulated by family members who recruited kin still living in Europe (1977:25–28; 1985). Helvetia's own mix of ethnic groups reflects this pattern of immigration. It is visible in the immigration of relatives outside the nuclear family, many of whom were coresident with their kin or took up residence as boarders with members of the same ethnic group.

But the community was also shaped by the R&P's particular hiring preferences. While the absence of several ethnic groups—Greeks, Croats, and Serbs, for instance—can be attributed to the flow of immigrant labor to other parts of the state with established ethnic communities, the complete absence of Irishmen and the paucity of Italians, of whom there were many in both the bituminous and anthracite fields (DiCiccio 1996:86–87; Hunt, Tryon, and Willits 1925:136), suggests the influence of the R&P's corporate ideology. This is also true in regard to the R&P's stated prohibition against hiring blacks, though indeed the workforce in western Pennsylvania's mining communities was overwhelmingly white throughout this period and the R&P Coal Company was but one of many operators in the state to exhibit this prejudice. In contrast to West Virginia, Maryland, and other Appalachian mining states, very few African Americans worked in Pennsylvania's coal mines but instead migrated to the area to find employment with the railroad or with the steel mills in Pittsburgh (Bodnar 1977; Bodnar, Simon, and Weber 1982; DiCiccio 1996:88).[13]

HELVETIA'S IMMIGRANT POPULATION

Why did Helvetia's foreign-born residents leave their homelands? Most of the town's English, Welsh, and Scottish miners (68%) immigrated to America well before 1890 and may have been recruited originally for their expertise as mining craftsmen, for such was the nature of coal mining in the United States prior to the mechanization of this industry (Dix 1988; Long 1989). Clearly, their intention was to remain in the country, as indicated by the length of residence in the United States prior to their arrival in Helvetia, and indeed 70 percent of all male British immigrants in Helvetia were naturalized citizens. The census schedules suggest they were mostly mining professionals (see Table 10), particularly those who immigrated prior to 1890, and that they were attracted to the supervisory positions offered by the R&P.

John Bodnar's examination of American immigrants from 1880 to 1930 provides some insight into the motivations of eastern Europeans (1985:261–275). His research shows that most emigrants from this region were not fugitives from "a culture of poverty," though certainly a dramatic rise in population during this period and a corresponding decline in the need for rural agricultural labor contributed to the impoverishment and the exodus of this landless class. Many also left to avoid military conscription. Bodnar's analysis suggests, however, that most emigrants from eastern Europe came from the middle to lower-middle classes in their countries of origin. Many were small farmers, and many were literate. For these individuals, the growth of commercial agriculture and the shortage of farm lands precipitated a crisis, forcing small landholders to emigrate, along with those who wished to farm but as yet had no land or had insufficient means to farm successfully. Many came to America with the intent of eventually returning home with enough savings to purchase the land they needed.[14] These emigrants, in fact, made "realistic decisions about familial and individual survival" (1985:267). With what he calls "peasant realism," they considered a number of factors in making the decision to emigrate: the difficulties imposed by land shortages, seasonal employment, and unpredictable weather conditions, coupled with low wages for agricultural labor, were weighed against the possibilities of year-round employment and the anticipation of higher wages paid to industrial laborers. Bodnar describes these people as "pragmatic" decision makers who were attempting to improve "their status in the rural world" (1985:269).

It is important to emphasize, again, that few of these immigrants had any prior training as miners.[15] In choosing to go into the mines to earn their living, they faced real hazards from their lack of experience as well as from an inability to speak the language of their supervisors. Many critics of the industry, including the United Mine Workers of America, argued that accidents and fatalities in the mines were much higher among newly recruited immigrants who did not speak English than among those who did (DiCiccio 1996:121–122). The three census schedules show that 55 percent of Helvetia's eastern Europeans learned to speak English at some time (Table 11), an act that would decrease their isolation from other groups in town and might potentially reduce the hazards of work underground. Whether English-speaking or not, they were entering an extremely hazardous industry in which fatality rates were nearly three times greater in this country than in Great Britain and several other European nations (DiCiccio

TABLE 11.

NUMBER OF ENGLISH-SPEAKING EMPLOYEES AMONG HELVETIA'S
EASTERN EUROPEAN IMMIGRANTS, 1900–1920, BASED ON U.S. POPULATION SCHEDULES

Nationality	English-speaking		
	Yes	No	Unknown
Austrian†	27	35	–
Hungarian†	10	8	–
Italian	1	1	3
Lithuanian	5	1	–
Magyar	6	8	2
Polish	47	48	–
Russian†	6	14	–
Slavish	28	1	–
Slovak	11	3	–
Slovenian	28	12	–
Total [305]	169 (55.4)	131 (43.0)	5 (1.6)

Note: For residents listed in more than one census, only the first census entry was used.
† Political country of origin only.

1996:121–127; Long 1989:46). In this context, then, the "pragmatism" shown by these individuals is especially remarkable, for knowing that they risked injury or death, they still chose the higher wages of industrial labor over the uncertainties of agriculture.

At this point, it is interesting to return to the census records to look at other types of information that help to define the qualities and characteristics of this community. In terms of the legal status of Helvetia's immigrant population (Table 12), the data show that 70 percent of Helvetia's immigrants from Great Britain applied for naturalization papers, versus 17 percent of eastern European immigrants. This discrepancy is in part a factor of the earlier immigration dates for most Englishmen, Scotsmen, and Welsh (Table 13). As noted earlier, 68 percent of these immigrants arrived before 1890. Most of Helvetia's Eastern European immigrants came to the United States between 1890 and 1909 (n=213 or 69.4%). Yet nearly one-fourth of the town's Slovaks, Poles, and Slovenes (n=45 or 25.1%) emigrated from Austria-Hungary during the 1880s as land shortages began to develop. Since, prior to 1941, immigrants could apply for naturalization within two to seven years of their arrival, depending on the laws of the state in which they resided, it appears that many eastern Europeans who arrived in the 1880s and 1890s did not choose to apply for citizenship. Given that some 43 percent of Helvetia's Eastern European workers did not learn to speak English, the fact that at least 60 percent did not apply for naturalization papers strongly suggests that many of these men did indeed intend to return to their native land at some future date.

The census schedules show that, on the whole, it was an educated population that came to Helvetia (Table 14). Seventy-two percent of Helvetia's eastern European workers could read, while 66 percent could write. The literacy rate was much higher for her English, Scottish, and Welsh immigrants (over 90 percent could read and write), yet this still represents a very high rate of literacy among eastern Europeans, a finding that is consistent with Bodnar's analysis of emigrants from this region.

TABLE 12.

RATE OF APPLICATION FOR U.S. CITIZENSHIP AMONG HELVETIA'S FOREIGN-BORN RESIDENT EMPLOYEES, 1900–1920, AS INDICATED BY THE U.S. CENSUS SCHEDULES

	Naturalized	Alien	Pending	Unknown	Total
English†	9	–	1	2	12
Scottish	22	5	–	6	33
Welsh	2	–	–	–	2
Subtotal	**33 (70.2%)**	**5 (10.7%)**	**1 (2.1%)**	**8 (17.0%)**	**47**
Austrian††	14	41	1	6	62
German††	1	–	–	–	1
Hungarian††	2	13	1	2	18
Italian	–	5	–	–	5
Lithuanian	1	2	3	–	6
Magyar	2	13	–	1	16
Polish	7	73	7	8	95
Russian††	2	14	1	3	20
Slavish	11	6	13	–	30
Slovak	4	9	1	–	14
Slovenian	9	13	1	17	40
Subtotal	**53 (17.3%)**	**189 (61.6%)**	**28 (9.1%)**	**37 (12.0%)**	**307**
Total	**86 (24.3%)**	**194 (54.8%)**	**29 (8.2%)**	**45 (12.7%)**	**354**

Note: For residents listed in more than one census, only the first census entry was used.
† Includes two residents for whom country of origin was not identifiable in census, but whose cultural affiliation was listed as English.
†† Political country of origin only.

TABLE 13.

DATE OF IMMIGRATION FOR HELVETIA'S FOREIGN-BORN RESIDENT EMPLOYEES
AS INDICATED BY U.S. POPULATION SCHEDULES

Nationality	Pre-1880	1880–1889	1890–1899	1900–1909	1910–1920	Unknown	Total
English	2	7	1	–	2	–	–
Scottish	5	17	–	6	4	1	–
Welsh	1	–	1	–	–	–	–
Subtotal	8 (17.0)	24 (51.1)	2 (4.2)	6 (12.8)	6 (12.8)	1 (2.1)	47 (100.0)
Austrian†	–	26	31	5	–	–	–
German	–	1	–	–	–	–	–
Hungarian†	–	6	6	5	1	–	–
Italian	–	–	–	–	5	–	–
Lithuanian	–	2	1	1	2	–	–
Magyar	–	–	4	8	3	1	–
Polish	1	5	52	22	13	2	–
Russian†	–	6	11	3	–	–	–
Slavish	–	4	3	17	5	1	–
Slovak	–	4	4	5	1	–	–
Slovenian	–	4	13	22	1	–	–
Subtotal	1 (0.3)	58 (18.9)	125 (40.7)	88 (28.7)	31 (10.1)	4 (1.3)	307 (100.0)
Total	9 (2.5)	82 (23.2)	127 (35.9)	94 (26.6)	37 (10.4)	5 (1.4)	354 (100.0)

Note: For residents listed in more than one census, only the first census entry was used.
†Political country of origin only.

   Helvetia's working population can also be characterized as one made predominantly of married men between the ages of 20 and 40 (Tables 15 and 16). Both Adrian Iselin and the Rochester & Pittsburgh Coal Company preferred to hire married men and they therefore built and maintained a stock of 124 family-style corporate housing units for their miners and unskilled workers, and offered services and amenities such as a school, a church, and medical care to attract these men and their families. The census returns indicate that 60 percent of Helvetia's resident miners were married or widowed. While the remainder of the town's male population—some 40 percent—was composed of single males, a closer look reveals that half of these individuals were under the age of 20 and were still living at home with their parents, and that most of these children and young adults (71%) were native-born Americans. Fewer than 20 percent of the town's miners, mine workers, or company employees, then, were single adult men. The largest groups of single adult males were Polish immigrants (34%) and native-born Americans (24%).

TABLE 14.

LITERACY RATES AMONG RESIDENT EMPLOYEES LIVING IN HELVETIA, 1900–1920,
BASED ON THE U.S. POPULATION SCHEDULES

	Read			Write			
	Yes	No	Unknown	Yes	No	Unknown	
Nationality							
American	141	2	–	140	3	–	
Subtotal	141 (98.6)	2 (1.4)	–	140 (97.9)	3 (2.1)	–	143
English	11	1	–	11	1	–	
Scottish	31	2	–	31	2	–	
Welsh	2	–	–	2	–	–	
Subtotal	44 (93.6)	3 (6.4)	–	44 (93.6)	3 (6.4)	–	47
Austrian†	42	20	–	39	23	–	
German	1	–	–	1	–	–	
Hungarian†	13	5	–	13	5	–	
Italian	4	1	–	4	1	–	
Lithuanian	3	2	1	3	2	1	
Magyar	15	1	–	15	1	–	
Polish	68	25	2	55	38	2	
Russian†	5	15	–	5	15	–	
Slavish	27	2	–	27	2	–	
Slovak	11	3	–	11	3	–	
Slovenian	30	10	–	28	12	–	
Subtotal	219 (71.6)	84 (27.4)	3 (1.0)	201 (65.7)	102 (33.3)	3 (1.0)	306
Total	404 (81.5)	89 (17.9)	3 (0.6)	385 (77.6)	108 (21.8)	3 (0.6)	496

Note: For resident employees listed in more than one census, only the first census entry was used.
†Political country of origin only.

In terms of length of residence, there are at least 50 families identified in the census schedules whose members were living and working in Helvetia for 10 or more years. These 50 families include 128 R&P employees between 1900 and 1920, nearly one-fourth of the working male population in town. Of these, 67 lived and worked here for at least 10 years. At least 12 were residents of this town for 20 or more years, while 2 miners are known to have been residents of this company town for at least 28 years. Recalling the data taken from the tax assessments for 1892–1899, these new figures would suggest that mobility was still extremely common between 1900 and 1920, partly as a result of Helvetia's decreasing isolation and the improvement in transportation networks. But coal mining rarely

TABLE 15.

MARITAL STATUS OF MALE EMPLOYEES LIVING IN THE COMPANY TOWN OF HELVETIA, 1900–1920, AS INDICATED BY U.S. CENSUS SCHEDULES

	Married	Single	Widowed	Total
American	43	96	4	
Subtotal	43 (30.1)	96 (67.1)	4 (2.8)	143
English	11	1	–	
Scottish	24·	7	2	
Welsh	–	–	2	
Subtotal	35 (74.5)	8 (17.0)	4 (8.5)	47
Austrian†	44	18	–	
German	1	–	–	
Hungarian†	12	5	1	
Italian	2	3	–	
Lithuanian	3	2	1	
Magyar	12	4	–	
Polish	53	41	1	
Russian†	15	5	–	
Slavish	20	7	2	
Slovak	13	1	–	
Slovenian	30	10	–	
Subtotal	205 (67.0)	96 (31.4)	5 (1.6)	306
Total	283 (57.1)	200 (40.3)	13 (2.6)	496

Note: For resident employees listed in more than one census, only the first census entry was used.
†Political country of origin only.

provided full-time employment during this period, and the mine at Helvetia was still subject to the same slowdowns, work stoppages, and variable working conditions as in its first decade of operation. After 1933, too, coal companies agreed to stop requiring their employees to live in company housing and this also contributed to the mobility of the workforce.[16] Yet an increasingly large percentage of Helvetia's families raised multiple generations in this town, often in the same house. While beyond the scope of this analysis, it is worth noting that testimony from former residents and documentary sources dating to the 1940s–1950s, including reunion materials and the list of names engraved on Helvetia's Honor Roll, clearly show that many of the families who were living here in the 1910s–1920s put down lasting roots in this town—deeply affective ties that were strained but not entirely severed when the mine closed and, later, when the town's last

TABLE 16.
AGE OF MALE EMPLOYEES LIVING IN HELVETIA, 1900–1920

Age of married male employees living in the company town of Helvetia, 1900–1920

	20–29	30–39	40–49	50+	Total
American	20	17	2	4	
English	2	4	2	3	
Scottish	5	9	·5	5	
Austrian†	14	18	10	2	
German	–	–	1	–	
Hungarian†	–	6	5	1	
Italian	1	–	1	–	
Lithuanian	1	1	1	–	
Magyar	1	8	2	1	
Polish	14	19	16	4	
Russian†	3	10	1	1	
Slavish	2	10	6	2	
Slovak	2	3	6	2	
Slovenian	7	9	14	–	
Subtotal	72 (25.45)	114 (40.3)	72 (25.45)	25 (8.8)	283 (57.1)

Age of widowed male employees living in the company town of Helvetia, 1900–1920

	20–29	30–39	40–49	50+	
American	1	1	1	1	
Scottish	–	1	1	–	
Welsh	–	–	–	2	
Hungarian†	–	1	–	–	
Lithuanian	–	–	1	–	
Polish	–	1	–	–	
Slavish	–	–	1	1	
Subtotal	1 (7.6)	4 (30.8)	4 (30.8)	4 (30.8)	13 (2.6)

Age of single male employees living in the company town of Helvetia, 1900–1920

	12–19	20–29	30–39	40+	
American	72	24	–	–	
English	–	1	–	–	
Scottish	2	4	1	–	
Austrian†	8	9	1	–	
Hungarian†	1	2	2	–	
Italian	–	3	–	–	
Lithuanian	–	1	–	1	
Magyar	–	4	–	–	
Polish	7	22	7	5	
Russian†	3	2	–	–	
Slavish	4	3	–	–	
Slovak	–	1	–	–	
Slovenian	4	6	–	–	
Subtotal	101 (50.5)	82 (41.0)	11 (5.5)	6 (3.0)	200 (40.3)
Total					496 (100.0)

Note: For resident employees listed in more than one census, only the first census entry was used.
†Political country of origin only.

residents were evicted (Metheny 1994). The second and third generations born of Helvetia's early miners were still firmly connected to the community when it began to die.

HOUSEHOLD STRATEGIES

While the census analysis thus far has focused on the mineworker, his role as wage earner and his status within the community must be studied within the context of the household. The household was the basic unit of social organization within the community, a key to the survival of many families, a stronghold of tradition and stability in times of change. All adult males in Helvetia were mem-

TABLE 17.
COMPOSITION OF HOUSEHOLDS IN HELVETIA, 1900–1920,
USING U.S. POPULATION SCHEDULES

	Nuclear	Extended	Augmented	Multiple family	Complex	Total
American	42	6	1	1	2	52
English	9	3	–	–	–	12
Scottish	17	6	–	1	1	25
Welsh	–	–	–	–	–	–
German	1	–	–	–	–	1
Austrian	25	–	6	1	1	33
Hungarian	5	–	2	–	–	7
Italian	1	–	1	–	–	2
Lithuanian	2	–	2	–	–	4
Magyar	2	–	2	–	2	6
Polish	19	4	13	2	5	43
Russian	1	1	3	–	2	7
Slavish	23	4	1	–	1	29
Slovak	8	3	–	–	1	12
Slovenian	20	–	2	2	–	24
Slovenian/ Polish	–	–	–	–	3	3
American/ Polish	–	–	–	–	1	1
Lithuanian/ Polish	–	–	–	–	1	1
Total	175 (66.8%)	27 (10.3%)	33 (12.6%)	7 (2.7%)	20 (7.6%)	262 (100%)

bers of a household, though in different capacities. For the purposes of this study, the household has been defined using several criteria set out by scholars who have examined this social unit closely for many years.

Laslett (1972:28) uses the term "co-resident domestic group" to denote "the fact of shared location, kinship and activity." The latter is defined as shared tasks performed inside the house but not outside. He classifies households into three groups: simple family households, extended family households, and multiple family households. Family and kinship are, however, secondary to coresidence because family members and kin are not necessarily coresident, while non-kin associates are frequently resident members of the household. This definition allows for the inclusion of servants and, under certain circumstances, visitors and lodgers within the household unit. As Beaudry (1984; 1988) and Carter (1984) have noted, however, definitions based on these three criteria are often problematic because they do not hold up cross-culturally. A more inclusive definition focuses on the household as a production unit. Carter, for example, uses cross-cultural data to define households as "task-oriented units" (1984:54). He states, "The household dimension of the domestic group . . . is defined by shared tasks of production and/or consumption, regardless of whether its members are linked by kinship or marriage or are coresident" (1984:45).

Each of these criteria works well in defining some of Helvetia's households, but not in characterizing all of them. For example, many individuals, though coresident, did not share in household tasks since they were boarders. They were provided with room and board in return for a fee but were not likely to share in household chores. Because of the complexities of household organization within this mining community, all three criteria—coresidence, family or kinship, and task sharing—were used to distinguish among the different household types found in Helvetia between 1900 and 1920 (Table 17).

More than half of Helvetia's households consisted of what Laslett calls simple family households or nuclear families (66.8%), with little variation on the basis of ethnicity; that is, the percentage of nuclear households for most ethnic groups fell within a range of 65 to 75 percent of the total. There are two notable exceptions to this. Eighty percent of American (native-born) households were simple family households. By contrast, only 44 percent of Polish households were simple in construction.

Some 10 percent (10.3%) of households in this company town included members of the extended family: fathers, mothers, in-laws, nieces and nephews, stepchildren, grandchildren, and adult siblings.[17] In a few cases, these households began as nuclear family units, but their structure changed after the death of the husband or father: the oldest sons became heads of household, for example, assuming responsibility for the surviving parent and their siblings. Many extended family members joined the core household after the loss of a spouse or parent. Immigration dates in the three schedules also indicate that many of Helvetia's miners arrived in this country alone but later sent for their families and their kinsmen. Extended family households were interspersed with other household types throughout the town, regardless of ethnic or cultural background.

A third type, what Bodnar refers to as an augmented household, included boarders and/or servants in its domestic arrangements.[18] In Helvetia, there were 33 such households (12.6%), all but one of which were eastern European in composition (97.0%).[19] Each of these households took in boarders to supplement their income. Interestingly, 30 percent of Polish households were augmented with boarders, the second largest household type for this ethnic group. Boarders were typically members of the same ethnic group as the head of household, most often single adult males (66.0%), but also married men without their families (27.2%). There were also a few small family units boarding in town (3.9%). Finally, there were three widowers boarding with other families (2.9%), one of whom had two small children with him. It is likely that childcare arrangements were shared through this particular household configuration, thereby allowing the widowed miner to return to work and contribute much-needed income to the household or family. Though rarely related to the head of household (there is at least one example), there were five pairs or groups of brothers identified among the boarders, which suggests again the importance of family networking to the immigration process.

In a few instances, housing units were shared by two distinct households; that is, the census enumerator listed two separate families, each with a head of household, who were sharing one-half of a doublehouse. There were seven multiple family households in Helvetia (2.7%). This type of social unit, the fourth type of household found in the community, does not seem to have been favored by any one ethnic group.

The last type of household organizational unit has been termed "complex" because 20 households (7.6%) in Helvetia are characterized by two or more of the household types defined above. There were seven extended family households containing boarders. An eighth household, that of the doctor, included extended family as well as a live-in domestic servant. There were four multiple family households in which one or both families incorporated their kinsmen into their domestic arrangements. There were seven multiple family households that shared their rooms with boarders. And there was one multiple family unit that incorporated both extended family members and boarders into the household. These types of households were found most commonly among immigrant families. Eighty-five percent of complex households were entirely or predominantly eastern European in origin.

It is also interesting to note that 5 percent of the households (n=13) in Helvetia were headed by widows, a surprising discovery since it was common for coal companies to evict widows from corporate housing, often without any grace period (e.g., Miller and Sharpless 1985:116; Hunt, Tryon, and Willits 1925:148–150).

Yet it appears that the R&P was very tolerant of widows living in company housing, regardless of whether they had sons or other family members in the mines. Remarkably, of the nine widows documented as heads of single-family households, four had no apparent source of income, and it is likely that the R&P allowed them to stay on rent-free. Helen McDonald, a 74-year-old widow, occupied a house with her 53-year-old widowed daughter. Mary Fisher, 67, was listed as the sole occupant of no. 269. The R&P evidently collected rent where it could and forgave the remainder, particularly if there was a prospect of gaining an employee for the company in the not too distant future. For Agnes Roger, who had five small children, and Mary Kosko, who was left with the care of four children, this concession by the company must have been an enormous relief, as the future of the miner's widow and his children was generally poor. In the five other simple-family households headed by miners' widows, a source of income can be identified. Usually these women relied upon their sons and, in some cases, their daughters to provide sufficient income for the family. Catharine Gundy held her family together with the wages earned by her two younger sons who worked in Helvetia Mine (the oldest son appears in the census as head of his own household of four) and by her daughter, who worked as a housekeeper.

Other types of households were headed by widows. Mary Vataha was head of an extended household that included her three young children, her widowed brother, and her nephew. Mary's brother worked for the R&P, and his wages provided the only source of income for this household. Mary, in turn, most likely assumed care for her nephew during her brother's shift at the mine. Veronica Andresky, a 37-year-old widow, took in two boarders to generate some income for herself and her small daughter. And Anna Kopinsky and Daisy Haag, both widows with young children, found themselves sharing half of a doublehouse with another family. It is not clear if they took in extra people to provide income, or if they moved in with other families or even relatives as a result of their changed status, but this step was apparently necessary to secure their future. Daisy was probably 33 when she was widowed. She and her children, including Sara Haag Crop, were relocated after James Haag, a salesman and later the manager of the company store, died in 1918 of the Spanish influenza. A short time after this loss, the family vacated no. 278, the store manager's single house, and they moved to another doublehouse just a few doors away. According to the census, the Haags shared their half of the doublehouse with another family, although Sara, who was nearly four at the time, had no recollection of this arrangement (Sara Haag Crop, Sept. 11, 1995).

While the average size of households in Helvetia was 5 to 6 members between 1900 and 1920, most households contained between 2 and 10 members. There were a few households with numbers in excess of 10, the latter usually but not always augmented households or multiple family households. The smallest household contained a single person—the widow Mary Fisher. The largest household contained 16 members, including 6 daughters and 8 boarders. The variety and size of households speaks to the range of strategies, both economic and social, used by immigrant and non-immigrant families to mitigate their entry into an industrial society. By broadening the composition of the household to include kinsmen or individuals outside the family, it was possible for some who might otherwise have had a very marginal existence to increase their financial resources or even to augment their savings by increasing the number of wage earners in the household. At the same time, such an arrangement allowed members to share the heavy burden of domestic chores—cooking, laundry, cleaning, and childcare. The latter was particularly important, as it freed many individuals to join the workforce.

A majority of households (73.3%) had only a single wage earner, though this number would have decreased as younger sons began to enter the mine (Table 18). As noted earlier, more than half of Helvetia's single male working population was age 20 or younger (see Table 16). Legally, boys could not begin to work for Pennsylvania's mining companies until age 12 or, after 1903, age 14, though many parents lied about the age of their son after child labor laws were enacted (Miller and Sharpless 1985:124; Long 1989:71–72).[20] The census records indicate that in most households children were expected to work in the mine when they reached an appropriate age, most often when the child was 14 or 15.[21] The number of children employed in the mine increased by age group thereafter. Most of these children were of eastern European descent, whether born in the United States or not, though the children of professional miners—the English and Scottish—were also apprenticed at an early age. Their jobs were variously listed as laborers, mule drivers, and miners, though the latter term was used in a very generalized way by the enumerators and does not indicate that they were skilled miners. Most likely they worked as loaders, assisted with the mules, or worked as trapper boys, responsible for opening and closing doors or partitions built to control air flow within the mine. Families with children in the mine constituted the majority of households with more than one wage earner.[22]

There are other income-earning strategies evident. In 21 households (8.0%), young, unmarried girls worked for wages outside the home. Catharine Dryna and Anna Duda, both 19, and Katie Pyne, 22, were bookkeepers for the company store. Jobs with the coal company were few in number, however, and there were not many local business establishments that provided employment for young women. The hotel was probably the only private employer in the area. Mary Kone was hired as a laundry girl at the hotel, and Katie Coprosky worked as a servant there. Mary Flynn, age 18, worked as a dining room girl, and Elizabeth Beloh, 16, worked as a waitress, presumably at the hotel. Agnes Brown was a teacher. Mary Hunter and Lottie Smulczenski worked out of their homes as dressmakers. All other employment was domestic in nature. Eight girls worked as servants in private homes, another four worked as housekeepers. It is not clear whether these

TABLE 18.
NUMBER OF WAGE EARNERS, MALE AND FEMALE, PER HOUSEHOLD,
1900–1920, AS INDICATED BY THE U.S. POPULATION SCHEDULES

	1	2	3	4	5	6	Total
American	47	5	2	–	–	–	54
English	8	3	1	–	–	–	12
Scottish	17	6	2	1	–	1	27
German	1	–	–	–	–	–	1
Austrian	30	4	1	–	–	–	35
Hungarian	6	1	–	–	–	–	7
Italian	2	–	–	–	–	–	2
Lithuanian	3	1	–	1	–	–	5
Magyar	7	–	–	–	–	–	7
Polish	37	8	4	2	–	–	51
Russian	5	3	1	–	–	–	9
Slavish	14	11	3	2	–	–	30
Slovak	7	3	1	1	–	–	12
Slovenian	22	4	2	1	–	–	29
Total	206 (73.3)	49 (17.4)	17 (6.0)	8 (2.9)	0 (0.0)	1 (0.4)	281

girls were working in Helvetia, with the exception of Helen Duda, 18, a servant in the home of Dr. Charles Maine, Helvetia's company doctor. There were also 14 young girls listed in 1910 as servants at home. They were not wage earners, but at least two provided much-needed labor in households with boarders.[23] Annie Duda, age 36, was the only married woman listed as a wage earner in the census. She took in laundry to supplement her husband's income.

The varied nature of the household in Helvetia meant the difference between a marginal existence and a living wage for many, while mitigating isolation and hardship with strengthened social and kinship networks for others within the community. The newspapers contain ample evidence that the lives of these miners and their families were often filled with tragedy. Every miner knew the risks of working underground, while wives and families learned to cope with the daily stress and fear that accompanied this hazardous profession. When disability or death occurred, often there were family or kinsmen or community networks to help the widow and her children. Regardless of occupation, illness and disease were also common to the period, and the newspapers record many events that were no less tragic than the accidents that could make a nineteen-year-old boy the head of his family and give him responsibility for the welfare of six individuals: smallpox in 1904, scarlet fever in 1909, outbreaks of cholera, and, of course, the Spanish influenza in 1918.

Such tragedies strike us forcibly in the present: though isolated snapshots, they are nonetheless compelling portraits from the past. An announcement of a wedding is found; the same names are located in the census. They appear for a third time in a front-page article about a murder-suicide in no. 393 (*DuBois Express*, Reynoldsville edition, Mar. 20, 1901, p. 4; *DuBois Courier*, Oct. 31, 1910, p. 1). The children are presumably taken in by their paternal uncle, now living in Tyler but still part of the household in Helvetia in 1910. A child who lives in no. 259 is horribly burned when he strays too near a trash fire in the backyard while his mother visits a sick neighbor. He dies of his injuries (*DuBois Courier*, June 3, 1912). Surely the presence of relations, including the brother who first came over with him in 1881, helps George Brent and his wife, Mary, cope with their grief. An infant daughter of a Helvetia family dies at nine months and is greatly mourned (*DuBois Courier*, Apr. 18, 1914). The process of getting to know these people is touched with sadness, yet it is clear that without extended family or the various bonds and social networks that grew out of a common cultural heritage, a religious preference, or a shared profession, life in this industrial community would have been much harder and, for many, their emotional and physical survival less certain.

ETHNICITY AND THE COMPANY

The last issue to be addressed in this chapter concerns the distribution of housing assignments by the R&P Coal Company in 1910–1920 and the impact of that ordering upon ethnic relations in the community. Many residents spoke of an uptown and downtown and felt there was a fairly rigid separation within the community on the basis of ethnicity. The perception that most assignments were based on ethnicity and religion, with eastern Europeans living in the eastern half of town, nearest to the Catholic church, and the Americans, English, and Scottish living downtown near the Protestant church, does not hold up under closer scrutiny, however. A look at the census returns shows that there was in fact considerable mixing of ethnic groups within certain sections of the town (Figures 18 and 19).

There are two distinct areas where little mixing occurred. The single and doublehouses on Second Street in the downtown were reserved for management. Since the upper level of the corporate hierarchy was filled by English, Scottish, and American-born workers, this area was exclusively occupied by English-speaking Protestants. Residents on this row included the company physician (no. 276), the Protestant minister on the corner of Second and Fourth (this house, no. 274, was later used as the doctor's office), the company store manager (no. 278) and some of his employees, the engineer, the mine foreman, the weigh master, the fire boss, and the blacksmith. Not all heads of household were management along this row, particularly in the doublehouses, but all were English, American, or Scottish.

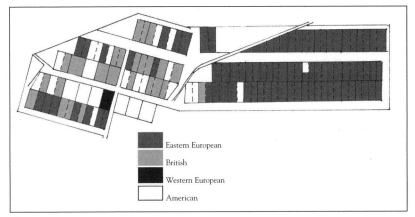

FIG. 18. Distribution of housing on the basis of ethnic background and nativity, 1910. Two or more shades within a unit block indicate the presence of multifamily, multiethnic households.

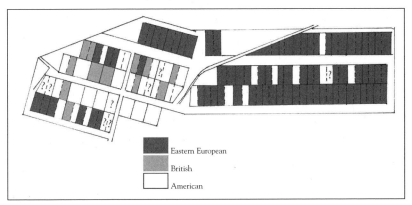

FIG. 19. Distribution of housing on the basis of ethnic background and nativity, 1920. A question mark indicates that no census data is available for that unit of housing.

A second area, the eastern half of town, or uptown, was predominantly eastern European in composition. Eighty-five to 90 percent of the households uptown on Second and Third Steet were Polish, Slavic, Lithuanian, and Magyar during this period. There were exceptions to this, however. The census schedules show that there were two Italian households, one Scottish household, three American households, and 10 households whose heads were American-born but were of Slavic parentage.

In contrast, there was considerable mixing of ethnic groups along the upper row of houses on Third Street downtown and in the area known as Bunker Hill. In 1910, Scottish, English, and American households accounted for 66 percent of the total along this row, but the remainder were Slovenian, Polish, and Magyar. By 1920, half of the households in this area were eastern European in origin.

One-fourth were headed by Americans. The remainder were English or Scottish. The other area that exhibits ethnic diversity is along the lower row of houses in the downtown area. Of the 12 housing units on First Street, 7 (58.3%) were occupied by the families of various eastern European nationalities in 1910, while five (41.7%) were rented by English, Scottish, and American families. This figure does not appear to change greatly in 1920, although two of the housing units were not accounted for in the census that year.

While some coal companies were known to use ethnic segregation as a means of creating discord and conflict among workers who might otherwise have united more quickly in their opposition to company practices, it is apparent that the R&P was more pragmatic in making its housing assignments, preferring instead to fill its houses with men who would generate profits for the company—regardless of location or ethnic group—rather than have its corporate housing vacant. Most, but not all of the American, English, and Scottish households were located in the western half of Helvetia. The uptown area was predominantly, but not exclusively, eastern European in origin. Excluding for a moment the houses reserved for management, the distribution of housing assignments throughout the rest of the community is largely a reflection of the composition of the workforce, which was predominantly eastern European in origin in 1910–1920, and the physical distribution of worker housing, two-thirds of which was located in the eastern half of town. Ray Kriner, whose maternal ancestors came to Helvetia when the town was first built, states that the miners drew for houses at that time (March 10, 1994). The integration of ethnic groups that is visible in some areas may then be the result of a housing lottery, a process that would most certainly have introduced a degree of randomness to the distribution of worker housing. Based on the above evidence, it is also possible that the perception of a division between uptown and downtown based on ethnicity was something that emerged not in the first years of Helvetia's operation but between 1930 and 1950.

The documentary analysis presented in this chapter begins the process of defining the identities of Helvetia's residents—who they were, where they came from and why, who they lived with, and what means or strategies they used to enter into the industrial landscape. It is an essential process, for these individuals had their own cultural practices, traditions, and beliefs—be they Americans, Slavs, Slovenes, Lithuanians, Magyars, Poles, Welsh, Scotch, or Englishmen—that shaped their individual, family, and community identities as much as, if not more than, the industrial workplace. In the chapter that follows, former residents speak of their experiences in Helvetia and their perception of life in a company town. The oral histories reveal that workers and residents actively sought to alter the company's regimen and to create a sense of place, often by incorporating elements of traditional lifeways into the industrial landscape. They show, in fact, a process of negotiation with the company that was continuous and thoroughly woven into the fabric of daily life in this community.

CHAPTER 5

ORAL HISTORIES FROM HELVETIA: A COMMUNITY REMEMBERS

Driving down this rural road, past the little church, past the crossroads, you would never know that a town stood here for nearly 100 years, that a bustling, ethnically diverse community of 800 or more residents once lived here in the many double- and single-family houses that lined its streets. All that remain are three houses, one of which is abandoned, and the old company store, a yellow brick building with a gas pump out front, down where the road turns sharply to the east. Surprisingly, the physical, aboveground evidence of this town disappeared only a few years ago. More surprising, perhaps, is how much of the town has been preserved, though you do not at first see it. Much of its history still lies within reach in the memories of the living.

The purpose of this chapter is to present an alternative perspective on life in a company town through the oral narratives of Helvetia's former residents and mine workers. The use of oral history is particularly appropriate to this study. It was through the recollections of my husband's grandfather that I was first introduced to the once-thriving mining town that had all but vanished from the landscape. The three interviews recorded with William "Rookie" Brown form the cornerstone of this research. But Helvetia's past actively lives on, too, in the collective conscience of its former residents who gather each year to meet old friends and family members, to reminisce about bygone days, and to renew and strengthen the bonds that have held them together across the years. Of the hundreds of people who have attended the Helvetia Homecoming over the years, only a small number remember the town's early days or can tell us what it was like to work in darkness far beneath the earth's surface. Indeed, a good percentage of those who attend these reunions did not themselves work in the mine at Helvetia. Nonetheless, most have deep roots within this community of coal miners. They come from coal-mining stock, from families whose husbands, sons, brothers, and even mothers and daughters worked for the Rochester and Pittsburgh Coal Company over several generations. All are potential informants whose memories may contribute to our understanding of the community that once resided in Helvetia.

Oral histories are an especially rich source of ethnographic data, not only for labor historians but also for the archaeologist who seeks to document more fully the lives of working-class families, both in and out of the workplace. Oral narratives help to reconstruct the day-to-day existence of these men, women, and children who are underrepresented or even absent from company documents and histories of the workplace. The oral histories collected for this project have a broader impact, however. For archaeologists, oral histories provide an emic perspective on the effects of industrialization and allow us to hear voices that are often muted or silent in company histories—those of the workers. By tapping into the memories of these individuals, it is possible to reconstruct the context in which material culture was used and discarded—indeed, the context in which the physical record was created. We may also gain insight into the cultural meaning—corporate and noncorporate—of material objects and the physical landscape, as well as the context and meaning of social action or performance within this industrial community. Further, we may discover worker perceptions about agency and the relationship between industry and labor. Oral traditions about the workplace may also contain elements of both "the world-as-lived and the world-as-thought" (Yentsch 1988:17). An analysis of oral narratives may therefore reveal how the working classes created a sense of place, a sense of community, even a working-class consciousness, in the industrial workplace.

In the present study, oral testimony has been integral to an analysis of the often conflicting sets of data derived from the material and documentary record of the site (Appendix B). The narratives collected from Helvetia's former residents and employees serve as an independent line of evidence, providing an emic view of working and living conditions in the company town as perceived and remembered by the coal miners and their families.[1] The oral histories add significantly to the reconstruction of daily life in Helvetia, but they also reveal the community's perceptions of the R&P's program of corporate paternalism and provide insight into the ways that Helvetia's residents actively and creatively shaped working and living spaces around them.

ORAL HISTORIES FROM THE WORKPLACE

To understand the heart of this community—the common bond that unified Helvetia's residents and gave this community social cohesion despite its diverse ethnic background—one must have an appreciation for the experiences of the coal miner who labored deep within the earth. Though well documented by historians, labor historians, and other scholars, oral accounts provide an immediacy and a connection to this industry and to its workers that other sources cannot supply. William "Rookie" Brown (1908–1995) was one of these workers, and his narrative provides such a link (Figure 20). His account is supplemented by the recollections of Thomas Crop, a longtime resident of Helvetia who, working side by side with his father, spent two years (1940–1942) loading coal for the R&P in Helvetia Mine.

William Brown was a longtime resident of DuBois, which, as noted earlier, is only six miles from Helvetia. Brown was unique among my informants because he did not grow up in a mining town, nor did he reside in Helvetia while working for the R&P at Helvetia Mine. Prior to our first interview, I had thought Brown was a career miner but discovered instead that he worked as a hand loader from 1930 to 1933, and only after being laid off from his job at the Vulcan Soot Blower Manufacturing Plant.[2] This was surprising to me because of his family's long association with the coal mining industry. Brown's grandfather and great-grandfather, both emigrants from England, were coal miners, as were his father-in-law and an uncle (Figure 21).[3]

Thomas Crop is the son of a coal miner (Figure 22). In 1928 his family moved to Helvetia from Eleanora, another R&P company town. Tom was seven years old at the time, and he stayed in Helvetia until he married. This is where he grew

FIG. 20. William "Rookie" Brown in 1991.

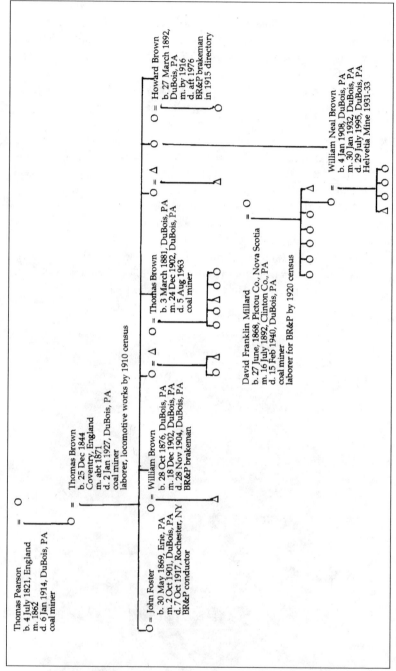

Fig. 21. Family reconstitution chart for William N. Brown.

up and came of age. His father, William Sr., was brought as an infant to America by his Scottish parents and he spent nearly 60 years working in the mines, beginning his trade when he was just nine years old (Figure 23). Both of Tom's grandfathers were coal miners. His grandfather Crop was killed in the mines when William Sr. was only four years old. Three of Tom's uncles (his father's half brothers) were miners, though one eventually left the mines for another trade. And Tom's three siblings—brother William and sisters Elizabeth and Ellen—worked in various capacities at the company store in Helvetia. Tom eventually went into the mines too, spending two years (1940–1942) working alongside his father in Helvetia Mine before leaving to join the Navy in 1942.

Tom's perspective on life and work in Helvetia is that of someone with deep roots in coal mining, who grew up in this town and briefly worked in the mines himself but then moved on to other employment, eventually marrying and moving to nearby Luthersburg. Though Tom knew who William Brown was in the 1930s, he did not know him well until many years later. Their experiences as hand loaders are separated by 10 years, their perspectives on life in Helvetia in the 1930s are defined (at least initially) by the difference in their ages—one a youth of 10, one an adult of 23—and by their relationship to the R&P within the company

FIG. 22. Thomas Crop in his Luthersburg home.

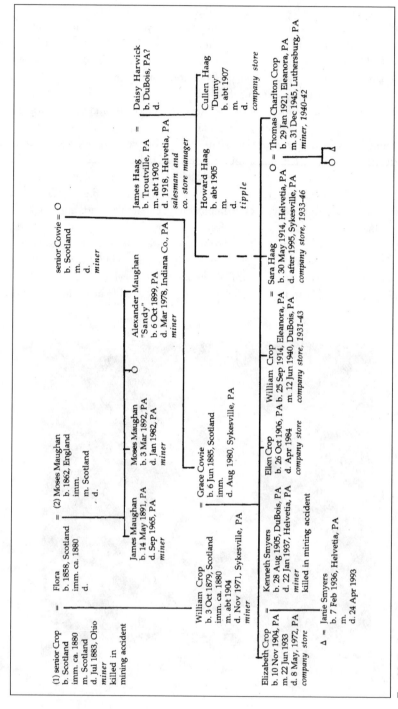

FIG. 23. Family reconstitution chart for Thomas Crop.

FIG. 24. *Left,* "Rookie" Brown, a hand loader who played ball for Helvetia. Papers of William Brown. *Right,* Tom Crop, seen here returning from the mine, lunch bucket in hand. Courtesy of Tom Crop. Rookie was photographed on Helvetia's ballfield, circa 1932. The photograph of Tom was taken in the side yard of no. 296, circa 1939.

town—one a resident, one a nonresident. But again, because of their common link to Helvetia, the two narratives complement each other in many respects (Figure 24).

Rookie Brown took his first job in a coal mine in 1930 at the age of 22 after he was laid off from the Vulcan Plant (Nov. 16, 1991).[4] "I was scared to death when I first went in there," he said. The mine, a country bank, produced house coal.[5] The shaft in which Brown worked was only 3 feet in height, the coal seam at the face was 27 inches high, and the only way to undercut the face was for Brown to use a pick while lying on his side in water. In retrospect, he said, these were good working conditions. Brown would drill holes into the face using a hand-operated breast auger. Charges of powder were inserted into the holes, then blasted to break down the coal. Coal was loaded by hand into a car. Brown's employer paid one dollar per ton of coal at that time, he said, but "I couldn't make three dollars a day consistent."

In February 1931, Brown took a job loading coal for the R&P in Helvetia Mine (R&PCC 1931a). It is probable that he was led to apply for work here through a family connection. His uncle, Thomas Brown, had previously worked at Helvetia Mine for an unknown period of time, but had left, according to his personnel card, for a painting job in DuBois; this same record indicates that he was rehired in August 1931 and was therefore working in Helvetia at roughly the same time as his nephew (R&PCC 1931b).[6] The clerk who filled out William Brown's card indicated that Brown had no previous experience as a miner, a point that conflicts with Brown's oral history. The record also indicates that he was given a physical examination at this time and that he had received first-aid training.[7]

Although the R&P provided worker housing at Helvetia, albeit primarily for families, Brown continued to live in DuBois. At the time of his hire, Brown listed as dependents his mother and an 11-year-old brother. As Brown was an only child, his "brother" might have been a cousin, though this has not been established. In actuality, he lived with his mother, at least one aunt, an undetermined number of cousins, and his uncle Thomas, all of whom shared a house on the corner of West Weber Avenue and South Franklin Street. Later, following his marriage in 1932, Brown lived with his new wife and his in-laws, the Millards, on First Street. At that time, trolley car service connected the town to area mines. The trip out to Helvetia and back cost him 25¢ a day.[8] He had to wake up at 5 A.M. in order to reach the mine in time for his shift.

The entrance to Helvetia Mine was a drift mouth, driven into the side of the hill above Helvetia Dam (Figure 25).[9] The man-trip or shuttle of miners and empty coal cars into the mine for the start of each shift was four and a half to five miles. Each man brought his equipment with him—an eight-pound lamp, miner's pick, auger, shovel, fuses, and blasting powder. The miners walked the distance from the tracks to their rooms and were ready to begin work by 6:45 A.M. Each shift was eight hours. When the shift was completed, the miners rode back out. The mine employed some 700 to 800 men as hand loaders at the time Brown was hired.

Helvetia Mine was worked using the room and pillar system, creating an underground network of rooms and tunnels (see Dix 1988:2–4, for a detailed description). The room, where the work of mining took place, varied in size according to conditions within each mine and according to the decisions of each operator. Its dimensions were defined by the large blocks or pillars of coal left in place to support the roof. At Helvetia, Brown said, the rooms were 5 feet in height and might average 20 feet in width. The length of each room depended on how much of the coal had been mined. Rooms were connected to each other via crosscuts and to the main heading or haulage way through one or more side entries or headings. In contrast to the country bank, where all labor was performed manually, at Helvetia the R&P used cutting machines to undercut the face of the coal to a depth of six inches. Often the face was cut before the shift started; if not,

FIG. 25. A group of unidentified miners and inspectors at the entrance to Helvetia Mine. Courtesy of Doris Andrulonis.

the miner had to wait until the cutting machine arrived. Brown and his partner would drill three holes into the face: the center hole, called the "buster," and two holes to either side, called "rib shots." They filled the holes with the charges that they brought down each day, but a shot-firer did the actual "shooting" once the fire boss had determined that it was safe to ignite the charges. The job of the fire boss was to check for the presence of gas in each section of the mine; he used the flame in his head lamp to detect the gas, judging by the flickering or the ex-tinguishing of the flame how much gas was present. Brown recalled that some men, determined or desperate to earn a decent wage, would flap a piece of burlap (part of the air ventilation system) back and forth in order to dispel the gas when they saw the fire boss coming, so as not to lose a day's work. Once the face had been blasted, the coal was hand loaded into the cars. When a car was full, the miner or his partner hung his check on it—a metal disc or tag on which each man's number was stamped, as well as something to identify the coal as machine-cut or pick coal (tonnage rates were set according to the type of coal). Loaded cars were sent first to the main haulage way and then to the surface using an electric motor. The miners then cleaned the room so that the cutting machine could move in to make the next cut in the coal face.

It is a characteristic of coal beds that they are found interlayered with deposits of sedimentary rocks. These deposits had to be mined along with the coal but were set aside in the gob or waste pile because it was too costly to remove this material from the mine. The miner was accountable for the quality of the coal he loaded, and if he sent up a car of "dirty" coal containing clay or slate, the car would be pulled aside and the miner penalized in some way. Most companies were quite stringent in their requirements, and Helvetia was no exception. Dockage— the impounding of the entire carload by the coal company—was a common penalty. Tom Crop described some of the R&P's practices:

> Of course, the company had rules in the mines, you know. If you loaded dirty coal, you got two days off. If you loaded it once in a month, you was all right. If you loaded it twice in a month, then you got two days off for dirty coal [July 29, 1994].

Tom is still laughing about the time he deliberately loaded all the dirt into his car so that he could get time off.

> I know I loaded dirty coal on purpose one day to get two days off. I wanted to go hunting. I never saw November so cold in my life. I was free and white, and—must have been about 19 years old or 20. I didn't have nobody to keep or anything. Dad wasn't looking. I shoveled [dirt] off the gob and the boney, throw it on there, you know. We came out that night, I looked at the board, and my number was on the board for dirty coal. He said, "They got you for dirty coal, buddy." I said, "Yeah. You know how it is, Dad. When you're a kid, Dad, they like to pick on you" [laughter]. He didn't know that I loaded it on purpose, and I might as well have worked because I never saw November so cold in my life. And you couldn't find a rabbit nowhere, wherever you went, and I had a good dog, but everything was so cold, the rabbits were all holed up [July 29, 1994].

Generally this concern was treated more seriously, and the miner had to be careful about the quality of the load to avoid having the entire car docked. Pointing to a map of Helvetia Mine, Brown said that it was difficult to avoid the shale and clay because "the farther down they went, the coal got dirtier. . . . I worked over there, and then I worked over here, and when it got down in here, Karen, the coal was that dirty that the men had a terrible time, but they worked it" (July 30, 1994). Miners throughout the coalfields complained bitterly about dockage, which they saw as an abuse by the coal companies because miners were paid by the ton, not by the hour (e.g., Dix 1988:14, 120; Long 1989:77–78). At Helvetia, a tonnage sheet was kept at the blacksmith shop to record the amount of coal sent up by each miner. This information was used to determine a man's earnings and, by extension, his credit at the company store. Since tonnage rates were low throughout the 1920s and 1930s—the result of a depressed market, overproduction, and intense competition—dockage was a great loss to the miner, affecting his family's welfare.[10]

The tonnage system created the potential for a number of other abuses by the coal companies, including short weighing. William Brown and Tom Crop both echoed a common complaint of the period, stating several times in their interviews that the R&P took advantage of the miner during the weighing-in process by fixing the scales (cf. DiCiccio 1996; Dix 1988; Long 1989). Before the mine was organized, Brown said, a full car might officially weigh in at 6,200, 6,400, or 6,700 pounds, but after the mine was unionized and a check weighman chosen by the miners was present, "the same car went 84, 87 [8,400, 8,700 pounds]. So you can see what they were stealing off the miners." Tom Crop made a similar complaint. Though the details varied (since the mine was unionized while Tom was a child, his knowledge must have been secondhand in this instance), the effect was the same: "I think when they got the union in, why, they found the company was cheating them on the weight of their coal. About 200 pound to a car. The scales were set that way. . . . But you take about 200 pound, you have 10 cars, you've got a ton of free coal" (July 29, 1994). Lloyd Gray, also a Helvetia resident, recalled similar complaints by the miners about the company's practices at weigh-in, stating that his father was not well treated as a loader and was paid the same regardless of whether the coal was level with the top of the car or mounded over the top (Sept. 11, 1995). The actual amount of coal taken by the company may have varied at every turn, as did the testimony of these informants, but it is clear from written and oral sources of the period that short weighing was an industrywide problem (see Dix 1988 for a general discussion of these abuses).

Brown also recalled the time that he and his partner hit a clay vein in their room and mined the face for a week without hitting coal. This type of labor is called "dead work." The miner was paid only for the amount of coal he loaded. Company men usually performed the tasks of timbering (putting timbers up to support the roof) and track laying along the main haulage and were paid a daily wage for their work. But the miner was not compensated for his time cleaning the room, advancing the track, timbering the roof, or performing any other tasks that were necessary for the work of mining. Brown knew they would not be paid much for mining the clay and that the company would not waste the time or expense to haul the clay out of the room, so he went out to the foreman and announced that he was leaving. The foreman sent him back, he said, promising to pay him and his partner for the dead work. On payday, Brown got wages of two dollars for 10 days work. "When I got that statement, 10 days, two dollars, my God, I cried," he said. "It didn't even cover the cost of the lights."

Brown stated that he attended union meetings in Helvetia before the union was recognized by the R&P. To Brown, the lack of a miner's union allowed the R&P and its managers to take advantage of the employees at Helvetia. "Well, I just barely made a living at it, and I'll tell you, it was rough," he said. "They had these people over a barrel when I was down here."[11] In addition to dockage, short weighing, and little or no compensation for dead work, he stated that the miners were exploited by management and company in other ways. Several former employees or family members complained of the foreman's control over hiring and firing, and the company's power to blacklist men whom they saw as undesirable, whether for their union sympathies or for disagreements between worker and employer. Betty Haddow Hamilton said that her father, a senior cutter in the mine, left Helvetia in 1939 because of problems with the foreman and the superintendent (July 14, 1995). He felt he could not make a living here, she said. Brown stated that he was fired by the foreman for refusing to load a car of coal for the motorman and the spragger, both company men who already earned a daily wage. The foreman wanted to give them some extra income that day. A loaded car represented probably half to a third of the miner's tonnage on any given day. Brown refused and was fired. "There I was—just married, a house full of furniture, and I got laid off." After several days, he went to the main office of the R&P Coal Company, explained the situation, said he had made a mistake and wanted his job back. Brown was told by management that there was no problem and he could return to work. But when he went down into the mine the next morning, the foreman gave him trouble. He was told to come back for the next shift. In the afternoon the foreman told him the same thing. "The next morning I go in there and he stuck me in a hole. I'll tell you, boy—this is when you talk about premeditated murder. I take the shovel . . . and the water [was] clear over 16-inch boots. I said to myself, 'Just make expenses, Bill, and get out of here'" (Nov. 16, 1991).

Other forms of favoritism were a cause for complaint. If you were buddies with the foreman or a close relative, Brown said, you might get more cars on a turn than another miner, or perhaps a better room assignment. His grandfather had also been subjected to unfair practices when he was still working underground, Brown said. In one mine, for example, the foreman assigned the pillars of clean coal ("and it wasn't pick coal at all, but 'squeeze coal'"—you could just knock the pillars down, he said) to his two sons.[12] They earned 90¢ per ton on that load of coal, while those who had mined the room had earned only 25¢ per ton, he said.

Stripped of any exaggeration or dramatic elements, the narratives by William Brown, Thomas Crop, and Lloyd Gray about working conditions at Helvetia, though different in their details, are nonetheless consistent internally. At their core are statements that such abuses occurred regularly before Helvetia Mine was organized and the effect of such practices was cumulative and detrimental to the miner, in many cases imposing severe hardship on the miner and his family by substantially reducing the miner's earnings.

"I couldn't make a living," said Brown. "It got tough." It was difficult for many to earn a living wage, for there were also expenses to be met. While Brown was an employee, each man had to pay for his lamp at a cost of 8¢ per day. He had to provide his own dynamite and detonation caps, costing 6¢ and 4¢ respectively for a single stick or cap. The company subtracted half a cent per ton from the miner's pay for sharpening augers and picks at the company blacksmith shop. Additionally, the R&P deducted a set amount—$1.00 each pay period was deducted from Brown's wages—for the cost of the company doctor (this fee paid both the doctor's salary and hospital expenses) and the company's baseball league (R&PCC 1931a). Rent (estimated to be $8.00 to $11.00 per month in the late 1920s and early 1930s) was also deducted from the pay of those who lived in company housing. Finally, some portion of the miner's pay might be deducted to pay for purchases from the company store. Brown did not pay rent, but he did have to pay up to $1.25 per week to ride on the trolley, depending on the number of days he worked.

Then there were conditions within the mine that could delay the miner or cost him a day's work—water at the face, rock and clay deposits, gas, slowdowns, and stoppages. Under ideal conditions, at a rate of 52¢ per ton, if Brown sent out three cars daily, each carrying approximately two to three tons of coal, he might earn about $3.00–$4.50 a day before expenses, but the number of empty cars on a turn varied—a miner might get only two empty cars on one day, three on another—and conditions were rarely ideal. When the company introduced the arc-wall cutter to its mines, the tonnage rate dropped to 25¢, making a grim situation more desperate. "It was terrible," Brown said. "We really beat our brains out" to make a living.[13]

Miners also risked injury, disablement, or death each day while working underground. While Brown felt that safety conditions at Helvetia were generally good and that the mine was run according to the rules and regulations of the U.S. Bureau of Mines, his narrative indicates that the observance of such restrictions was at times casual, even haphazard, on the part of the miner. During our first interview, Brown told me with much laughter of how he had once stored 24 sticks of dynamite behind the stove in his mother's kitchen (he would not say whether she knew or not). He also said that the miners would sometimes cut a niche into the side of the room, drive in a pin, and hang a bucket. They would cut a second niche beneath the bucket into which they inserted a white clay pipe—the kind, he said, that had a stamp on the bowl and cost one cent each. The pipe acted as a gas jet: the miners lighted the gas that leaked through the pipe and used the flame to warm their coffee. "In a place full of gas!" He said his grandfather had taught him how to do this. He also remembered that the miners used to "take five sticks of dynamite and stick a cap on it, roll wire around it and throw it like a football." Later he said, "Oh dear God! What chances [we took]! What chances!"

Despite this apparently casual attitude towards safety measures, the miners were well aware of the dangers that existed in the mines. Tom Crop said the coal miner knew that he "could be killed in a cave-in in there and the guys running motor, they knowed they could be electrocuted at times. And the spraggers, they could lose their hands, and they could lose their feet, and lose their fingers sometimes hooking up cars. And I know one fellow lost his whole hand—a young fellow. . . . There's—I know fellows that worked in the mines, and they had—they never worked again, they got hurt" (July 29, 1994).

Helvetia's families might be considered fortunate. The mine was never the scene of a major industrial accident, but Helvetia's newspaper column recorded accidents and fatalities by ones and twos—a miner horribly disfigured or disabled one week, a fatal injury the next. Tom Crop's brother-in-law, Kenneth Smyers, was killed by a runaway car in Helvetia Mine in 1937, leaving Tom's sister Elizabeth a widow at age 32. According to one resident, this was the same night that the Smyers's one-year-old daughter took her first steps (Thomas Steele, July 17, 1995). Brown recalled a man who watched his son, damp with sweat, electrocute himself when a machine short-circuited. The miner could also lose a limb operating equipment. Brown spoke of his fear of losing a leg while working temporarily as a spragger coupling cars. This fear led him to give up the job, despite the considerably higher wages (four dollars per day) he might earn.

Of all the dangers the coal miner faced, gas explosions and roof falls had the potential to claim the most lives. Brown spoke of a miner who "near blew his ears off" when his drill created a spark and ignited the gas in the air. He recalled a more horrifying incident at an area mine—an explosion on Easter Monday that had killed five men, he thought, including three company bosses and a motorman. The ventilation fans had been shut down for Easter weekend, he said. When these men opened the mine and threw the switch on the cars, the spark ignited the gas that had built up over the weekend, killing them all in the explosion.[14] The other great risk to the miner was a cave-in. One of Brown's favorite and oft-told stories began with a trip to see the Pittsburgh Pirates play the New York Giants in a baseball doubleheader. On the spur of the moment, Brown, his partner, and three others decided to take the afternoon off to go see the game. That day, he said, "the place that Lee and I had worked—was working in—caved solid. If we'd have been in there, they'd have never even bothered to look for us."

Despite these incidents, Brown's general impression of the safety conditions in the mine was positive, but mostly in the sense that the miners relied on each other, especially their partners, while in the mines and they never worked alone. "Two men to one place. One man couldn't work alone, because the other guy was part of his safety," he said.[15] "Your life depends on me." This life-or-death dependence fostered very close ties between mining partners and among miners as a group. Brown spoke of how he and his partner took along an older man who was hard of hearing, rather than leave him to work alone; unable to sound the roof, the miner would have been in constant danger from a cave-in. Tom Crop, who described his father as "a safe miner," stated firmly that "if it wasn't for his [father's] experience, why, I'd have been buried in there."

Because I didn't know the things to look for like he did. You're pulling back stumps and pillars, why—pillars and stumps, why—that's when you get into danger. You could hear your roof crack, your sandrock breaking—oh, oh, oh, break—and it makes you a little bit leery. Well, that night there wasn't no noise at all. And I thought, "That's good, that's good." And my dad went leery of it because there was what they call—a creep was on in the mines. There was stumps back there that they should have shot, and it couldn't get caving. If it would have caved and come straight down, you would have been all right, but it couldn't cave. It was just pushing its weight over and squeezing them stumps out, you know, just force, you know, forcing its way. It was squeezing. But my dad, he said, "Let's get out of here, buddy." He said, "There's something wrong. I don't like it." So we gathered up the tools and down the heading we went a little bit. He said—"Let's sit here for a little while," he said. "That's good. I think we've got a creep on up there." And he showed me out the head, he said, "You look up—you look up there at that coal, you see where it's squeezing loose." He said, "That's the sign of a creep." So we sit down there for, oh, maybe 10 minutes, and down she come up there, and, well, that car I had, it's still in there yet. I had it loaded up, my check number on it. It's still in the mines yet [July 29, 1994].

The struggles of the coal miner to earn a living wage and to survive, if not prosper, despite extremely harsh and dangerous working conditions are tragically well documented within Pennsylvania and across the country's coalfields.[16] Miners initiated a series of strikes and work stoppages in protest of these conditions; many were isolated protests but as the union movement grew, some strikes encompassed entire regions. In 1922, for example, the United Mine Workers of America called a strike that led to the closing of mines across the nation, including all of Pennsylvania's bituminous and anthracite fields. Nearly three-fourths of the country's miners were estimated to have walked off their jobs during the strike, which lasted into 1923. An investigation of the coal industry followed. The presidentially appointed U.S. Coal Commission was empowered to study problems within the industry and to make recommendations for their resolution (Hunt, Tryon, and Willits 1925; see also Dix 1988:137–148; Mulrooney 1989:26). The Jacksonville agreement, signed in 1923, led at least temporarily to the redress of some of these issues in the Central Competitive Field but could not be imposed on operators outside the field. Competition from these districts, and from nonunion operators who could undersell union coal because of their lower costs, led many owners to abrogate the agreement within the year. A period of union busting followed.

Faced with increasingly organized labor movements and the threat of unionization in the twentieth century, many owners engaged in a variety of tactics, both coercive and nonviolent, designed to control or silence the demands of miners for higher wages and better working conditions and to keep the union out. The company town with its associated institutions was one of the primary means used by coal operators to control their workforce. The R&P Coal Company was in a position as the leading mining interest in the region to provide a number of forms of welfare for its employees. Indeed, because of its paternalistic practices, the company was largely successful in its attempts to avert labor strikes and to keep the union out of its mines until 1933. These practices have been described in previous chapters. It is of interest now to look at the same policies and practices from the perspective of those who lived in the company town—the miner and his family.

ORAL HISTORIES FROM THE MINERS' DOUBLEHOUSE

How extensive was the company's influence in the town of Helvetia? And what were residents' perceptions of the R&P and of the programs and practices that were intended to influence and to exert control over the daily lives of every member of this coal mining community? To answer these questions, I have drawn together the oral narratives of several former residents and employees of the R&P. In addition to interviews with Rookie Brown and Tom Crop, I have used as my primary source of information a series of interviews with Lloyd Gray (Sept. 11, 1995), William and Sara Haag Crop (Sept. 11, 1995), and Veronica McKee (March 10, 1994; July 30, 1994), all former residents of Helvetia over a period that spans both the company's ownership and the sale of its operations to the Kovalchick Salvage Company.[17]

Lloyd Gray moved to Helvetia with his family in 1927 when he was seven years old (Figure 26). Lloyd's great-grandparents came over from Germany, and most of his family were from nearby Troutville or Big Run. Though Lloyd never worked in the mines, he said he spent nearly eight years working at the Amos Haag Farm, a company-owned farm on the hill above Helvetia (Figure 27). He served in the army during World War II (as did his three brothers, all of whom are listed on the town's Honor Roll). But most of his working career was spent at "the car shops"—the B&O railroad yards in DuBois—as a mechanic. Gray's family first occupied the western half of no. 387, the fourth doublehouse from the corner of First Street in Helvetia's downtown (Figure 28). In 1947, after the company sold the town to the Kovalchicks, his family rented no. 292 on Helvetia's main street. This was the same unit occupied by the Haags in the 1930s. Eventually, the Grays rented both sides of the doublehouse (nos. 290–292). Lloyd never married, and he continued to live with his parents in Helvetia until their deaths. He stayed on in this doublehouse by himself, leaving only in 1984 when his pension check was no longer sufficient to pay the bills, he said. In all, he was a tenant for 57 years, the longest tenure among all those interviewed for this project.

Veronica McKee was Helvetia's rent manager for the Kovalchick Salvage Company from 1947 to 1976 (Figure 29). She is also a former schoolteacher.

FIG. 26. Lloyd Gray, September 1995.

FIG. 27. As a young man, Lloyd worked on the Amos Haag farm above the company town. Photograph courtesy of Lloyd Gray.

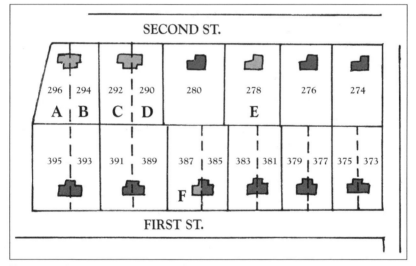

FIG. 28. Homes of oral history informants: (A) Thomas and William Crop, no. 296; (B) Betty Haddow Hamilton and Marlin Deitch (Dunlap family), no. 294; (C) Sara Haag Crop, no. 292; (D) Lloyd Gray, no. 290–292; (E) Sara Haag Crop and Veronica McKee, no. 278 (store manager's house); (F) Lloyd Gray, no. 387.

One of 12 children, she was raised in the mining town of Sagamore, located approximately forty miles southwest of Helvetia in Armstrong County. Her parents operated a hotel and tavern in that town for many years. Though married to an Englishman, she is herself of Czechoslovakian and Russian ancestry. McKee was divorced while her children were still young and she took the position of

FIG. 29. Veronica McKee in the kitchen of the single house that she bought in 1947. Photograph by Darryl Oblack (*DuBois Courier Express*, Mar. 28, 1989).

Helvetia's manager shortly afterward. She is the owner of no. 278, one of three company houses still standing in Helvetia today (see Figures 15 and 28).

William Crop is the older brother of Tom Crop. The Crops also lived on Helvetia's main street in no. 296 (see Figure 28). This family's long association with coal mining has already been recounted. William did not work in the mines, however; rather, he worked for the R&P as a clerk in Helvetia's company store, spending only one week in the mines while between clerking jobs for the R&P. William also married the girl next door in no. 292—Sara Haag, whose father had been company store manager. William and Sara (Figure 30) were married in 1940 and continued to live in no. 292 until 1951 when they moved to Sykesville with William's parents. Sara was the only one of my informants to have been born in Helvetia. She was born in 1914 in no. 278, the store manager's house, the same structure that has been Veronica McKee's home for more than 50 years. Sara was a resident of this town for 37 years, living in at least two, if not three, different company houses (see Figure 28).[18] Unlike most of my contacts, Sara's forebears were primarily farmers from the Troutville area. Sara's father, James, was the first to join the coal company, and he came to the R&P as a salesman. Nonetheless, after her father's death, both of Sara's brothers eventually went to work for the R&P—one on the tipple and one at the company store. Sara herself worked some 13 years in Helvetia's company store. In this capacity, then, and as a long-time resident, she shared many of the experiences of Helvetia's workers and their families.

To these narratives, collected principally between 1991 and 1995, I have added the recollections of other former residents, most of whom came by the excavation site after reading about the project in the local newspaper. Dozens of infor-

FIG. 30. William and Sara Crop in front of their Sykesville home, September 1995.

mal conversations took place at the site and notes were taken where possible. Other accounts of life in Helvetia were found in published form, primarily as recollections that were solicited by or submitted to the area papers. Many of these were collected during the last period of the town's existence, when the interest of former residents was heightened by the news that Helvetia's remaining tenants were being evicted and that all but four privately owned buildings would be lost to the strip-mining operation. Finally, a number of former residents who attended the Helvetia reunion in 1995 or saw articles about the excavation in the paper sent letters describing some of their experiences. Together, these narratives and personal accounts give us a very good sense of how Helvetia's families managed from day to day, how they felt about their lives in this company town, how they viewed their own position in relation to the coal company, and how they responded to corporate programs and practices.

"IT WAS THE PRETTIEST LITTLE MINING TOWN YOU EVER SAW"

When asked to describe what an individual would see when he or she first entered Helvetia, Tom Crop said, "If you was walking in from the church in the lower end, why, you would see nice mowed lawns, and the cement sidewalks, and you noticed, you know, how clean the town was."[19] And everybody had a garden. Time and again, when asked about Helvetia, people would mention the beautiful gardens and recall how neat the town was in its appearance. When asked to describe the company town at Helvetia, William Brown always mentioned the flower gardens. "It was the prettiest little mining town," he said in our first interview. "They tried to knock one another out trying to keep the grass growing real nice, and flowers and everything." Later, he repeated this assertion.

> It was the nicest little mining town in the country. The lawns were beautiful. The gardens were beautiful. Flowers that you wouldn't believe. And they kept them up, and it was just one nice little—it was the nicest mining town in the R&P Coal Company's—it was, boy, it was beautiful. And they took care of it [July 30, 1994].

Margaret Craig, whose husband was chief clerk for the Helvetia Mine Office from 1936 to 1940, lived for three years in nearby Stanley and made this observation:

> It is true that Helvetia was a beautiful small mining town and with the Power Plant and dam in the background, it presented an attractive picture. The people took pride in the appearance of their homes and surroundings. There were lots of gardens and lots of flowers which lent color to the whole town [Sept. 27, 1995].

What was it that set this town apart from others in the minds of its former residents and workers? How did the name of Helvetia become inextricably associated with gardens and neatly kept lawns? As described previously, the R&P Coal Company sponsored a number of organized activities outside of the workplace to instill a sense of pride among its families and to promote group solidarity within these mining communities. Gardening was encouraged by the company as a recreational activity, and at least as early as 1917 the company's president, Lucius W. Robinson, planned to institute yearly competitions for the best vegetable and flower gardens in each of its company towns. Written and oral histories describe prize-winning flower and vegetable gardens and company-sponsored competitions in many Pennsylvania mining communities, confirming the importance of this activity in the coal mining landscape (e.g., AIHP 1992; Brestensky, Hovanec, and Skomra 1991:42, 60; Miller and Sharpless 1985).

Many of Helvetia's former residents still talk about the yearly competitions. Betty Haddow Hamilton, who was born in Helvetia and for many years resided in no. 294, next to the Crop family, recalled Helvetia as "a model community where everybody vied each summer to win the prize the company gave for the most beautiful lawn and garden—I am happy to say my Dad won it several times" (*DuBois Courier-Express*, May 1, 1971). Tom Crop stated that his father's vegetable garden won first place one year, and that prizes in the amount of $20–$25 were awarded to the winners. Sara Haag Crop said her mother also won several times. Her mother was always in the garden, William added. Even Veronica McKee, who did not come to Helvetia until 1947 when the R&P sold the town to her brothers, told me with great pride that Helvetia was named the top mining town in the state for appearance in 1947 and that the R&P was then offering $100 prizes for its competitions (see also Kriner 1992:182).

Gardens were mentioned by every person who spoke to me about their experiences in Helvetia. Not because everybody grew vegetables to put enough food on the table—there were few who did not raise vegetables as part of their everyday subsistence. But oral testimony places this activity at another level. The gardens were, and still are, intricately woven into the community's identity and the sense of pride felt by many—not just as individuals, but as residents of the town and employees of the R&P Coal Company.

Margaret Craig stated that "there was a certain feeling among all [R&P] employees regardless of town that is hard to explain. The 'Company' seemed to be looked upon as one 'great parent' or some such feeling and the employees from all towns considered themselves to be a part of the family" (Sept. 27, 1995). Whatever else people thought about the company (and many of these narrators state quite bluntly that they disliked the company for a number of reasons), there is no denying that residents felt a great deal of pride in this town. Whether because of the gardening competitions, whether they remember something in Helvetia that raised it above other towns (past or present), whether that pride emerges from long-standing baseball rivalries or from their association with the many fine individuals they knew in this town, people continue to identify with the values they remember existing within this community.

Nearly all of the narratives collected or examined for this research contain statements about things that set Helvetia apart from her sister mining communities—the gardens, the cement sidewalks, the ball team, the brilliance of the town's lights at night. The narratives reveal perceptions about life in this company town that have to do with hard work, perseverance in the face of continual hardship, and community. Perhaps Helvetia's gardens and sidewalks and bright lights assume such importance in the eyes of the narrators because they stand in contrast to the drudgery and the uncertainties of daily life, and the difficulties of earning a living wage and putting food on the table. These day-to-day activities, though less noteworthy in the eyes of the town's former residents, were no less important than the gardens, however, in defining the identities of the miners and their families, whether at the level of the individual, the family, or the community at large. For this reason, we will look more closely at the miners' double-house, inside and out.

LIVING IN THE MINERS' DOUBLEHOUSE

Though Tom Bukousky, a resident of no. 296 from 1959 to 1964, was told that Helvetia's houses were brought to the site from one of the R&P's mines in Virginia (July 20, 1995), the documentary and archaeological evidence indicates that the company's houses were all built locally from the bottom up, with the bulk of the housing stock constructed before 1896.[20] These same structures were already some 20 years old when Sara Haag was born, and more than 30 years old when the Crops and the Grays first came to Helvetia (R&PCC 1916a). Lucius W. Robinson's very substantial renovations, begun in 1916, had reached or exceeded their intended lifespan by the early 1930s. The houses, in their renovated state, were considered by R&P officials to be adequate for the miners and their families for another 15 years.

Oral narratives indicate that the company carried out further renovations in the 1930s under the direction of Superintendent Sam Weldon, but they also dispute the company's definition of adequacy. The house leased to the Crop family in 1928 was "not much at first," according to Tom Crop.

> Well, I'll tell you, when we first moved in, it was cold. And we used to use the old slop jar or thunder mug, as it was called, and the urine would freeze at night in that big jar, or big mug, or bucket or whatever it was called. That's how cold it was. Of course, Mother always had a lot of quilts, you know, and you'd pile them on. And you heated your house with a cook stove, and you had a heating stove. And there was a hole cut in the ceiling for the heat to go upstairs. And later on, the company, they come along and they put shingles on the houses and they put new roofs [on]. That made a big difference keeping the heat, keeping the house warm [July 29, 1994].

Lloyd Gray, who moved to Helvetia just a year before Tom Crop, offered this description:

> When I first moved there, I think my mother and dad paid eight dollars a month rent and there wasn't no shingles. There was a wooden strip that went up—the boards went straight up and down, from the roof to the bottom, and there was wooden strips over the—well, some of them were pretty wide strips over the cracks. There wasn't no shingles and that on them [Sept. 11, 1995].

There was also no insulation, though the interior walls were plastered. The company put asbestos shingles or siding on the houses around 1929–1930, he said.

The roofs were sheathed with wooden shingles at this time, according to Lloyd, not the indestructible slate tiles that Veronica McKee remembered as being original to the houses. None of the doublehouses had furnaces. Instead, the interior of the miners' doublehouse was heated, as Tom Crop noted, with a coal stove in the kitchen and a heating stove. The coal had to be purchased from the company. Families without the means to buy coal resorted to collecting spillage from along the railroad tracks and near the tipple. Lloyd stated:

> A lot of the people hauled their own coal from over at the railroad tracks. My aunt hardly ever bought a load of coal. We went over on the railroad tracks, over to the coal yard where they stocked the cars. [The company] tipped the coal down the hill, and the coal dropped off. A lot of people uptown went over and filled their sacks and hauled it with a wheelbarrow or a wagon or that over from the tipple, where they would miss. Sometimes they would move the cars and they wouldn't shut the tipple off without a lot of coal would fall down on the ground, and they'd go shovel it up into their bags and carry it over to the house. That was the way a lot of people got their coal. They hardly ever bought a load. That's where we got most of ours. Of course that tipple was too far away for me to drag a sled or wheelbarrow—way up there where the tipple was [Sept. 11, 1995].

As mentioned previously, the company took measures against such practices, though the problem continued. Eventually, in the early 1930s, all of the houses were connected to the power plant, thereby providing other means of heating the miners' doublehouse. Veronica McKee said that the mining families were extravagant in their use of electricity, once connected, because it was free. She recalled a time when, as rent manager for the Kovalchicks, she went to close down a house after the occupant had died and found an electric heater in every room.

> In every room! Eight heaters . . . ! And the town at night was lit up like Times Square. Most unusual for a mining town, because they all had their lights on all night on the front porch and it was free. Oh, they loved to drive through here to see it all lit up [July 30, 1994].

This extravagance was no doubt justified, in the minds of most families, because of the hardships they endured for many years living in houses without adequate heat and without indoor plumbing or running water.[21] The doublehouses never had indoor toilets. "The voting precinct," as Tom called it, was therefore a steady feature in the landscape of this mining town. Water connections for the houses were not installed until the 1930s (R&PCC 1939).

When asked about the company's maintenance of its "investment," William Crop said, "They done it all." The company painted the exterior prior to the addition of siding (this is disputed by Lloyd Gray, who says he never saw the company paint "them old boards"), reputtied and painted the windows, refurbished the floors, and generally maintained the houses, he said. This was done every year or so. When asked what his father's responsibilities were, William said that the families maintained the insides of the doublehouses, but "there wasn't a whole lot to do inside. You'd get the company carpenter to do all that work for you." Yet his brother Tom described a makeshift scaffolding that his father erected to paint the walls in the stairwell. And Lloyd Gray said,

> You had to do that [maintaining the interior] if you wanted—of course, if the plaster fell off the roof—off the ceiling or that, or off the wall, they'd plaster it up for you. Then you'd put the paper on. And then after a bit, a lot of people started painting it, painting the paper, instead of painting them every year—[I mean] papering them every year [Sept. 11, 1995].

The miners were also free to make their own additions or renovations. William and Tom Crop and Lloyd Gray all described additions or changes made by their own fathers or by the neighbors. The various accounts indicate, then, that the company performed exterior maintenance "every year or so" and would undertake major repairs within the houses, but by and large left it to the mining families to maintain the interior and to make additions, provided these changes looked "respectable."

Informants were asked about the household economy. How did the families make ends meet? What kind of food did they put on the table and where did it come from? In short, I tried to reconstruct a picture of daily living conditions for the average mining household in the 1920s–1930s. While the census records indicate that between 1900 and 1920 three-fourths of Helvetia's households had only a single wage earner (Table 18), each of the individuals interviewed who were residents of Helvetia during the company's tenure came from a household with multiple wage earners (though three out of the four did not work until they completed high school, in contrast to the trend shown in Table 16, for the years 1900–1920). In the Crop household, for example, Tom went into the mine, William and Ellen worked at the company store, and Elizabeth washed aprons for the butcher. Lloyd Gray stated that two of his brothers went into the mine with his father, while he quit school early to work on the Amos Haag farm. And all three of Daisy Haag's children took up employment with the R&P. Though Sara was nineteen when she began to work full time for the company store, she was a part-time employee before that. Her brother Howard was working on the tipple by the time he was 15 years old.

Family reconstitution allows us to put this into a broader perspective, showing the interconnectedness of many families and suggesting ways in which they may have pooled their resources. Betty Haddow Hamilton's interfamily connections were reconstructed using oral testimony (July 14, 1995), the 1910 and 1920 census records, and a published narrative (*DuBois Courier Express*, May 1, 1971) (Figure 31). Betty's family lived in the eastern half of the doublehouse with the Crops (no. 294; see Figure 28) during the 1920s–1930s. Betty was actually born in no. 294 in 1922 and was, in fact, the third generation of her family to live in

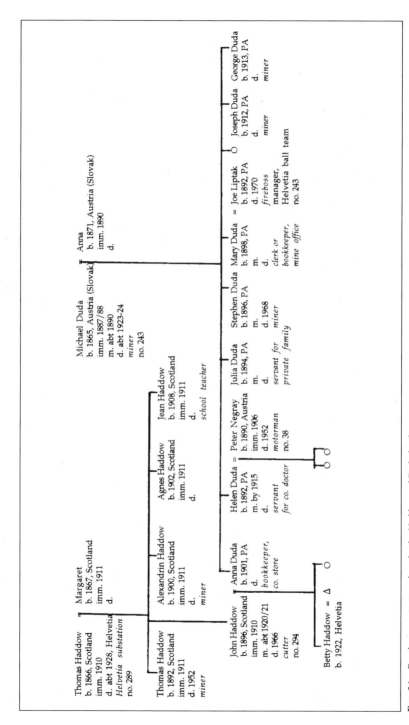

FIG. 31. . Family reconstitution chart for the Haddow and Duda families.

Helvetia. Her paternal grandfather, Thomas Haddow, emigrated from Scotland to the United States in 1910 with his 15-year-old son, John. They were followed the next year by his wife, Margaret, sons Thomas Jr. and Alex, and daughters Agnes and Jean. Tom Haddow was employed as a miner at Helvetia in 1920 along with his three sons, all in their twenties, though Betty's recollection is that her grandfather worked at Helvetia's substation. He died when she was in first grade (ca. 1928). The 1920 census places Betty's grandfather in house no. 289, across the street from her father's residence at no. 294. Betty's father, John, who came to the United States with his father in 1910, was a miner in Helvetia for some 20 years, as were her two uncles, Tom and Alex. Her aunt, Jean Haddow, became one of Helvetia's schoolteachers.

Betty's mother, Anna Duda, worked at the company store before she married John Haddow. Betty's maternal grandparents, Michael and Anna Duda, lived in Helvetia in the same house for 50 years (the census shows this was no. 243, located on Second Street in Helvetia's uptown). Both immigrated to this country from eastern Europe in the late 1880s–early 1890s. All three of their sons (Betty's uncles) worked the mines in Helvetia, while one of their daughters, Betty's aunt Mary, worked in the mine office here. She married Joe Liptac, a fire boss and manager of the Helvetia ball team for several years in the 1930s. The census records also show that Betty's aunt Helen was a live-in servant for the company doctor in 1910 before her marriage to Peter Negrey.

This reconstruction suggests that Betty's extended family—both the Haddows and the Dudas—readily accepted opportunities for employment with the company or within the town in order to contribute to the family's resources. The 1920 census provides an interesting window on the household economy of the Duda family, showing that the oldest children, Stephen, 24, and Anna, 19, were still single and living at home, contributing their earnings to the larger household. Mary, though not then employed in the mine office, and her husband Joe, who was working for the R&P, shared the Dudas's house at no. 243 with Mary's parents and all her younger siblings. The links between these families draw attention to the possibility of networks formed between households and relatives—from sharing living quarters to contributing wages and/or labor to the household's resources.

Oral histories also provide insight into other strategies used by mining families that were not recorded in the census schedules. Besides wage-earning strategies, the narratives reveal others involving food procurement, for example. Families relied greatly upon produce from their gardens, and many found the means to plant additional pieces of company property outside their own backlot. Tom Crop stated that. his father maintained a large vegetable garden in the backlot and a large potato patch across the alley. One year, he said, his father planted a bushel of potatoes that eventually yielded 17 bushels, enough to feed the family all winter. In addition, the Crops raised dozens of tomato plants, peppers, cabbage, carrots, cucumbers, rhubarb, beets, and dill for pickling. His mother canned much of the garden produce, again, in order to provide sufficient fare through the winter, and made pickles, ketchup, and tomato juice. Carrots were stored in a box of dirt in the cellar. Tom's narrative points to a variety of strategies and resources used by the Crops to procure food for the family, including the garden, shopping for bargains at area stores, and hunting.

> There wasn't much to fish around there. We used to do a lot of hunting, though. Rabbits and groundhogs used to taste pretty good when the mines worked one, two days a week sometimes. Groundhog anyhow. . . . They—groundhog's good. Nothing wrong with them. I've eaten them. I shot them and my mother helped me skin them. Made you feel good when you was putting the meat on the table and you was just a kid. . . . We used to shoot a lot of rabbits. They were plentiful in them days. I think—some of the families, I think, used to can them.

When I asked if he felt like there was enough food on the table, Crop answered:

> Oh, yes. Yes. We got enough to eat. And my mom always made—of course, that homemade bread, you could always fill up on that. She baked 13 loaves a week. And you had to use it to pack the buckets too, you know, for the mines. When I worked there, I'd have a bucket packed. When Uncle Jim stayed with us, he had to have a bucket packed. So it took a lot of bread. That's what you'd fill up on a lot of times if you was hungry [July 29, 1994].

In addition to their purchases from the company store, Tom said his family also went shopping for bargains in DuBois or Sykesville when they could. This was possible because the family had a car. His mother could shop for better prices outside of Helvetia and thereby maximize her purchasing power.

The Gray household consisted for the most part of Lloyd's parents and their four children, though his grandmother Gray lived with them for a few years and his three brothers left home after they married. The Grays did not have a car until after the war, so they made all their purchases at the company store for many years. Lloyd said everything the miner earned went to put food on the table, and often his expenses (the cost of powder, lights, etc.) exceeded his earnings. He recalled that people could buy goods and groceries on credit from the company store, and this was good because there was no relief or welfare at the time. Credit at the company store helped people to get along. He said too that in times of need, particularly when the mines were only working a few days a week, the company store would sometimes help the families in other ways.

> Some folks would [go to] the store, like I say, the store would go you for something. And the union, a couple times, they'd come around with some flour, a couple slabs of bacon. Sometimes I'd go up to the store and ask the butcher for a soup bone. You know the soup bone you get today is like this, shaved off—there ain't no nothing in it—you'd—back leg of the beef—he'd cut it up here and cut it here, and leave all that meat on there for you. You can take that off, put some

potatoes and cabbage or whatever with it. They'd throw all of them bones away or kept them for some kind of tallow or dye—kept them, or [there was] some place you could take them for fertilizer or something. Lot of times, I had to go up to the store and ask whoever it was, one of the butchers, ask them for a soup bone. If he didn't have one, he'd go cut one out for you [Sept. 11, 1995].

The soup bone, considered waste by the butcher, was readily given away when someone asked for it. Once, as he said, the miners' union gave his family some flour and bacon when the miners went out on strike, but such help was rare. Families could also go up to the Peacock Garden, Lloyd said, and take the extra vegetables left there by other residents. "I guess they helped each other out. Like I say, there wasn't no relief then. . . . Everybody took some vegetables up to the Peacock. Anybody could come in there—that didn't have anything—could take some." Tom Crop and Sara Haag Crop also stated that if there was extra, it was never sold but always given away to someone who needed it. Clearly there were forms of assistance or mutual aid available in town to help people through the worst of times, but the narratives all indicate that Helvetia's families needed to use several different strategies in order to put enough food on the table each day.

If there was cash, it went toward the purchase of food. The Grays supplemented their purchases with the potatoes, corn, and vegetables they raised in their garden (when they lived on First Street, Lloyd Sr. also had an extra patch across the road that he gardened) and with various foods that his mother canned during the year. They went hunting when they could. The family also raised a few chickens, but Lloyd said it was hard to feed animals in addition to the family, so the Grays did not keep a cow or hogs. They did have several hunting dogs and a Collie. Lloyd's brothers began to work in Helvetia Mine with their father as teenagers, but Lloyd quit school early and began to work at the Amos Haag farm, earning one dollar a day in return for his labors from morning until dark. Though his brothers eventually left home, Lloyd continued to live with his parents, contributing his wages from the car shop toward the cost of rent and food.

Documentary evidence from 1900 to 1920 shows that boarding was fairly common in Helvetia. None of the informants recalled having boarders in their household, though Lloyd Gray knew some families that did, "even when the mines was running." Tom Crop recalled that one of his uncles lived with them briefly. Relatives contributed what they could to the household. Tom's uncle "probably [gave] us 15 or 20 cents" each pay, he said. Both the Grays and the Crops added members of their extended families to the household at various times, while the 1920 census indicates that Daisy Haag, recently widowed, was sharing one half of a doublehouse with another family. The oral narratives suggest, however, that these particular families did not see boarding as an economic strategy they needed or wished to pursue.

Every day, the miner and his family dealt with the issue of food procurement, but the miner's wife, children, and extended family members had the daily task of food preparation and preservation, as well as the process of cleaning associated with this activity. Helvetia's doublehouses were not supplied with running water until the 1930s. A few miners surmounted this problem by running their own connection to the water line, as Lloyd Gray's father did. For most families, getting water meant going outside and fetching it from a series of pumps or spigots located within the town. Marlin Deitch, whose family moved into no. 294 after the Haddows left, said that one of the things his mother disliked most about living in Helvetia was walking out to the pump in the winter to find it frozen (Aug. 14, 1995). The work of filling containers, hauling them back to the house, and then heating the water on the coal stove was time consuming and laborious. The process would have to be repeated frequently to provide sufficient water for cooking, washing dishes, cleaning, laundry, and bathing.

The miner's wife also made bread each week. She prepared at least two meals a day (lunch was sent down to the mines in a bucket or pail, along with enough water for the miner to drink). She spent a great deal of time canning foods in season, because food preservation was critical. Canned foods could be stored in the crawl space beneath the house, according to Lloyd Gray.

> We kept food in there. [If you] knelt down at the opening, you could get in. That's where we had our canned goods and stuff. Kept it in the dark. Nothing froze. We patched up all the holes in the walls with clay mud. Nailed some cardboard around the wall to keep the frost out [Sept. 11, 1995].

And the miner's wife did most of the shopping. Since there were no refrigerators or icehouses in which to keep food from spoiling, most perishables were procured daily from the company store. All of these activities, in addition to weekly laundry, daily household chores, and childcare, were done without conveniences of any kind until the late 1930s–early 1940s. Children and extended family members assisted with the household chores and with the gardens. Lloyd Gray recalled helping his mother with the laundry and the dishes. "After you'd gone to school, you always had to do some chores around the house before you could go to play ball or go out and run around in the woods. Always was something to do."

In many company towns, the challenges of day-to-day living for the mining families were coupled with worries over the possibility of eviction. As described earlier, many leases were structured to allow coal companies to evict families with less than 24-hours' notice or with no notice at all. While a copy of one of the R&P's leases could not be located for this study, it is clear from Helvetia's oral narratives that the R&P was a better landlord than most operators and was unlikely to evict its families, even when the miners were out on strike.[22] Though people left town if they lost their jobs—as Lloyd said, "they couldn't live there long without working in the mines"—he didn't recall seeing anyone evicted.

> I didn't—a lot of times, I know—when the guy got killed, they let the woman live there, and if they had a boy, they'd give him a job. But they never kicked

them out. Different ones, they let them go ahead and live there. They'd take charge of rent, and they got a share if they had any income coming. If they didn't have any income coming, why, they wouldn't charge them any rent [Sept. 11, 1995].

Lloyd's recollections are supported by data in the census records. William Crop said that the R&P, in his mind, was a good landlord:

> If you didn't have no money coming, you didn't have to—they wouldn't—nobody got evicted, you know, for not paying rent. The longer you stayed there and worked at the mine—nobody was—if there wasn't enough money there for the rent, why, they didn't take it [Sept. 11, 1995].

Tom Crop did say that once a lease was signed, families had to abide by the company's rules, but the only thing the superintendent was a stickler about, he said, was keeping the yards clean.

> I know of only one family—one time, they—they just used to throw their cans and bottles out in the yard, and the superintendent of the mines, he told them that—he said—"I'll give you to noon to clean it up," he says, "or I'll move you out." And they had the power to do that, too, because when you signed your lease for the house, you know, they told you what to do. You didn't tell them what to do [July 29, 1994].

With this last comment in mind, the next section provides a look at the miner's backlot, at land-use practices in town, and at company regulations designed to keep up appearances and to maintain the company's housing supply.

LAND-USE PRACTICES

The company seemed to place heavy emphasis on keeping the houselots clean and orderly; indeed, their practices indicate a desire, if not a need, to maintain order in town and to maintain control over company property. Each housing unit had an associated coal shed, privy, and, later on, a garage along the alley, all standardized in form, construction, and location. Even the clotheslines appear to have been built by the company. They have a standardized look in photographs from the period and appear to have been set up in identical locations at the rear of each backlot.

Many of the families kept livestock in the backlots—cows, chickens, geese, pigs, and dogs. Residents built a variety of pens, sheds, runs or kennels, and barns along the alley or in the backlot to contain livestock at night, but many animals wandered freely through town during the day. According to Lloyd Gray, the coal company originally built fences around each house to protect the gardens from unsupervised ruminants. Allowing the animals free range had some obvious advantages for the mining families. The animals were able to graze on company land, leaving the families with less feed to purchase. The disadvantages were, of course, damage to the gardens and manure left throughout town. It was Sam Weldon, Helvetia's superintendent in the 1930s, who put an end to this practice. Weldon is remembered for cleaning up the town, removing the fences, tearing down many sheds, and moving the cows to a company pasture. Tom Crop said that Weldon's efforts had a measurable impact on the appearance of the town.

> They used to have chicken coops, and cow barns, and stuff up in the alleys, mostly up—in the ethnic groups mostly uptown, and there was some downtown had it too. They was—of course, they lived up in the upper row and there was a lot of fields back behind them there. They could have—they had barns up there, and then the place we called Bunker Hill, up there at the top, why, there was—a few of the families up there had cows. Then the company, they made them tear them down in the alleys, move them down on the lower row there towards the mines. Put them in there. And then the company, they fenced in a lot of land. You'd bring your cow down and put it in the pasture all day. Then you'd go down— someone had to go down at night and bring the cow home . . . they had barns for them at home, but they made them take them out of the alley down into the fields, see. Between the houses and the mines. Of course, the ones who lived— the upper row, up on Bunker Hill and that—why, they just left them alone. They didn't bother them. They just got the ones that was in the alleys, where people were walking by. That's when—Sam Weldon . . . he's the one that cleaned the town up. . . . He tore the fences down that went between the houses. That's when they put the sidewalks in. Then they moved their cow barns out of the alleys, down into the field there, further away from the houses. Then they could take their cow and they—I think it was a dollar a month they could put the cow in the pasture. That was taken off your pay at the mines. They done a lot of work, the company did, to fence that all in [July 29, 1994].

One result of this action, perhaps unanticipated by the company, is that when the superintendent began to charge residents for pasturage and to tell them where they could or couldn't leave the cows to graze, the residents found other ways to take advantage of the company's resources. Lloyd stated, for example, that there was "one old lady up here on top of the hill, she run around with a scythe and cut the grass for the cows, after the cows wasn't allowed to—[after she wasn't allowed to] keep the cows out here eating, she run around here and cut the hay and saved it for winter. She had big burlap sacks tied together. She had a big pile of—she'd cut the hay and leave it dry, and she'd pile on these big burlap sacks that she had tied together and roll it up. . . . Mrs. Bukousky. Cut her own hay."

Not only did Sam Weldon tear down the fences between the houses, the effect of which was to neaten up the town's appearance, but he also installed cement sidewalks in several parts of town. Sara Crop said that Helvetia was "the only mining town around that they did have cement walks. That was due to Sam Weldon." The superintendent also made sure that company property was protected. "He had a park down there, and if you destroyed any part of it, your dad was called to the office, and he [the superintendent] got the first [pitch]. He says, "If you can't control him," he says, "I will." He says, "You won't be working here" (William Crop, Sept. 11, 1995).

Some of the R&P's practices regarding the backlots were intended to maintain or improve sanitation. The R&P had the outdoor privies cleaned every year and hauled away the garbage from the houses each week. Trash was set out in the alley for collection. Most of the garbage was emptied into an abandoned airshaft or into a sinkhole that had opened up in an area of town that had been undermined (some areas of town, particularly First Street, were undermined to as little as 18 to 20 feet [5.49–6.10 m] below grade, according to Lloyd, giving cellar floors in this area a spongy feeling). Trash was also burned at the dump, Lloyd stated, but never in the backyard. "Always kept it—the place—cleaned up pretty good," he said.

This practice made it easier for families to maintain their backlots and improved the appearance of the yards, but it also reduced the risk of disease, improved safety for the families, and may have alleviated a problem with rodents. When asked if there was a problem in town with rats or mice, William Crop said, "No. Oh, every once and awhile, you'd catch one or see one, but, you know, there wasn't anything there. It never got—you know like some of these places that had a barn and a cow, you know—it was never a problem. It never caused any, you know—everybody had a gun and they'd shoot them." The latter part of this statement appears to contradict the first, and when set next to Lloyd Gray's testimony, suggests that despite regular trash pickup, the town still had its share of unwanted pests. Lloyd stated that there were quite a few rats and mice in the town and that his family stored their potatoes in the cellar using rivet kegs with screens on top to keep the rats out. He could hear them at night between the walls or the floors and in the attic of the house. The Grays used a lot of "rat nectar" in the house, and Lloyd said there was often an odor coming from the cellar from the rats and mice that died in there.

Some of the R&P's practices may have created health hazards. As previously noted, there was no indoor plumbing for the miners until after the company sold the town, though management had cesspools or cesspits for their indoor toilets.[23] In addition, then, to these cesspits, there were two outhouses for every double-house, set up along the alley, and there were ditches and, later, pipes draining wash water or water from the sink and carrying that wastewater away from the houses. Lloyd said the company kept the ditches free from rubbish and empty of standing water.

> Uptown, they just had a 50-gallon barrel . . . running out into the alley, down towards the dam. There was a lot of ditches along—open ditches—along the alleys, where the wash water from your sink or that would run out and down. They had it piped across the alley and they had ditches. The company—even

when the company owned it—they kept the ditches clean towards the creek or down towards the swamps from the town. They kept it clean [Sept. 11, 1995].

Tom said the old ball ground was frequently wet (eventually it was moved to the western end of town, opposite the Protestant church), and he believed that the problem was exacerbated by sewage or wastewater draining down from the company store. There is no data at present to indicate whether these practices were harmful to the residents. There is ample documentation, nonetheless, that pollutants and environmental hazards associated with coal mining were often detrimental to adjacent communities (AIHP 1992:49–49; Gordon and Malone 1994:124–126; Miller and Sharpless 1985:176–181, 323–324).

THE COMPANY STORE

Of all the institutions and programs associated with the coal company town, the company store was the most notorious. Yet with the exception of inflated prices, oral histories from Helvetia indicate that the worst practices associated with this particular institution were not duplicated by the Mahoning Supply Company. There is no evidence for the use of scrip, for example, and the testimony of former residents indicates that the company gave credit and other forms of assistance to families in need.

While Mrs. McKee stated that Helvetia's miners had to buy everything at the company store, there is plenty of evidence to the contrary. The store owned by J. M. Leis beyond the eastern edge of the town, though not a heavy competitor with the company store, was frequented by many families living within walking distance in Helvetia's uptown. By the 1920s, however, transportation networks were fairly well established and certainly less costly, and it was not uncommon for families to own cars. Those who had access to a car had the means to travel to DuBois or Sykesville to look for bargains at area stores. Lloyd Gray stated, however, that even after his family acquired a car, they continued to make most of their purchases at the company store.

> I figure you could get—you could buy—a lot of times buy it cheaper at the company store than you could buy it somewhere else. . . . Meat was better. The meat was better than you could buy any place else, I figured. My mother figured it was too [Sept. 11, 1995].

Veronica McKee stated that the miners also influenced the types of goods stocked at the company store:

> At one time, the store manager told me, "We thought we would get cheaper meat and cheaper canned goods," and he says, "Let me tell you, those miners knew the difference." They wanted their Del Montes, you know, canned goods. And they wanted good meat [July 30, 1994].

The company store carried everything a family might need too, William Crop said.

> You could get married there and get your whole set-up right there and never go
> to another store. Refrigerator, stoves, furniture. If you wanted to paint your
> house, they had paint, paint brushes. Hardware of any kind. Lawnmowers. Any-
> thing. . . . You had no need to go nowhere to get what you wanted—that you
> wanted to get. They sold everything. Meats. I don't know a thing that you would
> need—well, they didn't sell cars—that's about the only thing you'd have to go
> get—but they sold tires and all the equipment for them [Sept. 11, 1995].

William Brown described the store's contents as "top flight stuff," whether ladies
and menswear, groceries, meat, dry goods, or furniture. The Mahoning Supply
Company provided uniforms for the women who worked as clerks in the store.
These were dark green button-down-the-front dresses with white collars and
cuffs and accompanying dark blue sweaters (Evelyn Means, n.d.). The store was
conveniently located in the center of the mining town and it was open six days
a week. The company store also made deliveries. Informants were appreciative
of the high level of service and the courtesy of store employees.

Nonetheless, residents knew they were at a disadvantage in their relationship with the company store. Brown noted that Helvetia's families bought everything "on the book." "They couldn't work around it," he said. Few had cash in
hand for their purchases. The company gained additional control over the behavior of its employees by determining the amount of credit available to families and,
in some cases, by effectively taking away from their living wage to the point of
dependency.

> The company store, a lot of times you was—you could only buy so much, you
> know. They'd get the sheet from the mines and see what you loaded yesterday,
> to see how much money you had coming. You'd never get that much credit at
> the company store, you know. You needed this, you needed that. Of course, some
> people, they could get what they wanted. They would—they always paid their
> bills, you know, they stayed within their limits, and some people would run up a
> big bill, you know, and they didn't have enough money coming in to pay for it.
> . . . There was one—some of them, that was the only place they ever dealt with,
> the company store. They'd buy everything there. Maybe they never drawed a pay
> either because all their money went to the company to pay their food bill
> [Thomas Crop, July 29, 1994].

It is interesting to look at the company store from the perspective of those
who were intimate with its internal operations. Both William and Sara Haag Crop
worked full time as clerks in the company store beginning in 1933. Sara sold groceries, while William sold gas and powder at the mines. William argued that the
company store was increasingly competitive with other businesses in the area, but
he noted that the method of making purchases at the company store tended to

ORAL HISTORIES FROM HELVETIA

keep the miner perpetually in debt, regardless of whether prices were competitive or not. Everything was charged on account, he said, since most people didn't have any cash. "They was—you could maybe work there all day and then maybe there'd be two or three dollars worth of cash [in the till]. It was all charged."

> Well, the way they done it—you know, they known how much you was going to get. . . . They knowed what you was going to make. And as long as you stayed there . . . as long as you stayed there, they never bothered you. When you bought their furniture, you bought it, like, on a side account. You'd pay five dollars plus your groceries. And as long as you stayed there, if it took you 10 years to pay it— which it did some people—there was no carrying charge, you know, or what they have now—interest. . . . I put 10 years in, and we actually—I only think it— about two or three things that we ever repossessed, so you know, it wasn't—if you quit, [if] you signed this here lease, you know, they could come and get it [Sept. 11, 1995].

Lloyd Gray said that after deductions for rent and groceries, "a lot of times my mother and my dad and my one brother—they all owed money." But former store employees said the company rarely took everything. Evelyn Wilson Means, daughter of the power plant superintendent, worked in Helvetia's company store beginning in 1937, first as a clerk and later in the store office. Means recalled that they "went to the mine office once a month to take the money out of their pay [for purchases at the company store] but we never took all their money even if they owed more. You just couldn't take all of it" (Means n.d.)[24] There is suffi- cient testimony from the early 1930s to indicate that the miner often found deductions exceeded his pay, although this practice may have changed after the union came into the mines. Regardless, the economic state of the coal industry in the 1920s–1930s, the tonnage system, the practice of deducting for the cost of the miner's equipment, and the structure of institutions such as the company store meant that many families had to rely on credit from the company store. While most of the individuals interviewed for this study did not feel that the R&P took unfair advantage of the families in their position as debtors, except in the matter of inflated prices, there is no question that this system had the poten- tial to have an adverse effect on the families living in the company town.

CREATING SOCIAL COHESION

By contrast, the company's other paternalistic programs were viewed more favor- ably by residents. As described earlier, the company built the schoolhouse, the two churches, the band hall or election hall, and a park with a playground. With the exception of the park, which was installed in the 1930s, most of these buildings were in place during the first decade of the town's operation. Although Helvetia no longer had a band in the 1930s, it still had a baseball team. Each December, the company decorated a community Christmas tree at the doctor's office. Lloyd Gray and Tom Crop recalled that the children were given a special treat at Christmas. Tom said that "Santa Claus would come and give all us kids candy and an apple or an orange. Of course, that was all paid [for] by the company."

Perhaps the most important program was the company doctor. Along with credit from the company store, medical care was an essential for most miners, according to Veronica McKee. During the Great Depression, she said,

> instead of working five days a week, they were reduced to working three days a week. A tremendous hardship if you had a large family. Because there was no Social Security, no unemployment compensation, you see, no unemployment compensation. However, the coal company took quite a—I mean, the mining town was [better] than they [the miners] thought—good medical care from the company doctor. That was another thing that was free, you see. You got good medical care from the company doctor [July 30, 1994].

Medical care was not free. A flat fee was deducted from the miner's pay every two weeks—Tom Crop thought it was $1.00 to $1.50 from his dad's pay, though William Brown's employment card indicated that only 75¢ was deducted, perhaps because he was not yet married. But the doctor could be consulted an unlimited number of times and the fee never changed, regardless of the cost of medical treatment. Tom Crop said he would come to the house or see patients in his office as many times as needed.[25] The doctor delivered babies in the company houses. He also kept a horse and buggy or wagon in a barn behind his house, according to Lloyd Gray, in order to make sick calls. Only the very sick and severely injured would be sent to Adrian Hospital. The need for a doctor was constant, not only for injuries suffered in the mines but also for illnesses in the community. Epidemics were a severe threat throughout Helvetia's early years, as mentioned. And there were many births each year that required the attendance of the doctor. The availability of medical care at a flat rate must have been seen as a godsend by most families. Helvetia was fortunate too in that it had a series of competent resident doctors, as other accounts from the period indicate that in many mining communities, the company doctor was rarely available and medical care left much to be desired (Hunt, Tryon, and Willits 1925:142, 144; Korson 1943:57–59).

Other institutions of equal importance—churches and schools—were established by the company, though not under their direct supervision. "The people were all churchgoing," Veronica McKee said. "They went to church each Sunday." Early newspaper accounts indicate that attendance for both Protestant and Catholic services and religious meetings was regular. In addition, these institutions sponsored many other activities within the community, from church suppers, picnics, and religious festivals to feeding the baseball players on game night. The newspaper accounts and oral narratives suggest the churches provided social cohesion for many in town.

Schools that were built for the miners' children in each of the R&P's company towns were seen as a great advantage. Not all children attended a full 12 years of school, nor even eight. McKee stated that "usually the oldest son didn't attend high school, but the younger ones did because the older one went into the mines to get enough money to send the younger ones." But the census records from 1900–1920 indicate that most did attend for several years and nearly all of Helvetia's children could read and write. The oral narratives suggest too that by the end of the 1930s more families allowed their children to complete high school before joining the workforce and, further, that education was increasingly valued by families who hoped for a better life for their children. McKee described many of the students she had known from Sagamore and Helvetia who had gone on to become doctors, engineers, geologists, pilots, and professionals in other fields. Tom and William Crop and Sara Haag Crop all completed their high school education before joining the company. When Tom Crop was asked why he didn't start working before he had turned 19, he said, "Why, to finish my education." His parents wanted both Tom and William to finish school first, and they were able to manage without the extra income that these boys would have earned going into the mines at an earlier age.

A DIVERSE COMMUNITY

Mrs. McKee, who is of Slavic ancestry, said that mining towns were noted for their ethnic diversity and that this was, in fact, a good thing.

> One good advantage of the mining towns was the fact—it was like a great common denominator. You didn't have artificial [integration]. You went to school and you were all thrown together. You had Italians, Irish, Swedish, Russian, Hungarian, everything. . . . But they all got along very well. There was never any segregation. . . .
>
> When you walked down the streets of Helvetia, you could hear any accent because they were all either immigrants from Europe or descendants of immigrants. Helvetia had predominantly Scottish miners and Slovak miners. Unusual in that there were no Italian miners or Irish. . . . There might have been a couple of Irish, but they were all more or less Scotch and Slovak. . . . Which was most unusual because every mining town had practically every ethnic group—any ethnic group you wanted to meet [July 30, 1994].

The underlying reasons for the town's ethnic composition have already been explored. This section looks more closely at social interaction within the company town to understand how the members of Helvetia's diverse community interacted on a day-to-day basis. Most of Helvetia's former residents agreed that the town was divided into an uptown and downtown, based on ethnicity. Tom Crop said, "mostly the ethnic people was uptown, and the English people were downtown. And the company store was right in the middle." Asked if there was much mixing socially, he said:

> Well, they—well, I don't know how to say that. The company store seemed to be about the dividing line. You stayed on your side, and they stayed on their side. Like if we had ballgames or there was something doing, why then, there was nothing said because everybody had to come. Uptown to downtown to the ball-game, you know. And after it was over, they went up and went their way. When we was kids, we used to play baseball against each other, uptown and downtown. We never had no—we never had any trouble [July 30, 1994].

The narratives as a group suggest that the need to establish ethnic enclaves or to maintain a separateness was largely generational. If the adults had trouble mix-ing, the children rarely thought about it. In Helvetia all children went to the same school, according to Tom Crop, until the mid-1930s when a priest from DuBois opened a Catholic school in a building rented from J. M. Leis. Tom thought it only stayed open for a few years, however.[26] The children, in fact, went to school together for many years and played together regularly, whether on the ballfield, in the park, or at the dam.

Tom's narrative indicates that in most spheres of daily life in this town there was a separation but no tension between the different ethnic groups in town. Grace Hilliard, a forty-four-year resident of Helvetia, also described a division between the town's residents: "There were a lot of greenies that came from Europe who could not talk our language but the[y] sort of kept to themselves" (Sept. 22, 1995). Yet Lloyd Gray felt that there was not as much segregation as most people seem to remember. This feeling may stem in part from his own experiences liv-ing on First Street, where a mix of nationalities could be found in company hous-ing. Playing daily with the kids from uptown, Lloyd developed another perspec-tive on the town's ethnic divisions.

> Lot of people said uptown didn't associate with down the hill. I did. I went to school with them. I went swimming with them up at the dam. I had—I think I had all—I think I had more Polish friends than I had—we didn't always—I didn't always play with Tommy Crop and that guy that lived downtown here. I had a lot of different—like all them people that was up there yesterday at the reunion and every Homecoming—they were—I went to school with most of them. And they were most all foreigners or what you call them. They're as much American as we were. Most of them, their mother and dad came from—was born in another country [Sept. 11, 1995].

He did say that this interaction did not extend to marriage at first. "Wasn't nobody—they didn't allow the guys from downtown to marry the ones from uptown, but they started then, afterwards, to marry the different ones," he said. There were not too many mixed marriages according to the Crops, and Veronica

McKee stated such relationships also caused strain and discord in her hometown for some time.

> It was a hard period to live in also because the immigrants were terribly ostracized by the white Anglo-Saxon Presbyterians, but the thing is, their children didn't feel that way. When you went to school, you felt equal, you know. It was something the parents had, but they didn't transfer it to the children, or else the children refused to accept it. And when they started to intermarry, it was no longer a tragedy, you know [July 30, 1994].

It was the younger generation that overcame the difficulties of integration, not their parents. Speaking from her own experiences growing up in a Pennsylvania mining community, Veronica McKee also said that despite the ethnic diversity of the coalfields and the eventual breakdown of social barriers between groups, it was still difficult to be an immigrant.

> It was, in a way, a cosmopolitan way of life, because you had every kind of person there, you know. And yet it was a hard life, too, because you had the immigrants who were adjusting to their way—to this new way of life. And then you had those who had been here for a long time. And I have always felt, all my life, a divided personality, because I was first—shall I say—I was brought up under a Slav culture, and didn't even know that my name was Veronica until I started to school because I was called Verushka, which is a nickname. I told the teacher, you know, and I knew no English. Consequently, I always felt I was born between yesterday and tomorrow, and belonged to neither. Because you came home to a Slav culture and your mother didn't speak English, and she had no idea what a report card was. There was no way you could say "Thanksgiving Day" in Russian, you know, or "Valentine Day." And there was no way you could explain these things to her [July 30, 1994].

What mixing took place among the adults occurred primarily at the ballfield and at the company store, both places where the community gathered. William Crop said also that "when there wasn't no work, [the men] were all laying around the company store. . . . It was just a gathering—you know, standing around and talking—mostly the men." Lloyd Gray remembered "the older men used to hang out at that company store porch. . . . I don't remember the older people getting together until after the town got a little bit cleaned up [in the 1930s], and they built the new store. That's usually where they hung out at, but the younger guys, they'd always run up to the doctor's office" to play under the streetlight. The band hall or election hall also served multiple purposes in the community. "It was more or less a place for people to meet," said Tom Crop, noting that the older men also gathered in front of the doctor's office or at the playground. In the summertime, he said, the men used to pitch horseshoes and play quoits, a game they brought with them from Scotland that involved tossing a heavy metal ring.[27] The "three trees," Tom added, was a gathering point for the fellows in the upper part of town, suggesting that while interaction taking place at the company store or the ballfield was frequently mixed, the downtown and uptown each had their own meeting spot apart from these focal points in the community. The company did not sponsor many social gatherings. The community Christmas tree "was about the only social events there was then," Tom recalled. This statement overlooks the importance of the company-sponsored baseball league that was so popular in town, but it also implies that most socializing was carried out within ethnic groups and within each family, or among a few neighbors—an occasional birthday party or family celebration, perhaps—rather than taking place on a community level. It implies that very specific social networks were in place among the adult population, fairly narrow in their definition, except, again, when considering the baseball league.

Where were the women? According to Veronica McKee, the women went daily to the company store in the afternoon to make their purchases for supper, because there was no refrigeration. William and Sara Crop agreed that women might have an opportunity to socialize while doing the shopping, but most of their time was spent at home dealing with their domestic responsibilities. Marlene Fike stated, however, that there was a considerable amount of "neighboring" at night (*Sykesville Post-Dispatch*, Feb. 14, 1990)—visiting on the front porch or in the parlor—and this fits squarely with the observations of other former residents and employees. Rookie Brown frequently mentioned the sociability of Helvetia's townspeople, recalling the many invitations to sit down on the porch for a visit with the occupants. Veronica McKee talked about visiting during the evening hours too. At this time, she said, "they didn't have radio, and they didn't have TV. They didn't have cars. So you stayed home at night, and your friends would come over and you'd get out your knitting needles, and talk and sit around the coal furnace. You didn't go out like we do now." Sundays at church would have provided opportunities for families to meet as well.

Another gathering spot that residents mentioned was the Peacock Garden, down by Leis's store past the eastern end of town. This drinking establishment was frequented by many of the miners on Saturday nights, they said, though in many houses it was common to find "home brew" that was made up in the kitchen or the cellar. Home brew was tolerated by the company, according to Tom Crop. Though his father made it regularly, his mother "was dead set against it." And as long as you didn't try to sell it, he said, the company looked the other way. This is an interesting position taken by the company; it is at odds with company documents that complain of drunkenness and fighting, of hung-over miners who were careless or slack in their work as a result, of lost time occasioned by the many holidays and celebrations as well as day-to-day drinking. According to early news accounts of the town during its first two decades of operation, there were regular incidents involving drunken brawls, petty crimes, and even more serious criminal acts committed by miners while under the influence. Given the company's concerns about the loss of time and the decline in the quality of work in the mines stemming from the consumption of alcohol, its tolerance of home brew is quite interesting. How does this image fit with other accounts of cash shortages and the difficulties of putting food on the table?

It is also interesting to recall that in each oral account, the narrator remembered Helvetia as a quiet, peaceful community. And if there was any trouble, "it happened before our time." The town constable, it seems, was mainly employed escorting inebriated miners home and catching stray dogs, according to Tom Crop. Yet Elizabeth Wilson Means stated that there were several robbery attempts at the company store (Means, n.d.) and Margaret Craig had a wonderful account about meeting the infamous bank robber "Kid Millions," who, with the help of an FBI agent, had plans to steal the company's payroll for Helvetia Mine (Sept. 27, 1995).[28] There are also various newspaper accounts of brawls and drunken behavior. How do we reconcile these different images of the town?

It seems reasonable to presume that Helvetia lost much of its frontier quality with the passage of time, that the town may indeed have taken on a more tranquil atmosphere by the late 1920s and early 1930s, the period most often discussed by the narrators. It may also be that the narrators were thinking of trouble in terms of the conflict between the miners and the company, not the behavior of outsiders or criminal activity. William Crop spoke generally about earlier days when "the company [in a general sense, not the R&P] had too much say." He mentioned the Coal and Iron Police and said there were other towns nearby where "radicals" were causing trouble, but not Helvetia. "I don't think there was ever any—there wasn't no riots or anything, you know, or skull busting, or anything like that." It may also be that they were comparing past events in this small town with the events of today, or that they no longer remembered or wished to remember conflict within the town. The oral and written accounts provide an interesting contradiction that bears remembering. It does seem, however, that social relations within the town and between the company and the town residents were fairly harmonious for many years.

THE R&P BASEBALL LEAGUE

If anything defied the separateness with which these narrators characterized Helvetia's various ethnic groups, it was baseball. It was William Brown's participation in a company-sponsored baseball team that first led me to ask him about his experiences at Helvetia. Brown began playing organized baseball for the Elks as a 15-year-old and he described himself as "a pretty fair ballplayer at one time." He also played for the Vulcan Juniors and for the Peerless Eagles. It was his ability as a ballplayer that earned him the job at Helvetia Mine, he said. "I had to play ball for a job loading coal. . . . You had to make that ball team or you didn't have no job." Brown's bid for employment was successful: he landed a position as short-stop on the company baseball team and was given a job loading coal. Each week, the company deducted a fixed amount from his pay, and from the paycheck of every other miner at Helvetia, to finance the team. The company "took 50¢ a piece every pay from the coal miner to pay for that team," he said. William Crop recalled that the company "bought everything, you know, the individuals didn't have to pay—they would own their own glove or something like that, but—or shoes or something like that." But the company "furnished all the equipment." The miner's nonvoluntary contribution helped to pay for travel costs; team members were provided with uniforms as well (Figure 32).

The Helvetia ball team competed against teams from other coal mining towns in western Pennsylvania and was one of several teams that played in the company-sponsored R&P League (Figure 33). The team competed in other local leagues as well. Umpires were drawn from the community. The R&P League played two to three games each week during the baseball season, which lasted from May until September. Brown described the routine: the players would leave the mine at 11 A.M., go home, get cleaned up (he noted wryly that his teammates often had dark rings around their eyes from the coal dust in the mines—"We

Fig. 32. Helvetia's ball team, winner of the 1936 J. C. League (Jefferson and Clearfield County) championship. Most of the players are wearing the Chicago Cubs uniforms that the company bought secondhand that year (William Crop, Sept. 11, 1995). According to Rev. Leo Kramer (Aug. 14, 1995), a player who kept his uniform eventually sold the shirt to a collector for $11,000 because the name of the original Cubs player was embroidered on the shirttail. Photograph courtesy of James Haag.

look[ed] like owls," he said), and then board a bus for the trip to the ballpark. The team might travel as much as 50 to 100 miles to play a game that evening. Home games were held at Helvetia's ballfield, across from the Protestant church. Practices were held there after supper.

There were many good players on the team, Brown said, in part because ballplayers were given preference by the company when hiring. One season, when Brown played on the team, Helvetia won 33 games and lost only two. Brown's mining partner and teammate, Lee Gamble, later played four seasons for the Cincinnati Reds between 1935 and 1940, including an appearance in the 1939 World Series (Reichler 1984:978). But many of Helvetia's finest players also grew up in this town, and it was only natural for them to play on the team when they were of age. Former residents said that there were several players from Helvetia who went on to the major leagues, and some who turned down the opportunity as well.

For the coal companies, organized forms of recreation—particularly sports like baseball—were an especially effective device for creating a sense of pride, competitive spirit, and company loyalty among the miners and their families. And, indeed, the game found genuine support among the miners and created stronger bonds within the mining community.

> They loved to play baseball, I'll tell you that. You couldn't get a parking place down here when we played, and the ball diamond was down here. You couldn't

OFFICIAL SCHEDULE

Season of 1932

Lucerne 73
Waterman 86 miles
Iselin 97 "
Yatesboro 62 "

ROCHESTER

AND

PITTSBURGH

COAL LEAGUE

Kent, 78
One way. Guess will have to take our lunch along.

A. W. CUNNINGHAM, Chairman
R. E. PENFIELD, Secretary
D. N. LEWIS, Treasurer

Compliments of
MAHONING SUPPLY COMPANY

FIG. 33. This schedule for the 1932 season of the Rochester and Pittsburgh Coal League belonged to Rookie Brown. Participants in the R&P League played two to three games a week, from mid-May until mid-September, often traveling 200 miles roundtrip to meet the opposing team. On the cover Rookie noted the travel distances (one way) to several of the towns where Helvetia played; he added wryly, "Guess will hope to take our lunch along." Papers of William Brown.

get a parking place . . . ! They were here by the thousands! I'm not kidding you. We had a ball team that was really something [William Brown, July 30, 1994].

See, there wasn't that much else to do. And everybody went to the ballgame. That was—they—they'd get over a thousand spectators there at a ballgame [William Crop, Sept. 11, 1995].

William Crop explained that "they took off you 25¢ a pay [period] or something like that, and they give you a button to put on your hat. You could go anywhere under the R&P Coal Company and not pay to get in—just turn your head so the guy would see the button. It had R&P Coal Company on it. You could go and see the teams—there was one in Soldier over here, Adrian, Helvetia, Yatesboro, Numine, Ernest, Lucerne, Old Run, MacIntyre, Waterman—you could go to all those places, and nothing to get in. Just show your button."

"Baseball was the coal miner's hobby," said one former player (Seymour 1990:244). Another coal miner from southwestern Pennsylvania recalled that at this time "baseball was the biggest form of recreation in the mining town. Every patch in this area had its own team" (Brestensky, Hovanec, and Skomra 1991:50). The sport enjoyed considerable popularity among the miners because "baseball was a good way for [them] to relieve their frustrations from the living conditions or the work. And the miners enjoyed the activity" (1991:52). Certainly it was the most popular activity going in Helvetia. Although the baseball field is now over-grown and hardly visible to the eye, at one time it had bleachers and a wooden scoreboard. Nicknames were common among the players. "Ground Mole," Hel-vetia's pitcher, was a six-foot-four motorman. There was "Lefty" Powell and "Shorty" Steele and, of course, "Rookie" Brown, who was known by that name throughout his life.

But the coal miner's hobby also involved the whole community. Towns would empty out to travel to the ballpark for away games; often hundreds of people filled the stands and cars would line the roads for a mile outside of town. Each com-munity found a variety of ways to support their team. Dinner typically was pro-vided by the home team; at Helvetia, the Ladies' Auxiliary served meals to the players. Ballplayers received special treatment at the company store, Brown said, and were always welcome in town. The baseball team drew in participants and supporters from across the community. Children were filled with admiration for these players. Tom Crop, who watched Brown play while he was a boy, said that as a kid, "you tried to be like them."[29] And, indeed, Tom and William Crop both described the ballpark as their second home in the summer. The enthusiasm for the town's baseball players was carried over into neighboring communities as well. I found several newspaper clippings among Brown's papers announcing the birth of his first child, a son. One identified "the proud dad [as] one of DuBois' star baseball players." The third announced the birth of a new player for Helvetia:

we are told of another welcome addition sportdom will delight in hearing. . . .
"Rookie" Brown is a proud pop too and that means another ball player for Pearless,
Helvetia and others (Lets hope he gets to the majors).[30]

The importance of organized recreation from the standpoint of the R&P cannot be overestimated; indeed, it was perhaps the most successful of the company's
welfare practices because, through a series of competitions, the company was able
to promote group solidarity and redirect the antagonisms and emotions of the
miners away from management toward their competition in the field. For this
reason, the baseball league received considerable backing from owners and management over an extended period of time.

Seymour's study (1990) of nonprofessional baseball in America discusses the
history of the R&P League at some length. The league was controlled by the
R&P Coal Company; teams were run by the mine superintendents. This gave
the company control over hiring and player selection. As Brown related in his
narrative, the R&P could single out individuals for hire on the basis of their athletic skills; many teams actively recruited players. "A good ballplayer did not
have a difficult time getting a job," recalled one miner (Brestensky, Hovanec,
and Skomra 1991:52). Some players were enticed by offers of special treatment
or better money; other ballplayers, like Brown, were given a job because of their
abilities but did not receive any special treatment in the mine. The R&P continued such practices until union disputes forced the cancellation of the entire
season in 1933 (just after Brown quit his job at Helvetia). The company lost control of the league after 1934 when the union challenged the special privileges
accorded to ballplayers. Nonvoluntary deductions from the miner's pay ceased
and became strictly voluntary. Preferential hiring ceased as well. The R&P League
continued on for a few years but finally was dissolved in 1939 (Seymour 1990:253–
254). The league was greatly missed by many residents.

Company-sponsored baseball teams were not unique to the coal mines of
western Pennsylvania; indeed they were possibly the most visible and widespread
symbol of corporate paternalism in the early twentieth century. Organized
industrial baseball first found popularity in the 1910s, peaked in the 1920s, and
subsequently leveled off during the Depression years. This activity was heartily
supported by social and urban reformers as a cure for social ills and a means of
promoting healthier, happier lives, but proponents in industry also saw organized recreation as a possible counter to labor unrest (Seymour 1990:214). Thus,
the investment in teams and facilities was considerable—paid by the companies
outright or financed through nonvoluntary employee contributions. An elabo-
rate baseball park built by the Amoskeag Manufacturing Company cost the
company $40,000, for example. Textile Field, with a grandstand seat capacity
of 4,000, was considered "one of the finest athletic fields in New England"
and was touted as "one of the corporation's wonders, a symbol of its efforts to

advance . . . health and morale" among the Amoskeag's 14,000 employees (Hareven 1982:43, 49).

Competition was such that many businesses recruited semiprofessional and professional ballplayers. The Amoskeag team, which played against the Boston Red Sox and other professional teams, enticed professional ballplayers into the mill with the promise of an easy job and a position that was more secure than any they could have as professional ballplayers. This practice, harshly criticized by the unions, eventually ceased. Despite its many flaws, industrial baseball was immensely popular for many years. Though the level of competition has changed and the degree of corporate support has diminished with the passage of time, the company-sponsored baseball team continues to the present day.

The coal miner's baseball team was a significant part of the cultural land-scape as remembered and described by Rookie Brown and other Helvetia residents. When this phenomenon is examined in the context of community identity, social networks, and social boundaries, it stands out as a positive, strongly unifying force. The league also stands out as a remarkably successful program for the R&P in its efforts to mold its workforce.

HALF-DOLLARS AND SEEING STARS

How pervasive, then, was the company's influence? Certainly it was very strong in the workplace, affecting wages, the number of hours worked, and the type and quality of work conditions, though the lack of close supervision often translated into a lack of discipline in the mines and inadequate control over workers. Reports of drunkenness at work, underground smoking, and other forms of undesirable behavior point to the miner's continued disregard for certain corporate policies.

In the town, the company's presence was felt everywhere. As Tom Crop said when asked about a particular structure, "I don't know who built it. I don't know. They [the R&P] probably did. They built everything else, you know." Oral accounts indicate that superintendents enforced company regulations regarding land-use practices, the control of livestock, and the maintenance of the houses. They indicate, too, that the company's dictates shaped and even defined the structure of each resident's day, from the moment the miner left to start his shift and the miner's wife began her household chores until the time they went to bed. Company programs and institutions, from the company store to the baseball league, were also daily reminders of the R&P's authority.

What were residents' perceptions of the company and its practices? Narrators tended to separate the workplace from the company town when considering the R&P and its version of corporate paternalism. Tom Crop didn't like the company's practices in the mines. "I don't—weren't anybody liked the company, as far as that went. I liked the company, but I didn't like the mine foreman or the superintendents or something like that. Somebody had to be boss, you know, and someone had to run things. And if it wasn't run the way you liked it—like I say, someone had to do it." It was at this juncture that he talked about the practice of short weighing and other ways in which the company took advantage of the miner before the union came in, but then he went on to say that the company was generally fair in its role as landlord. When asked if this company town was well run, William Crop replied, "I'd say it was tops." William and Sara also felt the families were fairly treated by the company, though they knew this had not always been the case. "Well, whatever they [the company] said, that's the way it was," William said. "There was no changing things, you know, if they said it was this and that, there was no compromising or anything." When asked if people felt that they were treated fairly or that they were being taken advantage of, Sara Crop pointed out that, "They stayed there a long time. Some of them were there for years." William noted too that the company's influence changed over time. "See, you wouldn't always have to live in it. Well, lots of times, you know, getting to work and that, most people lived in town, and then it got to where you could afford an automobile, why, it [the company's policies] didn't matter too much."

Clearly, the company's influence diminished in many spheres as families purchased cars and had greater freedom to travel. Yet the R&P did not decide its towns were obsolete until the late 1940s, and many families, as the Crops indicated, lived in Helvetia for decades. Did families stay in Helvetia because they felt they were part of a large family, as Margaret Craig wrote? Did they stay for economic reasons? Were families unable to break the cycle of indebtedness or end their dependence on the company? Could it be, rather, that these mining families over time were able to create a sense of place in this community?

Return, for a moment, to a question raised earlier. What was it that people found in their community that today evokes so much fondness, pride, and nostalgia among the town's former residents? Was it the gardens, the sidewalks, the baseball team—all important features in the landscape of this company town? Oral narratives suggest that for many, these elements were central to the creation of place in Helvetia. Examined within the context of day-to-day living, their significance becomes clearer because they stand in contrast to the hardships of the coal miner's life.

Grace Hilliard, who with her husband and six children lived for more than forty years in Helvetia, said, "We were very happy living in the town, it was well kept" (Sept. 22, 1995). Her son Jack was one of the town's last remaining tenants and tried unsuccessfully to buy and save from demolition the single house in which he and his family lived. The census records indicate that many families stayed in Helvetia, often for several generations. But others left—particularly in the late 1930s and early 1940s—before the mine closed.

Tom Crop, who worked at Helvetia only a few years, joined the navy in 1942 and upon his release sought other employment in the area, determined to find work outside the mine. In our first conversation he said that having a son was an advantage over having a daughter, because a father could take his son to the mine, which increased the family's income and improved its living situation.[31] Tom Crop spoke with great pride of his father, William Sr., who worked as a coal miner for 59 years, beginning just a few months shy of his tenth birthday. In fact, each of the narrators showed pride in their coal mining heritage, in what their parents and kin endured.

One of the most interesting contradictions to emerge from the oral narratives, then, is that despite this heritage and pride in the achievements of their relatives, all four men—Tom and William Crop, Lloyd Gray, and William Brown—broke with the tradition of their fathers and grandfathers who otherwise would have passed along their knowledge to their sons. Each man either left the mines after a few years or never even took up the pick and shovel below ground. Neither Tom or his brother William took a job with the R&P until they had finished high school and neither chose mining for their trade. Tom said in one interview, "I don't know how long I'd have worked there, but Uncle Sam started to hire about 1942, and that's when I left the mines and went into the navy." He later said, however, that he had not applied for his mining papers before he entered the service, "because I wasn't interested."[32] This statement suggests that Tom had already considered the possibility of leaving the mines before he joined the navy. Lloyd Gray never worked in the mines at all. "My dad wouldn't take me in the mines," he told me. "Said he took two in and that was two too many." Rookie Brown worked for only three years as a coal miner. He left the mines for good in 1933. "I was fed up with it. I wasn't getting anyplace, and I didn't want to be messing around in the mines all my life," he said. On his last day, Brown said, he loaded everything into the cars: "dirt—everything went." He cleaned out the room, filling three cars with dirt and coal, and walked out with no regrets.

Why did these men break with tradition? As Lloyd Gray said, mining was a job and it was what they knew. But many of the men hated the mines. Tom Crop said, "Most of the fellows would sit around the doctor's office at night, and they'd talk about the mines. They all hated the mines, but all they could do was talk about it." In part, the break revealed in the oral narratives can be attributed to the start of the Second World War, as both William and Tom Crop and Lloyd Gray entered the service. And while many families still felt compelled to send their sons (and, in some cases, their daughters) to work for the company in order to make ends meet, it also appears that families increasingly recognized that the miner did not have to accept the risk of injury and death as part of his trade, for himself or for his children. Others seemed to recognize that coal miners faced a bleak future in an industry that was phasing out hand labor in the name of efficiency. Brown's recollections of a girl he dated are revealing:

There was a girl up there, boy, she was beautiful, and I dated her a couple of times. And you know, I despised that mines. I despised that mines. I could never make a good living at it. . . . And I said to myself—we had a little party down here by the ballpark, and it was just a sandwich and soft drinks, and it was—they [the R&P] never raised any ruckus, and I just said to myself, "Bill, you better get out of here or you're going to be working in that mines for the rest of your life" . . . . Now, this girl that I told you I dated a few times, I accidentally—at home I said—"A Fisher girl," I said [instead of Powell]. My mother says, "Who?" And I says, "A Fisher." And the other aunt says, "Helvetia?" And I says, "Yes." So then I got an earful! There was—when this place started, they had mules. And he got dragged to death with a mule in the mines—this girl's father. And my parents knew him. And I— like I say, I just saw stars this one night—"You better get out of here, buddy, or you're going to be working in the mines the rest of your life" [July 30, 1994].

Since Brown was married for more than a year before he finally left Helvetia (and not to this girl), this story may be apocryphal. Yet it is interesting that for Rookie Brown, the ballfield carried several associations. It was both the place where he found so much joy and satisfaction playing ball and one of the places where he said he realized that he needed to get out of the mines. It is interesting to specu- late on the reason for the latter association. Many have said that the ballfield was a symbol of the company's power over the miner. Did he recognize it as such? I think so, since he always spoke about the other players who made good by using the company's league as a jump-off into the majors. But if he despised the mine and despised the company's exploitation of the miner and his family, Brown also had many positive recollections of Helvetia. These memories, however, center on the people he knew there, rather than on the company.

There was something special about the town, though, with its neatly trimmed yards and its colorful gardens. It is interesting that at the time of our interview, Lloyd Gray, who never went into the mines at all, still carried in his pocket a sil- ver half-dollar from 1954, the year Helvetia Mine closed.

ORAL HISTORIES FROM HELVETIA

In Rookie Brown's testimony, there are inconsistencies in the family genealogy he presented and there is false information on his personnel record regarding his work experience and number of dependents. Perhaps he felt listing previous experience as a miner would be prejudicial to him in seeking employment from the R&P. He most likely lied about the number of dependents to demonstrate his need for employment. But the distortion is in the genealogy, not in his nar- rative of his experiences as a miner. If the embellishments are removed (and Brown was fond of telling stories), his narrative of underground mining is consistent with other accounts of abuses by management, of the dangers of mining, and the difficulties of making a living wage. If there is evidence in Brown's narrative of resistance by the worker, there is also evidence for action and negotiation by the worker—using his abilities as a ballplayer to get employment, negotiating with the company over pay for dead work, taking time off without authorization, using clay pipes at the face in violation of company regulations, turning down a sprag-ger's job, and ultimately quitting his job in the mine.

Veronica McKee's interview is especially valuable for her insights on events in the town after it was sold to the Kovalchick Salvage Company, but her pic-ture of life in Helvetia prior to 1947 is a composite, a carefully constructed image of life in a mining town prepared by a former high school English teacher. It was read to me at our meeting, a piece previously prepared for a local group. McKee's story was constructed primarily from secondary sources, newspaper clippings, and her own experiences as a child growing up in Sagamore, for she herself did not experience any of Helvetia's early history. Her account is faulty in many respects in terms of specific details about Helvetia's past, while many of her statements about the company store and violence during strikes contain elements of folk-lore. While true in other communities, they were not always true in Helvetia. Yet her narrative is generally representative of the miner's experience in the bitu-minous coalfields of western Pennsylvania and the immigrant's experience in the company town.

There is another level to this interview, lying just below the surface, that involves Veronica McKee's role as a self-appointed caretaker of Helvetia's history. She became an expert consulted by feature writers and reporters when Helvetia made headlines in the local paper. And in all likelihood, she adopted this role as a result of the struggle over the town's future in the early 1990s and, follow-ing its rapid demise, over the town's legacy. Players in this struggle were outwardly embroiled in arguments over the location of Helvetia's Honor Roll and whether there should be free access through the former alleyways of the town. But it is Helvetia's legacy that is at stake.

There is no question that almost all of the narratives have been affected by the town's destruction, heightening a sense of loss and a feeling of nostalgia. But when the narratives of Tom Crop, William and Sara Crop, and Lloyd Gray—all of whom grew up in Helvetia—are examined collectively, there seems to be ample justification for this nostalgia and for the pride that is so clearly expressed at each Helvetia reunion. Yet their perceptions of this company town stand in vivid contrast to those of the Chollocks, who were apparently quite bitter about some of their experiences in Helvetia. I had hoped to interview this couple—brother and sister—who were among Helvetia's oldest surviving residents and were of Slovenian ancestry. The sister first appeared in the 1910 census at the age of five. When approached about an interview, the brother stated that their experiences were so painful that they did not wish to talk about them at all. It is unclear to me, however, whether they were referring to their time as residents of the company town under the R&P Coal Company or their more recent experiences during the strip-mining operation, when they were evicted from their home of many years.

Without knowing more, we cannot say what has caused this disjunction. Clearly, much of it is generational—those who came of age in the town's earliest days and had to support their families under harsher living conditions will inevitably feel differently than those who grew up in town in the 1930s and 1940s, or those who came to Helvetia after it was no longer a company town. The remark by Peter Chollock begs the question—are there other disjunctions caused by ethnicity or religion that do not appear because of the small sample of informants? It is interesting to note in this context that Rookie Brown had never been to a reunion before I took him to the 1995 Helvetia Homecoming, and indeed he had never even heard about them. While he remembered the town as a special place and valued the friends he had made there, he always said that the mine closing was the best thing that ever happened to Helvetia's residents.

> I was going to tell you about up the valley when everything—mining was done, coke ovens were finished. And everybody started moaning, "What's going to become of us? What are they going to do? What about this? What about something else?" And the people have had it better ever since, you know [July 30, 1994].

He had no illusions about the dangers and hardships associated with coal mining. Perhaps this is the key to the Chollocks's unhappy memories.

Most are content, however, to remember Helvetia as a special place they once lived in. Tom Crop spent a considerable amount of time looking for a copy of a poem about Helvetia, written by a former resident, Pete Lafko. He said it really captured the feeling of Helvetia: "it was really good about the town, about the uptown and the downtown, and about the company store, and about the doctor's office and the dentist, you know, and the schools. And meeting their future wives, you know."

 Chapter 6

How the Miner Lives:
Material Culture and Worker
Identity in a Company Town

The miners' doublehouse was the center of daily life for Helvetia's mining families. The company's needs and schedules set the rhythm of each day. A typical day began with the men and the boys who were of age walking to the mine early in the morning to begin their shift. Their wives and mothers had already begun the day by preparing and serving breakfast and by packing a lunch for the men. Having seen their men off to work, these women began an unending list of household chores in a manner that was structured by the company in its role as landlord, by its paternalistic practices, and by policies that directly affected their economic standing and their strategies for day-to-day living. Nearly every activity was influenced in some way by the R&P's industrial regimen, whether it was food procurement, tending animals, or tending gardens.

As an example of how pervasive the company's practices could be, we have only to look at some of the most basic of everyday chores. Laundry was tedious, demanding, and probably the most labor intensive of all household activities. It had always been so, but it was particularly difficult for the miner's wife, who had to deal with the effects of coal dust not just in her husband's work clothes but on everything exposed to the dirty air that so often enveloped a coal town—curtains, linens, and other interior fabrics as well as articles of clothing. Perhaps smoke from a nearby coking operation contributed to the layer of grime that seemed to coat every surface in the town. The water itself contained ores and minerals, perhaps even discharge from the mine operation, that turned the water yellow and helped to discolor the laundry. Washday also involved hauling water for the washtubs since the company did not provide the miner's dwelling with running water. Instead, water was drawn from the hydrants or outdoor faucets erected by the coal company at various locations throughout the town. Doing laundry meant waiting in line with other families that shared the water supply.

For that matter, any water used during the day for drinking, bathing, cooking, cleaning, or washing dishes had to be hauled from the pumps. The coal used to heat the stove had to be purchased from the company or perhaps scavenged from alongside the railcars or the tipple. Finally, the clothes were hung to dry on clotheslines erected by the company in each backlot.

Food procurement is another example. Though a few families had the means of traveling to other stores, most prepared their meals with ingredients purchased at the company store or grown at home on parcels of land owned by the company. The women did most of the shopping. Many made the trip each day in the absence of refrigeration. Their purchases were determined in part by their individual needs and preferences, but also by the availability of goods selected by the company, and more so by the wage structure of the mine, by the system of credit and pay deductions used by the R&P, and by their economic status as mining families.

In the absence of a living wage, many families adopted a number of economic strategies to put sufficient amounts of food on the table each day. Gardening, raising livestock, and the addition of boarders to the household were all important responses to the policies of the company. Children also were expected to do their share. Those who were too young to perform wage work attended school in a building erected by the company, but at home they were given chores to help distribute the workload. They might take responsibility for a particular section of the garden, watch the younger children, help with the household chores, or tend the family's livestock in the backlot or in an area designated by the company.

At night, after the men had cleaned up from work and the chores and the evening's meal were complete, the miner and his family might head to the ballfield to watch a match-up between Helvetia's company-sponsored baseball team and a friendly rival from the R&P League, or perhaps attend a concert by the town band, also sponsored by the company. Or they might just sit out on the front porch and pass the evening chatting with friends and neighbors.

Through it all—day and night—families had to find ways to cope with the stress, tension, and fear associated with the hazards of the miner's work underground and with the threat of poverty and privation. This was perhaps the greatest impact that the company—that industrialization—had on Helvetia's families.

This portrait of daily life in the company town was constructed using various written and oral sources. A six-week archaeological investigation of a miner's doublehouse and its associated houselot adds another dimension to this reconstruction. The focus of this particular chapter is on the role of material culture in the creation of a living environment and in the negotiation of place and identity within the industrial landscape. As we have seen, the company's industrial regimen and its paternalistic ideology created a certain structure and certain relationships within which the miner and his family had to function each day. Nonetheless, Helvetia's families came to this town with their own identities and their own sets of cultural practices, traditions, and beliefs. The intersection of these two competing and often conflicting lifeways and mindsets will be most dialectic revealing of working-class behavior and worker agency in this setting, and it is this type of evidence that we are seeking in the archaeological record.

THE ARCHAEOLOGY OF A COAL COMPANY TOWN

The focus of the archaeological component of this study was a miners' double-house, the semidetached, two-story dwelling that was the standard building form used to house miners and laborers in Helvetia. The selection of an appropriate site for excavation was a complicated process, however, because very little of the town remained aboveground and initially it was not clear what part, if any, of the town site was undisturbed following a surface mining operation on the site of the former company town. Only four privately owned structures—the former company store, the engineer's house (no. 262), the store manager's house (no. 278), and one doublehouse (no. 74/76)—were extant on the town site proper (see Figure 11). It was necessary then to determine which areas of the town had been impacted by the strip-mining operation, how, and when.

After the R&P Coal Company sold the town site to the salvage company in 1947, the Kovalchicks continued to rent houses to the families under terms negotiated by the R&P. Despite these favorable terms, the number of residents began to decline after the mine closed in 1954. Some mining families continued to live in the town, having found employment in nearby communities and others having retired. New tenants, attracted by the low rent, moved in and out of the remaining houses throughout this period. But the town landscape began to change during this period. Many houses were torn down or fell into disrepair. Others were abandoned and stripped of their materials.

In 1989 the Kovalchicks made the decision to lease the town site back to the R&P, which still owned the mineral rights to the land and now proposed a strip-mining operation to recover the coal left beneath the town and from the hillside across the dam. Company officials were drawn back to this site for the same reason that Adrian Iselin was first attracted to this corner of Brady Township in the 1890s: a coal seam, 70 to 72 inches thick, that lies just a few feet below modern grade. In June 1989 the last tenants were evicted from the town (*DuBois Courier-Express*, Mar. 28, 1989; May 26, 1989; *Indiana Gazette*, June 13, 1989; *Sykesville Post-Dispatch*, Feb. 14, 1990). A videotape recorded by Ray Yusnukis (1989–1993) indicates that fewer than 20 houses were standing at this time, including the four privately owned structures. The video also shows that most of these houses had suffered from years of neglect. In anticipation of this large-scale surface-mining project, the salvage company razed all remaining structures on its property. The houses were burned, and in some cases the remains were bulldozed into the cellars. Some additional cleanup of the rubble took place in 1992 under an agreement with Brady Township officials.

Between 1990 and 1993 approximately one-half of the town site—Helvetia's entire uptown district and the area most associated with immigrant families from eastern Europe—was stripped to a depth of 20–25 feet (6.10–7.62 m) (Andy Kovalchick, telephone conversation, Mar. 9, 1994), destroying archaeological deposits in this area and permanently altering the landscape. All traces of the mining community were erased from this portion of the town site. The lower or western half of the town was not stripped, however; the company's application for a permit was denied because of the site's proximity to a wetlands area (*DuBois Courier-Express*, June 21, 1990).

There was some indication that portions of Helvetia's downtown had suffered minimal below-ground disturbance during the demolition phase and general cleanup of the house sites between 1989 and 1992. A walkover survey showed that the preservation of house foundations and their associated archaeological deposits was mixed. Many foundations were clearly disturbed by bulldozer activity; others were greatly overgrown and were difficult to access. But both oral testimony and the video recorded by Ray Yusnukis indicated that many of the doublehouses at the western end of town had fallen into disrepair and collapsed or had been knocked down well before the stripping operation began. Several houselots were subsequently tested along both sides of the main road in an effort to locate the undisturbed subsurface remains of a worker's dwelling.

The site of doublehouse no. 294/296, the westernmost dwelling on the south side of Helvetia's main street (Figure 11), was targeted after testing revealed intact deposits with historic-period materials in front of the house and in the backlot. A heavy weed cover was present across the entire houselot, but the site had remained relatively free of new tree growth. The discovery that this was the former residence of Tom Crop, an early contact and oral informant for the project, made the selection of this site ideal.

The houselot was explored in 1995 using several excavation methods (Figure 34). Areal or block excavation was used to give broad exposure to archaeological features and deposits along the front and sides of the house, including the foundation and the two front entries. Test trenches and excavation units were used to sample deposits and features within the backlot, including garden beds, trash deposits, and outbuildings. The investigation centered on the exterior of the structure and the surrounding houselot rather than on the cellar of the house, because of disturbances associated with the site's cleanup in the early 1990s.[1]

Exposed features, archaeological deposits, and living surfaces were analyzed for evidence of general living conditions and household activities, diet, health and sanitation practices, subsistence-related and/or income-producing activities, and activities associated with the maintenance, repair, or alteration of the houses.

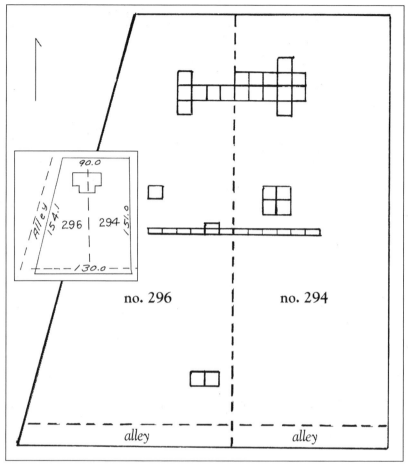

FIG. 34. Excavation areas were placed along the front and sides of doublehouse no. 294/296, located on the south side of Helvetia's main street (see inset). The backlot was also sampled.

Evidence of leisure-time or recreational activities, some sponsored by the R&P, was also targeted, with particular emphasis on the way that certain forms of material culture and land-use practices reflected ethnic traditions and worker identity.

WORKER IDENTITY IN A COMPANY TOWN

A number of assumptions were set up at the start of this project that could be tested archaeologically. Certain types of physical evidence were sought that would be indicative of foodways, material culture preferences, ethnic traditions, the cultural values of the occupants and, more broadly, evidence of working-class tastes and preferences.

John McClymer's study (1986) of late-nineteenth-century working-class standards of living and consumption patterns indicates that worker preferences are visible in choices made regarding diet, dress, and leisure activities. In terms of diet, for example, his research indicates that an increase in disposable income among working-class families living in Massachusetts in the 1870s did not lead to new consumption patterns modeled upon the standards for nutrition espoused by domestic reformers. Neither did these families begin to emulate the standards of middle- and upper-class households. Rather, these families made choices based on working-class notions of their own requirements or preferences. They did not necessarily increase the number of meals served daily with meat, fish, or vegetables, but instead increased the size of the portions served at each meal or purchased the more expensive cuts of meat (i.e., beef) and fish (1986:385–386). The various categories of data examined by McClymer (food consumption patterns, standards of dress, the quality of housing and furnishings) indicate a range of living standards among the working classes, and we would expect to find similar evidence of working-class preferences in an investigation of the miners' doublehouse.

Katherine Harvey's study of coal miners in western Maryland (1969) is also suggestive of the ways that working-class preferences are manifested. Harvey has compiled evidence that these miners, described as well-educated and cultured, negotiated wage rates through their union that left them sufficiently well off to purchase luxuries that most coal miners could not afford (1969:89–125). Pianos, organs, and lace curtains were common acquisitions among those families with disposable income. Harvey cited a 1902 news article that described the houses in Lonaconing as "tastefully kept, well furnished, the walls hung with pictures and the nucleus of a library is not uncommon, while many of them show refined taste and cultivation, an organ or piano adding a touch of artistic comfort and homelikeness [sic] to them, carpets floor the best rooms, and the kitchen, dining room and pantry show a love of good living that is decidedly appetizing and the miner lives well" (1969:96–97). McClymer's study of household consumption in 1875 shows that many working-class families in Massachusetts also furnished their homes with such items as pianos, carpets, and sewing machines, an indication not only of discretionary income but perhaps of status and working-class values as well (1986:389–390).

Several archaeological studies also demonstrate that evidence of worker preferences may be recovered from the physical remains of the past. For example, the faunal assemblage from Lonaconing, Maryland, indicated a preference for beef over pork among the town's residents based on the frequencies of certain species. Though researchers could not conclusively associate this preference with the ethnic backgrounds of the residents of Lonaconing, who were predominantly Scotch and German immigrants, the authors noted that it was nonetheless an interesting consumer choice for coal miners to make since the cost of beef was generally higher than other meats (Balicki, O'Brien, and Yamin 1999:102–103).[2]

I was also looking for data that would be useful in understanding the role of ethnicity and cultural tradition in the negotiation of identity and place in this industrial community. The presence of ceramic vessels with dates of manufacture that were significantly older than their date of deposition or were acquired from a source outside of the company store might be indicative of the transmission and survival of family heirlooms, for example—pieces that were valuable to the families and reflected their own ethnic traditions. Occasionally, material remains are found that are clear statements of worker ethnicity. At Eckley Miners' Village, excavators recovered a Catholic medal and what appears to be a rosary bead, items that demonstrate the religious preference of former inhabitants, if not their ethnic background (Warfel 1993:48, 211). Though such finds are rare, I thought it possible that we might uncover objects that expressed residents' cultural heritage.

I also expected to see evidence of accommodation—that is, the incorporation of new forms of material culture, particularly those provided by the company store, as a response to new conditions. Worker preference for certain items purchased from the company store might be indicative of adaptation to life in the company town and of changes to worker identity in response to the company's regimen. While store ledgers from Helvetia were not located, material evidence of store purchases was sought in an archaeological context, for example, through faunal remains or discarded food containers. Other questions presented themselves. Were the species of animals represented archaeologically consistent with the varieties and cuts sold by the company store or were they obtained from other sources, either from animals raised by the families themselves or from the wild? Was it possible to link the choice of particular cuts of meat or tinned foods to a particular cuisine? Would these choices indicate worker preference or merely the availability of goods through the company store? Was there evidence that families prepared meals in a traditional fashion or that they began to rely on ready-made or tinned foods provided by the store? A careful analysis of these categories of evidence would address the question of whether worker identity changed in response to new living and working conditions and, if so, how.

Within the corporate landscape established by the R&P—one that resonates with images and institutions of discipline, control, and domination—we would also expect to find evidence of resistance by the miners and their families. One striking image of worker resistance revolves around a common historical artifact, the clay tobacco pipe. As described by Rookie Brown, some coal miners used clay tobacco pipes to create a gas jet in the mine that was used to warm their coffee (Nov. 16, 1991). This action, recorded only in oral narrative, documents what may seem to be a fairly minor example of resistance to the company with little benefit to the miner. Yet such activity was in violation of company regulations, and miners caught with combustible materials faced possible fines and even discharge from the mine. I expected to find visible evidence of resistance to the corporate regimen and to specific company practices in the backlots of the doublehouses as well, but a central question, obviously, was whether resistance would be the main or only response of the mining families, or whether there would be more evidence of negotiation.

It has been difficult to answer some of these questions. The use of a landscape analysis, with its emphasis on the discovery and recording of landscape features and landscape sequences adjacent to the house foundation and, ultimately, the nature of the archaeological record itself, resulted in the recovery of comparatively few artifacts from the site, especially in front of the house. This was not the result of modern disturbance but rather the result of both corporate and tenant land-use practices that will be discussed in greater detail later. The backlot was somewhat different. Here more substantial deposits were discovered, yet these too were affected by the R&P's practice of regular trash removal and by the land-use practices of the occupants. Very little household rubbish or waste was disposed of in the yard except in discrete locations. And because the outhouses were cleaned regularly by the company as early as the 1920s, it was surmised that this normally informative repository would hold few cultural remains, if any, so the privies were not investigated at all. Despite the paucity of artifactual remains from the era of the coal company, we can still tease a fair amount of information from the objects themselves, from their context of deposition, and from their context of use by the coal miner and his family. The following section summarizes the data that can be gleaned from the artifacts themselves; it also demonstrates that oral history is often uniquely placed to amplify the archaeological and historical record, an especially valuable role when other sources are mute.

EVIDENCE OF DAILY LIFE
IN THE MINERS' DOUBLEHOUSE

Questions regarding the diet of residents of the doublehouse cannot be adequately addressed using the archaeological data from the site. Of the 92 bones or bone fragments that constitute the faunal assemblage from this site, nearly two-thirds are nondiagnostic fragments (Landon 2001).[3] The remaining one-third are mostly representative of domesticated species—primarily cow, pig, and chicken—but the remains from each taxon account for only one individual each. In addition, there are 16 bones or fragments that bear evidence of saw or shear marks. Several of these marks, found on cross-cut steaks, are consistent with "the work of a professional butcher" (Landon 2001:2), potential but unconfirmed evidence of purchases from the butcher at the company store. Landon states that, with two exceptions, the cuts of beef represented by the collection, "chuck, arm, round, and loin steaks . . . are all meaty cuts, ranging from moderate to more expensive in price." Though the assemblage is disappointingly small and fragmentary, the findings are consistent with our expectations based on documentary and oral sources, even if they do not add significantly to our knowledge.

Interestingly, there are also remains of a rabbit, a woodchuck, and a freshwater bass, though none bears evidence of butchery marks that would indicate human consumption. Such finds are certainly consistent with the oral testimony of Tom Crop, who recalled fishing and hunting as a youth to put food on his family's table (July 29, 1994). This discovery is even more compelling in light of Tom's mention of eating groundhog (woodchuck, *Marmota monax*). But again, the faunal data are at best only suggestive; each species was represented by a single bone.

There is little additional evidence related to foodways in the assemblage. No prepackaged food containers, glass or tin, were found in these deposits. The only materials related to food preservation are the remains of glass canning jars (Atlas and Mason jars) and the glass liners from the lids. The jars themselves cannot be closely dated, nor do they offer any insight on the types of foods preserved by this method. Instead, we must rely upon the oral testimony of former residents for data on foodways and subsistence-related activities.

The artifact assemblage contains little evidence of health and sanitation practices. One small cylindrical glass bottle may have been used for medicinal purposes (e.g., medicinal spirits, elixirs, tonics) or some other type of household solution. The bottle, recovered from a unit behind no. 294, was mold-blown with a flanged lip for a cork or glass stopper, suggesting a late-nineteenth- to early-twentieth-century date of manufacture. The remnants of at least six patent medicine bottles were also recovered that date to the late nineteenth and early twentieth centuries. With the exception of four comb teeth, no other artifacts related to personal hygiene were recovered.

Not surprisingly, ceramics are the best represented category of household artifacts recovered from the site. The assemblage from the doublehouse includes the highly fragmented remains of a variety of ironstone, semivitreous, semiporcelain, and porcelain vessels from the late nineteenth and early twentieth centuries (Figure 35). It is often difficult to distinguish among these ware types, even when the sherds are marked with the company's name, yet period mail-order catalogs did make distinctions among these ceramic types on the basis of price, decorative motif, and their availability as matched sets or open stock. Differences in wear patterns and the degree of vitrification are also evident. Though all ironstone, semivitreous, and semiporcelain wares were advertised as highly durable and resilient household ceramics, ironstone had a tendency to discolor during use. Staining and exfoliation of the glaze are common on archaeological specimens.

Ironstone, a refined earthenware, is the predominant ceramic type found at the site. American companies were manufacturing ironstone in large quantities by 1870, most notably in New Jersey and Ohio, and this ceramic type remained

FIG. 35. Assorted ceramic tablewares from the doublehouse. Ironstone is predominant, although the assemblage also contains several refined earthenwares, a variety of semivitreous and semiporcelain wares, as well as American and English porcelain. Photograph by Michael Hamilton.

quite popular through the 1920s. It was also the cheapest ceramic available on the market in the late nineteenth and early twentieth centuries. While plain and relief molded decorations (e.g., scalloped and beaded edges) are common in the assemblage from the doublehouse, reflecting the popularity of such styles in the late nineteenth century, a number of plate rims, bowls, and teacups are also decorated with gilded rim bands, with a flow blue technique, or both (Table 19). Several body sherds also bear a printed floral or vine motif. Plates and cups constitute the bulk of the assemblage, though one sherd with a substantial foot ring is most likely from the base of a large vessel such as a soup tureen or other serving dish.

Several pieces of semivitreous and semiporcelain dinnerware (variously called hotel china, stone china, or graniteware) were also recovered at the site, in both undecorated and ornamental forms (Table 19). Flow blue, gilding, and molded relief are the most common forms of ornamentation. One plate from the site bears the mark of Homer Laughlin, a manufacturer from East Liverpool, Ohio. The mark postdates 1897, the year in which the company name was changed from Laughlin Brothers to Homer Laughlin, but can only be dated generally to the period 1900–1910 (Lehner [1895] 1988:247–249). A second piece, marked "La Francaise Porcelain," was manufactured by an American firm, the French China Company, between 1900 and 1932 (Lehner [1902] 1988:156).

Several sherds of refined porcelain were also recovered from the site. Again, plates, cups, and bowls constitute the bulk of the assemblage. While most of the assemblage consisted of undecorated body sherds, others were embellished with rose swags or floral sprigs, rim bands, and gilding (Table 19). These patterns are typical of the dinnerware sets advertised in period catalogs (Montgomery Ward [1895] 1969; Sears, Roebuck, & Co. [1902] 1969).

Though poorly represented, three utilitarian ceramic types were identified in the assemblage. The remains of several stoneware vessels were present: a buff-bodied stoneware with brown exterior glaze; two variants of a gray salt-glazed stoneware; a heavy, dark brown stoneware; and a gray-bodied salt-glazed stoneware vessel with a dark brown interior slip reminiscent of an Albany slip. The rim diameter suggests the latter two vessels were storage jars. Several sherds of a coarse redware with a brown interior glaze were also recovered but were too small to indicate vessel form or function. Finally, two sherds from a yellowware bowl with a brown interior glaze and a molded base were identified.

The assemblage of glass also can be divided into decorative and utilitarian wares. A number of serving dishes were identified with scalloped or beaded rim decoration, one with starbursts, another with stippled relief. At least two vessels had a molded wheat or leaf pattern. Several also had press-molded relief, in an imitation cut-glass design that is common for the late nineteenth and early twentieth centuries. Several fragments of an iridescent orange tableware with a beaded rim were also recovered. One badly deteriorated piece appeared to be a cut-glass stopper or perhaps the stem of a serving dish. A few tumblers or drinking glasses were represented in the assemblage, several of which were fluted and several others that were apparently etched, but none were diagnostic. Most of the glass was from bottles or utilitarian containers but, again, with the exception of the canning jars and medicine bottles, nearly all of the fragments were nondiagnostic or of a very recent vintage, beer and soda bottles being most prevalent.

Most categories of household goods were unrepresented or underrepresented in the site assemblage. No tinware, enameled ware, or any kind of metal kitchenware was recovered from the site. No kitchen utensils were identified. The incompleteness of the physical record indicates that most household rubbish was

TABLE 19.
DECORATED TABLEWARES FROM NO. 294/296

Refined Earthenware	N
Black transfer print, floral motif	1
Cobalt blue glaze	3
Molded relief, hand-painted motif	1
Rockingham glaze, mottled with green, molded relief	1
Subtotal	6
%	5.9
Whiteware	
Blue transfer, geometric motif	3
Subtotal	3
%	3.0
Ironstone	
Floral motif	10
Floral motif, molded relief	1
Flow blue, gilding	1
Flow blue, gilding, molded relief	2
Flow blue, polychrome floral motif	1
Flow blue, transfer	1
Fluted body	1
Gilded band	1
Gilded rim	7
Gilded, beaded rim	1
Molded relief	5
Molded, beaded rim	1
Scalloped rim, feather edge	1
Scalloped rim, molded relief	1
Scalloped, beaded, overglaze floral	1
Scalloped, gilded rim, molded relief	2
Subtotal	37
%	36.6
Semivitreous	
Cobalt blue glaze	1
Floral decal	2
Flow blue	1
Flow blue, molded, gilded swag, floral	2
Gilded band, molded relief	1
Gilded rim	3
Molded, beaded rim	1
Pale blue glaze	1
Rockingham glaze, molded exterior	1

TABLE 19. (CONTINUED)

Scalloped, gilded rim		1
Scalloped, beaded rim, garland		1
	Subtotal	15
	%	14.9
Semiporcelain		
Brown transfer print, oriental motif		1
Gilded rim		1
Gilded exterior band, relief molding		2
Interior floral motif		3
Molded relief		2
Molded relief, floral decal motif		2
Scalloped, gilded, overglaze floral		1
	Subtotal	12
	%	11.9
Porcelain		
Black and gold rim bands		1
Geometric rim motif		1
Gilded band		1
Gilded rim		1
Gilded rim, molded relief		1
Gilded rim, rose swag		1
Gilded interior motif, molded rim		1
Hand-painted motif		9
Monochrome rim band, overglaze motif		1
Monochrome wash		5
Monochrome wash, molded relief		1
Molded relief		2
Overglaze floral decal		1
Scalloped, beaded rim, rose sprigging		1
Scalloped, gilded rim		1
	Subtotal	28
	%	(27.7)
	Subtotal	101 (100.0%)
% of Ceramic Assemblage		
Refined earthenware		1.2
Whiteware		0.6
Ironstone		7.4
Semivitreous		3.0
Semiporcelain		2.4
Porcelain		5.6
	Subtotal decorative	101 (20.2%)
	Total tablewares	502 (100.0%)

disposed of elsewhere on site or, more likely, off site. The archaeological record therefore tells very little about daily living conditions in the doublehouse.

Yet the excavated materials do show that some of the tenants residing in no. 294/296 possessed decorative glassware and tablewares, including sets of matching dishes (particularly plates and teacups) and serving pieces. The selection of ironstone, semivitreous, and semiporcelain dinnerwares indicates that these families preferred vessels that were inexpensive, resilient, unlikely to craze or break, and therefore very practical, yet the rim sherds demonstrate that many of these vessels were also ornamented in some way. Gilding and molded decoration were most common.[4] The presence of porcelains also suggests that pieces were purchased that were not for everyday use. Whether these dinnerwares were purchased for daily use or special occasions, their presence may be interpreted as a visible expression of worker identity and perhaps as an indicator of working-class status.[5] Such findings are consistent with data from nineteenth-century working-class communities in Paterson (Yamin 1999), Lowell (Beaudry, Cook, and Mrozowski 1991), and Lonaconing (Balicki, O'Brien, and Yamin 1999), though it is evident that many families also chose other types of material goods to express their working-class identity, and these choices varied over time and space (e.g., Yamin 1999:115).

PERSONAL DRESS AS AN EXPRESSION OF WORKING-CLASS IDENTITY

The materials excavated from the vicinity of the doublehouse have somewhat more to say about worker identity as it relates to personal dress. While Katherine Harvey (1969) described the coal miners of western Maryland as "The Best-Dressed Miners" because of their atypically high standards of living, researchers have also commented on the dress of New England's mill girls and laborers, suggesting that other members of the working classes placed considerable importance on their personal appearance (Dublin 1979; Eisler 1977; McClymer 1986; Prude 1983:139; see also Beaudry and Mrozowski 2001:123–125; Beaudry, Cook, and Mrozowski 1991). McClymer's study of working-class families in late nineteenth-century Massachusetts indicates that two-thirds of the households sampled were considered "well-dressed" by the Bureau of Labor, despite the fact that many of these families were living in substandard housing or served only one meal with meat per day (1986:387–388). McClymer does not indicate what criteria the Bureau of Labor used to distinguish between those who were well-dressed and those who were not, but the archaeological evidence from Lowell, Massachusetts, suggests that small items of adornment were as integral to workers' notions of dress as the quality and style of clothing. Beaudry and Mrozowski (2001:123–125) contend that the many decorative buttons, hair combs, and pieces of costume jewelry found at the site of a Lowell boardinghouse are not only indicative of the frequency with which items of personal ornament were used by the residents, but they are also markers of an emergent working-class identity or subculture.

The small finds from the miners' doublehouse in Helvetia are also indicative of worker identity and suggest that personal appearance was important to these working-class families. Among the many household and construction-related materials in the site assemblage are several items of dress and personal adornment, including a brass cufflink made in a dumbbell pattern with a blue enameled and gilded fleur-de-lis motif; three pieces from the internal workings of a pocket watch; a gilded clasp from a small bag or purse; and a copper-alloy pin with beaded edgework, perhaps a woman's lace pin or beauty pin (Figure 36). The latter, also identified as a belt pin, was described in 1902 as "the best [idea] for waist or skirt ornaments, both useful and ornamental" (Sears, Roebuck, & Co. [1902] 1969:90). Several glass and faux-pearl beads were found. A small, pocket-sized brass container, tentatively identified as a lipstick tube, was also recovered. The 10 sides or panels of the container show traces of gilding and are marked with linear striations, while the base has a gilded motif resembling a coat of arms (a crown with two shields below and garland). The assemblage also includes a number of buttons made from glass, ceramic, wood, and shell. Among the more ornamental of these are two black glass buttons with molded leaf decorations and a stamped metal button with a flower—possibly a thistle—and two leaves in the center. There is also a fabric-covered button, woven from a coarse thread or fiber.

Each of these items contributed to the well-dressed appearance of its wearer. Yet the presence of such items among the material remains of these miners' households is indicative of something more. When we remember that the occupants of these houses used a variety of economic strategies to put food on the table while living on a coal miner's wages and that many times these families would have had little—if any—discretionary income, it is not unreasonable to suggest that such objects were considered by their owners to be important, if not integral, to the construction and maintenance of working-class identity and to the negotiation of an individual's place within the community.

LEISURE-TIME ACTIVITIES

If anything can be said to be revealing of worker identity, it is surely leisure time—that is, the activities selected according to personal preference by the working classes when they were not on company time or performing tasks associated with their daily subsistence. The most obvious example of leisure-time activity near the doublehouse is to be found in the garden, where both vegetables and ornamental flowers were grown, and this will be discussed in detail in a later chapter, but there is other evidence from the houselot that is revealing of such activities.

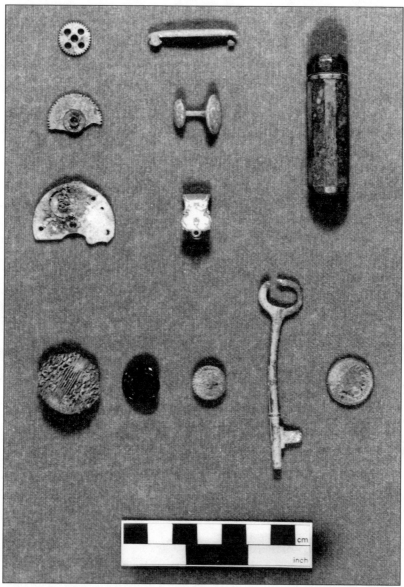

FIG. 36. Items of dress and personal adornment from the miners' doublehouse: *top row, left and below,* three pieces from the internal workings of a pocket watch; *top center,* a copper-alloy lace pin with beaded edge work; *second row, center,* a brass cufflink made in a dumbbell pattern with a blue enameled and gilded fleur-de-lis motif; *third row, center,* a gilded clasp from a small bag or purse; *upper right,* a gilded, 10-sided pocket-sized container with a coat of arms on the base, possibly a lipstick tube; and buttons made from glass, ceramic, metal, celluloid, wood, and shell. Among the more ornamental of these are a button covered with a coarse thread or fiber *(bottom, left)* a black glass button with leaf and vine motifs *(bottom, second from left),* and a stamped metal button with a flower, possibly a thistle *(bottom, third from left).* Other small finds include a brass key and an Indian head penny dated to 1899 *(bottom, right).* Photograph by Michael Hamilton.

Perhaps the most visible expression of leisure time appears in front of the house. As noted, the deposits excavated in front of the doublehouse had little artifactual material compared to the backlot, and, indeed, much of the assemblage was architectural in nature. There was, however, an abundance of children's toys recovered in this area—from Dale Evans on her horse and an assortment of cowboys or cowboy-related objects, to the 22 clay marbles found in association with the front porches, to a panoply of soldiers (Figure 37). We did not find any lead soldiers as described by Betty Haddow Hamilton (July 14, 1995), handmade from scraps found along the railroad. The clay marbles are stratigraphically associated with the earliest years of tenancy under the company, however, the range of toys recovered from the site is indicative of favorite childhood activities from all periods of occupation. Indeed, these materials represent a sizable portion of the overall assemblage from no. 294/296. This is not surprising, given that those most likely to have leisure time were children. In addition to the more common finds of marbles, slate pencils, and, later on, soldiers, cowboys, and cars, several bisque doll fragments were found in association with both units of the doublehouse, suggesting that at least two families chose to purchase such items. Part of a miniature porcelain teacup or teapot was recovered as well. Three pieces of baked clay—one is a head with a face scored into the clay, the others are hats made by pinching and shaping pieces of clay to fit on top of the head—highlight the contrast between store or catalog purchases and handmade items.

The majority of artifacts associated with the front of the house, including the toys, are small finds—things that very likely fell out of pockets or fell through cracks in the porch or the walk. In addition to the remarkable assemblage of toy soldiers, cowboys, and marbles, there were small beads, coins, buttons, slate pencils, and a jack knife. These finds were clustered around the two entryways, indicating that much time was spent on the porches by the families and that a variety of leisure-time activities took place there, from children's play to socialization and relaxation by the adults. The oral narratives contain many references to social visits and family leisure time spent on the front porch. In this context, the presence of so many small finds near the entries is not at all surprising.

When asked about the activities of the miners after hours, Tom Crop stated that many of the men living downtown played horseshoes or quoits at the park, went hunting, worked in the garden, or simply sat on the porch (July 29, 1994). Archaeological evidence suggests that much of the time spent on the porch was occupied with smoking. Numerous fragments of clay tobacco pipes were found across the site, but particularly in front of the doublehouse, suggesting again the importance of the front porch during leisure hours and the social and symbolic import of sharing a pipe with friends, neighbors, and coworkers. The pipes from the Helvetia doublehouse were made of both white ball clay and terra-cotta (Figure 38). Though one pipe stem was marked "GERMANY," most were unmarked

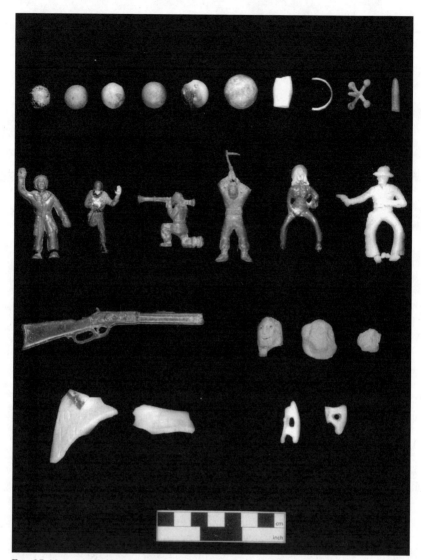

FIG. 37. Numerous children's toys were recovered during excavations, particularly from the front of the doublehouse. The assemblage reflects childhood activities from all periods of occupation at the site, with artifacts ranging from marbles, jacks, slate pencils, and plastic soldiers, to a Dale Evans figurine (*second row, second from right*), cowboys, and metal cars. In all, 39 clay and glass marbles were found on the site, most near the front walks or the front porches. Two small porcelain handles, perhaps from a miniature tea set, were also found behind no. 294. Several bisque and china doll fragments (*top, fourth from right and bottom row, left*) provide an interesting contrast to a small clay head, made with two separate hats (*third row, right*). Photograph by Michael Hamilton.

and most likely manufactured in Bristol or Scotland. All the terra-cotta pipe bowls were ribbed. Several of the white clay pipe bowls had molded decoration, including one with an eagle's wing. The recovery of a vulcanite mouthpiece and a terra-cotta pipe bowl with stem shank indicates that composite pipes were also used. Several studies link the activity of smoking with the leisure hours of the working classes, both in public spaces (Balicki, O'Brien, and Yamin 1999:95, 98–100; Cook 1989, 1997; Yamin 1999:147–149) and private (Beaudry, Cook, and Mrozowski 1991; Beaudry and Mrozowski 2001). The presence of so many pipes in association with the doublehouse suggests that smoking continued to be a favored activity of the working classes.

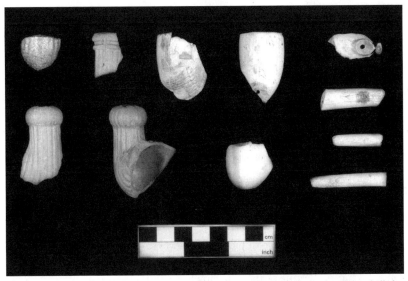

FIG. 38. Clay tobacco pipes from the Helvetia doublehouse were made primarily of white ball clay or terra cotta. Though one ball clay pipe stem was stamped "GERMANY" (*right, second from top*), most were unmarked and most likely manufactured in Bristol or Scotland. Several of the white clay pipe bowls had molded decoration, including one with an eagle's wing (*top row, third from left*). Composite pipes were also common. Photograph by Michael Hamilton.

The most intriguing artifact from this category is a thin brown stoneware pipe bowl fragment with the letters "PING" and a molded hand extended outward (Figure 39). The motif, which appears to symbolize a helping hand, has not been identified. Emblems and symbols associated with the miners' union or the miners themselves have been researched, but as yet nothing has been discovered to shed light on its meaning. It does suggest at least the possibility of a symbol associated with the union or with the working classes, or perhaps a religious or fraternal organization, rather than anything related to ethnicity or to contemporary politics.

FIG. 39. Portion of a stoneware pipe bowl with the letters "PING" and a hand. Photograph by Michael Hamilton.

In contrast to the excavations behind the boardinghouses in Lowell or in the working-class communities of Lonaconing, Maryland, and Paterson, New Jersey (Balicki, O'Brien, and Yamin 1999; Beaudry, Cook, and Mrozowski 1991; Bond 1989; Yamin 1999), the investigation of the double-house did not produce any direct evidence of alcohol consumption, either in association with the house or in more discrete locations in the backlot. There is considerable oral testimony regarding the manufacture of home brew in many households, including no. 296, as well as evidence of consumption at locations outside the company town, thus it appears that this activity took place openly and there was little need for the town's male residents to drink covertly. There are also numerous company memoranda complaining of the effects of drinking among the miners, most often as part of a religious holiday or ethnic celebration. This suggests that there may be some differential behavior associated with drinking based on ethnicity among the men. We cannot speak at all, however, to the issue of behavioral differences on the basis of gender.

ETHNICITY IN THE COMPANY TOWN

Documentary and oral evidence presented elsewhere in this volume indicates that the cultural traditions, practices, and beliefs of the town's residents remained intact within the setting of the company town and indeed were integral to the negotiation of identity and place within the industrial landscape. Historical research has suggested that the preservation of cultural traditions and even the enhancement of ethnic identity and consciousness among the working classes occurs under the influence of external economic and social forces—under repressive social conditions, for example, when mobility and wages are restricted, or when economic gains are not followed by increased social and political power, particularly in single-industry company towns or towns with a very powerful social elite (Bodnar 1977:150–153; Couvares 1985; Gutman 1977). In his study of Steelton, Pennsylvania, John Bodnar (1977:144) found that in times of repression and struggle there was a strengthening, if not a resurgence, of ethnic traditions and a withdrawal or retreat into traditional ethnic communities and networks. Bodnar also found that under such conditions, ethnic groups moved away from intermarriage or even intergroup socialization (see also Bodnar, Simon, and Weber 1982).

Archaeologically, material evidence of ethnic identity has been preserved at several working-class sites: pipe bowls bearing Irish symbols or slogans were found at Lowell and Paterson (Beaudry, Cook, and Mrozowski 1991; Yamin 1999); preferences for beef or pork appear to be related to the ethnic background of groups living in Lonaconing, Maryland, and the Five Points district in New York City (Balicki, O'Brien, and Yamin 1999; Yamin 1998); vineyards were built by Italian families living in Paterson's working-class neighborhoods (Lauren Cook, personal communication, 1994). Though I hoped to find some visible expression of the diverse ethnic background of Helvetia's mining families in the archaeological record of the doublehouse, such evidence was not forthcoming.

Again, it is clear that we must turn to other sources to address the question of ethnicity. There is ample evidence for the survival of ethnic traditions and the incorporation of existing practice into the industrial regimen of the R&P in the oral narratives of former residents of the town. Veronica McKee indicated that in her hometown of Sagamore, ethnic groups continued to prepare traditional foods and, indeed, were known within the community for those dishes, whether it was halupki, kohlrabi, noodles, beef, or potatoes (July 30, 1994). Other cultural survivals are evident from the oral accounts. Veronica McKee has kept a number of hand-painted Easter eggs and many pieces of embroidery and lace made in the Slavic tradition by her mother. Tom Crop stated that many of the older men played quoits, a game with direct ties to Scotland, the country of origin for many of the town's miners. There is also testimony as to the separation—the boundaries—maintained between Helvetia's ethnic groups, and the institutions that encouraged the maintenance of distinctive cultural and religious traditions. St. Anthony's Roman Catholic Church and Bethel Union Church each helped to sustain and reinforce social and ethnic networks within the community, not only through Sunday services but through picnics, religious holidays and festivals, and social groups such as the Ladies' Auxiliary or the Sisters of the Greek Catholic Union, No. 183, of Helvetia (*DuBois Daily Express*, May 5, 1914). The hierarchy within the coal company also promoted ethnic separateness within the mine.

There is ample documentary evidence too, from the R&P archives, for the continuation of traditional cultural practices among the miners and their families, particularly as they relate to leisure activities. In numerous letters and memoranda, company officials complained about the loss of production in the mines as a result of the many ethnic festivals and religious holidays observed by the company's employees:

> We did not expect to match the May tonnage, June having five Sundays and several Holidays, all of which are observed among the different nationalities, all

being idle to some extent when there is any holiday, either religious or National. L. W. Robinson, July 3, 1913 [R&PCC 1913].

Dear Sir. We made a start this morning at Helvetia mines but the start was very poor. About 50 men all told was all that came. These were mostly english [sic] speaking men. All the foreigners are drunk and celebrating today and will be for several day [sic] as is their usual custom at this time of year. We may have double this amount tomorrow. . . . J. Harvey, Supt., Helvetia, Aug. 24, 1916 [R&PCC 1916i].

While the ethnicity of former residents of no. 294/296 is not visible archaeologically, there is nonetheless ample evidence from documentary and oral sources that the cultural practices of Helvetia's mining families—from foodways and leisure activities to social gatherings and religious traditions—were successfully incorporated into the industrial regimen and that the ethnic identities of its residents were maintained within the environment of the company town.

NEGOTIATION AND RESISTANCE: THE COMPANY AS EMPLOYER AND LANDLORD

The many architectural remains found on this site—from the machine-cut nails and the hexagonal asbestos siding fragments to the ceramic doorknob and the hundreds of fragments of window glass—are all evidence of the coal company's role as owner and landlord, evidence of the physical environment within which Helvetia's families negotiated their daily existence. Two other artifacts found at the site speak to the miner's relationship to the company as an employee and capture both the miner's acceptance of and resistance to certain aspects of the company hierarchy and corporate policy: a brass coal check and a United Mine Workers pin from the Dixonville Local 1515 (Figure 40). Both items were recovered near the backdoor of no. 296, a transitional space between work and home.

The brass coal check, stamped with the initials of the R&P and the number "5," is particularly interesting. It is a pick coal check, given to the men who were assigned to pull out the stumps or pillars supporting the roof when the work of mining was complete. In explaining how the coal check system worked, William Crop's narrative reveals not only the difference in pay represented by a pick check in his day—99¢ a ton for pick coal as opposed to 50¢ per ton for machine-cut coal—but also other feelings and images associated with the pick coal check (Sept. 11, 1995). These include the anger many miners felt over the mechanization of work in the mines, the frustration of the cutter who did not earn as much for his labor as the man with the pick coal check, the competition among the hand loaders for the higher-paid pick coal, and the dangers of working underground.

Tom Crop recognized the UMWA pin as having once belonged to his uncle Sandy (Alexander) Maughan, who at one time worked in Dixonville, a town located 35 miles south of Helvetia. Interestingly, the coal check evoked a stronger

FIG. 40. Coal check and United Mine Workers pin found near the back entry of no. 296. The brass tag bearing the number "5" and "RPCC" is for pick coal, which earned a higher tonnage rate for the miner than machine-cut coal. The UMWA pin for the Dixonville local belonged to Thomas Crop's Uncle Sandy (Alexander) Maughan. Photograph by Michael Hamilton.

response from the Crop brothers than did the UMWA pin, perhaps because the pin postdated the recognition of the union by the R&P in 1933 and was worn during a period with fewer labor disputes. The UMWA pin is the most obvious statement of resistance by the miners to the practices of the coal companies, but both artifacts speak volumes about the coal miner's existence, from his fight to have union representation in the mine to his unceasing struggle to earn a living wage each day.

Despite the paucity of material culture remains from the doublehouse, there are some noticeable similarities with the archaeological assemblages from Lowell, Paterson, and Lonaconing. At each of these sites, the ceramic assemblage, the small finds, and the tobacco pipes—the remnants of daily life—help to tease out variations in working-class households and standards of living, but they also provide evidence of the active construction and maintenance of working-class identity. In Helvetia, it can be argued that these artifact categories demonstrate the preferences of the mining families with regard to leisure-time activities, certain household goods, and personal dress—preferences that were integral to the creation of a living environment. There is also evidence of resistance to, as well as the acceptance of, some aspects of the industrial regimen, eloquently expressed by a small brass tag and a union pin, but the artifacts from the doublehouse speak primarily of the active negotiation of worker identity and place within the company town.

 CHAPTER 7

THE MINERS' DOUBLEHOUSE:
AN ARCHAEOLOGICAL PERSPECTIVE

Though the material remains from this site had the potential to speak about working-class values, identity, and agency, or the company and its paternalistic practices, there were in fact very few artifactual remains that could be subjected to an analysis of this type, and even fewer with such obvious symbolism as the UMWA pin and the coal check. I therefore turned to material evidence writ large upon the landscape: the miners' doublehouse, the most obvious statement of corporate power and ideology on the lot.

By looking at the doublehouse as artifact—a house built and maintained by the company, an unmistakable representation of corporate control, but also a home inhabited, furnished, and altered by working-class families—the sequence of repairs, alterations, and maintenance that is visible in the archaeological record becomes more significant. While there are contemporary sources indicating the company houses at Helvetia were well constructed and well maintained, oral testimony provides conflicting views from former residents. There are also oral accounts stating that the miners made their own alterations to corporate housing, to improve, enhance, and positively shape their living environment. One way to examine the general question of living conditions, then, is through an analysis of the archaeological deposits surrounding the front entries to the house as well as various features and deposits found in the backlot. When viewed in conjunction with documentary and oral sources, the archaeological data from the company house on lot no. 294/296 provide compelling evidence of worker agency.

THE MINERS' DOUBLEHOUSE
The average miners' dwelling, according to Veronica McKee, had two rooms and a pantry on the first floor. The upstairs floor plan included two bedrooms and a hallway. The attic was accessible only through a scuttle. Since Adrian Iselin and

the R&P preferred to hire married men with families, the basic form of corporate housing in Helvetia was a semidetached dwelling that provided two families or households with an identical room plan. The 1947 town plat indicates that Helvetia's two-story doublehouses were built to standardized dimensions, 40 x 20 ft (12.19 x 6.10 m), with a divided, two-story rear ell, 10 x 20 ft (3.05 x 6.10 m), projecting from the center rear of the house. The houses were of wood frame construction, the exterior clad with board-and-batten siding for some forty years, the roofs covered with wooden shingles. Later, asbestos siding and roofing tiles were added. The walls, which were not insulated, were covered with plaster and lath on the interior. The foundations were constructed of a local sandstone, and as the houses were built slightly above grade, each house had at minimum a small crawl space underneath. Those that were built into the hillside generally had larger cellars. Cellars and crawl spaces were divided by a partition wall. The doublehouses were also constructed with a front porch for each entry, set at opposite ends of the facade.

Archaeological evidence suggests some variation to the standard doublehouse as mapped in 1947. The foundation of no. 294/296 was completely exposed along the front of the house and partially delineated along the sides during excavation (Figure 41). An effort was made to trace the walls with chaining pins as they continued around the back of the structure, though the rear and side dimensions were not easily deciphered because of disturbance from the bulldozer. The dimensions recorded during fieldwork do indicate a front facade of no more than 35 ft (10.67 m) in length, however (Figure 42), and an adjustment to the length

FIG. 41. The foundation of doublehouse no. 294/296.

Fɪɢ. 42. Plan view of the front foundation wall.

of the main block alone changes the total living space in the structure to a figure that is closer to 1,800 square feet, rather than the 2,000 square feet of the doublehouse depicted on the 1947 town plat. Since the house was divided into two units, each household had the use of approximately 900 square feet of living space as originally constructed. This included the ell, which would have been divided on each floor into a 10 x 10 ft (3.05 x 3.05 m) room for each unit.

A figure for gross living space is best appreciated in the context of the number of residents per unit. Although the list of tenants for no. 294/296 cannot be completely reconstructed, the figures do not suggest that these particular units held more than six or seven occupants at any one time while under the ownership of the company (Table 20). The average was closer to four or five occupants per unit. In another part of town, however, the same size unit held 16 occupants, in one instance, and, as shown previously, there were many households in Helvetia between 1900 and 1920 with 10 or more members. When the area required for the stairwells on the exterior side wall of each unit is deducted from the length of the main block, the adjusted living area would provide rooms of approximately 14 x 10 ft (4.27 x 3.05 m) downstairs and something slightly less upstairs, depending on the configuration of the hallway. The space beneath the stairwell was used for storage or as a pantry. The standard room plan and the room dimensions are consistent with those observed in other western Pennsylvania doublehouses. Mulrooney's survey suggests that room size in the typical doublehouse averaged 12 x 14 ft (3.66 x 4.27 m), with kitchens averaging 10 x 10 ft (3.05 x 3.05 m) to 12 x 12 ft (3.66 x 3.66 m) (1989:16, 21).

By contrast, the dimensions recorded in the extant engineer's house (no. 262) are substantially larger. This structure was surveyed, measured, and photographed during the summer of 1994 (Figure 43). The measurements are consistent with the specifications recorded on a 1923 company blueprint that was located after the survey. They indicate a single block with overall dimensions of 24 x 30 ft (7.32 x 9.14 m), with three rooms downstairs (living room, dining room, and kitchen) and four bedrooms and a bathroom upstairs. No. 262 is one of four singles built along Helvetia's main street in 1923. Living space for company officials in these houses was substantially greater—by 60 percent—than for the company's laborers. Each of the four units had a total gross living area of 1,440 square feet. Room size ranged from 20 x 14.6 ft (6.10 x 4.45 m) for the living room, and roughly 12 x 16 ft (3.66 x 4.88 m) each for the dining room and kitchen, to 12 x 10–14 ft (3.66 x 3.05–4.27 m) for bedrooms (variations in room dimension were caused by the construction of a bathroom at the end of the hall). In addition, each of these houses had a full basement and both front and back porches. The houses were furnished with indoor plumbing, with a sink in the kitchen and a bathroom with tub on the second floor, a clear reflection of the company hierarchy. Bathrooms and bathtubs, as noted earlier, were not added to the miners' doublehouse until after the company sold the town to the salvage company.

TABLE 20.

Tenants of no. 294/296, East and West Halves of a Miners' Doublehouse

No. 294

Year	# Occupants	Tenants
1892–1910	–	Unknown
1910	3	John Woodhead, 30-year-old motorman, emigrated from Scotland in 1902; wife, Martha, 31; and 2-year-old son Ellis
ca. 1921–1939	4	John Haddow, Scottish immigrant; wife; 2 daughters; Betty Haddow Hamilton born here in 1922
1939–1954	6	Clyde Dunlap, employed at power plant; wife, Clarice Kephart Deitch; sons, Clyde W. and Howard Dunlap (sons from first marriage to Martha Bellingham); 2 stepsons, Dean and Marlin Deitch
ca. 1962–1963	–	Calvin McKee
after 1964	–	Tom Nesbit/David Brown

No. 296

Year	# Occupants	Tenants
1892–?	–	Unknown
?–1898	–	Isaac Johns, miner (Brady Township 1898, Reel 178), moved family to Walston in 1898 (*DuBois Express, Reynoldsville Edition*, Sept. 23, 1898)
1898–1910	–	Unknown
1910–?	5	William Morgan, 37; wife, Anna; son, Walter; father, Thomas (b. 1840, 69-year-old Welsh immigrant and 20-year resident of Helvetia; grandfather of informant Raymond Kriner); and 1 boarder (Evan Williams, Welsh, a 64-year-old widower)
1928–1951	6	William Crop, Scottish immigrant; wife, Grace; daughter, Elizabeth; daughter, Ellen; son, William; son, Thomas; granddaughter, Jane Smyers after 1937
1951–1959	–	Unknown
1959–1964	–	Bukousky
after 1964	–	Tom Nesbit/David Brown

Sources: U.S. Population Schedules (1900, 1910, 1920); Brady Township (1892-1899, Reel 178); oral history interviews.

In addition to the four single houses built in 1923, there were seven single houses of an earlier vintage, one of which is presently owned by Veronica McKee and was the store manager's house (no. 278) (see Figures 11 and 15). These houses were slightly smaller in terms of gross living space than the units built in 1923.

FIG. 43. The engineer's house, no. 262, was photographed and surveyed in 1994. The house was used as a field office by the R&P during the strip-mining operation but is now derelict.

Six of the houses had a two-story 30 x 20 ft (9.14 x 6.10 m) main block with a single-story 10 x 5 ft (3.05 x 1.52 m) front entry and a two-story gable on the front of the unit, providing the families of company officials with some 1,250 square feet of living space. The seventh single house (no. 273), located on the corner of Second and Fourth streets, also had a main block of 30 x 20 ft (9.14 x 6.10 m) but is shown on the 1947 plat with an ell attached to the left rear of the unit. This last unit apparently differed from the other single houses in its overall appearance as well, having a three-bay front facade and a central entryway. Oral tradition suggests the house was standing prior to the construction of the company town at Helvetia, and it is said to have been the site of a house or log cabin built by James Woodside. Woodside, the first settler in Brady Township, is known to have settled on Stump Creek in 1785 near the present-day site of Helvetia (Brady Township Bicentennial Book Committee 1976:1–2; Kirk 1929; Kriner 1992:5, 16). Though no evidence has been found to prove or disprove such a claim, it is more likely that this particular house was an earlier form of single-family dwelling built by Adrian Iselin between 1891 and 1896.

No. 274 is the only other house known to have differed in its construction from the three basic house types recorded on the 1947 plat. This building served as the doctor's office (his residence was next door in no. 276). Though its configuration appears to be identical to that of the adjacent single houses, albeit with dimensions of 40 x 20 ft (12.19 x 6.10 m) for the main block, the building appears in a videotape (Ray Yusnukis, 1989–1993) as a three-bay, one-and-a-half-story structure with a shed dormer and a covered front porch, approximately 10 x 5 ft (3.05 x 1.52 m).

These are but minor variations, however, in a town that overall conveys an appearance of uniformity in its layout and its construction, whether we are viewing it in plat form (Figure 11), in panoramic view (Figure 9), or in an aerial photograph (Figure 44). The three major housing styles—the 62 doublehouses built for Helvetia's miners and laborers, as well as the two types of single houses for company officials—appear as standardized house forms neatly laid out on parallel rows of streets, with little to differentiate one house from the next. Oral tradition states that all of the company houses were originally painted red (Tom Bukousky, July 20, 1995), and, indeed, an undated postcard of the town shows Helvetia's houses painted a bright red, in common with many other coal towns of the period (AIHP 1992:48; DiCiccio 1996:90) (see Figure 9). By the 1930s, each house was uniformly clad in asbestos siding. Oral accounts indicate that the company alternated the color of siding from one house to the next, forming a pattern of green and rusty red up and down the streets (Thomas Crop, July 29, 1994).

By the time of Helvetia's founding, coal company towns in western Pennsylvania were notable for a standardization in house forms, materials, and town

FIG. 44. An aerial photograph of Helvetia, 1939, captures the uniformity of the mining landscape. The street grid and the housing forms of the coal company town create an appearance of regularity from this perspective. The mine is located in the bottom center, while Helvetia's downtown and the ballfield are visible in the upper left corner of the photograph. Courtesy of Tom Bukousky.

plan. Outwardly, the same is true of Helvetia. On the surface, it would appear that the only distinction to be drawn is between those built for management and those built for everyone else. This apparent uniformity is belied, however, by the immense variation in facades, enclosures, additions, and alterations to the houses of Helvetia, making each one individual in its appearance and character—changes that were in fact made not by the company but by Helvetia's mining families.

ALTERING THE DOUBLEHOUSE

Architectural, archaeological, and oral evidence shows that residents of Helvetia altered both the interior and exterior construction of company houses to suit their personal tastes or to meet changing economic needs, and that over the years many improvements were made by the residents to facilitate drainage, heating, cooking, and sanitation. We have already seen how tasks associated with food preparation and storage, laundry, and other household chores were affected by the company's practices and by the services provided by the R&P. All meal preparation and the clean-up that followed were done without the convenience of running water for many years. A coal stove, essential for these tasks and for heating the houses in winter, was provided by the company, but the coal had to be paid for with the miner's wages. In response to these conditions, or perhaps independent of them, Helvetia's miners made a number of changes to their surroundings.

Bake Ovens and Summer Kitchens

Some families built their own bake ovens outside or set up summer kitchens with kerosene or oil stoves behind the house (see also Warfel 1993). Documentary sources show that in the backlots of other Pennsylvania mining towns some immigrant families built outdoor bread ovens made of stone or brick, surely an expression of ethnicity and a survival of past cultural practice (AIHP 1992:9; Brestensky, Hovanec, and Skomra 1991:60; DiCiccio 1996:91) (Figure 45). At least two separate studies have tied this type of brick or stone oven construction to Italian and Greek immigrant families.[1] Some of Helvetia's families, like the Crops and Haddows, built and enclosed a side porch or built an addition to the ell and used the new space for a summer kitchen (Tom Crop, July 14, 1995; Betty Haddow Hamilton, July 14, 1995). Tom Crop recalled that his family set up a kerosene stove on an enclosed side porch and that a box was set on top for baking. In the adjacent unit, an oil stove was set up in the enclosed side porch (Marlin Deitch, July 21, 1995). This action effectively increased a family's workspace while helping to alleviate the problem of added heat in the house during the summer months. In substituting oil or kerosene for coal heat, families reduced their consumption of coal. This may have been a cost-saving measure, but the biggest advantage was that when the stove was no longer needed, it could be turned off and would not continue to burn fuel or give off heat like a coal stove.

AN ARCHAEOLOGICAL PERSPECTIVE

FIG. 45. Undated photograph of a mining family's garden in Phillips, Pennsylvania. A stone bread oven is visible to the right of the wooden walk (AIHP 1992:9). Courtesy of the Penn State Fayette Coal and Coke Heritage Center.

Water and Sewer

There is archaeological evidence in the backlot of no. 294/296 for other types of improvements made by the tenants of this doublehouse. When he visited the excavation site in 1995, William Crop stated that his father rigged a connection to the main water line before the company did so, bringing running water to the enclosed side porch of their unit (July 25, 1995). William and Tom both indicated that their father and John Haddow dug a ditch and laid a pipe from the company line (which extended only as far as no. 290/292) to the side porch of each unit. William said that his father also installed a pipe to drain water from the basement to the alley.

During fieldwork, excavators uncovered several pipe trenches and drainage pipes in the houselot of no. 294/296, including evidence for the improvements made by William Crop Sr. A pipe trench and an iron drainage pipe were uncovered just off the southwest corner of the house. The pipe runs westerly from the house toward the alley and drops in elevation as it moves away from the house. Numerous late-nineteenth- to early-twentieth-century materials were identified in the stratum overlying both pipe and trench. These in turn are overlaid by a brick walkway that, according to oral testimony, was built by William Crop Sr. in 1933. This walk was built to replace an older wood or plank walk that crossed the backlot when the Crops moved into the house in 1928 (Thomas Crop, July 29, 1994; William Crop, July 25, 1995).

Altering Living Space

Families also added to their living space or altered the interior of their homes. Oral narratives tell us, for instance, that extended families sharing an entire double-house often cut a doorway through the partition wall to facilitate the use of space (Tom Crop, July 29, 1994; Lloyd Gray, Sept. 11, 1995). The stairwell, which was originally boxed or enclosed with a pantry or storage area underneath, was opened up by some families—to make it fancier, according to Tom Crop (July 29, 1994). The wall and doorway were removed and replaced with an open balustrade.

Many families added pantries or additional kitchen space onto the side or rear of the ell and then converted the second downstairs room from a kitchen into a dining room. When six former residents of this doublehouse were questioned about room layout and the number and types of porches, each remembered the units somewhat differently and did not always agree on the floor plan. In fact, the confusion over the floor plan is a clear indication of how often families altered their living space to suit their needs.

Betty Haddow Hamilton stated that her father built and later enclosed a side porch that had been added to the east side of the ell. This addition then served as an eating area for the Haddows and later was used as a pantry by the Dunlap family, which resided in no. 294 after the Haddows moved away. Marlin Deitch

FIG. 46. Photograph of Jane Smyers taken at the rear of no. 296, looking toward no. 294. Taken in 1938–39, the photograph clearly shows the back entry for the western unit, reached by a series of wooden stairs. Notice that the rear wall of no. 296 also projects farther out from the structure than the rear of no. 294. A brick walkway is visible at the base of the stairs and can be seen curving around the bottom stair, presumably toward the entrance to the crawl space for no. 296. The Crops' clothesline pole is visible to the right (south) of the brick walk. Behind it is a wooden shed built by the tenants in no. 294. The photograph shows the rear of the ell and the pantry addition for no. 294 as well as the cement walk leading from the front of the eastern unit to the privy at the rear of the backlot. Courtesy of Tom Crop.

FIG. 47. Dean and Marlin "Bruz" Deitch (right) in front of the eastern wall of no. 294, 1951. This view captures the eastern wall of the enclosed sun porch as well as the northeast corner of the pantry addition. The two wooden steps at the bottom left of the photograph are for the side door. Also visible are the cement-covered walks leading to the front entry of no. 294 and around the side of the house toward the rear of the backlot. A close-up of this photograph reveals a series of small plantings, possibly shrubs, along the foundation. Courtesy of Marlin Deitch.

recalled that the pantry had an oil stove and sink. The back door, he stated, was located on the side wall of the pantry (July 21, 1995). The addition to the ell of no. 294 is visible in a photograph taken from behind no. 296 in the late 1930s or early 1940s (Figure 46). The image captures the southern wall of the addition, and it confirms the absence of a rear entry for no. 294. The addition is also covered with the same siding as the rest of the house, suggesting that the changes described by Betty Hamilton and Marlin Deitch were made prior to the residing of the houses by the company in the 1930s. A second photograph, from about 1951, shows the northeast corner of this addition, which appears to be flush with the main block, and two wooden steps leading to the side entry (Figure 47). This suggests an addition approximately 10 ft (3.05 m), the length of the ell, by perhaps 7.5 ft (2.29 m), the width of the pantry, or some 75 square ft of additional living space.

The Crops also enclosed a porch on the side of the ell in the adjacent unit, and the family used this space for a sink and the kerosene stove. No. 296 had a back entry, accessed by wooden stairs that led into the kitchen (Figure 46). There is disagreement over the size of the addition to no. 296 as remembered by Marlin Deitch, Tom Bukousky, and Tom Crop. The previous photograph clearly shows that the rear of this unit projected several feet further into the yard than no. 294, and the alignment of the sidewalk exposed behind no. 296 suggests the addition may have extended nearly five feet beyond the back wall of the ell. Tom Crop

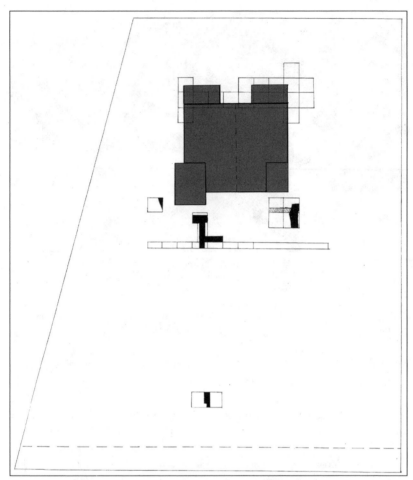

FIG. 48. Conjectural footprint of the doublehouse with subsequent additions, based on oral testimony, period photographs, and archaeological evidence. Brick walks behind the house are shown in black. The cement cross walk is indicated by hatch marks. The brick walks provide key evidence regarding the size of the rear addition on no. 296.

also stated that the western wall of the enclosed porch extended several feet past the main block. The room, then, estimated to be 14–15 x 10 ft (4.27–4.57 x 3.05 m), would have added as much as 140–150 square feet of living space to the unit (Figure 48).

Cellars and Crawl Spaces

Other modifications were made to the cellars of the doublehouses. Oral accounts indicate that the cellars were essential for food storage and preservation (as well as for making home brew and, according to Lloyd Gray, root beer) and were used

AN ARCHAEOLOGICAL PERSPECTIVE

regularly for this purpose. Marlin Deitch stated that his family deepened the cellar for no. 294 in order to maximize use of what had been essentially a crawl space (July 21, 1995). The crawl spaces were accessed by doors cut into the rear wall of the house (Figure 46). A frame of wood or brick is evident in the area just south of the opening in the foundation, suggesting that the crawl space for no. 294 was accessed by a set of exterior stairs by the late 1930s or early 1940s.

Front Porches and Rear Stoops

One of the most noticeable expressions of individuality and identity by the miner and his family is evident in the alteration or creation of porches by the tenants. Archaeological evidence suggests that the front porches were original to the doublehouses; certainly they were constructed by Adrian Iselin or the R&P. No evidence was found for an earlier living surface beneath the porches or for earlier entryways in front of the doublehouse. Several photographic images taken throughout the town also show a uniformity to the open woodwork that framed the porches on each doublehouse, suggesting a single episode of construction or at least a single agency responsible for their construction. Yet a comparison of the porches in these images also shows some variation in the woodwork enclosing the gable ends of the porch, changes that were most likely made by the tenants, not the company. Indeed, the oral, historical, and archaeological data from this community suggest that many porches were modified, renovated, or added to the miners' doublehouse during the R&P's tenure. Most important, the combined evidence shows that decisions on how to use and alter these spaces were made by the miners themselves.

While the physical evidence from the front porches at no. 294/296 dates largely to the time of original construction or to changes made during the post-company era, the oral and photographic data reveal several interesting differences in the ways the porches were used by the tenants of the doublehouse during the coal company era. The excavation revealed that both porches were between 12 and 13 ft long and 5 to 6 ft wide (3.66–3.96 x 1.52–1.83 m) as originally constructed. While the Crops lived in no. 296 (1928–1951), the west porch remained open (Figure 49) and served as a focal point of leisure-time activity. William Sr. in particular is remembered as spending many hours there relaxing or visiting with friends and neighbors (William Brown, July 30, 1994). As described in the previous chapter, the artifacts found beneath the porch reflect the use of this space for leisure-time activities. These objects were predominantly small finds—items that might drop from someone's pockets when he or she was sitting on the front porch or on the steps, and objects that could easily slip (or be pushed) through the cracks and knot holes in the floorboards or could be pushed through the lattice screen by a child.

Tom Crop said that most people left the porches open. "If you wanted to close them in, you could," he said, "but you done it—if you was a good enough carpenter" (July 29, 1994). While the Crops were content to use the porch as built by the company with only the addition of a wooden swing, other mining families enclosed their porches, including the tenant on the eastern side of the double-house. John Haddow enclosed the front porch at no. 294 to create some 60 to 70 square feet of additional interior living space—space that was screened from the public. This new space was used as a sunroom (Figure 50).

The archaeological record does not document this change by John Haddow, nor does it record the construction of a ramp leading to the porch of no. 296 by Tom Bukousky's family sometime in the late 1950s or early 1960s. Instead, the strata adjacent to the house foundation reflect the use of the porches over their estimated 80-year life span. The deposits are consistent with what one would expect to find under a raised, covered porch: rodent burrows and animal deposits, as well as the previously mentioned small finds. No evidence of alteration is visible archaeologically until the removal of the porches during the post-company era.

It is fortunate that the evidence of John Haddow's changes is preserved in the oral and photographic record. Most archaeological evidence for alterations by the tenants of no. 294/296 is found in the areas immediately adjacent to the porches. Excavation units placed directly in front of no. 296 exposed several features associated with the porch and front entry (Figure 51 and Table 21), including a

FIG. 49. Tom Crop standing southwest of the front porch for no. 296, circa 1939. The open-work on the porch railing is consistent with that seen on other doublehouses, but the woodwork covering the gable end of the porch has a scal-loped edge. Notice the brick walkway that extends from the street to the front porch and around the western side of the doublehouse. Courtesy of Tom Crop.

FIG. 50. Front view of the enclosed sun porch built by John Haddow at no. 294, early 1950s. The doublehouses in the row behind are barely visible through the trees lining the front sidewalk and the side boundary of no. 294. Courtesy of Marlin Deitch.

AN ARCHAEOLOGICAL PERSPECTIVE

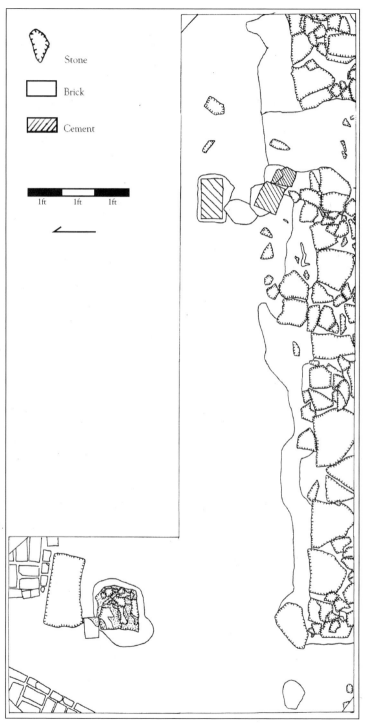

Fig. 51. West front entry. Plan view of archaeological features, including foundation, builders' trench, porch support, front walks, and front stoop.

Stone

Brick

Cement

1ft 1ft 1ft

TABLE 21.

FEATURES ASSOCIATED WITH THE WEST FRONT ENTRY OF NO. 296

Feature	Unit	Description
Walkways		
41	19	Brick walk connecting front entry to company sidewalk and to Feat. 40, the brick walk leading to the rear of the lot
40	19/23	Brick walkway connecting front walk to rear of house
Front entry		
39	19	Rectangular flagstone at the base of porch steps, abuts the front walk (Feat. 41), 2.0 x 1.0 ft. (0.61 x 0.30 m)
West porch		
46	19	Mortared stone pad or sub-base for NW porch support, 1.5 x 1.5 ft. (0.46 x 0.46 m)
63	19	Fill above the NW porch support (Feat. 46)
	5F	Drip line along western edge of porch
4	4	Rodent burrow beneath the porch
26	10	Small feature containing a deposit of animal bones beneath porch
Other		
30/31	10/12	Cement paving stones, in vicinity of SE porch support but different construction; function unknown
64/65	10/12	Fill surrounding cement paving stones (Feats. 30–31)
23	12	Disturbance to foundation created by bulldozer
32	5	Possible posthole for fence line along front of no. 296

rectangular flagstone placed at the base of the porch stairs, the brick walk that connected the company's cement sidewalk to the front entry of no. 296, and a brick walk that connected the front of the house to the backlot along its western side. These features were installed by the mining families living in no. 296, not by the company.

It is significant that this treatment of the front yard and entry for the western unit was not replicated on the eastern side of the doublehouse (Figure 52 and Table 22). Though roughly contemporary in construction and use, different materials were chosen for the walks in front of each unit, indicating the exercise of individual preference in their design and construction. The walkways surrounding the doublehouse will be discussed in greater detail in the next chapter, but within the context of their association with the porches—as a transitional space between the streetscape and an exterior, semipublic space used for leisure activities (no. 296), or between the streetscape and a private, interior space (no. 294)—

they provide further documentation of the miner's efforts to shape activity areas in front of the doublehouse.

The videotape made by Ray Yusnukis (1989–1993) and numerous photographs of the company town show a variety of alterations to the front porches of numerous doublehouses. Many of these changes can be dated to the era of the company and were clearly made by the miners themselves. Helvetia's families made changes to the rear entry, as well, including the installation of different stoops, porches, and an assortment of coverings, as well as the actual relocation of the rear access. Again, these alterations are evident in photographs taken in town before 1947 and in the oral record of the community. John Haddow's conversion of the east front porch at no. 294, his construction and subsequent enclosure of a porch on the side of the ell, and William Crop's relocation of the rear entry for no. 296 are excellent examples of the ways that Helvetia's mining families shaped and altered their living environment in accordance with their personal preferences and the needs of the household. But these are not isolated examples. The combined evidence confirms that such alterations were not unique to the occupants of no. 294/296, but rather were undertaken by many tenant families.

INSIDE THE DOUBLEHOUSE

Though there is virtually no archaeological evidence for interior furnishings, period photographs and oral accounts give us some idea of what the miners' doublehouse looked like inside.[2] The use of each room varied according to the individual preferences of the tenants. The front room downstairs generally served as a living room or parlor; the room behind it served as either a dining room or kitchen. The ell on the rear of the house might be used as either pantry or kitchen. Tom Crop stated that his family used the two main rooms downstairs for a front parlor and a living room. The family enclosed a side porch adjacent to the ell, and the combined area served as kitchen, pantry, and eating area. Upstairs were two bedrooms and a clothes press. The stairs, located on the exterior wall of the unit just behind the front door, were left boxed with a door at the bottom to close off the stairwell.

The miner's family made adjustments to the interior of the house in other ways, not just by changing the function of existing rooms or adding on additional living space. The selection of furnishings also shaped the living environment of the doublehouse. The walls were papered in many of the houses, including no. 296, while many families regularly repainted the plaster or painted over the existing wall paper each year (Tom Crop, July 29, 1994; Lloyd Gray, Sept. 11, 1995). Tom Crop also stated that his family put down rugs over the hardwood floors— something, he noted, that not everyone could afford. No. 294 also had hardwood floors, according to Betty Haddow Hamilton, but her family laid a Wilton rug on the floor of the front room (July 14, 1995). Tom recalled that linoleum was a common floor covering in many houses, particularly in the kitchen. Oiled floor

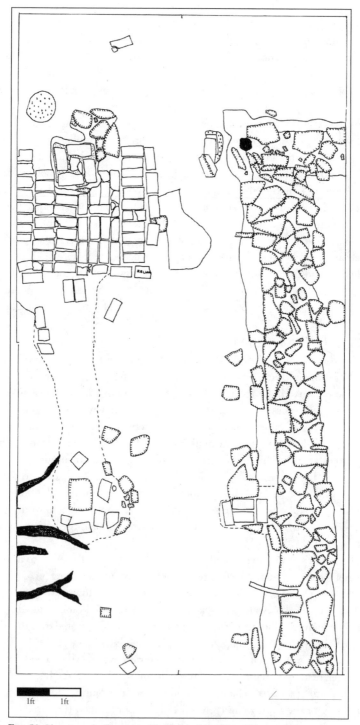

FIG. 52. Plan view of archaeological features in front of no. 294, the eastern unit of the doublehouse, including the house foundation, builders' trench, several walkways, porch supports, planting holes, and garden beds.

TABLE 22.

FEATURES ASSOCIATED WITH THE EAST FRONT ENTRY OF NO. 294

Feature	Unit	Description
Front walkway		
2	–	North-south cement walk at grade level, 15 ft (4.57 m), connecting east front entry with company sidewalk; cement poured over earlier brick walk (Feat. 61)
61	–	North-south mortared brick walk; visible in west profile, Unit 15
21	–	Sub-base or fill for Feature 61, north-south brick walk; visible in west profile, Unit 15
Front entry		
60	2	Stone fragments adjacent to and lying beneath brick paving (Feat. 3) along its southern terminus; remnants of earlier walk?
10	2	3 dark, sharply rectangular stains with remnants of wood, from bottom boards for porch steps, 2 ft (0.61 m) north of foundation
3	2/7	Brick paving associated with front entry; postdates sun porch
Porch supports		
19	13/17	Disarticulated remains of NW porch support, brick and stone scatter, associated disturbance from tree north of excavation area
28/62	9	SE porch support, 3 stacked bricks off northeast corner of foundation, with the third brick set into feature fill (Feat. 62)
29	2/7	NE porch support, mortared brick atop stone pad, 1.2 x 1.2 ft (0.37 x 0.37 m); located beneath brick paving (Feat. 3); imprint from upper layer of brick visible in mortar
37	3/6	SW porch support, dry-laid brick dug into builder's trench (Feat. 6)
Cross walkways		
18	15	East-west brick walkway connecting front entry and front walk (Feat. 2) with sidewalk to rear of the house (Feats. 7, 59); some bricks have mortar, indicating reuse
20	15	Sub-base or fill for Feat. 18, east-west walk
Side walkways		
7	11	North-south cement walk leading to rear of east unit; cement poured on earlier mortared brick walk (Feat. 59)
8	1	Fragmented cement slabs mortared to brick, identified as broken-up section of Feat. 7, north-south walk along side of house
59	11	North-south brick walk, serving as sub-base for later cement walk (Feat. 7), connected with back walk (Feat. 33) at rear of unit
27/44	1/11	Sub-base for north-south brick walk (Feat. 59)

cloths would have been another alternative. A photograph of the front room or parlor in no. 296 shows a very pleasant decor with wall paper, drapes and a window shade, rugs on the floor, pictures on the wall, and a large radio next to the upholstered armchair (Figure 53).

McGuire (1991:103) states that during the nineteenth century, "workers could afford few of the products of their labor and maintained very low levels of consumption, especially of durable goods." Though we are only looking inside a single domestic unit, the photograph and oral testimony about the interior of no. 296 in the early twentieth century stand in contrast to McGuire's assessment of nineteenth-century working-class households. The archaeological evidence also suggests a different picture. Material remains from the site are sparse, as noted, but indicate that at various times these units were also furnished with matching dinner sets, decorative glassware, and porcelain. Families would have chosen furnishings and household goods that were suited to their economic means and their own personal preferences—items not necessary to the family's daily subsistence.[3] Jewelry, cuff links, and other small finds are also indicative of the ways that Helvetia's families shaped their living environment: they reveal choices about the allocation of disposable income, as well as aspects of working-class culture and identity.

It must be acknowledged that the institution of corporate paternalism and the advent of welfare capitalism meant real gains in income and in living standards for many workers, though others maintained a precarious existence on the edge of or below the poverty line despite the benefits offered under a paternalistic system. The documentary and oral evidence presented in this volume does not suggest that many of Helvetia's families had much, if any, disposable income, though the image constructed from the physical evidence of daily life in no. 294/296 suggests a comfortable existence for some of the families. But rather than looking only at durable goods as the primary measure of the mining family's standard of living, we should also weigh the importance of the physical alterations made to the doublehouse by the miner. In each of these units, whether through the addition or reconfiguration of living space,

FIG. 53. Interior of no. 296, circa 1939. Tom Crop is seated in an upholstered armchair with a guitar in his lap. His niece, Jane Smyers, is next to him. Courtesy of Tom Crop.

AN ARCHAEOLOGICAL PERSPECTIVE

through alterations to the structure, or through the use of furnishings, the tenants of no. 294/296 actively shaped and changed the living environment of the double-house to suit their own preferences and needs.

Within the community at large, the numbers and types of alterations made by residents undoubtedly were influenced by the size of the family or household (the number of mouths to feed) and the number of wage earners, as well as the status of the miners within the company hierarchy. McClymer has argued that standards of living were fluid among the working classes (1986:396). Those who were native-born, those who were skilled workers, and those with few or no children had more opportunity and greater means to influence their living conditions than did those who were foreign-born or unskilled laborers and those with more than two children. While the standard of living in no. 294/296 was perhaps higher than that of eastern European households in Helvetia, the oral and historical evidence suggests that the alterations described in this chapter were not by any means limited to Helvetia's downtown or to the households of native- and British-born workers or even to its skilled workers. The standard of living would certainly have varied from one family to the next, yet the changes made to the living environment in each miner's household are indicative overall of the worker's ability to influence his family's physical and economic well-being.

LAND-USE PRACTICES IN THE BACKLOT

An examination of the use of space in the backlot must begin with a definition of that space. The 1947 town plat records lot dimensions of 90 x 151 x 130 x 154.1 ft (27.43 x 46.02 x 39.62 x 46.97 m) for no. 294/296 (see Figure 34). This was a corner lot, so its dimensions were somewhat different from those of the other lots in town. No. 294/296 was bordered on two sides by the alley that rounded the southwest corner of the lot as it curved around the parcel to connect with the street. Most lots, on average, were 100 ft wide and 150 ft deep (30.48 x 45.72 m), though many were as much as 130 ft wide (39.62 m), and others were as much as 182 ft (55.47 m) in length (see Figure 11). Dimensional variations were created by the topography of the site and by the grid of streets and alleys. Helvetia's streets in the downtown were 50 ft (15.24 m) wide but were as much as 90 feet (27.43 m) wide uptown. The alleys were consistently 15 feet (4.57 m) in width. Each family or household, then, had rights to a lot approximately 50 x 150 ft (15.24 x 45.72 m). The distance from the back of the house to the rear alley averaged 100 feet (30.48 m), so the backlot for each unit had dimensions of roughly 100 x 50 ft (30.48 x 15.24 m). These dimensions are consistent with the average lot size recorded in Mulrooney's survey of southwestern Pennsylvania company towns (1989:16). In her report, Mulrooney stated that the backyards were deliberately kept this size to act as firebreaks between the wooden houses.

The backlot was also the location of various outbuildings provided by the coal company and the setting for a variety of utilitarian tasks. Photographs of western Pennsylvanian coal towns invariably capture an accumulation of structures and materials in the backlots. Some—privies, coal sheds, fences, and clotheslines—were built by the coal companies, but others—washhouses and sheds, ovens, wood-piles, vegetable gardens, animal pens, and additional fences and clotheslines—were built by the miners and their families (Bennett 1990:8, 17–21). Bennett notes that alleyways were typically constructed between rows of houses to allow for fire access, coal delivery, privy cleaning, and access to the sheds and, later, to the garages. In like manner, the R&P built a coal shed, a privy for each unit, and a garage along the rear alley behind each doublehouse (Figure 54). As residents of the end unit, the Crops had their own coal shed. The Haddows shared theirs with the Haags in no. 294. These structures are no longer standing, but the locations of the two priv-ies behind no. 294/296 and the Crops garage were recorded during a survey of the backlot. Clotheslines, built by the company, were set in the back of the lot near the privies, according to Tom Crop and Betty Haddow Hamilton (July 15, 1995). The clothesline near the alley behind no. 294 is extant but nearly invisible behind a dense screen of vegetation.

Helvetia's families used their backlots in a number of ways that, as in the doublehouse, show evidence of the active use or modification of the corporate landscape, often for purposes not originally intended by the company. As noted, barns built during the early years of the town's operation were converted into garages by some families in the 1920s. The company later replaced the barns with

FIG. 54. In the background of this photograph, a company clothesline can be seen adjacent to the privy behind no. 8 in Helvetia's uptown. The alley and the privy for the house in the next row are visible just beyond. The boy in the foreground, posing beside Stephen Chollock's 1946 Plymouth, is Bob Bowers. Courtesy of Gary Chollock.

AN ARCHAEOLOGICAL PERSPECTIVE

garages that were also used for multiple purposes, especially by those families without cars. The Crops used their garage for a workshop, for example (July 29, 1994). Residents also built a variety of structures and outbuildings in the backlot to serve a variety of purposes. In early photographs, a shed is visible just to the right of the Crops back door (Figure 46). Betty and Tom both recalled that it was the Haddows's (no. 294), and it may have served as a washhouse for John Haddow or perhaps for storage. Marlin Deitch did not remember the shed at all, an indication perhaps that it was removed shortly before or just after his family moved to this house in 1939. No evidence of this outbuilding was visible in the units behind the house, though debris that may be associated with its demolition was recorded behind no. 294. A survey of the backlot did reveal a cement block foundation for a shed, approximately 5 x 3 ft (1.52 x 0.91 m), to the west of the doublehouse, near the alley. The Crops did not have any additional sheds for their unit, however. While its purpose and its temporal association remain uncertain, the materials are inconsistent with those used by Iselin or the R&P to construct accessory structures behind the doublehouses, suggesting that this shed dates to the post-company era.

Other utilitarian structures were erected in the backlots by the residents. Summer kitchens and outdoor bake ovens were built by some miners. Families often set up a second clothesline nearer to the backdoor of the doublehouse. A wood post for a clothesline was erected just a few feet behind no. 296. Marlin Deitch stated that his family also set up a second clothesline about five feet off the back of no. 294. The poured concrete footer for this structure was discovered, along with several clothespins, while excavating the intersection of the east-west walk behind the house and the north-south walk that led to the privy and the company's clothesline. Again, oral testimony reminds us of the importance of such everyday features—for example, Marlin Deitch's comments about his mother's experiences in Helvetia and how she hated walking to the pump or to one of the outbuildings in the cold weather (Aug. 14, 1995). The same was surely true on washday, whether in winter or summer. Having a second clothesline closer to the house was a simple and inexpensive improvement that quickly proved its worth for the miner's wife.

There is no record of livestock kept in the backlot of no. 294/296, but many residents kept cows, chickens, pigs, and geese—particularly the eastern European families who lived uptown and along the top row of houses on the hill in Helvetia's downtown. The oral narratives described previously indicate that families erected any number of structures to house their animals. Cow barns, pens, and kennels were erected along the back alleys, for example. An abandoned chicken coop was found during a walkover survey of the backlot at no. 289/291, just across the street from the excavation site.

Many of Helvetia's families allowed their animals to roam freely, in a sense treating the company's land as land held in common—a preindustrial tradition turned on its head. In a clear example of how the company responded to the actions of its tenants, company memoranda and oral accounts document efforts by R&P officials in the 1930s to set aside an area in town for pasture and to remove the livestock then roaming through the streets. Fences that had been erected between the houses to keep out wandering pigs and cows were torn down by the company after the pasture was created. Fees were charged for pasturage and fines were levied against anyone who violated the prohibition against wandering livestock in town.[4] In this instance, there is a dialectic—the company encouraged employees to raise their own food (produce and livestock), residents incorporated agrarian behaviors of the preindustrial age into the corporate landscape by allowing their animals to graze freely and by building an assortment of pens and barns to house their animals, and the company responded to its lack of control by penning the animals, tearing down many of these barns, and charging a fee for pasturage. Yet at least one resident continued to cut and feed to her animals the hay and grass that grew on the hillside above the town on land owned by the company.

MATERIAL EXPRESSIONS OF THE WORKER WRIT LARGE UPON THE LANDSCAPE

Larry Lankton has described company housing as "a tangible expression of the bond between employer and employee," however tenuous that relationship might have been at times (1991:148). He went on to note that

> workers paid a price for occupying a company house. They had less choice and selection at the mine than in neighboring independent villages. They had to take what their employers gave them, and what the ordinary worker received was a solid dwelling that expressed no individuality and had few frills. . . . Companies, too, paid a price for serving as landlords. They invested capital in structures that did not return a profit directly. They employed men to build and maintain the houses. As the standard of living went up, workers came to want more, so managers endured an onslaught of requests for modernization. They had to bother with leases and rent collection, with public works matters like streets, garbage collection, and water hook-ups [Lankton 1991:148].

Clearly there was a dialectic of attraction and control in place within the company town, an important element defining the relationship between company and worker. It may be argued, however, that this relationship was also based on the negotiation of competing interests. Through the lens of the doublehouse and the backlot, we can see a dialectic between company and worker that speaks of negotiation, and renegotiation, of both the industrial regimen and the structure of daily life in a company town. Despite Lankton's observations about the faceless quality of housing in such communities, the ordinary workers in Helvetia gave their homes individuality through the many alterations and additions to the doublehouse, through the furnishings they employed and the cultural tradi-

AN ARCHAEOLOGICAL PERSPECTIVE

tions they carried on, and also through a dialogue with company officials about services as well as the use of space on company property.

In this chapter we have seen many examples of how the miners and their families altered their living space to improve their general well-being and to shape the physical environment to suit their needs. In this context, it is interesting to look again at the condition of these houses after the R&P divested itself of its company towns. By 1989, most of Helvetia's houses had deteriorated so much that they had long since collapsed or had been razed by the salvage company. The state of decay found in Helvetia less than 100 years after its founding stands in strong contrast to the neatly kept homes under the company. What is the change that occurred?

Al Miller, real estate manager for the Rochester and Pittsburgh Coal Company at the time of this project, remarked that Helvetia was always less well kept than other former R&P towns, particularly Lucerne, Homer City, and Ernest— company towns that have embarked on a second life as privately owned communities. Miller stated that "coal miners do not have housing values like other occupational groups" (personal communication, July 7, 1994), implying that efforts to maintain the appearance of each company town came from the coal companies themselves, not the residents. Once the R&P withdrew from Helvetia, the houses and infrastructure began to decay. The videotape made by Ray Yusnukis and the testimony of former residents and the Kovalchicks' rent manager seem to support this assertion. Without the structure and order imposed by the R&P's officials, the town of Helvetia began to deteriorate. Fewer than two dozen houses were still standing prior to the start of the strip-mining operation in 1989. From the exterior, most of the remaining houses appeared to be poorly maintained, their accessory structures near to collapse. Under the salvage company, both landlord and tenant failed to maintain the symbiosis that had previously characterized tenant-owner relations in this town. A few homes were proudly maintained, but with the caveat that most of these were privately owned.

Yet Miller's statement is problematic on a number of levels. First, Helvetia was home to many different families after the mine closed, not just coal miners. Many of these newcomers had no vested interest in the community other than the low monthly rent and utility fees. It also appears that while they repeatedly expressed the desire to purchase their homes, town residents were never given the opportunity to make the important transition to ownership, unlike residents of Lucerne, Ernest, and other former company towns where the R&P's company houses, now encased in vinyl siding, have survived the post–coal mining era. According to Veronica McKee, the Kovalchicks elected to sell a limited number of houses in the other towns in order to make the first payment on their purchase:

> See, I worked for Kovalchick, you know, when they bought these towns, and that involved 2,000 houses, see. And to make the first payment, they had to sell some, so I sold 800 houses—800 houses among all these towns, you know [Conversation with William Brown, July 30, 1994].

Much blame has been leveled at the salvage company (as well as the coal company for selling out), but in Veronica McKee's view, this was unavoidable because of an agreement between the salvage company and the R&P. The Kovalchicks agreed not to raise the rent on Helvetia's houses for 20 years, she said, because

> the coal company didn't want trouble with the miners, you see, or with the union, see. So they made this commitment, but it almost broke the [salvage] company because everything went sky high, like . . . liability and property damage, fire insurance. Cleaning the outside privy went from three dollars each to 10 dollars each. You can imagine. . . . Carpenter wages went up. Materials to repair the houses went up. And it almost reached the point where they almost lost the properties. They had mortgaged themselves to the hilt, until 1967, when they finally were free of this commitment and they tripled the rent [July 30, 1994].

The owners of the salvage company contributed to the decline of the town's housing stock by encouraging the remaining tenants to scavenge materials from the vacant houses when they needed something to repair their own home (William and Sara Crop, Sept. 11, 1995; Lloyd Gray, Sept. 11, 1995; Ray Yusnukis, 1989–1993). Residents, too, bear some responsibility for the condition of the houses.

When we reexamine Al Miller's statement about coal miners, however, we realize that the decay he described cannot be attributed to a lack of housing values on the part of the miner. True, the changes to Helvetia occurred after the mine closed and the company sold its towns, when the town's population was not made up exclusively of coal miners. Yet judging from the emotions raised by the process of eviction (and from the high level of interest in the annual Helvetia Homecoming), it is clear that there was and still is a great deal of pride among the town's last tenants. The problem, however, is with the perception of Helvetia's miners as individuals unconcerned about their homes, as individuals unwilling to invest in the care and maintenance of their homes. This perception is fully contradicted by the archaeological, oral, and documentary evidence from Helvetia during the era of the coal company. The many modifications to the miners' doublehouse indicate substantial interest and investment on the part of the tenants, while the landscape itself, as shown in the next chapter, is an eloquent witness to the feeling of pride that residents placed in their homes and in their community. What the evidence from the doublehouse reveals, in fact, is that efforts to maintain the appearance of the town and its dwellings came from both the coal company and the residents of this company town, and that Helvetia's coal mining families were particularly active in shaping the living environment in this community.

CHAPTER 8

CREATING ENVIRONMENT: THE PHYSICAL LANDSCAPE OF THE MINING TOWN

The coal company town, the coal camp, and the mining patch stood apart from other communities, whether in the bituminous fields or in the anthracite region. As George Korson said, "The typical village was in the country, but not of it" (1943:32). The absence of grass and flowers was as conspicuous as the coal dust, smoke, and cinders from the coke ovens and the constant noise from the colliery or the tipple. The streets were generally unpaved, often deep in mud, and there were no sidewalks to raise passersby above the dust or the mud. Often there were no fences, and livestock wandered freely through the streets and the backlots.

In many ways, Helvetia did not fit with the picture painted by Korson. Helvetia's landscape brought notice to this small community—indeed, it was one of the town's highlights. Not only did former residents offer detailed descriptions of flower and vegetable gardens and gardening competitions, but they also remembered the cement sidewalks and how different it was in town after the company took steps to confine the livestock and improve the appearance of its houses and yards. It is important, then, to look more closely at the physical landscape in Helvetia—at its construction, use, and perception; its role in the cultural landscape of this mining community; and how that landscape changed over time—for Helvetia was not always as green as it is remembered.

This chapter considers, too, the use of landscape as a means of negotiating identity and place in an industrial society. Landscape is both the context of daily life and a force in shaping that existence. Like material culture, landscape shapes and reflects the identity of those who inhabit the land, who manipulate its appearance, who construct its meaning. Indeed, the use of the land is integral to the formation of identity. It is not only related to subsistence and housing, but it is also the context for socialization and discourse. It is the setting for the construction of individual, family, and community identities. A close analysis of place may reveal kinship networks, residence patterns, social networks, and ethnic background. Landscape may be used by different parties to actively construct and signify their values and beliefs and to exert power in a positive or productive context (Rodman 1992:29). Those values and meanings may be encoded in and intertwined with its physical features.

It is the process by which a landscape is created and used that is most revealing of social relations and social structure, cultural identity and social conflict, and human perception of place, both past and present, across time and space. Visual imagery and the emotional associations revealed by oral narratives are integral to this task. Rodman has argued that landscapes are multilocal, that "a single place may be experienced quite differently" by many individuals, and as such, they carry multiple meanings "for different users" (1992:647). Many features within the company town—the ballfield, the company store, the miner's dwelling and backlot—convey a duality of meaning that arises from the intersection of the corporate/industrial landscape with the traditional lifeways of those who came to work the mines and subsequently altered the physical and cultural space around them. Thus, they reflect both corporate ideology, working-class values, and worker identity.

The combined archaeological, oral, and historical evidence from Helvetia suggests that this was so because the physical landscape was central to the negotiation and construction of identity and place by residents. Through the lens of landscape, we can see the different relationships and different types of discourse that developed between the miner and the R&P Coal Company: that of landlord and tenant as it relates to land-use practices in the backlots and within the town; that of a propertied landowner and a landless class; and that of a paternal authority and the various members of this corporate family. The evidence of discourse speaks again to the agentive role of workers in shaping their living environment, from negotiation over the use of space to the assignment of meaning to that space and to other features within the landscape of the company town.

LANDLORD AND TENANT

The landscape of the company town expressed and shaped the relationship between landlord and tenant from 1891 to 1947. The R&P, as landlord, implemented land-use practices that were intended to impose order and control across the landscape, from regular trash pickup and disposal to policies concerning the use of yard space. The company dictated the location of certain utilitarian structures within the yard, directing the flow of household activities to the backlot, particularly those related to animal husbandry and domestic chores. As tenants, the miner and his family were bound by company restrictions on behavior and land use, enforceable by eviction, yet Helvetia's residents imposed their own preferences over the company's, constructing their own outbuildings or other structures as needed, changing the location of activity areas, and selecting the plants and seeds that they used to cultivate their gardens and ornament their yards.

Archaeologically, we can catch a glimpse of the R&P in its role as landlord just off the west front porch of the doublehouse. This locus contains a small, roughly circular feature 0.5 ft (0.15 m) below modern grade. The profile resembles that of a posthole, while the absence of a mold suggests that a post was removed and the hole filled in. There are no diagnostic artifacts from the fill, but given its depth and its location directly off the northwest corner of the house, it is suggestive of an early fence line near the front of no. 296, one that was most likely removed in the early 1930s by order of Superintendent Weldon.

The most significant and visible of the R&P's practices involved trash removal and the maintenance of the yard areas. The perception of former residents is that Helvetia's yards were kept clean by the tenants, in part as a response to company policy, but also out of individual pride. Archaeologically, the findings are fairly consistent with this perception. Though the front of the doublehouse was used intensively, particularly the front porches, the yard remained relatively free of debris because activities were largely confined to socialization and leisure time.

As noted in the previous chapter, the accumulated soil matrix in front was for the most part very thin and overall contained very little material except that associated with the demolition of the house or with the period when the house was vacant and the lot untended. The distribution of artifacts from the era of the coal company does, however, clearly reflect the use of the yard area as ornamental space. Artifacts were found primarily in association with the porches, the front walks, and planting beds. Most materials found in the first context were small finds that fell through the cracks of the porch or were lost beneath the stairs or in the spaces between the bricks, while finds from the latter deposits are very small and fragmented, suggesting that they were constantly churned up during planting. There were no trash deposits and no caches of materials discovered in the front yard. This is consistent with the findings from Lowell regarding the use of space around the boardinghouses (Beaudry 1989; Beaudry and Mrozowski 2001). The Boott Mills Corporation imposed its ideology of order and control on that portion of the landscape visible to the public, thus the front yards remained largely ornamental and the facades were well maintained. Only the backlots were unscrutinized, and these spaces were found to have been used heavily by the operatives for a variety of purposes.

The low number of artifacts in the front yard of the doublehouse suggests that efforts were made to keep the front areas free of debris while living under the company. Most of the artifacts were very fragmentary and well mixed throughout the soil profile, indicative of constant foot traffic and the compacting of the yard surface over time. The absence of any loam or humic layers beneath the modern sod level also suggests the possibility that the earliest yard surface in front of the house was a swept dirt surface. Most materials cannot be tightly dated, but those household artifacts found in the lower levels of the soil matrix beneath the demolition debris seem to predate the 1930s when the Crops and Haddows began to make substantial alterations and upgrades to the doublehouse and the associated yard areas. Despite their infrequency and fragmentation, the presence of ceramic and glass in front of the house does suggest that in the early days of the company town Iselin and the R&P were either less stringent in their requirements about front yard maintenance or that rubbish disposal was not then offered by the company.

There is additional evidence on the matter of trash disposal. Several rich artifact-bearing deposits were found in the backlot, in quantities and sizes that

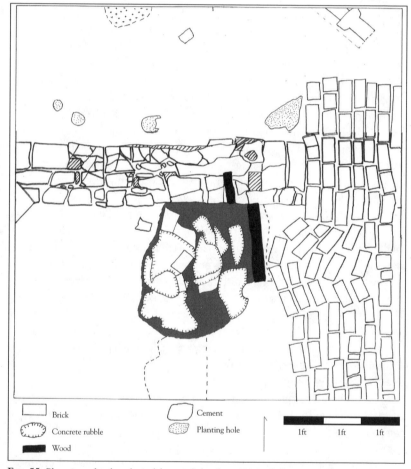

Brick   Cement

Concrete rubble   Planting hole   1ft   1ft   1ft

Wood

FIG. 55. Plan view of archaeological features behind no. 294, including two walkways, a drainage pipe, planting holes, and a cement footer for a clothesline. The north-south brick walk was compressed under the weight of a bulldozer.

are not consistent with the company's known history of rubbish collection and disposal, nor with the character of materials found in front of the house. The greatest quantity was located behind no. 294, on the south side of the crosswalk at its juncture with the long north-south walk that leads to the privy (Figure 55). Early photographs indicate that John Haddow's garden, and later the Dunlaps's garden, came right up to the walk on the east side, but to the west they reveal that a shed was located just off the back of no. 294.

Despite expectations of finding evidence for the shed in one of the four units opened behind no. 294, no structural remains were found. The photographs suggest that prior to 1939–1940 the shed stood just to the west of the clothesline, however, and in close proximity to the excavation units. It has been suggested that the shed was built by one of the tenants for storage or perhaps was used as a washhouse for the miner returning home at the end of the workday, but its function has not been conclusively determined. The assemblage from these units, though mixed with modern debris, contains the remnants of numerous broken dishes, storage jars, discarded glassware vessels, bottles, clay tobacco pipes, and other types of household goods from circa 1890–1910, and in significantly larger pieces. This is the location of the intact medicine bottle, for instance, as well as a substantial percentage of the ceramic tablewares found on the site.

While their relationship to the shed remains uncertain, the presence of household goods from the first several decades of occupancy under the company is significant. These materials are present in sizable quantities as well as in significantly larger pieces, indicating primary deposition of household rubbish by one of the families occupying no. 294, presumably during a period when the coal company did not see a need for its involvement in trash disposal or when officials were less concerned about maintaining the appearance of the backlots. This evidence is consistent with the testimony of former residents who described the efforts of Superintendent Sam Weldon to clean up the town in the early 1930s, implying that there was a need for such action. By reviewing the correspondence of Adrian Iselin Jr. and Lucius W. Robinson, however, we can surmise that the R&P made efforts to impose its ideas concerning maintenance and sanitation—an ideology of order and control—upon the tenants as early as 1916–1917.

The backlot was sampled in other areas to develop a sense of land-use practices across the site. Again, no trash pits were exposed, though we might expect some from this earlier time period. The two units opened near the west privy at the rear of the lot were nearly devoid of household rubbish. There were some household materials found within the organic soils of the gardens. These were much fragmented—evidence of the constant mixing of soil and the heavy use of this yard space for cultivation. But in contrast to the front yard and these other locations, relatively large quantities of company-era materials were found behind the doublehouse in close proximity to the walkways and outbuildings on the upper portion of the backlot. In addition to the four contiguous excavation units behind no. 294, a fifth unit was opened off the southwest corner of the house, behind no. 296. This area of the site also produced a substantial number of household goods, again in a less fragmented condition, again in greater quantities than seen in the front. These remains were found just east of the walk that connects the front of the house to the rear door of the unit. A difference was also visible in the quantity of household materials found in an excavation unit approximately 20 feet to the southeast, still behind no. 296, at the juncture of the crosswalk and the brick walk leading to the privy for that unit. The assemblage collected off the rear of the doublehouse points once again to primary deposition of household rubbish by the tenants.

On a related point, some of the materials recovered from the garden soils behind no. 296 were burned. Small pieces of glass and ceramic that show evidence of burning and melting were found with pieces of coal slag. Was household debris burned by the tenants and then deposited in the garden? Lloyd Gray said that his family never burned rubbish and that there was no need for this because of trash pickup (Sept. 11, 1995). Several oral accounts indicate that families commonly brought over coal ash from the power plant to use in the gardens, though Marlin Deitch said that William Crop Sr. was very particular about removing impurities and slag from the ash before tilling it into the soil (Aug. 14, 1995). Regardless, the coal ash from the power plant cannot be the source for these bits of household goods. The materials are present nonetheless, and many are burned. Coupled with the documentary evidence for rubbish fires and the evidence from behind no. 294, the presence of these materials is a clear indication that at some point in time the occupants of no. 296 were burning and disposing of household rubbish in the backlot.

The combined evidence suggests, then, that in the town's early days, the houselots were less vigorously maintained by the coal company, and the tenants were accorded more freedom with respect to certain land-use practices in the backlots, though the front yards were still kept relatively free of rubbish. Again, this finding is consistent with oral accounts and company papers that document the cleanup of the town in the 1930s and the company's extensive renovations to its housing stock in 1917 and again in the 1930s. It is not unlikely that regular trash removal began during this period. And the efforts to control sanitation and land-use practices in the backlots through trash removal are paralleled by the company's decision to confine roving livestock and to lessen the health risks associated with that practice.

The archaeology also confirms what Lloyd Gray suggested in his interview—that despite the practice of off-site rubbish disposal that most likely began between 1917 and 1930, there is evidence of rodent activity on site. Rodent burrows and faunal remains in the deposits along the front foundation and under the porches provide direct evidence that from time to time the doublehouses had unwelcome guests. Most telling, however, is a paper wrapper found near the garage and privy in the backlot of no. 296. Two words are still legible: "KILLS RATS."

MORTAR, CEMENT, AND NAILS

Mulrooney (1989:21), Corbin (1981:67–68), and others have argued that the inherently unstable nature of owner-employee relations that characterized the coal company town would have constrained if not restricted the interest (and the economic means) of the miners in making the improvements to house and yard that a homeowner would more readily undertake. DiCiccio (1996:89) also states that even those few who could actually afford to buy their own homes would have been reluctant to make any investment because they never knew how long the mine would function. The evidence from Helvetia suggests just the opposite. The archaeological and oral data described in the previous two chapters provide multiple examples of the active role of mining families in the creation and alteration of the living environment of the doublehouse, a practice that carried over into the backlot as well. In such simple materials as cement and mortar, used to bind together the different activity areas within the houselot, there is evidence that Helvetia's residents influenced the use of space in the backlot behind the miner's dwelling in a manner that was external to, or exclusive of, company needs or requirements.

While the coal company gave some structure to the use of space by fencing in the houselot, at least initially, and by locating accessory buildings along the alleyways, the miners themselves created the internal structure that allowed the families to determine the manner in which they accessed and used the various spaces within house and houselot. This is most visible in the sequence of walkways constructed over time by the tenants of no. 294/296 and in the variety of materials used to surface the walks (Table 23).

A series of walkways was built by the occupants of no. 294 to connect the front and side entries of the house to the road and the company sidewalk, to the tenant-built shed behind the house, and to the privy and coal shed at the back of the lot. Moreover, many of the walks were replaced or refurbished over time. At least two different walks led to the front door of the east unit (see Figure 52). Upon closer examination of the extant cement walk that once connected the house to the company sidewalk, it was apparent that the cement had been poured over an existing brick walk. The brick and mortar walk, and its sub-base, were recorded in profile when the adjacent unit was excavated. A small scatter of fieldstone at the base of the brick paving and at the bottom of the front steps suggested the possibility of yet another, even earlier walk in front of no. 294. There are also several bricks beneath the sub-base for the brick walk that are visible in the unit profile and are also suggestive of earlier construction, but further investigation will be needed to identify their function. Oral accounts indicate that

TABLE 23.

Feature	Unit	Description
		No. 296 (west)
Front walkway		
41	19	Brick walk, basket-weave pattern with two rows of stretchers lining the edges, connecting front entry to company sidewalk and to Feat. 40, brick walk leading to the rear of the lot
Side walkway		
40	19/23	North-south brick walkway, basket-weave pattern, connecting front walk to rear of house along its west side
Cross walkways		
47	S61.2W70	East-west brick walk, basket-weave pattern, connecting side walk (Feat. 40) to backdoor and to rear walkway (Feat. 48)
51	22/29	East-west brick walkway, basket-weave pattern, connected to rear walk (Feat. 48), may cross garden in an easterly direction
Rear walkways		
48	24/27	North-south brick walkway connecting back of house to privy and coal shed at back of lot; continuous row of bricks laid side to side with a course of stretchers lining each side; dry laid; a section also exposed behind house from S70W26 to S63.7W26
58	27	Three parallel, linear soil stains marking the location of wood planks or runners from earliest walk
		No. 294 (east)
Front walkway		
2	–	North-south cement walk at grade level, fifteen feet long, connecting east front entry with company sidewalk; poured on earlier brick walk (Feat. 61)
61	–	North-south mortared brick walk; visible in west profile, Unit 15
21	–	Sub-base or fill for Feat. 61, north-south brick walk
Cross walkways		
18	15	East-west brick walkway connecting front entry and front walk (Feat. 2) with side walkway to rear of house (Feats. 7, 59); some bricks have mortar, indicating reuse
20	15	Sub-base or fill for Feat. 18, east-west walk

TABLE 23. (CONTINUED)

Side walkways

7	11	North-south cement walk leading to rear of east unit; cement poured on earlier mortared brick walk (Feat. 59)
8	1	Fragmented cement slabs mortared to brick, identified as broken-up section of Feat. 7, north-south walk along side of house
59	11	North-south brick walk, serving as sub-base for later cement walk (Feat. 7), connected with back walk (Feat. 33) at rear of unit
27/44	1/11	Sub-base for north-south brick walk (Feat. 59)

Crosswalks

34	18/21	West cement walk poured over existing brick walk (Feat. 66), connecting shed rear of house to back walk (Feat. 33)
36	18	East cement walk across the top of the garden
66	18/21	East-west brick walk beneath poured cement walk (Feat. 34).

Rear walkways

33	18/20	North-south brick walk connecting the house to the privy and coal shed at the back of the lot; installed by John Haddow

John Haddow laid all of the brick walks on this side of the doublehouse, while the photographic record suggests that the Dunlaps resurfaced the front walks with cement in the early 1940s. The cement walk that connects the front and rear of the unit was also found to be poured over an existing brick walk, while photographs indicate that the adjoining crosswalk at one time had the same cement covering.

This practice of use and reuse was followed across much of the houselot. The crosswalk in front of no. 294 was originally a dry-laid brick walk, yet several of the bricks have mortar traces on them, suggesting that these materials were used previously and then were scavenged or recycled. Among the many soft-mud bricks used to build the various walkways on the houselot are stiff-mud bricks—stamped, occasionally glazed, sometimes perforated—bearing the names of several Pennsylvania brick manufacturers, including Monro, Woodland, Clearfield, Marion, and Reliance, all made between the 1920s and 1940s (Gurcke 1987). This suggests again that bricks were recycled or brought from somewhere off-site as the opportunity arose.

On the west side of the doublehouse a similar network of walkways was built for the convenience of the miner and his family, again using a variety of materials to surface or resurface the walks. A brick walk connected the front entry of

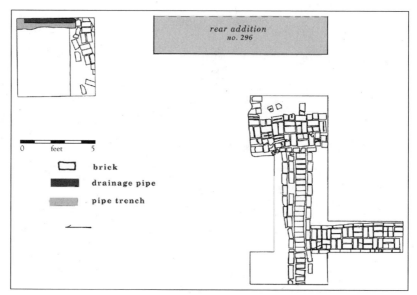

Fig. 56. Plan view of excavation areas and archaeological features associated with the rear entry to no. 296, including several brick walkways and a drainage pipe installed by William Crop Sr. The location of the back wall of no. 296 is conjectural.

no. 296 with the road and company sidewalk (see Figure 51). The bricks were dry-laid in a basket-weave pattern (repeating pairs of bricks laid in opposite directions) with a row of stretchers lining either side. A second brick walk curved around the side of the house to the back of the lot and it was laid in identical fashion to the one in the front yard. This second brick walk can be seen in a photograph taken of a youthful Tom Crop in the late 1930s (see Figure 49). Behind the house, another series of walks was evident (Figure 56). A brick walk led to the backdoor and the entry to the crawl space. A second east-west section, located 5 ft (1.52 m) to the south, may have been built to cross the garden behind the house. Unlike the other walks, this section was partially constructed using perforated yellow and red masonry bricks as edgers. The width of the walk was also reduced in this area. From the back entry, a third brick walk extended south across the backlot to the privy and coal shed. A portion of this walkway was exposed near its terminus at the back of the lot. It was also narrower and laid out in a slightly different pattern than those at the opposite end of the lot. Here, a continuous row of bricks was laid side to side down the center with two rows of stretchers lining each edge.

The brick walkways are the second set of walks used by the tenants of no. 296 to connect the various parts of the lot. According to Tom and William Crop, the original walkway was made of wood and was removed or covered over in 1933

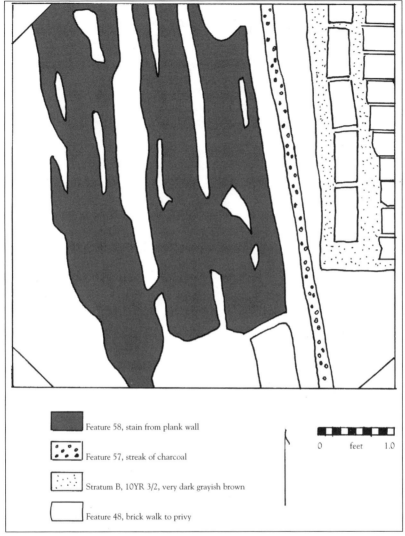

FIG. 57. A series of linear soil stains was exposed at the back of the lot adjacent to the north-south brick walk laid by William Crop Sr. in 1933. The stains mark the location of an earlier wooden walk that once connected no. 296 to the privy and coal shed at the rear of the backlot.

when William Crop Sr. installed the brick walkways (July 11 and Sept. 11, 1995). Evidence of the earlier plank walk was found next to the brick walkway at the rear of the lot. Parallel stains in the soil mark the location of the wooden runners (Figure 57). According to Tom, cross boards were nailed to the runners like railroad ties on a track (July 29, 1995).

Wooden walkways are visible in period photographs from Helvetia as well as from other Pennsylvania mining communities. Often they were just planks laid end to end. They contrast vividly with the neat, finished cement sidewalks built along the road by the R&P. The variation in material and the frequency with which new walks were built and older walks resurfaced serves to emphasize the freedom with which families altered their surroundings. The company may have decided where to put the "voting precinct," but it was the miner who elected how best to access the privy and connect the various activity areas within the backlot.

HOMEGROWN

Though the image we have of Helvetia is that of a pretty little town with an abundance of flower and vegetable gardens, we cannot really speak about the earliest years of the town's occupation. To date, there is no documentary evidence relating to the miner's backlot for this period, nor is there oral testimony. Archaeologically, garden and landscape features are inherently difficult to date because of their continuous use and cultivation. The few artifacts that do find their way into the garden soil are moved about with the tilling of the soil and so become part of a matrix that often includes more recent materials. It has not been possible to date the landscaping features and garden beds that were identified in the lot surrounding no. 294/296. But it is clear that by the 1920s–1930s most of Helvetia's families had large vegetable gardens behind the doublehouse. The residents of no. 294/296 grew many items, including tomatoes, peppers, cabbage, carrots, rhubarb, potatoes, and beets. Much of this produce was canned for later use.

Helvetia's families kept vegetable gardens as part of an economic strategy that allowed them to supplement the miner's wages. There is no evidence, documentary or oral, that it was ever an income-producing activity, though there are certainly instances where miners' households sold extra produce to supplement their income (DiCiccio 1996:91). Each informant stated that gardens were a necessity to the miner and his family, and there was never anything extra to sell. Gardens, they said, were especially important when the miners were not working regular days, particularly during the summertime when the mine typically slowed its production. In an interview with the *Sykesville Post-Dispatch*, Marlene Fike stated that "her parents would pick their own fruit and plant gardens so they could then can everything they had to ensure that there was always food on the table in case of work stoppages or long coal mining strikes" (Feb. 14, 1990). And gardens were often essential for families to manage through the winter months. Both Lloyd Gray and Tom Crop said their fathers planted additional fields of potatoes for this purpose. Canning and food preservation were important parts of this strategy. Lloyd Gray's mother canned strawberries and blackberries and made jelly out of elderberries and apples. Tom Crop's mother canned pickles, tomatoes, and just about everything else, he said.

Families did what they could to maximize the space under cultivation. William Crop Sr.'s garden filled the western half of the backlot behind no. 294/296. When asked to estimate its size, Tom Crop indicated that the garden's dimensions were approximately 50 x 60 ft (15.24 x 18.29 m) near the back of the house where the lot was at its widest, but then it shrank down to an area approximately 50 x 30 ft (15.24 x 9.14 m) to conform with the lot's irregular shape in back. Despite the constraints placed by the alleyway, William Sr. kept some 4,500 square feet of garden under cultivation in the backyard, according to Tom's description (July 29, 1994). Many informants said that the family's garden took up most of the space in the backlot, and there really was not any place to play there as children— which is why they were so often found at the ballfield or the dam. A photograph of the backlot behind no. 294/296 shows the eastern half of the garden with the beds extending to the very edges of the walk that leads to the alley, suggesting that the Haddows and the Dunlaps also put as much space as they could into cultivation. Lloyd Gray said too that when they lived in no. 292, next to the Dunlaps, his father's garden extended the length of the backlot and was 30–40 ft (9.14– 12.19 m) wide. Each miner had an area approximately 100 x 50 ft (30.48 x 15.24 m) behind the house, as noted earlier, so after subtracting the area for the garden, the Grays would have had just enough space remaining for the walkway and a clothesline.

Several former residents of Helvetia also recalled that the company would let the families plant just about anywhere in town. William Crop said that you didn't have to ask the company for extra space to garden: "They was glad you did it because it made it look nice, you know" (Sept. 11, 1995). Families that lived on the outer edges of town were able to plant particularly large gardens. The Crops, who lived in the doublehouse on the end of the row, were able to plant a field of potatoes across the alley. When the Grays lived on First Street, Lloyd's father hired Ray Kriner to come with a team of horses to plow part of the bottom area for additional garden space (Kriner also plowed the field appropriated by William Crop for his potatoes). Other areas in town were kept under cultivation by the families, including some land out past the Protestant Church. Lloyd stated that,

> our last superintendent, he kept planting potatoes in that piece around out there and he said, go out and plant—he says, any place you want to plant a garden, he says, on company property, you can go out and—well, my dad, he—above the church on the hill, my dad and my uncle pulled the old stumps and that—or old trees—they wasn't very big then—they pulled the stumps or pulled the trees out, and plowed 'em, planted potatoes and corn. Anybody that wanted to, they was allowed to plow up any place they wanted [Sept. 11, 1995].

While families maximized the amount of land that could be put under cultivation, they also took steps to enrich and replenish the soil. An excavation trench placed across the rear of the lot behind no. 294/296 revealed a thick organic garden soil containing lenses of coal ash and slag. Marlin Deitch's testimony states that ash from the power plant was screened and used to enrich the soil; his neighbor, William Crop Sr., put a lot of extras into the garden soil, he said. Others recalled that their gardens were manured regularly. Lloyd Gray said his family did not make compost—most of the leftover food scraps were fed to the dogs—but the Grays would buy horse or cow manure from the farm, while other families collected manure from their own animals.

In this context, the landscape again expresses a dialectic between the tenants and the coal company. Veronica McKee stated that families were encouraged by the R&P to plant and grow as much as they wanted (July 30, 1994). The company encouraged the miners and their families to plant gardens, and for years offered incentives for gardeners in the form of cash prizes. This activity certainly instilled pride of place, it gave the families something to do in their leisure time, and it contributed to the miner's sense of well-being—clearly an advantage for the company. The R&P benefited, too, from the labor invested by residents in their efforts to create an orderly, well-maintained landscape. Families in turn relied heavily upon homegrown produce to supplement their diet, and indeed gardening was one of the primary strategies used by families to manage economically on the miner's wages. It supplied much-needed food that families did not have to buy from the company store. Many families asked the company for more ground or took it freely, asserting a right to common use of land they did not own.

Clearly, garden produce was essential for subsistence in many households, but the garden landscape was more than a source of food to many of the families. It was a place where they chose to spend their leisure hours cultivating the fruits and vegetables they most preferred and gardening in a manner that was deeply rooted in cultural and ethnic traditions.

Of Cabbages and Kin

If the miner's garden is an extension of his identity and that of his family, it may also reveal the social and ethnic characteristics of Helvetia's residents. Care for the garden was of course a family activity, with responsibilities divided among members of the household, perhaps on the basis of gender, perhaps on the basis of age. Clyde Dunlap's boys, for instance, were each responsible for one-fourth of the family garden behind no. 294 (Marlin Deitch, Aug. 14, 1995). Lloyd grew many of the family's vegetables, particularly after his brothers married and moved away (Sept. 11, 1995). In the Crop household, William Sr. did the planting, but Tom remembered spraying the potato plants with kerosene to kill the potato beetles while his mother evidently determined what vegetables she needed for canning and which herbs she needed for food preparation and preservation (July 29,

1994). Next door, in no. 292, Daisy Haag was always in the garden, according to her son-in-law (William Crop, Sept. 11, 1995). With her children working and herself widowed, most of the responsibilities fell on her shoulders.

Oral testimony is most revealing of family relations and household responsibilities in the garden, but there is also some evidence of social relations within the larger community—from townwide gardening competitions to support networks that seemed to be in place when families had extra produce to share with those in need, whether they were kin, members of the same ethnic group, or anonymous figures who went up to the Peacock Garden in search of assistance.

The coal miner's garden was also said to be "a continuation of a European rural tradition" (AIHP 1992:54), with plantings as diverse as the families that raised them. Veronica McKee stated that the types of vegetables would vary according to the cultural background of the household (July 30, 1994). Slavs, she said, would plant lots of cabbage, potatoes, and kohlrabi, from which they would make a variety of ethnic dishes. "There wasn't anything they couldn't do with cabbage," she said. Yet potatoes seem to have been universally appreciated for their value as a food source that preserved well and would last through the winter when other vegetables were scarce, while many families, regardless of ethnic background, planted cabbage, turnips, leafy vegetables, and so on. The oral narratives suggest, rather, that it was primarily the process of food preparation and presentation that allowed for the expression of ethnicity. Cabbage might be used for coleslaw downtown and for halupki uptown. The one noticeable difference that might be evident in the types of plants cultivated by mining families is surprising since there were historically very few Italians living in Helvetia under the company. Immigrant Italian families were remembered for terraced gardens where they planted grapevines for making wine (Veronica McKee, March 10, 1994; July 30, 1994). There is some evidence for this pattern of planting from the working-class neighborhoods of Paterson, New Jersey, where Italian immigrants also planted grapevines in the backlots (Lauren Cook, personal communication 1994). Clearly, the potential is there to distinguish archaeologically between plant types on the basis of ethnicity, but oral testimony regarding traditional ethnic dishes is less elusive and helps to flesh out this aspect of daily life.

LANDSCAPE AND WORKER IDENTITY

Helvetia's miners and families imprinted their identity upon the landscape in very personal ways, primarily through the selection of ornamentals, fruit trees, and vegetables, and their decision on how to utilize space within the backlot and, in some cases, on other company-owned land. Lloyd Gray planted apple trees along the sidewalk in front of no. 292. A pear tree was identified on the backlot of no. 280 near the alley. And Rookie Brown told me there were plum trees uptown. On one visit, he recalled seeing "one row of houses here—I'll bet you there was 200 plum trees. . . . And they were just loaded with plums. And they were good plums too—good" (July 30, 1994).

Coal mining landscapes were characteristically dirty, dusty, and gray, lacking vegetation and color. In contrast to its lush, overgrown appearance today, early photographs of the Helvetia town site show an area largely devoid of trees and ornamental plants (Figures 8 and 9). A visitor or resident looking toward the dam and the entrance to the mine while it was still in operation would be able to see the rock dump and the slag heap, the mining plant containing the tipple, powerhouse, and other structures, as well as other physical evidence of the mining operation. The absence of vegetation was in part attributable to the impact of mining on the surrounding environment. The close proximity of the town site to the coal mine and its associated industrial plant meant that much of the surrounding landscape would be enveloped in "clouds of smoke, piles of waste material, and fine particles of coal dust [that] discouraged any new growth" (Mulrooney 1989:21). But the dearth of vegetation also stemmed from the failure of operators to provide for green space in their planning. Trees and grass were not seen as necessary to the coal miner's existence in most company towns. In Helvetia, as in other Pennsylvania mining towns, the coal companies were generous with their lot sizes, but they were rarely so generous in landscaping or providing parks and green space except in the few model coal company towns. It was up to the miners and their families, then, to turn their patch of earth green.

Whether Helvetia's earliest families did so or not cannot yet be determined. But certainly by the 1920s–1930s residents began to alter the physical landscape of the company town and the miners' doublehouse with lasting effect. Archaeological evidence for landscaping in front of no. 294/296 includes planting beds, organic soils, and grass-lined walks near the entry on the east side of the house. Spruce trees were planted in front of no. 294—one on either side of the front walk and two that lie just south of the company sidewalk—to screen the house from the road, though it took many years to achieve this effect. Betty Haddow Hamilton remembered that her father planted the spruce trees in front of the house. She also remembered that he planted grass along the walks. The soil profile from an excavation unit placed to the east of the front walk was difficult to interpret, consisting of many lenses of soil with pockets of gravel and clay as well as many fragmented artifacts, all within a rich, organic soil matrix. Overall, the sequence is suggestive of planting beds that were frequently turned over and replenished. This was the only area in the front yard where the overburden above subsoil was well developed. While the evidence conflicts with Betty's recollection of unbroken lawn in front (and with the later photographic evidence), there is every reason to think that garden beds were maintained by early occupants of the house. Later, as shown in a photograph from 1951, the side of the house was landscaped with small shrubs or plants along the foundation (see Figure 47). Evidence of one

FIG. 58. Jane Smyers in the flower garden planted by her mother, Elizabeth Crop Smyers, in the side yard of no. 296, circa 1939–1940. Courtesy of Tom Crop.

of these plantings was exposed near the northeast corner of the doublehouse. A small circular planting hole just over half a foot (0.15 m) in diameter was identified next to the foundation wall.

There was little evidence of landscaping in the units placed in front of no. 296, primarily because these areas were filled with architectural features. A side view of the front porch (see Figure 49) shows a small evergreen shrub alongside the porch, signs of which are still visible archaeologically in the soil profile of an excavation unit and in the disturbance to deposits created by root activity. This is the only archaeological evidence of planting near the foundation, but oral accounts state that Tom's sister grew flowers in the side yard. After her husband Kenneth was killed in a mining accident here in Helvetia, Elizabeth Crop Smyers moved back to no. 296 with her infant daughter. She planted a flower garden, which she maintained yearly, to provide cut flowers for her husband's grave at the cemetery in DuBois (Figure 58). The bed was lined with white stones, Tom said (July 29, 1994).

Lloyd Gray stated that his mother planted flowers, too, both on First Street and behind no. 292 (Sept. 11, 1995). Many flowerbeds were cultivated throughout the town, according to descriptions of the gardening competition. Most everyone raised vegetables, but uptown, Lloyd said, there were actually a few families that planted only flowers. Growing flowers was not a necessary activity, but it was a frequent and natural use of leisure time among the mining families. Tom

Crop also said that "a lot of the people, why, they had a little—along maybe the edge of the garden or something—they always had part of the garden, you know, to plant some flowers into" (July 29, 1994). Sara Haag Crop said there were more flowers in Helvetia than in a lot of other mining towns (Sept. 11, 1995).

While the main street through Helvetia's former downtown is still lined with tall, majestic spruce trees, these are actually post-company additions to the landscape. The Kovalchick Salvage Company was responsible for planting most of the trees seen today along the main road. According to Veronica McKee, the salvage company began to plant maples and evergreens along the street in 1947 under her direction as town manager (July 30, 1994). The trees were provided at no cost by the Commonwealth of Pennsylvania. "It was a beautiful street," she said. But well before the era of the coal company ended, Helvetia's mining families had begun the transformation of what had been a mostly barren town site. During a plant survey on lot no. 294/296, we recorded a number of spruce trees, juniper, and other species of conifers that are known to have been planted by the mining families who once lived here, as well as several well-established rose bushes and an old lilac. The adjacent lot contained several apple trees and a horse chestnut. Taking the oral and photographic evidence together with data from the plant survey, it is clear that the miners and their families were responsible for planting nearly all of the trees and shrubs in this coal town.

Clearly, yards were landscaped to suit the miner's tastes, varying according to individual, ethnic, and cultural preferences and traditions. Informants were able to identify various trees that family members had planted or could point to the location of a prized flower garden. The interviews also suggest that the reasons for planting ornamental species and gardens were as diverse as the types of plants selected. Tom Crop's sister maintained her flower garden on the west side of the house to provide flowers for the grave of her husband, an act associated with sorrow and remembrance. Other people grew their flowers for the chance to win the gardening competition, from pride in appearance, and for recreation and personal enjoyment. Though not necessary to the miner's subsistence, ornamental species were integral to the creation of a living environment around the doublehouse and an important element in the construction and expression of the miner's identity.

A WELL-ORDERED LANDSCAPE

Rookie Brown, in describing this pretty little mining community, said "they took care of it." This begs the question of who took care of the town's landscape and maintained the houses—the company or its residents? The evidence presented thus far indicates an overwhelming amount of initiative displayed by Helvetia's residents over the years. The company may have installed cement walks along the road downtown, maintained the exterior of the houses, and encouraged residents to garden, but the landscape expresses far more of the miner's identity and preferences than it does a corporate ideology. Though driven by economic necessity to plant vegetables, Helvetia's mining families invested a substantial amount of leisure time in gardening for pleasure as well as for subsistence needs. Sara Haag Crop recalled that "there wasn't too much to do in a place like that and people would like a garden, you know, to have [something to do]" (Sept. 11, 1995). Gardening, then, was a recreational activity as much as it was a necessity.

Gardening competitions were sponsored by the coal company as early as 1917 and cash prizes were awarded to families with the "best kept up yards and house surroundings" and the best gardens (R&PCC 1916b; 1916c). Sara's mother won several prizes, and Tom and William Crop's father won first prize one year. The prizes represented a lot of money for the mining family. During the early years of the competition, prizes of $25 were typical, though by 1947 the company was evidently offering prizes of $100. "This was a tremendous sum to a coal miner. It spurred them on to do their best," Veronica McKee said (July 30, 1994). But winning first place also involved recognition among other members of the community and perhaps a certain status among the families. The competition certainly made a significant impact on residents and visitors, both visually and emotionally, judging from the prominence of the gardens and the competitions in the oral narratives of former residents.

While the R&P's organized activities and competitions helped to impose order and control over the town landscape, it may be argued that the care and fastidiousness observed by former residents and employees of the company and the many varieties of ornamental species speak more to personal preferences and the expression of worker identity. Meticulously maintained yards and ornamental garden beds were part of an image, an outward face turned toward the community and visitors (Figure 59). The cultivation of certain vegetables for use in the preparation of traditional dishes was an important element of worker identity, indicating not only the survival of an Old World culture or ties to a New World agrarian past, but also a negotiation and reworking of the industrial landscape to suit the needs and desires of working families.

One could also argue that the well-ordered landscape was less a result of corporate influence and more a matter of individual preference and community pride. Gardens were first and foremost a family activity, centered on an important economic need. It is noteworthy that the gardening and yard competitions were usually—although not exclusively—won by male residents of the town, indicating a substantial use or investment of leisure time in this activity by individuals who typically spent 8 to 10 hours a day in the darkness underground. Clearly, the practices of the R&P—from organized gardening competitions to specific policies regarding land use and rubbish disposal—were integral to the creation of this mining landscape, but it was the action and initiative of the mining families that ultimately shaped its appearance. The evidence from the garden is consistent

FIG. 59. Two young girls in Buffington, Pennsylvania, show off loaves of newly baked bread while their mothers look on. Here at least a portion of the family garden is planted on the side of the doublehouse. Notice also the wooden plank walk crossing the garden and the bare, hard-packed yard surface behind the house. Courtesy of the Penn State Fayette Coal and Coke Heritage Center.

with that presented from the backlot and from inside the doublehouse: Helvetia's miners and their families constructed a sense of place for self, family, and community through the "creation" of environment.

DUALITY IN THE CORPORATE/INDUSTRIAL LANDSCAPE

Helvetia's cement sidewalks were remembered as a unique feature among mining towns (Figure 60). When told that Rookie Brown thought Helvetia was the prettiest town he had ever seen, Bill Crop immediately mentioned the cement sidewalks: "Well, you've noticed there, they had cement walks, you know. That's the only town under the company that had cement walks." Veronica McKee made the same comment. This is interesting, given that she had traveled a great deal more than most mining families, not only to other mining towns, but also out of the mining region to some of the big cities on the eastern seaboard.

> It was the only mining town to my knowledge that had cement sidewalks . . . which meant a great deal to the coal miners' wives because the other towns would be inundated in mud during the spring and when the big snows came [July 30, 1994].

While the sidewalks were such a prominent feature in this little mining town as well as in the recollections of its former residents, it is interesting to note that

FIG. 60. The cement sidewalk, installed by the R&P Coal Company in the 1930s, is one of the few vestiges remaining from the era of the company town. The former company store is in the distance.

the walks did not extend throughout the town. Rather, it appears that sidewalks were constructed only in the lower town, not in Helvetia's "ethnic" uptown. According to Lloyd Gray,

> The company put sidewalks down this lower row [First Street], from out here at the road out across here, and people built brick sidewalks, or laid cement. My dad had cement sidewalks we put in. And up on Main Street, they had it run from the company store clean to the [Bethel Union] church. On the Main Street up here. Uptown, they didn't put any, the company didn't put no sidewalks on. . . . The company put this one in, down near the road out to the ball ground, and up to this last house out here, then up round Main Street [Sept. 11, 1995].

Since the sidewalks were installed in the 1930s, according to most testimony, this suggests that the company felt there was no need for cement sidewalks uptown, but only in the lower portion where management lived. Certainly this is evidence of the preferential treatment accorded to management by the corporation. We might also see this as an example of the prejudicial treatment of

Helvetia's eastern European immigrants by the coal company, but as discussed in an earlier chapter, the census data suggest that housing assignments for miners were determined more on the basis of availability or by lottery than on the basis of ethnicity.

The sidewalks invite a comparison, however, a look at the duality of meaning expressed and encoded within certain features of the corporate landscape. On the one hand, there are the paved cement sidewalks in the downtown, built mostly for the benefit of the company's managers and officials who lived closest to the mine. The company sidewalks stand in contrast to the multiple walk sequences and resurfacings that are evident in the backlot of no. 294/296. The formal, institutional appearance of the company sidewalks also contrasts vividly with the diverse materials used by the miners to construct their own walkways. It is interesting that there is evidence of some vegetative screening between the doublehouse and the sidewalk. While the corporation attempted to impose its sense of order and control over the streetscape and the exterior of the houses, when we step inside the miner's dwelling or out into the gardens, it is clear that the corporate landscape has disappeared and we find ourselves instead in a space that has been altered to suit the individual tastes, preferences, and needs of its occupants.

This multilocality, as it is termed by Rodman (1992), is also evident in some of the town's more prominent features and among several corporate institutions within Helvetia. The ballfield is a symbol of corporate ideology. The company-sponsored baseball team that played on it has been described as an instrument of social and economic control, used by corporations in a variety of industries to exert a subtle, yet powerful, influence over their employees. I would guess that some of the miners also recognized this aspect of control in Helvetia's baseball team—certainly there were many objections to the mandatory "contributions" taken out of each miner's pay. Rookie Brown was well aware of the duality of purpose and the underlying ideology of the ball team. It was here at the ballfield that Brown realized he had to leave the mines soon or stay there the rest of his life. But it was here that Brown also turned this form of institutional control on its head, using his abilities as a ballplayer to get a job loading coal for the company and to do something he enjoyed so very much—playing ball. Many former residents also remembered with pride those miners who parlayed their time with the R&P League into a spot in the majors.

The baseball team was undeniably popular throughout Helvetia, and this was true in most mining towns. Entire communities were drawn out of their homes to share in the hopes and disappointments of their players. But the miners—and their children—played baseball because they enjoyed it, whether on teams sponsored by the coal company or on teams made up on the spot between uptown and downtown—not because the company desired complacent workers and residents. And they continued to play ball after the R&P League collapsed in the mid-1930s. Again, it raises the question of whether a dominant ideology, masked or overt, can be imposed unilaterally upon a subordinate group, or whether there are in fact multiple meanings contained within the landscape—evidence of discourse and competing interests within the larger industrial landscape. It may be argued that worker identity and agency are as strongly present as corporate ideology in the baseball diamond and in the wooden bleachers alongside.

Indeed, the ballfield became a social gathering place within Helvetia, a place where lines between ethnic groups blurred, a place where family, friends, and fellow residents came to express their support for the players and to express their individual preferences for this leisure activity, but also to interact with other members of the community. This was also true at the company store, an equally prominent feature in the corporate landscape. This institution of social and economic control became a daily gathering place for residents. Members of the community met within its doors or out on the front steps to exchange greetings or share the latest news, and to gossip; in short, the company store became a place where the many social networks in town intersected, allowing residents to maintain those networks on the very doorstep of the corporation. Granted, there were many other meeting places in town, differentiated on the basis of age, sex, and ethnicity, yet the company store was a very blatant symbol of corporate power, the ballfield only slightly less obvious.

Helvetia's Honor Roll of war veterans also exhibits this duality of place and meaning (Figure 61). The Honor Roll is and was a powerful symbol for the town's

FIG. 61. The Helvetia Honor Roll lists the names of former residents who served their country in World War II. The memorial presently stands adjacent to Bethel Union Church.

residents, its meaning derived primarily from associations unrelated to the coal company. The memorial nonetheless carries some level of corporate meaning, not only because members of the R&P corporate family left the company town to serve their country, but also because the memorial was located for many years on company property next to the doctor's office. In recent years, its location has been the subject of dispute among the town's remaining residents, in part because of the memorial's continued symbolism. Today, however, it is also representative of a struggle over land-use rights in the post-company era. These disjunctions suggest that the negotiation of identity and place is still ongoing within the former company town.

LANDSCAPE AND IDENTITY

A final area remains to be explored in the realm of landscape. As noted at the beginning of this chapter, the landscape of the company town expressed multiple relationships between the R&P and town residents. Having looked at the physical expression of the relationship between landlord and tenant, and that of a paternal authority and its family members, we must now consider that of a propertied corporation and landless individuals and how that relationship was expressed in the landscape of the company town.

Landscape is in part a socially constructed phenomenon. People without claims of ownership to a piece of land may still establish a sense of identity and place within a community. One anthropologist has argued that landless individuals may be individuals without place, but "use rights, nevertheless, are a modicum of power" (see Rodman 1992:650). Helvetia's residents had no rights of ownership, but they claimed "a right of use" to land held by the corporation, a claim that aided in the construction of a sense of place in this company town. A discourse of negotiation over the worker's place in the industrial landscape is evidenced by the many alterations and additions to houses the miners did not own, by the cultivation of gardens in the backlots they used but did not possess, by the mental appropriation of company institutions and features within the corporate landscape through use and through an alteration of meaning, and by the active, physical appropriation of company lands "by claim of right."

The latter is demonstrated by the many oral accounts of families who began to plant their gardens on land that was separate from the backlots, on lands across the alleys and on the peripheries of the town. It is also demonstrated by the actions of some of Helvetia's earliest residents, many of whom let their livestock roam freely through the town and left them to graze on lands owned by the company. By exercising this claim, Helvetia's mining families entered into a dialogue with the company over land use, identity, and place.

Not all of Helvetia's residents were able to develop a sense of place within this company town or within the industrial landscape. This was undoubtedly a factor in the development of a mobile workforce, as discussed earlier. There are some who stayed but failed to adjust to the parameters of life in a company town, as evidenced by several tragic accounts of suicides within Helvetia. But again, by looking at the census data and other documentary sources, we can see that many of Helvetia's families stayed for years, even generations, suggesting that they were successful in altering their living environment to suit their own preferences and needs. The construction of landscape, identity, and place within Helvetia was not based on a discourse of resistance. Rather, it speaks of an ongoing dialogue between employer and employee, between landlord and tenant, involving the active construction of a living environment.

CHAPTER 9

NEGOTIATING PLACE: SOCIAL DISCOURSE IN A COMPANY TOWN

In his assessment of the impact of the industrial revolution on people and places in eighteenth- and nineteenth-century England, Barrie Trinder reminds us that industrial landscapes "comprehend much more than machines and buildings" (1987:3). This simple statement eloquently expresses the underlying thesis of the present study. The history of the laborer and his or her family must be an essential component of the study of industrialization; such study should encompass the impact of working-class behavior upon the industrial process and upon social relations within the workplace but should also comprehend the impact of their actions and choices upon the industrial landscape, from the isolated company town to the urban working-class neighborhood. This study provides an example of how scholars may refocus on workers and begin to address issues of working-class culture and identity and, most important, worker agency within the industrial landscape.

In this volume, an alternative view to social and economic relations within the industrial landscape has been presented—one that highlights the positive and agentive role of the working classes in shaping the course of their daily lives. The crux of this study has been to explore the ways that mine workers and their families constructed their individual identities and their sense of place within the controlled environment of the coal company town. The evidence presented here indicates that residents of Helvetia actively and creatively shaped the physical and cultural landscape of the company town as they successfully sought to alter or modify for their own needs the industrial regimen established by the Rochester and Pittsburgh Coal Company.

The dynamic of industrial relations has been examined carefully within the setting of this company town in order to address issues of working-class behavior. Through the lens of material culture and landscape, it is evident that residents were actively engaged in a series of relationships with the coal company and with other members of the community. Helvetia's mining families entered into and maintained a dialogue with officials of the Rochester and Pittsburgh Coal Company over the creation of a living environment within company housing and over the use of space within the backlot of the doublehouse and the town at large. The evidence is found in contemporary written sources, in the oral narratives of former residents and employees, and in the archaeological evidence from the miners' doublehouse.

This interaction is best described as a dialectic. The corporation established the structure of its industrial community. The miners entered into a dialogue with the Rochester and Pittsburgh Coal Company over its institutions, its regulations, and its paternalistic practices. Some actions by Helvetia's mining families centered on the incorporation of different aspects of traditional lifeways and working-class culture into the corporate landscape. Other actions involved the alteration or appropriation of physical space. In many instances, the actions of the miners evoked new responses from the R&P. This dialogue was continuous and ongoing, though its form may have varied over time and according to gender roles, age, ethnicity, and cultural background. The negotiation of place also occurred at the level of the community, through the construction and maintenance of social and economic networks, the retention of ethnic identity and cultural practice, the use of space and material culture, and the appropriation of cultural space and meaning.

It is important to recognize that the miner's ability to influence living conditions for himself and his family did not necessarily extend to the workplace. Tonnage rates were not subject to negotiation except in the context of organized protest and labor strikes. For many years, Helvetia's miners banded together to demand an increase in wages and to complain of abuses by the company. Few issues were permanently resolved before the union was recognized by the R&P in the 1930s. But as noted earlier, it seems that economic conditions—depressed markets or increased demand for coal—were often more influential than the efforts of the miners in extracting concessions from the coal company. Similarly, there was no recourse against termination and blacklisting during the company's earliest days. And as often there was little to be done about safety conditions in the mine without the power of the union, except for a few measures the miner might take on his own—working with a partner he knew and trusted, sounding the roof, learning to read the warning signs within the darkened rooms of the mine. Yet personal acts of resistance are evident—from the clay pipe used to heat coffee at the face to carloads of dirty coal—as well as negotiation with the foreman, for example, over pay for dead work. There were also many employees who felt they could not adequately change working conditions within the mines and opted to leave. The most significant improvements underground were made through the miner's union, but this does not lessen or negate the importance of individual acts of negotiation and resistance.

Within the context of the company town, however, there is another side of industrial relations. Helvetia's mining families exerted considerable influence over living conditions within the doublehouse and in the backlots of those dwellings. Eviction was a threat, a constant source of worry in many communities, yet the miners and families of Helvetia seem to have mediated a stable existence within the company town; indeed, the relationship between the R&P and its residents may be described as symbiotic. Not every family pursued the same course or took the same actions in this ongoing dialogue. But the evidence indicates that from the town's earliest days its mining families developed strategies that helped them to adjust to or cope with certain aspects of the industrial regimen while enabling them to incorporate elements of traditional lifeways or individual needs and preferences into that regimen.

DISCOURSE IN THE INDUSTRIAL LANDSCAPE

As described in the preceding chapters, the actions taken by Helvetia's mining families to shape the physical and cultural landscape are visible in several contexts, defining the range of social and economic relationships established between Helvetia's families and the coal company, from inter-household and intra-household relations, to those of tenant and landlord, employer and employee, paternal head and corporate family, as well as propertied corporation and landless individual. Material culture and landscape were integral to this discourse, part of the miner's negotiation of identity and place, used to communicate meaning, construct identity, create and enforce social boundaries based on ethnicity and cultural practice, and negotiate between the competing interests of the company and its workers.

The evidence from Helvetia suggests that creation of a sense of place leads to stability within such communities. Generations of the same families stayed in Helvetia, many occupying the same doublehouse for decades (Figure 62). Fathers and grandfathers, brothers and sons all walked to the mine entrance and rode the mantrip into the darkness over a succession of years. It is interesting to contrast these findings with Allyson Brook's (1995) concept of anticipated social mobility in western mining communities, which she linked to violence, social and economic disruption, and a corresponding lack of social and economic stability. Was it the miner's active role in shaping the living environment of the company town of Helvetia that gave stability to this community's members? It may be argued that in many cases the answer is yes. A closer look at the spectrum of social and economic relationships between the company and its tenants and among the residents of the town reveals that the process of negotiation was thoroughly and deeply woven into the fabric of daily life.

FIG. 62. *Left,* a wedding-day portrait of Stephen and Margaret Chollock in the side yard of no. 25, July 19, 1941. *Right,* Ann Sokloski, Margaret's sister and matron of honor, Frank Sokloski, her husband, and their daughter, Marian, behind no. 27 (Joseph and Ann Chollocks' home). Margaret and Ann were third-generation Helvetia residents. Ron Chollock (Stephen and Margaret's son) purchased the former company store from the salvage company and is one of Helvetia's last private landowners. Photographs courtesy of Gary Chollock.

Household

The household was the center of the miner's existence, and it is the context in which we see the most evidence of worker agency. It began with the composition of the household itself, which varied in accordance with the needs of the families. The census data reveal that while many of the town's residents lived in simple family households, approximately one-third of Helvetia's households contained extended family members and/or boarders. Many families welcomed boarders because they provided an additional source of income. Wright (1981:196) has stated that "economic pressures meant that between one quarter and one half of all working-class households, in cities and in company towns, included boarders or lodgers." Clearly there were economic benefits to this arrangement, from the generation of additional household income to the pooling of labor and resources among kin. But there were social benefits as well, and often the two went hand-in-hand. Family and kin were important for getting a job in the mines, particularly during hard times, and for learning the tools of the trade through apprenticeship. Many of Helvetia's households also contained unmarried relatives and immigrants newly arrived from the same native village. The household served as an entryway into industrial society for many newcomers.

SOCIAL DISCOURSE IN A COMPANY TOWN

Lamphere notes that strategies for income production and for the allocation of labor within some working-class households at times reflected cultural values (for instance, in certain ethnic groups women were expected not to work without a male chaperone), but in other instances these strategies were dictated by the manpower needs of local industries and the "exigencies of the labor market" (1987:30–31). Thus, in some areas, local industries might depend exclusively on heavy physical labor and would rely upon the male population to build their workforce, while other industries, less physically demanding in their requirements, encouraged the employment of women. This is particularly evident in the textile mills and in the shoe and garment industries (Blewett 1988; 1990; Hareven 1982; Lamphere 1987). Many industrialists were quick to take advantage of the large population of unemployed women and young girls in Pennsylvania's mining communities. In the anthracite region, silk mills were erected near the mines so that employers could draw upon the large pool of unmarried girls who were available to perform wage work (Miller and Sharpless 1985:193, 199).

In Helvetia, household economic strategies differed on the basis of gender and age. Young boys were typically sent to the mines with their fathers as soon as they were of age. Until the 1930s–1940s, it was expected that sons would follow their fathers and brothers into the mine, and families counted upon both the careful supervision that these boys would receive under a relative and on the additional income they brought home. The coal company offered only a few paid positions to women, as clerical workers in the office or as clerks in the company store. Thus, women would look for or make their own opportunities for wage work. Unmarried daughters looked outside the home for work as schoolteachers, domestic servants, and waitresses, or they took in work as laundresses and seamstresses. They also stayed home to help with childcare and domestic chores, which were demanding enough for a single family and even more so for an extended family or a houseful of boarders. Few, if any, married women worked outside the house.

Instead, women invested much of their time and effort in constructing a support network for their husbands and their families. The primary response to the inadequacies of the miner's wages was to take in boarders to provide additional income. Women also took on responsibilities in the gardens that were so necessary to family subsistence. While certain tasks such as the selection of plants, the enrichment of the soil, and the cultivation of the beds may have been allocated on the basis of gender or age, food preservation was primarily the responsibility of the miner's wife, who was known for canning "anything she could get her hands on." There is no evidence to date that Helvetia's families sold their extra garden produce, or perhaps butter or eggs, as documented in other mining communities, though the possibility exists.

The oral histories suggest, however, that the most important contribution these women made to the household economy was through the careful budgeting and expenditure of family income, through their efforts to stretch or supplement those wages sufficiently to put food on the table every day and to keep a roof over their heads. These contributions were not insignificant, for the efforts of these miners' wives enabled many families to survive the slowdowns and work stoppages at the mine, as well as the months-long labor strikes that occurred with increasing frequency in the 1920s but historically extended back to the earliest days of the mine's operation. The miner's wife gave some stability to the household, and her efforts often kept the family from slipping into poverty and even destitution in times of trouble. As one report has noted, "poverty and the threat of poverty existed daily, slowly chipping away at a family's fragile security" (AIHP 1992:52), so while few were able to save for emergencies, miners' wives pursued a diverse set of strategies that were essential to their family's economic well-being, allowing many to avoid what would otherwise have been a very tenuous, even marginal existence.

Carol Giesen (1995) has written extensively on the importance of family and social networks for coping with the emotional stress and anxieties associated with the hazards of the mining industry and the constant threat of injury, disability, death, and loss of income. The miner's existence was fraught with economic hardship: strikes, work stoppages, mine closings, termination, injury, and death meant the loss of wages upon which the family depended for its survival. The role of the miner's wife encompassed any number of duties: picking up the burdens and responsibilities of the household, sometimes earning extra income for the family when her husband was unemployed, adjusting the family's schedule around the husband's when he was on shift work, keeping a clean house to show pride of appearance, and loyalty and support for the miner. Though Giesen interviewed the wives of present-day coal miners in West Virginia, the anxieties they described and their responses to these daily challenges would be the same in any mining household, regardless of time or geographic location. Helvetia's wives were no different, and the responsibilities they shouldered provided the cement that held many families together.

It is at the level of the household, too, that we see the most significant changes to the physical environment of the miners' doublehouse, from additions, alterations, and the reconfiguration of space, to the construction of pipes to bring running water to the house and to drain the excess away. Families built summer kitchens or added on to the rear ell to increase their living area and to improve the inner workings of these important domestic spaces. They cut doors between the adjoining units when sharing a house with their kinsmen. They furnished their homes according to their individual preferences and economic means, using fabrics and rugs, wall coverings and window coverings, glassware and ceramic dishes, and other types of household goods to shape the living environment of the doublehouse. They added on porches, enclosed them, and covered them.

They constructed a network of walkways to provide structure to the many utilitarian spaces within the backlot for the convenience of those who used them. They found the materials they needed for these improvements from a variety of sources, combining new purchases with materials that were handmade, recycled, or scavenged from another location. And they created a landscape surrounding the doublehouse that reflected their cultural and ethnic background, and their own tastes and needs. They raised beds of vegetables and cultivated fruit trees for their subsistence, planted shrubs along the foundation, planted trees to screen the house from the road, and planted garden beds with flowers that could be cut to fill the house with their scent or to cover the grave site of a loved one. In each of these acts, Helvetia's mining families not only altered and improved their living environment but thereby constructed and expressed elements of a working-class identity to others in the community.

Kinship

The act of negotiation is also visible in the establishment of kinship networks in this mining community. Extended family members contributed to the support networks created by each household, through the pooling of economic resources and the sharing of labor associated with domestic chores and childcare. The presence of an adult who could not go into the mine—whether from age or disability—but could provide supervision or labor at home meant that another—one younger or more fit—might be freed to take his or her place among the household's wage earners.

Kinship networks also provided a link to the familiar. For newly arrived immigrant families, the presence of kinsmen in the same community contributed to the retention of cultural practices and the maintenance of social networks created long before these families came to Helvetia. The importance of chain migration was discussed briefly. The census records indicate that at least 10 percent of Helvetia's households incorporated members of their extended family—often brothers and sisters or parents who immigrated to this country in the footsteps of another.

Regardless of ethnic background, extended family networks provided a foothold for in-laws, stepchildren, half brothers, and half sisters. These networks were especially important to the women and children who suddenly found themselves without husband and father one day. With the core social group broken apart by the mine, kin groups provided a safety net for those who might otherwise face privation and marginalization without assistance.

Kin networks were often replicated in the industrial workplace. Despite the existence of an official company hierarchy, men often hired their relations or provided the connection that was needed to find employment within the mine. In families with more than one person working in the mine, kinsmen often worked together as partners, as much for their protection as from a mutual preference to work with someone they knew. For those unfamiliar with the language of mining, the presence of a family member often meant the difference between life and death.

Ethnic Groups

Helvetia's families were an ethnically diverse group from the mine's inception. For many in the community, the presence of other members of the same ethnic background meant that support networks were in place, that others were nearby who practiced the same customs and placed value on the same traditions and beliefs. The ethnic communities that constituted Helvetia's population were integral to the construction and maintenance of group identity. The data suggest that in the early years of the town, the company deliberately created a separation between Helvetia's eastern European immigrant families and those of American or British origin by placing the Protestant and Catholic churches at opposite ends of town. And, generally speaking, most eastern Europeans lived up town. But not all.

Housing assignments in the 1900–1920 census schedules show in fact that considerable mixing occurred downtown and to a lesser extent uptown. That mixing indicates a randomness in housing assignments that stemmed from the availability of units and most likely from the use of a lottery, suggesting that ethnicity was only one of several factors that may have affected the distribution of housing assignments. If residents perceived a separation between uptown and downtown, it is primarily because they constructed and maintained boundaries of their own that were based on language, custom, and religion and were maintained at least into the 1940s. The differences between Helvetia's many subgroups were given expression through the creation of fraternal organizations and benevolent societies, church groups, and for a period of time a separate schoolroom. Social mixing was for the most part limited to interactions at the company store, the schoolhouse, and the ballfield. Intermarriage between ethnic groups was not common before the 1940s either. The second and third generations of Helvetia's mining families, brought together at the schoolyard or at the ballfield, did not feel this separation as much as the adults, and it was this younger population that eventually brought these diverse communities together.

While the archaeological component of this study did not recover evidence of specific practices or materials related to the ethnic background of the tenants of no. 294/296, oral and documentary evidence indicates that cultural practices associated with each ethnic group—from celebrations and religious holidays to leisure activities and foodways—were incorporated into the industrial regimen within the company town. The data addressed in this study confirm the findings of other scholars with respect to the retention and resiliency of cultural traditions in an industrial society. The decision to emigrate or to enter into the industrial economy did not mean that these people were abandoning traditional rural lifeways. Bodnar has argued that immigration led to an intensification of traditional religious and cultural values, and that "many steadfastly rejected change" (1985:270; see also Gutman 1977). Oral histories from Helvetia are particularly clear on this point. Though the narrative of Veronica McKee suggests that the intersection of multiple cultures and ethnicities often created problems in identity for some individuals—a feeling that they were neither one nor the other—the traditional ethnic customs that were passed on to Mrs. McKee by her mother are still deeply rooted in her identity today.

Community

In a study of verbal and nonverbal forms of communication in colonial South Africa, Yvonne Brink (1992) brings into focus the role of material culture and landscape in social discourse. Brink has suggested that the act of visitation was akin to the reading of text in material form. A message was conveyed through architecture and the display of household furnishings. Social visits served a discursive role that permitted the reading, interpretation, and exchange of text and meaning (1992:135–145). Did the various types of social interaction that occurred within Helvetia involving both the company and the residents of this town play a similar role in the ordering of the industrial landscape and in community formation and definition?

For a number of years, the *DuBois Express* carried a column that reported on activities in each of the area's mining towns. These are wonderful documents that tell who had a birthday, who was visiting or had gone visiting, who had been promoted or had left the area, who was ill, who was convalescing, and what local meetings and social gatherings had occurred. Weddings, baptisms, and christenings were reported alongside the scores from the baseball games played by Helvetia's own team. Accounts of criminal activity in the town were a regular feature. A column published on December 2, 1892, noted that a prayer meeting had unfortunately been passed over by some in favor of a dance.

These documents, as well as the accounts of former residents, suggest that social interaction within the community was varied in its makeup and often representative of the different subgroups within Helvetia. These were distinguished on the basis of ethnicity, religion, age, and/or sex. The data further suggest that each such exchange or gathering had the effect of strengthening the ties, associations, and networks between families, neighbors, fellow residents, and fellow workers. While the miners' union was a key to organized protest and worker agitation, and notices and reports of many miners' meetings were carried by the *Express*, the union was rarely able to assist within the community for any length of time. Instead, there were many community-based associations and networks that provided social and economic support for Helvetia's residents. These groups, organized on the basis of a common ethnic background or shared religious faith, were prevalent in Pennsylvania's mining communities (AIHP 1992:54; R&PCC 1901g) and took the form of benevolent societies, fraternal organizations, religious organizations, and ladies' aid societies. But the community was also home to more informal alliances that were not described in the newspapers, though the emotional and material support they provided was just as significant. From gifts of food, childcare, and the sharing of resources, members of these networks reached out with assistance when family life was disrupted by illness, injury, or death, providing a safety net for those in need.

In each exchange reported in the newspaper or remembered in the oral narrative of a former resident, we see the process of group formation and definition as well as the construction and maintenance of worker and community identity within the corporate landscape. Oral accounts indicate, for instance, that the women of the community would all go down to the company store around 2:30 each afternoon to buy food for supper and to socialize with friends. In an example of the appropriation and co-option of space and meaning, the company store became a daily gathering place for the families, a center of community activity, the daily context for the formation and maintenance of networks and alliances within the community. Though the company store was a symbol of economic exploitation, it also carried positive associations for residents in the context of these social gatherings. Other corporate-sponsored activities, such as the gardening competitions and the baseball team, provided important settings for social discourse in this town despite their association with corporate ideology. The frequency with which these sites are mentioned in contemporary documents and in oral histories suggests that these locales had a meaning for Helvetia's residents that was separate from their corporate/industrial meaning.

Return for a moment to the front porch of the doublehouse, a face turned outward to the community. What text or meaning is conveyed by social visits within this space? From the porch a visitor would be able to look out on a well-kept yard and perhaps see some flowers or shrubs in bloom. The company sidewalk might be visible, but would just as likely be obscured or overshadowed by trees the miner had planted alongside. The contrast between this formal, institutional walk and those built by the miner would be immediate and obvious to the visitor, and the latter would be recognizable as one of many improvements made by the occupants in the creation of a living environment surrounding this doublehouse. The choice of plantings and the care expended upon their cultivation would be recognizable not only as an expression of the occupant's personal preferences but also as an expression of identity. Behind the visitor perhaps the front door would be open to reveal the interior of the doublehouse with its many alterations and its furnishings that expressed the identity of its occupants. Maybe something would point to their ethnic background, something from the Old Country that transcended the facelessness and dehumanization of workers that was so common in the industrial landscape. The visitor, invited to sit for a while on the porch and to perhaps take some refreshment, would see all these things and recognize in them an expression of identity and place that was separate from the ideology of the company town and the demands of its owners.

LANDSCAPE AND MEMORY

For William Brown, who never lived in Helvetia but worked in the mines over several years in the early 1930s, what was most memorable about this mining community was the congeniality of the town's residents and the well-kept appearance of the town and its many gardens. Oral histories from Helvetia recall a time when social visits were exchanged on the front porch of the doublehouse. Whether you were a close friend, a coworker, or a visitor to town, people would invite you up for refreshment and to set a spell on the porch. The mine was viewed as a separate experience from the town; Brown saw his job in the mine as one to be left as soon as possible. Thomas Crop remembered Helvetia as a nice place to grow up in the 1920s and 1930s. The cement sidewalks, a rarity in coal towns, were ideal for kids with roller skates; other childhood activities were recalled with pleasure as well. As a child and later as a young adult, Tom did not feel the company's presence in the town was exploitative. The R&P was a good landlord, he said. There was no trouble here between the miners and the company. For Veronica McKee, whose personal experiences growing up in another western Pennsylvania coal town are often merged with her retelling of Helvetia's past, mining towns were for many years places of exploitation by the coal companies, places of conflict and confrontation, of social and ethnic barriers. These different views of Helvetia suggest rightly that social and economic structures changed over time within the company town.

What comes through clearly, however, whether we look at the documentary evidence, the oral narratives of former residents, the broken clay tobacco pipes from the yard of the doublehouse, or the brick and mortar used to build walks across the backlot, is that throughout the period of the coal company, Helvetia's families actively shaped the physical and cultural landscape of the doublehouse and the company town in order to influence their social and economic well-being. Granted, there are many examples of resistance, from minor infractions to severe violations of company policy to the efforts of organized labor. Yet to speak only of resistance is to present a one-sided and incomplete view of industrial relations.

The R&P's corporate presence is irrefutable, its power undeniable, yet there is also no doubt that the miners and their families were actively engaged in discourse with the company and were not merely the passive recipients of corporate ideology. The actions taken by Helvetia's mine workers and families to establish a sense of place and identity within this corporate landscape were woven into the fabric of daily life, through the use of material culture and the physical alteration of space and meaning, and through the incorporation of various aspects of traditional lifeways and working-class identity into the industrial regimen of the company town. It was, in fact, in the living of their daily lives—the celebration of religious and ethnic holidays, weddings and baptisms, the cultivation of their gardens, the preparation of traditional foods, the furnishing of their houses, and the landscaping of the backlot—that Helvetia's families negotiated their entry and continued place within the industrial landscape. The evidence may be found, if we look closely, in the miners' doublehouse.

Appendix A
Select Papers of the Rochester
and Pittsburgh Coal Company

Lucius W. Robinson, August 14, 1916, to Adrian Iselin Jr.

Dear Sir:-

I have your letter of the 10th inst. and have attended to the matters in connection with the church at Helvetia, which ought to straighten everything out in good shape and give them a fresh start.

I note your idea that we should make our mining towns the most attractive of any in the country and no doubt it is a most desirable thing to do and ought to some extent at least attract the better class of men. We have the same desire and ambition but have been handicapped to some extent at least by not having any surplus funds available to do what might be done along this line. There is no doubt but what many improvements could be made, and where the expenditure would not be relatively large in taking in all our mining towns and carrying out what we have in mind we would like to do, at the same time it would run into a considerable amount. We have the last year and this had a considerable force of men on constantly painting up our towns and I hope conditions will warrant our following this up with other features of beautifying at different places, perhaps furnishing some amusement halls and encouraging their bands, which we find does a good deal of good, and this might be followed by certain efforts and offering of prizes for the most attractive looking yards, etc., although before much can be done along this line it would be desirable whenever we find we can afford to do it to consider something in the way of laying walks perhaps some little piece here and there and building fences for gardens, furnishing amusement halls for the young people and many things we have in mind if we had the money available for the purpose. We will go over this matter, however, further and would be glad to carry it out along any line you may desire to meet your views in the matter.

I note your acknowledgment of my letter of the 9th inst. in answer to your letters of the 1st and 4th and shall be very glad to give you any further information along the same line, and hope to have an opportunity in the near future to further discuss such matters. I trust you are having an enjoyable trip and if the weather is such as we have here it will be a very agreeable change.

Very truly yours, Lucius W. Robinson, President

[R&PCC 1916e]

Lucius W. Robinson, August 24, 1916, to Adrian Iselin Jr.

Dear Sir:-

Further concerning character of our mining towns and answering your letter of Aug. 21st, I will say that our new mining towns so far as character of houses is concerned are certainly at least equal to the best in the country and superior to the average. Our old mining towns, built years ago, are certainly far from what they should be, but at the time built were about the standard usually recognized as the proper thing to do. There is very wisely a growing tendency, not only in mining towns, but in connection with all industrial affairs, to furnish labor employed better accommodations. This has grown out of the desire on the part of employers to do all possible for their workers, and somewhat of a necessity also to attract the most desirable labor.

This year we have improved all the houses in all our Indiana County towns. We have had all of last year and now have and will have all of this year a large force of painters in charge of a general foreman engaged in this work, and we have spent considerable in this improvement.

The most practical thing to do do [sic] as I view it is, as we have funds available, to furnish each mining town an amusement hall which can be used for entertainments, and cater as well to the amusement and recreation of the women and children. Our idea of these amusement halls is a place where they can have a respectable dance, hold church entertainments, have moving picture features and be used in the winter for basket ball and band practice, etc., and in this connection encourage the bands in different towns, furnishing a band stand, contribute what is necessary to the bands and ask them in return to give frequent concerts during the year. In the meantime we propose to offer prizes for the best kept up yards and house surroundings, and in the spring the same feature for the best gardens and yards and surroundings.

We can at least make some improvements along the above lines and where it will cost considerable, even going this far, we have no doubt it is a good thing to do from all stand points. For instance, I instructed Mr. Fritchman when last in Indiana to start at Luciusboro mine which is rather isolated and impossible to get out of the town without great inconvenience, that we proceed at once to provide an amusement hall which would be available for the coming winter, and I would like very much to follow this up every where, especially in our newer towns. We have some places where possibly being near some of the larger towns where the people can get in for amusement, it may not be necessary or policy to make any great investment along these lines. We can, however, see that our towns are kept well cleaned up and do something substantial in the way of amusement. I deem it quite as necessary to look after the interest of the families in that I find the men appreciate this even more than for their own special amusement. As to whether large bath houses would be successful or not, it is an open question. I find at some operations where this has been tried out and expected to be a great feature, they have not been successful. Others report that they have done considerable good. We may decide to try out this also in addition to what I have mentioned above.

We have had all these matters in mind for some time but things have not been very favorable for carrying out such plans and we will have to do such work as we can spend the money. Of course, some of our companies, having surplus and available funds, can move along these lines without any embarrassment.

I will take this matter up further with you from time to time and report what we think can be accomplished along practical lines. Where we have done less than some people in the way of amusement and furnishing amusement features, the character of our towns built the last year years [sic] has certainly been strictly up to date.

Very truly yours, Lucius W. Robinson, President
[R&PCC 1916f]

Memorandum from Lucius W. Robinson, September 7, 1916, to F. N. Fritchman, General Manager; Mr. James Craig, Superintendent; Mr. I. J. Harvey, Division Superintendent; Mr. F. Pardee, Assistant General Manager; Mr. L. W. Robinson Jr., General Manager.

Gentlemen:-

As we have been discussing informally for some time past the question of improvements to our mining towns, making them as strictly up to date as possible, improving to the greatest extent possible their general appearance and features of convenience and also the question of furnishing some kind of amusement and attraction at our towns for the men, women and children, I will say that I want this matter very carefully considered between now and next spring that we may have definite, concise plans formulated that at all points we may feel that this work is going along proper lines; and I take it up now and invite all concerned to express their views of what seems to be best for your particular surroundings. In order to get the matter started we will outline briefly what conclusions we have come to so far as the matter is thought out.

Our miners' houses in Indiana County for the past two years have been very thoroughly repaired where needing same and all thoroughly painted with two coats. This in itself has greatly improved the appearance of these towns which along this line has been pretty easy of accomplishment in that the houses are of more modern construction than in the old region, very much better buildings and easier kept in perfect condition. Where we have not done this work, I want recommendations as to what buildings you [illegible] which are worthy of embellishment in the way of painting. Of course, we have some very old towns and some very old low [illegible] buildings which probably it would not be policy to spend any money on. You can recommend, however, such as you deem best.

Commencing next spring in the way of further embellishment my idea would be to offer prizes in our different mining towns for the best kept yards and gardens, offering a small cash prize at each place and possibly the further inducement of those who have specially good gardens and kept their premises in best condition to be furnished with a good garden fence.

At points where we have bands I would suggest that a band stand be erected and the band encouraged to give semi-weekly concerts. In connection with this band stand I would call to your attention one that has recently been built at Yatesboro at a cost of $300, which combines some very desirable features.

Next for summer amusement I would suggest that where you have a grove or some shady spot at or near our mining towns we put in a few inexpensive facilities for children play ground. This has been very successfully worked in some of the cities and would be we think very much appreciated by the women and children. In this connection I will say that our theory is that we should keep in mind in preparing summer and winter amusements the welfare of both the women and children as well as the men, and I think you will find they will be greatly appreciated by our workers as they will want to work at places where they have schools, churches and some amusements for their families and they will be more contented as workmen if their families are thus provided for in some way at least.

Now so far as winter amusements are concerned, we have found that where we have permitted nickelodeons to be built by some outside party, that they have furnished amusement and attraction that has been rather successful, and we would approve of any reliable party putting up nickelodeon halls in any of our mining towns, giving them ground rent free and making such contract as we have with those existing.

Now as to swimming pools or bath houses, I would advise you that investigation of this matter shows there have been as many failures as successes. Where the question of swimming pool has been agitated and recommended in some of our mining towns, I would not approve of this for on thinking it over carefully it will occur to you that a swimming pool is very expensive and unless properly run is a most unsanitary proposition. You are no doubt aware that in cities where they have swimming pools no one is permitted to use them until they have gone through a most thorough bath outside of the swimming pool before using same, and it would hardly be practicable to furnish the facilities for properly operating in a sanitary satisfactory way swimming pools in our mining towns. It is barely possible that shower baths would be the preliminary step in any event to a swimming pool and might in some cases be worth considering, and I would be glad to have any recommendation along this line.

Now as to winter amusement it would seem to us that the most practicable thing that could be done at all points would be to furnish some kind of amusement hall where church festivals, roller skating, band practice and any kind of social entertainment might be held; perhaps in some cases putting in a basement mainly above ground that would serve as a winter play ground for small children.

These suggestions are simply intended to roughly outline the matter and to have each of you give this careful consideration between now and spring, realizing, of course, that we have got to go pretty slowly in the entire matter and find out by experiment what is most satisfactory and how far we should go.

There is another matter which could be probably in some of our mining towns progressed with excellent results and that is the setting out of Lombardy Poplars which are very rapid growers and which would soon make a considerable showing planted with in the yards or along the streets. They are very cheap and the expense would not be large for setting out a considerable number of these in many of our mining towns.

Very truly yours, _____ President"

[R&PCC 1916g]

Lucius W. Robinson, August 21, 1902, to George L. Eaton, Secretary.

Dear Sir:-

I write you now to advise you the prospects are very poor for getting anywhere near our normal tonnage next week, August 25th. to 30th. and probably for a few days thereafter. I wish you would advise Mr. Yates of this so he will understand it and also post Mr. Merchant as he states he can save some money on the railroad by knowing it ahead. My main objective is to let you arrange so what coal we do load can go where needed worst, as it will be a badly broken up week at best. We have the State Firemens Convention commencing Monday for two or three days and the annual Punxsy. Fair commencing Tuesday and lasting the balance of the week. Tuesday is big day with the firemen when they have hose races, a parade and other attractions too great for the average miner to miss, and Thursday is big day at the Fair, so that these two days, with the usual extra allowance for recovery, will break up our week badly, especially so far as the mines at this end are concerned. Then this will be followed up by Labor day Monday the 1st. which is always a big holiday with the miners and on which day we do not expect to do anything at any of the mines. It will take us a couple of days to recover from that, so that if, during this period we are able to get our coke drawn and ovens charged every day we will be doing well. This is a tough proposition to meet and rather a blue forecast, but the fact of the matter is, and all our Supts. so advise, and I know it is true, that our men are working very indifferently, coming out at all hours of the day and are not at all ambitious to work either six days per week nor very many hours of the days they do work, since they can make a living on shorter time. These conditions are in nowise peculiar to our employees but apply throughout all the mining regions. I do not know just how badly we will be affected but know that the cut in our tonnage will be serious after Monday of next week for at least a week thereafter.

Very truly yours, Lucius W. Robinson, President

[R&PCC 1902h]

Appendix B
Using Oral Histories
from Helvetia

Although oral history has been an accepted component of historical archaeological investigations for many years (Adams 1976; Brown 1978; Schuyler 1978), its use has been limited. Most investigators, given the opportunity to collect and work with oral testimony, have tended to focus their inquiries on what their informants can tell them about specific features of a site. Yet oral history is more. It is ethnography, folk history, ideology. Studies by Yentsch (1988), Yamin and Bridges (1996), and Purser (1992), who integrated oral histories and traditions into their interpretations of past peoples, opened the doors for new avenues of historical archaeological inquiry, and there are now several excellent studies that draw upon these unique resources. Indeed, oral sources have become an inextricable and often dramatic part of many archaeologists' reconstructions and interpretations, whether historical ethnography, ethnohistory, or historical archaeology.[1]

Oral history has been used as a component of several archaeological studies of industrial landscapes and communities (Beaudry and Mrozowski 1987a; Costello 1998; Wood 2002). Brashler's use of oral history (1991) to explore gender relations in the logging camps of West Virginia is a fine example of what may be done in this regard. Here the oral evidence is incorporated into a study of the different stages of development within the logging industry, along with the archaeological evidence of shanty camps, mill towns, and company-owned family camps. Margaret Wood's recent study of women's labor in the coal camp of Berwind, Colorado, is also an excellent example of how oral, historical, and archaeological sources may be woven together to examine gender roles and ethnicity among mining families (2002).

When we look at the sum total of archaeological studies that use oral sources, however, we can see that the application of this valuable resource has been uneven at best. Only rarely are oral data truly integrated with the process of archaeological inquiry and interpretation. The use of oral history was critical to the study described in the present volume. Given the uneven tenor of past studies as well as the uneasiness many archaeologists feel toward oral sources, and by way of explication for those who are intrigued by its use in this study, I include here a brief summary of oral history methods and the specifics of this inquiry.

WHAT IS ORAL HISTORY?

What is oral history, or oral documentation? The term "oral history" has variously been defined as the process of collecting and preserving oral accounts or narratives by "interviewing living historical informants to record the remembered past for posterity" (Sitton, Mehaffy, and David 1983:152) and as "primary source material obtained by recording the spoken words—generally by means of planned, tape-recorded interviews—of persons deemed to harbor hitherto unavailable information worth preserving" (Starr 1996:40).[2] Many oral historians argue persuasively that oral history is as much a process for the collection of historical data as it is a study of human perceptions. Ron Grele, for example, has written that oral history may elucidate "the ways in which memory and historical construction guided the ways in which people made their histories and lived in history" (Grele 1996:67).

To prepare for this component of the study, I undertook a review of the literature on oral documentation, comparing research techniques and theoretical differences among anthropologists, folklorists, historians, and oral historians. I began with basic texts for oral history practitioners, such as Baum (1987); Sitton, Mehaffy, and Davis (1983); Davis, Back, and Maclean (1977); and Yow (1994). Carl Oblinger's booklet, *Interviewing the People of Pennsylvania: A Conceptual Guide to Oral History* (1990), was especially helpful in creating a general framework of questions and research topics that are appropriate for working-class communities, and for this mining town in particular. I then turned to several volumes that focus on theoretical issues associated with the practice of oral documentation—for instance, the relationship between interviewer and narrator—and with the process of interpreting oral narratives (Allen and Montell 1981; Dunaway and Baum 1984, 1996; Grele 1985; Henige 1982; Thompson 1978; Vansina 1985; Yow 1994).

THE PRACTICE OF ORAL HISTORY

There is much overlap among the various disciplines that record and interpret oral narratives, be they interviews with public figures or private citizens, collections of folksongs and poems, oral traditions, or local legends. While many oral historians and historians conduct interviews to preserve information about previously neglected groups or minorities—ethnic groups, women, or the working classes, for instance—or poorly documented periods of history, anthropologists will use many of the same techniques to construct ethnographies of both contemporary and historical peoples, analyzing oral traditions and narratives for what they reveal about social structure, cultural practice, cultural meaning, and worldview in the past and the present (Glassie 1982; Purser 1992; Schmidt 1990; Vansina 1985; Yentsch 1988). Oral history has been shaped greatly by the cross-disciplinary exchange of theory and method over the last two decades. Many practitioners and interpreters of oral history have been influenced by the post-modernist movement, for example, and have broadened the dialogue within this field to address issues of subjectivity, oral history as performance, oral history as text, and other topics that are familiar to archaeologists and anthropologists alike (Dunaway 1996; Dunaway and Baum 1984, 1996; Frisch 1990).

The importance of critical analysis to the process of interpreting oral sources has been highlighted by these debates. Scholars in this field (Allen and Montell 1981; Friedlander 1996; Henige 1982; Hoffman 1996; Moss 1996) have answered challenges regarding memory: its fallibility, the tendency to embellish, indeed, the inherent subjectivity of oral histories and the selectivity of human memory. For many historians who are uncomfortable with the use of oral history, it is often a question of authority and reliability, a reluctance to use oral sources that stems from an inherent bias toward the "objectivity" of written sources. Glassie's ethno-graphy of the people of Ballymenone in Northern Ireland (1982), which he wove out of a multiplicity of sources—material culture, landscape, oral tradition, and oral history, as well as written materials—serves as a critique of traditional his-toriography. This work challenges "professional historians [who] feel the land, its fields, houses, and buried broken crockery, cannot serve truly as documents. [To them,] artifacts, even spoken texts, are suspect. Only the written word is mean-ingful and useful" (1982:603). Because of this, Glassie argues, "the historian's story retains its dreary elitist bias, since few of the past's people wrote and most of them were tied to an upper-class minority" (1982:603). The same bias against oral sources is often to be found among archaeologists who are cautious about relying upon materials that may be purposively ideological in their origin.[3] Yet oral histories, conducted with the appropriate methods and subjected to verifi-cation, are in no way less reliable than supposedly "objective" written documents. Both sources have the potential to mislead without critical review.

For practitioners of oral history, there are internal and external tests that may be used to validate the content and reliability of oral narratives, steps that have become part of a standardized procedure for processing interviews and other oral accounts (e.g., Allen and Montell 1981:67–76). Reliability has been defined as

> the consistency with which an individual will tell the same story about the same events on a number of different occasions. Validity refers to the degree of con-formity between the reports of the event and the event itself as recorded by other primary resource material such as documents, photographs, diaries, and letters [Hoffman 1996:89].

The oral historian working with several related narratives, for example, will examine their content for consistency and logic. He or she will also analyze the source of the account—whether it comes from personal experience or is based on secondhand or even thirdhand accounts—and ask what biases are involved in the recounting of these narratives, because, as Peter Friedlander notes, "the structure of memory is related to the structure of perception, and the latter is itself rooted in culture, education, and experience" (1996:155). External tests involve the verification of accounts using written, material, or physical evidence.

A determination of validity and reliability is important, but narratives that are not strictly "factual" can also be revealing when their content is analyzed for their underlying meaning. Interpreters must ask why there are discrepancies or inconsistencies within the narratives and then seek to determine the meaning and significance of those disjunctions. As noted by a number of scholars, oral history is a social document, a dialogue about the past in the ethnographic present, that reveals perceptions, traditions, and beliefs about the past (Grele 1985, 1996; Purser 1992:26; Vansina 1985:94–123; Yentsch 1988). As Allen and Montell have observed, too, a primary organizing principle of oral narratives—whether tacit or acknowledged, whether embodied in visual imagery or hidden within the narrative—is emotion (1981:26). The emotional associations of the informant will guide the flow of the narrative. Brought to the surface, these associations may reveal much about how people think about the past and why. Oral history, then, is as much an exercise in verification as it is learning how people create their own versions of the past and determining the meaning of those constructions.

How do we penetrate the layers of meaning within oral narratives in order to get to the underlying truth? How do we sort out what is perceptual from what is actual, and what meanings are contained within? Deconstruction of the narrative is called for. The analyst may begin by breaking the interview or narrative down into its component parts. Allen and Montell (1981:25–40, 71–83) have written extensively on this subject, detailing the characteristics of oral sources that appear again and again, regardless of geographic origin or time period. Embellishment is perhaps the most common tendency of all narrators, and many accounts contain "floating narrative embellishments"—that is, folklore themes or dramatic elements, often described as motifs, that are repeatedly transferred from one narrative to the next. Strip these elements away and the narrative may reveal a factual, verifiable reference to a historical event or person at its core.

Many oral sources show a disregard for standard chronology. This characteristic often appears in the form of telescoping as the narrator collapses, compresses, or extends time as he or she establishes his or her own relationship with that time, event, or person (Allen and Montell 1981:26–29, 80; Henige 1982:98–101). In her study of house histories, Yentsch (1988) found that oral traditions associated with houses often projected individuals into direct association with their ancestors or created cultural connections to certain ideological beliefs, and that this process often led to the displacement of other individuals or entire families from local memory.

Visual imagery also serves as a key to understanding meanings that are submerged within oral narratives. An orange, remembered as a precious gift at Christmas by a miner's daughter, and a clay tobacco pipe, used illicitly in an underground mine, are images that carry with them deep emotional associations that may reveal perceptions about modern-day welfare and minimum wage levels, for instance, as much as they convey working-class attitudes regarding the power of corporations over their daily lives (Metheny 1992, 1998).

ORAL HISTORIES FROM HELVETIA

As a "facilitator of the process of memory" (Sitton, Mehaffy, and Davis 1983:21), the oral history interviewer has the potential to guide the structure of the encounter, to focus questions upon activities, events, or people most relevant to the study, and to then look closely at the underlying meaning contained within those accounts. Therefore, the present project makes limited use of existing oral history collections, but instead focuses extensively on a series of interviews conducted between 1991 and 1995 with former residents of Helvetia and with former employees of Helvetia Mine. By conducting an oral history component as part of this study, I was able to set up the structure of each interview in advance, prepare a general framework of questions, guide the narrators toward a discussion of events or people associated with the particular research problems addressed by this project, and then return to items I wished to discuss further. As the collection of oral histories is an interactive process—"a shared authority," in the words of Michael Frisch (1990)—it is not surprising that I found the flow of each narrative often led in directions I had not anticipated, just as the narrators, responding to my questions, often answered in a manner I did not expect. Yet as a participant in this process, I was able to redirect the conversation if needed or pursue that avenue of inquiry further.

A good interviewer, be she anthropologist, historian, or layman, will also ask what constraints she brings to the process as interviewer and interpreter. Purser's recounting of her association with an oral history project in Paradise Valley, Nevada, and her own odyssey—the stages by which she learned as a collector of oral histories to listen and interpret—is highly informative (1992). In asking myself these questions, I recognize that the oral history component for this project has been constrained by several factors, including time, travel distances, the interview format, and the lack of formal training for conducting oral history interviews. The latter, for example, is evident in some of the earliest interviews I collected. I can point to mistakes that I made (technical problems with the tape recorder or the setup, for example, or questions I should have asked or wish now that I had asked), but I believe that these faults were largely compensated for or corrected in subsequent interviews and, of course, by the experience I gained with each interview.

More significant, perhaps, is the type of interview format selected for this project. Because I wished to elicit information about and perceptions of land-use practices, the role of the company, and the responses of workers and residents to corporate policy, I chose to use directed interviews of approximately one hour in length, subject to follow-up questions and/or multiple interviews with the narrator. For this reason, the interviews that I collected do not provide a complete spectrum on daily life in this company town. They are not life narratives. The decision to use directed interviews over life narratives means some topics—child-rearing practices, for instance, or the experience of going to school and church within the company town—and some time periods—employment histories following the closing of the mine, for example—were not addressed by this project. Given the relative abundance of oral history collections related to Pennsylvania's coal miners, however, there was no need to duplicate those sources, and every reason to pursue directed questions that might elicit information specific to the research questions addressed in this project.[4] All of these resources provide contextual material for the Helvetia study, yet my particular interest was in the landscape and its role in the negotiation of place, and I had questions specific to this community that could not be answered using existing collections. It was with these concerns in mind that I determined to conduct interviews directly with Helvetia's former residents and began research into the practice and critical analysis of oral histories.

The scope of what I hoped to achieve also narrowed as the study evolved, largely as a result of time constraints and travel distances. I was not able to collect narratives from as broad a sample of Helvetia's residents as I would have liked. I was unable to interview any descendants of eastern European immigrants, with exception of an individual who moved to the town after its sale by the company. In addition, the selection of informants was by necessity heavily influenced by the current proximity of former residents to the town site. As it turns out, this sample represents a fairly narrow cross-section of Helvetia's population. They are primarily descendants of American, Scottish, or English families who lived in Helvetia's downtown. Another bias occurs because all but two of these individuals grew up in Helvetia in the 1920s–1930s and they did not become heads of household in Helvetia until the end of the company's tenure was near. These people have, I believe, a perspective on life in the company town that differs considerably from that of its earlier residents. A further consideration, resulting from the demographic background and the age of my informants, is that at present I have, for example, no firsthand accounts of the daily experiences of women residing in this company town prior to the introduction of labor-saving devices or the introduction of running water to company housing. Many of the narratives do contain secondhand accounts and experiences, however. They describe events or people as related to these individuals by family members or acquaintances, or convey their perceptions of the experiences of others. Recognizing the limitations of the materials I was able to collect in no way diminishes their value, and, as clearly shown, the narratives are an integral part of this study.

The oral history component of this study began with two formal interviews conducted in 1991 and 1992 with William N. Brown of DuBois, a former employee of the R&P Coal Company from 1931–1933 and one of Helvetia's many non-resident miners. These oral history interviews were undertaken in conjunction with a graduate seminar project. A series of informal interviews with former residents was then conducted in 1994 in preparation for writing a dissertation proposal. As part of my dissertation research, I conducted in-depth oral history interviews with these and other individuals. Formal interviews took place in 1994 and 1995. Interview data sheets were prepared to record biographical and genealogical information. All interviews were taped and have been transcribed for archival purposes following the recommendations of Baum (1987), Allen and Montell (1981), and others. Release forms were prepared and signed. The transcripts have been published in a separate volume (Metheny 2002).

As noted, the formal interviews were structured to address specific research questions. Each interview began with a list of questions to ascertain a basic chronology (dates of birth, dates of residence or employment in Helvetia, employment history) and a family history for each individual. The interview continued with a discussion of the physical appearance of the town and questions about the homes in which these informants once lived. Houses and landscape features often serve as mnemonic devices (Rodman 1992; Yentsch 1988, 1996), and it was my hope that by having these informants describe, for instance, what a person would see as they entered the town from its western end, certain features would recall additional memories, revealing emotional associations with particular elements in the landscape of the company town. Once the interview process was well established, my intent was to begin with narrowly focused questions about the miner's houselot and to then work outward from there to explore the community at large.

Thus my interviews often began with specific questions about the household. What did they eat? What were their responsibilities within the household economy? How did the family get along on a miner's wages? Questions were asked about land-use practices, beginning with family gardens and the maintenance of yards and houses by miners' families, then moving outward to discuss company regulations regarding sanitation and the upkeep of corporate-owned property. In an effort to reconstruct interactions within the community, informants were asked about social and economic activities outside of the workplace. Where did members of the community gather socially? With whom did they interact? What was the nature and role of social networks or alliances in the community? Were these based on family, culture, ethnicity, or economics? What role did cultural traditions play, if any, among Helvetia's diverse ethnic groups as they worked to create a sense of place within the industrial landscape? Finally, informants were asked for their views about the coal company, about corporate rules and regulations and the impact of such rules on their lives, and their perceptions of—or reactions to—the R&P's corporate regimen.

Again, questions were directed so as to reveal associations and meanings within the landscape of the company town (e.g., the ballfield, the Honor Roll, the company store) and to elicit individual perceptions of company policy as well as responses in the workplace and at home that could be set against the written and archaeological evidence. Interviews were analyzed, then, for those associations and what they might reveal about the past. As seen in the text of this volume, the interviews not only revealed emotions and tensions stemming from the hardships and tragedies experienced by many individuals and families (whether or not these things happened as a direct result of their employment by the R&P or from their residence in the company town), but also from conflict with the coal company and from conflict, as yet unresolved, over the custody of Helvetia's past in the present.

These formal interviews were supplemented by dozens of informal conversations at the site or over the phone. Notes were made of these talks and meetings when possible and were kept as part of the record for this project or were noted in a daily journal kept during the excavation (Metheny 1995). Other forms of orally communicated data were reviewed. The latter included anecdotes, personal recollections, or narratives in the form of poetry or song, for example—orally communicated data that have been preserved in written form through the publication of newspaper articles, local histories, family histories, or reunion materials, and may represent firsthand accounts or accounts that have been transmitted over several generations. Many of the materials reviewed in this study are associated with a particular landmark or person from Helvetia; others speak to the relationship between the company and the miners.

As stated earlier, these sources must be read critically, for when viewed as a collection, it is easy to see how certain stories, repeated through the years, were translated into "fact"; having taken on a voice of authority, these "facts" were subsequently reproduced in a variety of media (often the same authors are involved). This is most evident in recent newspaper articles and in materials assembled for the Helvetia reunion. The source of information is most often one of the town's former residents, several of whom are well versed in local tradition about the mine, the company, and the town. It is interesting to note that in response to a letter I sent to a local historical society inquiring about tax records, I received, much to my surprise, a brief summary of Helvetia's history based on the researcher's conversations with a former resident and with Veronica McKee, my own informant. The information was presented as factual, yet was based on secondary sources without any cross-checks of primary materials, and much of it was erroneous. This incident serves as a cautionary tale of its own. As Allen and Montell note, narrators are likely to have "well-developed repertoires of firsthand accounts dealing with significant events in their lives. Such stories are usually highly polished from many retellings" (1981:48). Such was the case with several of my own informants, though follow-up interviews and external tests bear out much of what they related. The narratives are in general quite reliable. Yet my experience with the historical society, which I had assumed would be the purveyor of factual material, highlights the need for caution even when working with "objective" sources such as newspaper accounts and local experts.

All oral sources reviewed for this project, whether interviews or orally documented materials of another type, were therefore evaluated for their reliability and accuracy through a series of internal and external tests, described previously. The source of each account was determined where possible. Follow-up interviews with three of the six primary informants for this project show that interview data were consistent over time. The data collected from these interviews or from other oral sources were compared against data from primary written sources (chapters 3–4) and the archaeological evidence recovered during excavations in 1995 (chapters 6–8). Discrepancies were analyzed for their significance and are discussed more fully in these chapters.

I found this interactive approach to be ideally suited for the Helvetia project. The oral narratives complement, enhance, and at times challenge the archaeological and documentary evidence of life in this community. Oral histories from the workplace and the backlot place working-class families at the forefront of study and allow us to construct an alternate view of industrial relations in the company town. It is through such an approach that the stories of these ordinary people, the miners and families of Helvetia, may best be told.

NOTES

INTRODUCTION

1. See Hunt (1989) and Frisch and Walkowitz (1983) for a discussion of more recent trends among historians, especially the movement toward a "new cultural history" and a "new social history." Frisch and Walkowitz note particularly the importance of Marxist historians E. P. Thompson and Eric Hobsbawm and labor historians Herbert G. Gutman, David Brody, and David Montgomery to a new social history of the working classes (1983:ix–xi, xvii, n. 2–3). The *Annales* school, particularly the work of Fernand Braudel, also has contributed to this shift (Hunt 1989). The influence of this approach is evident in a number of community studies and close examinations of family, race, class, gender, and working-class culture (Blewett 1988; Corbin 1981; Hareven 1982; Hareven and Langenbach 1978; Lewis 1987; Trotter 1990; Walkowitz 1978).

2. Originally organized as the Rochester and Pittsburgh Coal and Iron Company in 1881, the company was reincorporated in 1927 as the Rochester and Pittsburgh Coal Company (Cooper 1982:10, 90). In this study I have used the latter designation or, simply, the R&P.

3. An interesting contrast is found in Paul Mullins's examination of potters in nineteenth-century Rockingham County, Virginia. Mullins argues, in opposition to other Marxist models, that in the transition to industrial capitalism in this part of rural Virginia, some potters used "decorative preferences, functional variation, and production strategies [to] negotiate social change" (1996:152). These potters chose to retain elements of the earlier nonindustrial craft, including traditional styles of vessel decoration and labor structures organized around established social networks (including kin-based networks), while selectively introducing some of the newer technologies into their workshops. These choices are seen as an exercise of agency by the potters as a means of negotiating their entry into the industrial landscape.

4. The authors note that they are building on the ideas of E. P. Thompson (1978), who saw the need for studies of class "from the bottom up," and Henry Glassie (1982), who urged a contextual approach to the study of human behavior from "the inside out," particularly for those who have previously been left out of our histories (Beaudry, Cook, and Mrozowski 1991:156).

5. Alison Bell (1994) has observed that responses to industrialization varied by class as well as by sex: while working-class women and children often worked outside the home, whether as part of an economic strategy or in response to conditions of industrial production, middle-class women were strident in their opposition to the use of female and child manual labor, arguing its immorality while injecting an ideology of separate spheres into reformist programs.

6. When this project was first undertaken, there were no archaeological studies of coal company towns that specifically addressed the issue of worker agency (Balicki, O'Brien, and Yamin 1999; Gradwohl and Osborn 1984; Warfel 1993). A more recent endeavor, the Colorado Coalfield War Archaeology Project (CCWAP), promises to contribute much to this discussion, however. In this project, researchers are undertaking testing and excavations at the site of the twentieth-century company town of Berwind and at the site of the Ludlow tent colony. The latter site was occupied by striking miners in 1913–1914 and was the scene of the infamous 1914 Ludlow Massacre. The team has set as one of its goals an examination of the role of worker agency in effecting changes to living conditions in the Southern Colorado coalfields (CCWAP 2000, 2002; Wood 2002).

7. Bell's study of female laborers in England (1994) indicates that working-class identity was at odds with a middle-class ideology as well. Not only did working-class families with multiple wage earners have little use for the middle-class ideology of the separation of spheres, but the sexual division of labor among the working classes differed considerably. Bell documents many examples of women performing the jobs of men in certain professions, something anathema to a middle-class identity. Working-class behavior and preferences also clashed with those of the middle class. Bell notes that working-class women were often seen smoking tobacco pipes, drinking after-hours, and socializing with men in public establishments. A contemporary complained that they "often enter the beer shops, call for their pints, and smoke their pipes like men" (Bell 1994:8).

1. CORPORATE PATERNALISM AND THE COMPANY TOWN

1. This figure was compiled by the Bureau of Labor Statistics in 1930 (Crawford 1995:2; Magnusson 1917).

2. See Miller and Sharpless (1985) for an interesting discussion of the mutual growth of transportation concerns and the anthracite industry in Pennsylvania.

3. Crawford also argues that in traditional Marxist interpretations, the design of the company town is seen only as a "one-dimensional" response to economic forces, with the focus on capital with a capital "C" (1995:5). She calls for the contextualization of studies of company towns, noting variation in form and in the historical, social, and economic context of their construction.

4. This conceptualization is helpful in considering emergent forms of paternalism, but, as stated, Scranton's model does not account for changes in the ideology of corporate paternalism once an industrial economy was fully established, nor does it treat the importance of this ideology in sustaining industrial modes of production in the late nineteenth and early twentieth centuries.

5. The concept of a paternal authority also developed under the influence of evangelical Christianity (Crawford 1995; Wallace 1972). Many owners and managers felt it was their Christian responsibility to ensure the physical and moral welfare of their workers, and their

brand of paternalism was shaped accordingly. Wallace discusses the effects of evangelical or Christian capitalism at length in his study of Rockdale, an early-nineteenth-century industrial community in Pennsylvania (1972).

6. Samuel Slater's correspondence shows that he often referred to his younger operatives as "my Children" (Prude 1983:45).

7. Candee has also argued the need to distinguish between independent, single-enterprise Waltham-style mills and the interlocking multicorporation mill complexes of Lowell (1992:113).

8. There are numerous examples of armed conflict and repression within company towns during this period. Among the most infamous are the conflicts at Lattimer, Pennsylvania, in 1897 (Miller and Sharpless 1985:214–239); Homestead, Pennsylvania (1892), site of Andrew Carnegie's vast steel works (though Homestead had no company-owned worker housing, it was nonetheless a company town in the broadest sense of the term) (Demarest 1992; Serrin 1993); Virden, Illinois, in 1898; and Rock Springs, Wyoming, the site of ethnic rioting in 1885 (Gardner and Flores 1989:46–50). In the latter instance, company officials failed to protect Chinese miners and their families from rioting by white miners. The riot resulted in the destruction of the homes of the Chinese miners and the loss of more than two dozen lives. All of the aforementioned towns, with the exception of Homestead, were coal company towns. The rise of model towns in the late nineteenth and early twentieth centuries did not entirely displace the closed company town, and conditions remained harsh and oppressive in some regions and industries. See, for example, the coal camps operated by the Colorado Fuel and Iron Company and, in particular, Ludlow, Colorado, site of the Ludlow Massacre in 1914 (CCWAP 2000, 2002; Crawford 1995:81; Roth 1992:179).

9. While it was common to house railroad laborers and loggers in boxcar bunkhouses that were moved from site to site, in many company towns that were more or less permanently located, immigrant laborers and ethnic minorities were often made to live in shelters built from railroad boxcars (Roth 1992:176; Turner 1982:33; cf. Gardner and Flores 1989:170). There are also examples of workers who, during the depression years, eked out an existence living inside of abandoned coke ovens (AIHP 1992:52).

10. If one reviewed the history of conflict in company towns, there would be little change to this list of worker responses, except in the frequency with which each type of response was used. Indeed, some of these behaviors—strikes, walkouts, absenteeism, transience—still characterize worker responses in our own time. The more extreme acts of murder, such as swept the anthracite fields during the time of the Molly Maguires (Kenny 1998; Miller and Sharpless 1985:136–170), are rare today, although there have been exceptions—the disappearance of teamster boss Jimmy Hoffa, for example.

2. BUILDING THE COAL COMPANY TOWN

1. To a lesser extent, the standardized houses built for ironworkers on early iron plantations such as Hopewell Village, Pennsylvania, may have influenced the form of worker housing (Gordon and Malone 1994:83–84; Mulrooney 1989:10–11). Mulrooney also speculates that the two-story semidetached, gable-end dwelling so characteristic of miners' dwellings in Pennsylvania was modeled after the masonry row houses built for Welsh miners in the 1830s and 1840s; these in turn are, she believes, reminiscent of British urban house forms of the period (Mulrooney 1989:126, 141 n. 2, 142 n. 3).

2. See also Harvey (1969:74–88, 103) for a description of mining communities in Mary-land. Here the company towns had a reputation for being cleaner and better built than their counterparts in Pennsylvania, primarily because companies were not the exclusive holders of real estate in these settlements and did not exercise the same feudalistic authority over workers as was practiced in the closed company towns of Pennsylvania. A large percentage of miners' housing in Maryland, although company built, was owned by private individuals, particularly after the Civil War when companies began to sell off extra land and worker housing (Balicki, O'Brien, and Yamin 1999). Miners could not only own property but could build their own houses in these communities as well. The State of Maryland also outlawed the company store in 1868, a decision that helped to loosen the control of mining interests in the state.

3. Mulrooney (1989:142 n. 4) feels that this term describes vertical plank construction, a common method used to build miners' dwellings in Pennsylvania, Maryland, and West Virginia. House frames were, according to a period account, sheathed with "undressed planks set up vertically with weather strips covering the cracks between the boards" (1989:131).

4. The basis for Mulrooney's study was a 1987 survey of industrial sites in two southwestern Pennsylvania counties conducted by the Historic American Buildings Survey (HABS) and the Historic American Engineering Record (HAER) under the auspices of the America's Industrial Heritage Project (AIHP). A second survey, conducted in 1987 by the Pennsylvania Historical and Museum Commission (PHMC), provided a broader understanding of the region, examining industrial sites in nine counties: Bedford, Blair, Cambria, Fayette, Fulton, Hunting-don, Indiana, Somerset, and Westmoreland.

Though not part of the AIHP or PHMC studies, Clearfield County, in which Helvetia is located, is also part of Pennsylvania's main bituminous coalfield. Geographically, Clearfield County lies directly east of Indiana County and north of Cambria County. Approximately one-third of the county comprises part of the eastern edge of the main field, while the remain-ing two-thirds contains semibituminous or "smokeless" coal (DiCiccio 1996:9–13). In terms of a "mining culture" (Mulrooney 1989:27) and miners' housing, there is no distinguishable difference between the AIHP study area and any part of central or western Pennsylvania.

5. The typical anthracite miners' house did differ in one important respect. The main block of the two-and-one-half-story structure with its attached rear ell provided families with an average of five and one-half rooms, according to Mulrooney, versus a four-room plan in the main block of the bituminous miners' house (Mulrooney 1989:14).

6. Many of Pennsylvania's coal mines were "captive" mines in that they were owned and operated by steelmakers, railroad companies, and other industries to supply the needs of their owners (DiCiccio 1996:102).

7. Maryland's company towns also diverged in form and function from their counterparts in eastern Pennsylvania as the coal companies sold off both their extra lands and their existing housing stock after the Civil War and as company controls were weakened within the state.

8. The economic structure of the anthracite industry was such that small, independent operators dominated the lower field where the coal was most difficult and most costly to access and extract, while larger corporations dominated the upper field. As a consequence, the mines were capitalized at grossly divergent levels, affecting both the quality and consis-tency of worker housing as well as working conditions in the mines and the degree of corpo-rate or owner control. The changing composition of the workforce and the increased flow of

immigrant labor after 1840 were also significant. The treatment of workers was a reflection of social currents and the ethnic prejudices of the operators, as well as a response to labor unrest. Finally, the geology of the anthracite region required deep mining, creating difficult and hazardous working conditions (Kelly 1998:47–49; see also Miller and Sharpless 1985, chapters 4–5; Wallace 1988).

9. There is an interesting study of unionization in West Virginia by Corbin (1981), in which he discusses the development of a working-class consciousness among West Virginia's miners. Though historically the most oppressed and brutally treated workers in this industry, these coal miners resisted unionization for decades. Corbin argues that most worker responses occurred outside of the union because the interests of the state's miners were not the same as those of the union until the 1920s.

3. IN THE COAL FIELDS OF WESTERN PENNSYLVANIA

1. These documents are found in a collection of official correspondence and company ledgers that has been archived in the Special Collections at Stapleton Library, the Indiana University of Pennsylvania (IUP) in Indiana, Pennsylvania.

2. The railroad was organized in 1881 as the Rochester and Pittsburgh Railroad Company. As was common with such ventures, however, the company was not successful financially, and the railroad went into receivership in 1885. The railway and all of its stock in the R&P C&I Company were purchased by Adrian Iselin, a New York City banker and one of the original investors in both the railway and the coal company. Iselin consolidated all of his rail interests in 1887 and renamed the entire network the Buffalo, Rochester, and Pittsburgh Railway (Cooper 1982:23–24). The BR&P severed all direct ties with the coal company in 1906 after railroads were prohibited from transporting goods in which they held an interest (Cooper 1982:78).

3. A letter to A. G. Yates, dated June 2, 1890, suggests that Iselin notified the R&P of his intent to open the mine only after he had purchased sufficient lands to make the venture a success, but he assured them that, as a large stockholder of the BR&P, he would do nothing to injure the R&P (Rochester and Pittsburgh Coal Company [R&PCC] 1890a).

4. Of particular interest are several references to the town and plant in the Brady Township tax records (1891:39–40; 1892:50–52; 1895:46–47) and in the R&P archives (R&PCC 1890–1893:8, 38, 145; 1891; 1894b). For references to the coking operation at Helvetia, see Brady Township 1895:46–47; 1898:97–98; 1916:112–113; R&PCC 1892a, 1892b, 1895a, 1895b.

5. The R&P's largest coking operations were at Walston, which had nearly 1,000 ovens. Walston was famous for having the longest continuous row of coke ovens in the world, reportedly one and one-quarter miles in length. The company stopped building new ovens at Walston in 1904 (Cooper 1982:19–20, 48).

6. For a breakdown of these improvements, see Brady Township 1891:39–40, 1892:50–52, 1893:39–41, 1894:47–48, 1895:46–47, 1896:42–43; R&PCC 1890–93:8, 25, 55, 84, 1892c, 1892d, 1895c, 1898a, 1898b, 1901a, 1901b, 1901c; *DuBois Express,* Sept. 2, 1892, p. 8, Dec. 2, 1892, p. 8.

7. Based on the newspaper account of Iselin's visit to Helvetia and his correspondence concerning the construction of the mine and the new town, it seems likely that the original

company store was located across the valley from the town site, nearer to the entrance to the mine. This is also suggested in several oral history interviews conducted for this project (Thomas Crop, July 29, 1994; Lloyd Gray, Sept. 11, 1995).

8. The town was also served by at least one privately owned boardinghouse, known as Smith's Boardinghouse, and a hotel. The former may have been located at Stanley or in Leis' Town on the eastern fringes of Helvetia (*DuBois Express*, Feb. 9, 1894). The hotel, given the improbable name of the Hotel Eldorado, was operating in Leis' Town by 1892 (*DuBois Express*, Sept. 23, 1892, p. 8). The Eldorado was quickly renamed the Exchange Hotel just a few years later by a new proprietor (*DuBois Express*, Reynoldsville edition, March 2, 1894). It was destroyed by fire in 1911.

9. Mules were used at Helvetia for nearly 40 years, long after the mine was electrified. Iselin's letters indicate his desire, if not his intent, to have Helvetia motorized from the onset of production (R&PCC 1890c, 1890d), and the tax rolls indicate that many parts of the mining operation were motorized by 1900, including a haulage system. The same tax rolls show, however, that the company maintained a stable of up to four dozen mules until 1927 (Brady Township 1892–1927; R&PCC 1901d). It is likely that the company continued to rely upon mules to bring the cars to the main track or perhaps to haul the cars in areas of the mine where the build-up of gas made it too dangerous to use an electric haulage system (David Kuchta, e-mail, Jan. 26, 2001; see also DiCiccio 1996:119).

10. R&P company records do not indicate that the housing supply for employees and officials of Helvetia Mine ever exceeded the 62 double-block house and 10 single-family houses built by Iselin (134 units) by more than one or two buildings. In a letter to Adrian Iselin Jr. concerning the need for repairs at Helvetia, L. W. Robinson stated unequivocally that there were 73 houses in the town (R&PCC 1916a). Presumably the figure printed in the newspaper in 1892 represented an overall estimate of both housing units and nondomestic structures built or planned by the owners. The 1947 plan of Helvetia, recorded for the conveyance of the town to the Kovalchicks, shows 60 extant double-block houses and 11 extant single houses (131 units), with indications that one single house and one doublehouse were no longer standing (134 units). A company blueprint indicates that four of the single houses on the Kovalchick plat (nos. 258, 260, 262, and 264) were constructed by the R&P in 1923 for officials at the power plant and for the mine foreman. It is not clear, however, whether these were built as replacements or as new construction. The same document confirms that no. 258, the mine foreman's house, burned down in 1939 (R&PCC 1923).

11. See entries from the *DuBois Express*, Reynoldsville edition, May 15, 1896, p. 7, Sept. 9, 1898, p. 8, Feb. 22, 1899, p. 6; *DuBois Courier-Express*, Aug. 21, 1981; Kriner 1982:99; R&PCC 1916b, 1916c, 1916d.

12. In a letter to Superintendent John McLeavy, Adrian Iselin Jr. wrote: "Dear Sir:- I have a telegram from Mr. Yates [then president of the R&P] saying that you decline the offer of Deputies and new men he made you. I have replied to him that I could not, or would not, interfere with your judgment in this matter, and wish to leave it entirely to you to do what you may think best in Mr. Iselin's interest, to have his mines started as soon as possible. My only instructions to you are that Mr. Iselin is willing to pay as high wages as anybody pays in competing regions. . . . As I wrote you a few days ago, it is, however, very unjust that Mr. Iselin's houses should continue to be occupied by men who refuse to work at what you consider fair and just wages, the same being 5 cents higher per ton than those paid at Horatio

and also, I am told, in the Cumberland [Maryland] region, both of which compete with our coal in the market" (R&PCC 1894d).

13. Local newspaper columns regularly featured news from Helvetia and its sister mining communities. In Helvetia, residents were attending concerts, revival meetings, socials, dances, and picnics as early as 1892 (*DuBois Express,* Sept. 9, 1892, p. 8).

14. Helvetia's baseball team was playing in the 1890s, and references to the town band date back to the early 1900s as well.

15. Interestingly, the figures from Helvetia show that its miners were largely divided on this vote, and, indeed, the returns show that many communities were strongly opposed to settlement: "Gentlemen:- The result of the vote for accepting the contract made by the officials of the U. M. W. of A. and the Operators, so far as we have the figures, was very largely in favor of accepting [a two-year agreement]—in fact of 4084 votes cast, there were only 1191 against, this among our own mines and those of part of the Clearfield Region. Most all of our mines voted in a very pronounced way for resumption. As an illustration at Ernest 251 for and 7 against; Lucerne 245 for and 4 against; Soldier Run 173 for and 73 against; Trout Run 117 and 7; Helvetia 136 and 97; Adrian 121 and 26; Florence 30 and 6; Jacksonville 102 and 4; Yatesboro No. 5 104 and 42; Yatesboro proper 291 and 14. The vote at Eleanora and Iselin was not as favorable, but still Eleanora carried by a slight majority of 4 and Iselin would certainly no doubt start if we wanted the men to go to work" (R&PCC 1914b).

16. One document written by Lucius W. Robinson while president of the R&P Coal Company mentioned that both "good houses" and "good shanties" were available to newly recruited laborers; he did not, however, specify which R&P towns had shanties (R&PCC 1902c). A second letter to Helvetia's superintendent requests a report on recent improvements to the mine and town, including the "building of houses, shanties, and coke ovens," but the wording as such does not confirm the presence of these structures in town (R&PCC 1900c). I have found no evidence to date—oral or historical—that shanties were built in Helvetia. It is also interesting to note again that in describing the improvements to be made to the town in 1916–1917, Robinson indicated that unlike many coal operators, the R&P viewed its company housing as a "paying investment" (R&PCC 1916g).

17. The courts of West Virginia ruled that the relationship between the company and the miner was one of master and servant (Corbin 1981:9–10). As in other communities, the company police force was empowered to evict families at any time of day or night. Families' furnishings were quite literally carried out of the house and set down in the street (Corbin 1981:10; Mayer 1989:81–83; Michrina 1993:25–26). During the notorious Paint Creek–Cabin Creek strike in West Virginia (1912–1916), company guards actually evicted a woman in labor (Corbin 1981:10).

4. WE LIVE IN THIS PLACE

1. The 1930 census was not available to researchers when this study was undertaken.

2. Employment records for individuals were available upon request through the main office of the Rochester and Pittsburgh Coal Company, but it is unclear whether these records were preserved following the R&P merger with Consol Energy in 1998.

3. Tax assessments were reviewed through 1932 and no additional listings by house number were found after 1898.

4. At present it is not possible to discern the logic by which the houses were numbered, nor the reason for the discrepancy.

5. Three of the 28 cows listed between 1892 and 1899 were recorded in more than one year, for a total of 25 cows owned by 25 (16 percent) of the 159 individuals identified as Helvetia residents in the rolls. Likewise, of the 45 dogs listed, 4 appear on 2 or more tax rolls, leaving us with 41 dogs owned by 38 different individuals (24 percent).

6. For a discussion of geographic mobility by West Virginia's coal miners, see Corbin (1981:40–43) and Shifflett (1991).

7. There are many recorded examples of mobility by Helvetia's miners; e.g., *DuBois Express*, June 10, 1892, p. 8, July 15, 1892, p. 8, Sept. 2, 1892, p. 8, Sept. 23, 1892, p. 8; *DuBois Express*, Reynoldsville edition, Sept. 23, 1898, p. 8.

8. Summertime was typically the slow season for coal production as the demand for heating fuel declined during the warm weather, yet a seasonal reduction in the number of workdays, though a hardship, did not necessarily mean unemployment and therefore would not account for such a large number of vacancies.

9. The Coal Commission reported that in 1922–1923 approximately 50 percent of all bituminous coal miners lived in company housing, though the rates varied regionally. Half of Pennsylvania's soft coal miners lived in company towns. By contrast, two-thirds to four-fifths of bituminous miners lived in company housing in the Appalachian coal fields. Some 90 percent of West Virginia's miners lived in company-owned housing. Illinois and Indiana had the smallest percentage (9 percent) of miners living in company towns (Hunt, Tryon, and Willits 1925:139–140; see also DiCiccio 1996:93–94).

10. Raymond Kriner stated, for instance, that his family rented a farm near Helvetia for some 10 years, during which time they mixed mining and farming (Raymond Kriner, March 10, 1994).

11. Industry-wide figures from 1922–1923 indicate that 40 percent of America's bituminous miners were foreign born. In Pennsylvania, however, that figure increased to more than 55 percent (Hunt, Tryon, and Willits 1925:136).

12. See Bodnar (1985) for an analysis of the various waves of immigration during this period.

13. Most black miners in western Pennsylvania were "imported" from the South as strike breakers (Lewis 1987:79–118).

14. Bodnar cites a return rate ranging from 25 percent to 60 percent, depending on place of origin (1985:269).

15. Only 10 percent of Polish, Magyar, and Slovak immigrants who came to the United States after 1880 had previous experience as miners in their native countries, compared with some 80 percent of Scottish immigrants (DiCiccio 1996:88).

16. This concession was reached as part of a settlement between the UMWA and coal operators. The settlement, called the Appalachian agreement, was signed on October 2, 1933 (Dix 1988:192).

17. This number actually rises to 15 percent of households in Helvetia (n=40) when complex households containing extended family members are included in the count.

18. The term, as used by Bodnar, differs somewhat from the definition of a corporate household as used by Beaudry and Mrozowski in their analysis of the boardinghouses at Lowell (1988:5). While both types of households are based primarily on coresidence (thereby permitting the inclusion of boarders or servants in the definition of the household), rather than on kinship or task sharing, augmented households in Helvetia were not at all similar to the corporate-controlled boardinghouses established in Lowell. Rather, miners' families often took in extra boarders to supplement their income. For this reason, the term "augmented" is preferred.

19. Again, the number of augmented households increases to nearly 19 percent of the total households in Helvetia (n=49) when complex households containing boarders or servants are included.

20. In 1885, Pennsylvania set the minimum employment age at 12 for work above ground, and 14 for work below ground. Those ages were raised, respectively, to 14 and 16 in 1903.

21. The 1900 census shows that at least one family sent their 12-year-old son to work for the R&P, while a second included a 13-year-old boy who was listed in the census as a mine worker.

22. In three of these households, members found employment outside of the company. Alexander Knyziwski worked as a tailor out of the home of his father-in-law. Sixteen-year old Joseph Hunter worked as a servant for a private family. He subsequently went to work as a miner for the R&P. Alexander Kortz was employed as a bookkeeper in an area tannery. Outside employment was rare, however.

23. It is not certain why these girls were named in the 1910 census in this manner, as there is no consistent relationship with this type of employment and the presence of boarders, nor is there any correlation with the use of this title and the girls' attendance or lack of attendance at school. The census is quite clear, however, that none were wage earners, despite the occupational title of servant.

5. ORAL HISTORIES FROM HELVETIA

1. For a discussion of oral history methods and the specifics of this inquiry, see Appendix B. The transcripts of these interviews are found in Metheny (2002).

2. Soot blowers were used to clear boiler tubes that "coked up" while burning coal.

3. Thomas Brown immigrated to the United States in 1862 at the age of 18 and worked as a coal miner until some time between 1900 and 1910. Thomas Pearson left England in 1871 when he was in his forties and was employed in the coal mines of Pennsylvania until retiring between 1900 and 1910 (Metheny n.d.). William's uncle Thomas was a coal miner with at least 17 years of experience when he was rehired by the R&P in 1931 (R&PCC 1931b). And William's father-in-law, David Millard, an immigrant from Nova Scotia, was a coal miner for many years. Despite the strong tradition of coal mining among his kin, however, William Brown did not pursue similar employment. One likely reason for this is that most of these men eventually left coal mining for the locomotive works in DuBois. Census records show that, with the exception of Rookie's uncle Thomas and his grandfather Thomas Pearson (who at age 70 still listed his employment as a coal miner), nearly every one of Brown's male relatives (including his future father-in-law) had taken up employment with the BR&P by 1920, well before William Brown began to look for work (Metheny n.d.).

4. All subsequent references in this chapter to Brown's narrative about Helvetia are taken from the November 16, 1991, interview unless otherwise indicated.

5. A country bank refers to a small underground mine, usually accessed by a drift mouth and generally owned by local farmers or small independent operators. Because of the mine's small size and the lack of capital investment, labor would have been performed completely by hand (DiCiccio 1996:18).

6. Thomas Brown's Personal Record Card contains no additional information. It is not known when he first worked at Helvetia, nor how long he continued to work there after being rehired in 1931 (R&PCC 1931b).

7. A certificate for first-aid training, issued by the U.S. Bureau of Mines, was found among Rookie's papers after his death in 1995.

8. Oral history interview, July 30, 1994.

9. Bituminous coal deposits in western Pennsylvania lie in flat beds close to the surface. A drift mouth, or straight corridor, dug into the hillside was a common method of entry into these deposits. The drift was driven slightly upward to allow groundwater to drain.

10. For the coal mining industry, the period between 1925 and 1933 was a poor one economically (Dix 1988:142). The demand for coal was low, production exceeded demand, there was increasing competition from oil and natural gas, and technical improvements in coal burning reduced the amount of coal needed to produce energy. The price of coal dropped in response to these outside market forces through the mid-1920s and 1930s. At the mines, wages were cut along with the number of days worked, or miners were simply laid off. Many companies simultaneously increased their efforts to modernize their operations. This also had a direct impact on the miner, as many hand loaders saw their earnings greatly reduced as a result of lower tonnage rates, while others were displaced from the mines altogether.

11. Oral history interview, July 30, 1994.

12. Pillars were pulled only when work in the room was complete.

13. Oral history interview, July 30, 1994.

14. The incident he described is most probably the explosion that occurred at Kramer Mine, April 21, 1936; nine men were killed, all company officials (Kriner 1992:173).

15. Oral history interview, July 30, 1994.

16. One of the most moving accounts is found in *Harlan Miners Speak* (Dreiser et al. [1932] 1970), a volume that assembles oral testimony along with the reports and writings of diverse members of a committee asked to investigate and report on the poor living conditions of the miners in Harlan County, Kentucky, the systematic violation of their constitutional rights, and acts of violence and terror carried out against them by coal operators in the early 1930s.

17. All subsequent references to Veronica McKee's narrative are drawn from the July 30, 1994, formal interview unless otherwise noted.

18. Again, the 1920 census lists the family of Daisy Haag as sharing a house with the Weber family. The enumerator listed the house number as no. 396, which does not correspond with the town's numbering system. Given the order of visitation, it is possible that the house number might be no. 296 or even no. 294, both of which are missing from the enumeration, but it clearly cannot be no. 292. The census shows another family residing in no. 292 in 1920.

19. All subsequent references in this chapter to the oral testimony of Thomas Crop are taken from the July 29, 1994, formal interview unless otherwise noted.

20. As the R&P did not establish any mining operations out of state until 1947 (Cooper 1982:103–105), I have no explanation for this piece of local lore.

21. The company never installed toilets for the miners (Bill Crop said he believed it was pressure from the union to install bathrooms that led the R&P to sell off its company towns), and the company did not provide running water for the doublehouses until the early 1930s. As to the quality of the water, Lloyd Gray said it was rusty at times, when there were leaks in the main line. Given the town's proximity to the mine, where sulfur, acids, and other toxic wastes were regularly discharged into the groundwater supply, the town's water was probably tainted to some degree.

22. No evidence of evictions has been found, though that does not mean they did not occur. But the narratives suggest that unlike Adrian Iselin, who threatened his employees with eviction during a dispute in 1894 (R&PCC 1894a, 1894c, 1894d), the R&P found it less desirable to evict the men and their families over labor and wage disputes. In a company document from 1914, L. W. Robinson wrote that the coal company had made "liberal deductions for house rent and other features due to [the] suspension" of work a week earlier (R&PCC 1914a).

23. The R&P's intransigence on indoor plumbing for the miners is typical of coal operators of the period, and by all accounts Helvetia's residents were much better treated than many mining families, in both the anthracite and bituminous fields. Coal companies just did not see the need to supply indoor plumbing for those at the bottom of the company hierarchy. Yet as Veronica McKee said to me while describing the beautiful mansion and gardens built for Lucius Robinson, the R&P's president, on Coal Hill just above Helvetia, "He could have put an indoor bathroom in every house in all these towns for what he paid for that, you know!"

24. A clipping of this article was sent to me by Tom Bukousky, without a date or page number, but the contents suggest the article was written after the start of the strip mining operation in Helvetia.

25. Informal interview, March 10, 1994.

26. Telephone interview, June 13, 2001.

27. A *quoit* is a flattish ring of metal (usually iron) that is tossed or pitched at a pin set in a clay-filled box. The quoit can weigh as much as 14 pounds and is pitched 18 to 21 yards to the pin, depending on which version of the game is being played. The game of quoits is most commonly associated with England, Wales, and Scotland. It was primarily played by agricultural and working-class people, particularly those in the mining industry.

28. This incident took place between 1937 and 1940 while the Craigs resided in Stanley. Mrs. Craig wrote that the payroll was normally delivered by train to Sykesville by the state police and then taken to Helvetia under escort with guards in the lead and rear cars. When this incident occurred, all seven men were armed, but none of the weapons was loaded. Thereafter, all the guards carried loaded weapons.

29. Informal telephone conversation, March 9, 1994.

30. None of the clippings was dated. One was cut from the *DuBois Express*, but the source for the other two clippings could not be identified.

31. Informal telephone interview, March 9, 1994.

32. Informal telephone interview, June 13, 2001.

6. How the Miner Lives

1. Oral accounts indicate that the house had collapsed well before plans were devised for a strip-mining operation. Archaeological and oral evidence confirm that the remains of no. 294/296 were burned during the clean-up of the town site (1989–1992). The foundation walls were sheared off at grade level and pushed into the cellar with a bulldozer, but damage to subsurface remains was confined to the rear of the structure. For these reasons, the back of the house and the cellar fill were not investigated. For a more detailed discussion of excavation methods, see Metheny (2002).

2. The report noted that similar evidence was found in Cumberland, Maryland (Cheek, Yamin, and Heck 1994), and the authors cited Katherine Harvey's research (1969) on western Maryland coal miners, which suggested that much of their disposable income was spent on expensive cuts of meat.

3. An analysis of the faunal collection was made by Dr. David B. Landon of the University of Massachusetts-Boston (2001). The report details taxonomic representation, including a minimum number of specimens and minimum number of individuals, identification of body parts, and presence of butchery marks, gnaw marks, and/or burning. For a complete list of faunal remains, see Metheny (2002).

4. By contrast, ceramic assemblages from late nineteenth-century Paterson and Lonaconing both show a predominance of undecorated ironstones (Balicki, O'Brien, and Yamin 1999:100; Yamin 1999:116). There is insufficient evidence from Helvetia for a meaningful comparison, but the assemblage suggests that the households in no. 294/296 may have owned more decorative wares than working-class families in these other communities. Though the deposits from Helvetia cannot be tightly dated, we do know that they are somewhat later in date (ca. 1892–1930) than those from Paterson and Lonaconing, and the variation that is evident in the ceramic assemblage may simply be a result of this temporal difference. Certainly the variety of wares and patterns advertised in mail-order catalogs from the 1890s and early 1900s suggests that such decorated dinnerware was preferred by many families over plain or relief molded ironstone or granitewares (Montgomery Ward & Co. [1895] 1969; Sears, Roebuck, and Co. [1897] 1983; [1900] 1970; [1902] 1969).

5. Comparable sets of dinnerware were advertised in a 1902 catalog at prices ranging from $4.95 for 100-piece sets of granitewares or semivitreous wares with molded rim decoration and $5.98 for semiporcelains to as much as $19.95 for refined porcelains and chinas from England or France (Sears, Roebuck, & Co. [1902] 1969). Thus, nearly all working-class families would have been able to afford a set of matching, decorated graniteware dishes, but the working-class family with more discretionary income might be able to purchase the more refined wares. Archaeologically, one would expect to see a range of patterns and styles that reflects the variation in living standards maintained by the working classes and perhaps varying levels of status within the working-class community.

7. THE MINERS' DOUBLEHOUSE

1. See Julia Costello's article (1998) on bread ovens built by Italian immigrants who traveled to California's mining region. Priscilla Wegars (1991) has also studied the stone ovens built by railroad workers, looking at the ethnic backgrounds of their builders and their users, the techniques of construction, and the date and distribution of such structures.

2. Samples of wallpaper and paint colors were collected from no. 262, the extant engineer's house, during the 1994 survey, but no samples were recovered archaeologically from no. 294/296 with the exception of some fragments of linoleum that, though heavily discolored, appear to have been white or white with narrow dark green stripes.

3. In addition to the company store, Helvetia's families could have used mail order catalogs for their purchases, though it is interesting to note that at least one such company, Sears, Roebuck, & Co., self-billed as "the cheapest supply house on earth," for many years only accepted orders with cash payments in advance. No installment plans were available, no credit was issued. This policy was mentioned with particular reference to inquiries about pianos, organs, and similar goods ([1902] 1969), suggesting that consumers who purchased such extras often had to save the entire sum up front rather than budget monthly payments. By contrast, the Montgomery Ward catalog from a few years earlier ([1895] 1969) stated that the company would accept cash-on-delivery orders or payment through an installment plan.

4. A similar problem arose in the R&P's company town of Adrian. In a letter to A. W. Calloway, Adrian's Superintendent, dated May 3, 1901, L. W. Robinson wrote: "Dear Sir:- I am glad to have your letter concerning the farm at Adrian. In driving by there recently, I noticed a large number of cows on it and several people tramping across it. I would suggest that you continue your efforts to keep up the fences, as you would have to do anyway in converting it into pasture lands, and then instead of trying to farm it or spend any more money on it, turn it all into pasture, charging whatever you can get for each cow, and arrange to keep a check on them and collect proper charges for the pasture. I anticipate it will be difficult to get collections from all, but you will have to devise some means to accomplish this, and if you find any one putting cows in without first making proper arrangements, charge them an excessive price until they make a proper contract. I believe we will get more out of this farm in this way than to farm it as we have been. It will not do to let the fences get down, as all cattle would run in then indiscriminately, and as we have so many houses close to it, I do not believe it would pay to farm it any longer. Very truly yours, Lucius W. Robinson, General Manager" (R&PCC 1901d).

APPENDIX B: USING ORAL HISTORIES FROM HELVETIA

1. The works of Spector (1993), Ryder (1988), Costello (1998), and Terrell (2000) are good examples of how ethnohistory and oral history are being used by the archaeologist as storyteller. See also Ogundiran (2000).

2. Oral history is generally distinguished from folk history or folk narratives by the informant's relationship to the events or people described. While oral histories most often record the firsthand experiences of individuals, folk narratives and traditions recount information, customs, or cultural practice that have been transmitted orally over one or more generations (Brunvand 1978). Often, however, there are elements of folklore present in an oral history interview in the form of local knowledge or family lore, for instance, and the source of these accounts must be teased out through the analytical process (Allen and Montell 1981:71–75,

157–160; Brunvand 1978:99–124; cf. Yentsch 1988; Yamin and Bridges 1996). Tales of ghosts who return to warn of impending disaster in the mine are an excellent example of this (Miller and Sharpless 1985:130–132; Long 1989).

3. I would include written sources here, as well, and note that this concern is most evident in the study of complex, state-controlled societies such as developed in Egypt or Mesoamerica, for example (cf. Vansina 1985:96–100, 103–106).

4. There are a surprising number of oral history collections documenting the experiences of coal miners in Pennsylvania, most of which are archival in nature; that is, the interviews were most often collected as life narratives, not to answer a particular research question (cf. Magda 1981; Oblinger 1990; Shopes 1993). Cultural surveys by the Federal Writers Project and the WPA gave impetus to the collection and preservation of oral histories in the state, thus a substantial amount of testimony on the daily lives of workers and their families has been collected, though many of the narratives are in raw, unanalyzed form or have been broken into disconnected topics (Bodnar 1983; Brestensky, Hovanec, and Skomra 1991; Oblinger 1984, 1990; cf. Michrina 1993). Many of the earliest collections document the harsh working and living conditions of the anthracite miner in eastern Pennsylvania (Bodnar 1983; Oblinger 1984; Roberts 1984), while several recent initiatives in the western part of the state have recorded the experiences of bituminous miners, many under the auspices of the America's Industrial Heritage Project (Brestensky, Hovanec, and Skomra 1991; DiCiccio 1996; Mulrooney 1989; see also Michrina 1993). Oral histories related to coal and coke production in southwestern Pennsylvania have been collected under the auspices of the AIHP's Folklife Division since the 1980s (Shopes 1993:435). Two of the six folklife documentation centers established under the AIHP serve as repositories for materials and oral interviews concerning Pennsylvania's bituminous miners: the Patchwork/Voices project at Pennsylvania State University–Fayette and the Special Collections and Archives at Stapleton Library, Indiana University of Pennsylvania. To this body of oral testimony must be added the earlier works of Korson (1943, 1964), who preserved images of the miner, the coal company, and the coal company town through the collection of miners' songs, and the many oral narratives collected across the country by a diverse body of scholars and professionals (Dreiser et al. [1932] 1970; Murphy 1997; Schwieder 1983; Schwieder, Hraba, and Schwieder 1987; Shifflett 1991:241–243).

References Cited

Oral Interviews

All interviews were conducted by the author and were recorded on tape unless otherwise noted. Transcriptions of key oral interviews appear in Metheny (2002). A complete set of transcriptions will be deposited with the DuBois Historical Society in DuBois, Pennsylvania, at the completion of this project.

Brown, William N.
1991   Videotaped oral interview, Nov. 16. DuBois, Pennsylvania.
1992   Oral interview, Jan. 3. DuBois, Pennsylvania. Handwritten notes.
1994   Taped conversation, July 30. DuBois and Helvetia, Pennsylvania.
Crop, Thomas
1994   Informal telephone interview, Mar. 9. Handwritten notes.
        Informal interview, Mar. 10. Luthersburg, Pennsylvania. Handwritten notes.
        Oral interview, July 29. Luthersburg, Pennsylvania.
1995   Informal conversation, July 14. Helvetia, Pennsylvania. Handwritten notes.
        Oral interview, Sept. 11. Luthersburg, Pennsylvania.
2001   Informal telephone interview, June 13. Handwritten notes.
Crop, William, and Sara Haag Crop
1995   Informal conversation, July 25. Helvetia, Pennsylvania. Handwritten notes.
        Oral interview, Sept. 11. Sykesville, Pennsylvania.
Gray, Lloyd
1995   Informal conversation, July 20. Helvetia, Pennsylvania. Handwritten notes.
        Informal conversation, July 21. Helvetia, Pennsylvania. Handwritten notes.
        Oral interview, Sept. 11. Sykesville, Pennsylvania.
McKee, Veronica
1994   Oral interview, Mar. 10. Helvetia, Pennsylvania. Handwritten notes.
        Taped conversation with William Brown and Karen Metheny, July 30. Helvetia, Pennsylvania.
        Oral interview, July 30. Helvetia, Pennsylvania.

ORAL SOURCES/WRITTEN NARRATIVES

Bukousky, Tom
> 1995   Informal conversation, July 20. Helvetia, Pennsylvania. Handwritten notes.

Craig, Margaret C.
> 1995   Letter to Mr. Thomas Bukansky [Bukousky], *Tri-County Newspaper/DuBois Courier-Express*, Sept. 27. Forwarded to Karen Metheny at the request of the author. Indiana, Pennsylvania.

Deitch, Marlin
> 1995   Informal conversations, July 21, 24, Aug. 4, 14. Helvetia, Pennsylvania. Handwritten notes.

Hamilton, Betty Haddow
> 1971   "From the Scratch Pad: Remembers Helvetia." Letter to the editor, reprinted in the *DuBois Courier-Express*, May 1.
> 1995   Informal conversation, July 14. Helvetia, Pennsylvania. Handwritten notes.

Hilliard, Grace
> 1995   Letter to Karen Metheny, Sept. 22. DuBois, Pennsylvania.

Kramer, Rev. Leo
> 1995   Informal conversation, Aug. 14. Helvetia, Pennsylvania. Handwritten notes.

Kriner, Raymond
> 1994   Informal conversation, Mar. 10. Brady Township, Pennsylvania. Handwritten notes.

McKee, Calvin
> 1995   Informal conversation, July 14. Helvetia, Pennsylvania. Handwritten notes.

Means, Evelyn Wilson
> n.d.   "Helvetia: Big Run Woman Remembers Working at the Company Store." Article from the *DuBois Courier-Express* relating the recollections of Evelyn Wilson Means. Undated clipping without page references.

Steele, Thomas
> 1995   Informal conversation, July 17. Helvetia, Pennsylvania. Handwritten notes.

Fike, Marlene, and Violet Henry
> 1990   "Memories of Thriving Town Survive Demise of Helvetia." News article relating the recollections of Marlene Fike and Violet Henry, former residents of Helvetia. *Sykesville Post-Dispatch*, Feb. 14.

Yusnukis, Raymond
> 1989–1993 Videotaped narrative and walkover survey of Helvetia, Pennsylvania. Copy of video in possession of author.

UNPUBLISHED SOURCES

Brady Township Tax Assessment Records, Assessment Office, Clearfield County Court-house Annex, Clearfield, Pennsylvania
> 1891–1902 Microfilm Reel 178.
> 1903–1932 Microfilm Reel 179.
> 1947   Microfilm Reel 182.

Rochester & Pittsburgh Coal Company (R&PCC). Records, including ledgers, files and official correspondence. On file, Stapleton Library, Special Collections and Archives, Indiana University of Pennsylvania, Indiana, Pennsylvania.

1890a   Adrian Iselin to A. G. Yates, June 2. Ledger copybook, Adrian Iselin, Coal
           Properties, Helvetia Mines, 1890–1896, pp. 13–15. Collection 51, Series 1,
           Box 1, Early Correspondence.

1890b   Adrian Iselin to A. G. Yates, Sept. 23. Ledger copybook, Adrian Iselin,
           Coal Properties, Helvetia Mines, 1890–1896, pp. 43–44. Collection 51,
           Series 1, Box 1, Early Correspondence.

1890c   Adrian Iselin to J. A. Haskell, Apr. 23. Ledger copybook, Adrian Iselin,
           Coal Properties, Helvetia Mines, 1890–1896, pp. 1–4. Collection 51, Series
           1, Box 1, Early Correspondence.

1890d   Adrian Iselin to J. A. Haskell, Apr. 29. Ledger copybook, Adrian Iselin,
           Coal Properties, Helvetia Mines, 1890–96, pp. 5–6. Collection 51, Series 1,
           Box 1, Early Correspondence.

1890–1893 Ledger 135, Journal 1, 1890. Helvetia Mines, 1890–1893. Collection 51,
           Series VI, Box 140B.

1891   Adrian Iselin to J. A. Haskell, Jan. 12. Ledger copybook, Adrian Iselin,
           Coal Properties, Helvetia Mines, 1890–1896, p. 59. Collection 51, Series 1,
           Box 1, Early Correspondence.

1892a   Adrian Iselin to John McLeavy, Superintendent, Helvetia, Nov. 2. Ledger
           copybook, Adrian Iselin, Coal Properties, Helvetia Mines, 1890–1896, p. 218.
           Collection 51, Series 1, Box 1, Early Correspondence.

1892b   Adrian Iselin to John McLeavy, Superintendent, Helvetia, Nov. 11. Ledger
           copybook, Adrian Iselin, Coal Properties, Helvetia Mines, 1890–1896, pp.
           220–221. Collection 51, Series 1, Box 1, Early Correspondence.

1892c   Adrian Iselin to John McLeavy, Superintendent, Helvetia, Aug. Ledger
           copybook, Adrian Iselin, Coal Properties, Helvetia Mines, 1890–1896, pp.
           142–148. Collection 51, Series 1, Box 1, Early Correspondence.

1892d   Adrian Iselin to John McLeavy, Superintendent, Helvetia, Sept. 12. Ledger
           copybook, Adrian Iselin, Coal Properties, Helvetia Mines, 1890–1896, p. 194.
           Collection 51, Series 1, Box 1, Early Correspondence.

1894a   Adrian Iselin Jr. to John McLeavy, Superintendent, Helvetia, June 20.
           Ledger copybook, Adrian Iselin, Coal Properties, Helvetia Mines,
           1890–1896, p. 344. Collection 51, Series 1, Box 1, Early Correspondence.

1894b   Adrian Iselin Jr. to George E. Merchant, President, Rochester & Pitts-
           burgh Coal & Iron Co. Ledger copybook, Adrian Iselin, Coal Properties,
           Helvetia Mines, 1890–1896, p. 293. Collection 51, Series 1, Box 1, Early
           Correspondence.

1894c   Adrian Iselin Jr. to John McLeavy, Superintendent, Helvetia, June 4. Ledger
           copybook, Adrian Iselin, Coal Properties, Helvetia Mines, 1890–1896, p. 339.
           Collection 51, Series 1, Box 1, Early Correspondence.

1894d   Adrian Iselin Jr. to John McLeavy, Superintendent, Helvetia, June 13. Ledger
           copybook, Adrian Iselin, Coal Properties, Helvetia Mines, 1890–1896, p. 342.
           Collection 51, Series 1, Box 1, Early Correspondence.

1894e   Adrian Iselin Jr. to John McLeavy, Superintendent, Helvetia, June 25.
           Ledger copybook, Adrian Iselin, Coal Properties, Helvetia Mines,
           1890–1896, p. 345. Collection 51, Series 1, Box 1, Early Correspondence.

1895a   Adrian Iselin Jr. to John McLeavy, Superintendent, Helvetia, Nov. 21. Ledger
           copybook, Adrian Iselin, Coal Properties, Helvetia Mines, 1890–1896, p. 344.
           Collection 51, Series 1, Box 1, Early Correspondence.

1895b   Adrian Iselin Jr. to John McLeavy, Superintendent, Helvetia, Nov. 29. Ledger copybook, Adrian Iselin, Coal Properties, Helvetia Mines, 1890–1896, p. 400. Collection 51, Series 1, Box 1, Early Correspondence.

1895c   Adrian Iselin Jr. to John McLeavy, Superintendent, Helvetia, June 25. Ledger copybook, Adrian Iselin, Coal Properties, Helvetia Mines, 1890–1896, p. 382. Collection 51, Series 1, Box 1, Early Correspondence.

1898a   Lucius W. Robinson to Mr. A. W. Calloway, Assistant Superintendent, Adrian, July 27. Ledger copybook, L. W. Robinson, 1898, p. 149. Collection 51, Series 1, Box 1, Early Correspondence.

1898b   Lucius W. Robinson to Al Cole, DuBois, Pennsylvania, Sept. 13. Ledger copybook, L. W. Robinson, 1898, p. 684. Collection 51, Series 1, Box 1, Early Correspondence.

1900a   Lucius W. Robinson to Mr. D. Fleming, Superintendent, Eleanora, Pennsylvania, Aug. 21. Ledger copybook, L. W. Robinson, 1900, p. 277. Collection 51, Series 1, Box 1, Early Correspondence.

1900b   Memorandum from Lucius W. Robinson to R&P Superintendents, Aug. 10. Ledger copybook, L. W. Robinson, 1900, p. 205. Collection 51, Series 1, Box 1, Early Correspondence.

1900c   Lucius W. Robinson to T. S. Lowther, Superintendent, Helvetia, Pennsylvania, July 30. Ledger copybook, L. W. Robinson, 1900, p. 60. Collection 51, Series 1, Box 1, Early Correspondence.

1901a   Lucius W. Robinson to George A. Sheldon, Helvetia, Pennsylvania, May 29. Copy ledger, Lucius W. Robinson, General Correspondence, Apr. 18–June 26, 1901, p. 584. Collection 51, Series 1, Box 1, Executive Correspondence, R&P C&I Co., 1896–1918.

1901b   Lucius W. Robinson to George A. Sheldon, Helvetia, Pennsylvania, June 4. Copy ledger, Lucius W. Robinson, General Correspondence, Apr. 18–June 26, 1901, pp. 655–656. Collection 51, Series 1, Box 1, Executive Correspondence, R&P C&I Co., 1896–1918.

1901c   Lucius W. Robinson to A. W. Calloway, Superintendent, Adrian, Pennsylvania, May 3. Copy ledger, Lucius W. Robinson, General Correspondence, Apr. 18–June 26, 1901, p. 209. Collection 51, Series 1, Box 1, Executive Correspondence, R&P C&I Co., 1896–1918.

1901d   Lucius W. Robinson to George A. Sheldon, Helvetia, Pennsylvania, May 24. Copy ledger, Lucius W. Robinson, General Correspondence, Apr. 18–June 26, 1901, p. 524. Collection 51, Series 1, Box 1, Executive Correspondence, R&P C&I Co., 1896–1918.

1901e   Lucius W. Robinson to All Superintendents, June 14. Copy ledger, Lucius W. Robinson, General Correspondence, Apr. 18–June 26, 1901, p. 830. Collection 51, Series 1, Box 1, Executive Correspondence, R&P C&I Co., 1896–1918.

1901f   Lucius W. Robinson to All Superintendents, May 1. Copy ledger, Lucius W. Robinson, General Correspondence, Apr. 18–June 26, 1901, p. 165. Collection 51, Series 1, Box 1, Executive Correspondence, R&P C&I Co., 1896–1918.

1901g   Lucius W. Robinson to Jacob L. Fisher, Esq. of Punxsutawney, June 12. Copy ledger, Lucius W. Robinson, General Correspondence, Apr. 18–June 26, 1901, p. 769. Collection 51, Series 1, Box 1, Executive Correspondence, R&P C&I Co., 1896–1918.

1902a   Lucius W. Robinson to Rev. C. Wienker, July 25. General Correspondence Ledger, Lucius W. Robinson, July 2–Sept. 13, 1902, p. 305. Collection 51, Series 1, Box 1, Executive Correspondence, R&P C&I Co., 1896–1918.

1902b   Lucius W. Robinson, President, to Adrian Iselin Jr., Vice President, BR&P, July 7. General Correspondence Ledger, L. W. Robinson, July 2–Sept. 13, 1902, pp. 78–81. Collection 51, Series 1, Box 1, Executive Correspondence, R&P C&I Co., 1896–1918.

1902c   Lucius W. Robinson, President, to A. J. Davis, July 11. General Correspondence Ledger, L. W. Robinson, July 2–Sept. 13, 1902, pp. 137–139. Collection 51, Series 1, Box 1, Executive Correspondence, R&P C&I Co., 1896–1918.

1902d   Lucius W. Robinson, President, to All Superintendents, July 23. General Correspondence Ledger, L. W. Robinson, July 2–Sept. 13, 1902, p. 280. Collection 51, Series 1, Box 1, Executive Correspondence, R&P C&I Co., 1896–1918.

1902e   Lucius W. Robinson, President, to Mr. Charles E. Patton, Punxsutawney, Aug. 16. General Correspondence Ledger, L. W. Robinson, July 2–Sept. 13, 1902, p. 589. Collection 51, Series 1, Box 1, Executive Correspondence, R&P C&I Co., 1896–1918.

1902f   Lucius W. Robinson, President, to Mr. John J. Davis, Aug. 30. General Correspondence Ledger, L. W. Robinson, July 2–Sept. 13, 1902, pp. 793–794. Collection 51, Series 1, Box 1, Executive Correspondence, R&P C&I Co., 1896–1918.

1902g   A. W. Calloway, Florence Superintendent, to Lucius W. Robinson, President, July 7. General Correspondence Ledger, L. W. Robinson, July 2–Sept. 13, 1902, p. 109. Collection 51, Series 1, Box 1, Executive Correspondence, R&P C&I Co., 1896–1918.

1902h   Lucius W. Robinson, President, to George L. Eaton, Secretary, Aug. 21. General Correspondence Ledger, L. W. Robinson, July 2–Sept. 13, 1902, p. 671. Collection 51, Series 1, Box 1, Executive Correspondence, R&P C&I Co., 1896–1918.

1902i   Lucius W. Robinson, President, to Mr. T. S. Lowther, Superintendent, Helvetia, and Mr. T. R. Johns, Superintendent, Walston, Sept. 11. General Correspondence Ledger, L. W. Robinson, July 2–Sept. 13, 1902, p. 973. Collection 51, Series 1, Box 1, Executive Correspondence, R&P C&I Co., 1896–1918.

1902j   Lucius W. Robinson, President, to T. R. Johns, Superintendent, Walston, July 9. General Correspondence Ledger, L. W. Robinson, July 2–Sept. 13, 1902, p. 109. Collection 51, Series 1, Box 1, Executive Correspondence, R&P C&I Co., 1896–1918.

1902k   Lucius W. Robinson, President, to Mr. W. M. Wall, Punxsutawney, Sept. 1. General Correspondence Ledger, L. W. Robinson, July 2–Sept 13, 1902, p. 820. Collection 51, Series 1, Box 1, Executive Correspondence, R&P C&I Co., 1896–1918.

1908   Adrian Iselin Jr. to Lucius W. Robinson, Mar. 27. Executive Correspondence, A. Iselin Jr., Oct. 25, 1906–Mar. 18, 1909. Collection 51, Box 2. Executive Correspondence, R&P C&I Co., 1904–1912.

1910   B. M. Clark, Office of the Solicitor [legal department for the R&P Coal Co.] to L. W. Robinson, Oct. 27. Executive Correspondence, L. W. Robinson, Oct. 20–28, 1910. Collection 51, Series 1, Box 2c, Folder 10, Early Correspondence. Executive Correspondence, R&P C&I Co., 1904–1912.

1913   L. W. Robinson to Messrs. A. Iselin & Co., July 3. Executive Correspondence, L. W. Robinson, June 2–July 31, 1913, Collection 51, Series 1, Box 3, Early Correspondence. Executive Correspondence, R&P C&I Co., 1913–1923.

1914a   L. W. Robinson to Messrs. A. Iselin & Co., Apr. 20. Executive Correspondence, L. W. Robinson, Jan.–June 1914. Collection 51, Series 1, Box 3, Early Correspondence. Executive Correspondence, R&P C&I Co., 1913–1923.

1914b   L. W. Robinson to Messrs. A. Iselin & Co., May 5. Executive Correspondence, L. W. Robinson, Jan.–June 1914. Collection 51, Series 1, Box 3, Early Correspondence. Executive Correspondence, R&P C&I Co., 1913–1923.

1916a   L. W. Robinson to Adrian Iselin Jr., Sept. 21. Executive Correspondence, Adrian Iselin Jr., 1916. Collection 51, Series 1, Box 3, Item 20, Early Correspondence. Executive Correspondence, R&P C&I Co., 1913–1923.

1916b   Lucius W. Robinson, President, to Adrian Iselin Jr., Aug. 4. Executive Correspondence, Adrian Iselin, Jr., 1916. Collection 51, Series 1, Box 3, Item 20, Early Correspondence. Executive Correspondence, R&P C&I Co., 1913–1923.

1916c   Lucius W. Robinson, President, to Rev. John Lorenz, Aug. 4. Executive Correspondence, Adrian Iselin Jr., 1916. Collection 51, Series 1, Box 3, Item 20, Early Correspondence. Executive Correspondence, R&P C&I Co., 1913–1923.

1916d   Lucius W. Robinson, President, to I. J. Harvey, Division Supt., Helvetia, Aug. 9. Executive Correspondence, L. W. Robinson, July–Aug. 1916. Collection 51, Series 1, Box 3, Item 23, Early Correspondence. Executive Correspondence, R&P C&I Co., 1913–1923.

1916e   Lucius W. Robinson, President, to Adrian Iselin Jr., Aug. 14. Executive Correspondence, L. W. Robinson, July–Aug. 1916. Collection 51, Series 1, Box 3, Item 23, Early Correspondence. Executive Correspondence, R&P C&I Co., 1913–1923.

1916f   Lucius W. Robinson, President, to Adrian Iselin Jr., Aug. 24. Executive Correspondence, L. W. Robinson, July–Aug. 1916. Collection 51, Series 1, Box 3, Item 23, Early Correspondence. Executive Correspondence, R&P C&I Co., 1913–1923.

1916g   Lucius W. Robinson, President, to F. H. Fritchman, General Manager; J. Craig, Superintendent; I. J. Harvey, Division Superintendent.; F. Pardee, Assistant General Manager; and L. W. Robinson, Jr., General Manager, Sept. 7. Executive Correspondence, Adrian Iselin Jr., 1916. Collection 51, Series 1, Box 3, Item 20, Early Correspondence. Executive Correspondence, R&P C&I Co., 1913–1923.

1916h   Lucius W. Robinson, President, to Adrian Iselin Jr., July 24. Executive Correspondence, Adrian Iselin Jr., 1916. Collection 51, Series 1, Box 3, Item 7, Early Correspondence. Executive Correspondence, R&P C&I Co., 1913–1923.

1916i   I. J. Harvey, Division Superintendent, Helvetia, to Lucius W. Robinson, Aug. 24. Executive Correspondence, L. W. Robinson, May–Apr. 1916. Collection 51, Box 3, Item 23, Early Correspondence. Executive Correspondence, R&P C&I Co., 1913–1923.

1917   L. W. Robinson to Adrian Iselin Jr., Aug. 21. Executive Correspondence, L. W. Robinson, 1917. Collection 51, Series 1, Box 3, Item 28, Early Correspondence. Executive Correspondence, R&P C&I Co., 1913–1923.

1923   Blueprint for 24' x 30' Standard Mine Forman's House. Drawn by Consoli-
           dated Lumber & Supply Co. Construction Department, Indiana, Pennsylva-
           nia, for the Rochester & Pittsburgh Coal Co., Feb. 9, 1923. Four pages.
           Basement file, 622-973-1499-102. Map drawer 49.
1939   Town Plan and Water System, Helvetia, Brady Twp., Clearfield County,
           Jan. 1939. Amended, Mar. 4, 1947. Map drawer 49.
1942   Supplemental Agreement between James Mark, President, District No. 2,
           United Mine Workers of America and L. W. Householder, Vice President,
           Rochester & Pittsburgh Coal Co., Jan. 31. Collection 52, Box 110.
1947   Kovalchick Plan of Lots, Helvetia, Brady Township, Clearfield County.
           Drawn by Thos. Pealer, Indiana, Pennsylvania, for Kovalchick Salvage Co.,
           Nov. 1947. Map drawer 49.

Rochester & Pittsburgh Coal Company (R&PCC), Main Office, Indiana, Pennsylvania
1931a   Brown, W. N. Personal Record Card. Helvetia Mine.
1931b   Brown, Thomas. Personal Record Card. Helvetia Mine.

NEWSPAPERS
Clearfield Progress
DuBois Courier-Express
DuBois Daily Express
DuBois Express
DuBois Express (Reynoldsville Edition)
DuBois Morning Courier
Indiana Gazette
Jefferson Democrat
Sykesville Post-Dispatch

GOVERNMENT DOCUMENTS
Commonwealth of Pennsylvania
1927   Report of the Department of Mines of Pennsylvania, Part II—Bituminous,
           1923–1924, 1925–1926. J. L. L. Kuhn, Harrisburg.
U.S. Bureau of the Census (USBC)
1900   Twelfth Census of the United States, Schedule No. 1-Population. Luthersburg
           Precinct of Brady Township, Clearfield County, Pennsylvania. Supervisor's
           District 10, Enumeration District 54. June 21. Sheets 150A-154A. Document
           on microfilm, National Archives, Waltham, Massachusetts.
1910   Thirteenth Census of the United States: 1910 Population. Helvetia (Mining
           Town), Troutville Precinct, Brady Township, Clearfield County, Pennsylvania.
           Supervisor's District 17, Enumeration District 54. Apr. 25–30. Sheets 4A–13A.
           Document on microfilm, National Archives, Waltham, Massachusetts.
1920   Fourteenth Census of the United States: 1920 Population. Helvetia
           Precinct, Brady Township, Clearfield County, Pennsylvania. Supervisor's
           District 15, Enumeration District 110. Jan. 6–22. Sheets 1A–11B. Document
           on microfilm, National Archives, Waltham, Massachusetts.
U.S. Geological Survey (USGS)
1924   Topographic map, DuBois Quadrangle, fifteen-minute series.

PUBLISHED SOURCES

Abercrombie, Nicholas, Stephen Hill, and Bryan S. Turner
  1980   *The Dominant Ideology Thesis.* Allen and Unwin, London.
Adams, William H.
  1976   Silcott, Washington: Ethnoarchaeology of a Rural American Community.
              Report of Investigations No. 54, Laboratory of Anthropology, Washington
              State University.
Albert, Richard C.
  1980   *Trolleys from the Mines: Street Railways of Centre, Clearfield, Indiana and Jefferson
              Counties, Pennsylvania.* Printed by Harold E. Cox, Forty Fort, Pennsylvania.
Allen, Barbara, and William Lynwood Montell
  1981   *From Memory to History: Using Oral Sources in Local Historical Research.*
              American Association for State and Local History, Nashville, Tennessee.
Allen, James B.
  1966   *The Company Town in the American West.* University of Oklahoma Press,
              Norman.
America's Industrial Heritage Project (AIHP)
  1988   Berwind-White Coal Mining Company Eureka No. 40 and the Windber
              Mines, Cambria and Somerset Counties, by Demain Hess. Historic American
              Building Survey/Historic American Engineering Record. U.S. Dept. of the
              Interior, National Park Service, Denver Service Center.
  1990   Blair and Cambria County, Pennsylvania: An Inventory of Historic Engi-
              neering and Industrial Sites. Edited by Gray Fitzsimons. Historic American
              Building Survey/Historic American Engineering Record. U.S. Dept. of the
              Interior, National Park Service, Denver Service Center.
  1991   Huntingdon County, Pennsylvania: An Inventory of Historic Engineering
              and Industrial Sites. Edited by Nancy Shedd. Historic American Building
              Survey/Historic American Engineering Record. U.S. Dept. of the Interior,
              National Park Service, Denver Service Center.
  1992   Coal and Coke Resource Analysis: Western Pennsylvania, Northern West Vir-
              ginia. U.S. Dept. of the Interior, National Park Service, Denver Service Center.
  1993   Indiana County, Pennsylvania: An Inventory of Historic Engineering and
              Industrial Sites, by Richard H. Quin. Historic American Building Survey/
              Historic American Engineering Record. U.S. Dept. of the Interior, National
              Park Service, Denver Service Center.
Balicki, Joseph, Elizabeth O'Brien, and Rebecca Yamin
  1999   Main Street in "Coney": A Study in Landscape Archeology. Data Recovery–
              Maryland Route 36, Lonaconing, Allegany County, Maryland. Archeological
              Report 195. Prepared for Maryland State Highway Administration, Project
              Planning Division, Environmental Evaluation Section. John Milner Associ-
              ates, Inc., Alexandria, Virginia.
Baugher, Sherene
  1982   Hoboken Hollow: A 19th Century Factory Workers' Housing Site. *North-
              east Historical Archaeology* 11:26–38.
Baum, Willa K.
  1987   *Oral History for the Local Historical Society.* 3rd ed., rev. American Association
              for State and Local History, Nashville, Tennessee.

Beaudry, Mary C.

1984   Archaeology and the Historical Household. *Man in the Northeast* 28 (Fall):27–38.

1988   Comments on the Historical Archaeology of North American Households. Paper presented at the Annual Meeting of the Society for Historical Archaeology, Reno, Nevada.

1989   The Lowell Boott Mills Complex and Its Housing: Material Expressions of Corporate Ideology. *Historical Archaeology* 23(1):19–32.

1990   Review of "The Recovery of Meaning: Historical Archaeology in the Eastern United States," edited by Mark P. Leone and Parker B. Potter Jr., Smithsonian Institution Press, Washington, D.C., 1988. *Historical Archaeology* 24(3):115–118.

1993   Public Aesthetics Versus Personal Experience: Worker Health and Well-Being in 19th-Century Lowell, Massachusetts. *Historical Archaeology* 27(3):90–105.

1996   Reinventing Historical Archaeology. In *Historical Archaeology and the Study of American Culture*, edited by Lu Ann De Cunzo and Bernard L. Herman, pp. 473–497. Henry Francis du Pont Winterthur Museum, Winterthur, Delaware.

Beaudry, Mary C. (editor)

1988   *Documentary Archaeology in the New World.* Cambridge University Press, New York.

Beaudry, Mary C., Lauren J. Cook, and Stephen A. Mrozowski

1991   Artifacts and Active Voices: Material Culture as Social Discourse. In *The Archaeology of Inequality*, edited by Randall H. McGuire and Robert Paynter, pp. 150–191. Basil Blackwell, Oxford.

Beaudry, Mary C., and Stephen A. Mrozowski

1988   The Archeology of Work and Home Life in Lowell, Massachusetts: An Interdisciplinary Study of the Boott Cotton Mills Corporation. *IA, The Journal of the Society for Industrial Archeology* 14(2):1–22.

2001   Cultural Space and Worker Identity in the Company City: Nineteenth-Century Lowell, Massachusetts. In *Archaeologies of Urban Landscapes*, edited by Alan Mayne and Tim Murray, pp. 118–131. Cambridge University Press, Cambridge.

Beaudry, Mary C., and Stephen A. Mrozowski (editors)

1987a   Interdisciplinary Investigations of the Boott Mills, Lowell, Massachusetts. Vol. 1, Life at the Boarding Houses: A Preliminary Report. Cultural Resources Management Series 18. Division of Cultural Resources, North Atlantic Regional Office, National Park Service, Boston.

1987b   Interdisciplinary Investigations of the Boott Mills, Lowell, Massachusetts. Vol. 2, The Kirk Street Agents' House. Cultural Resources Management Series 19. Division of Cultural Resources, North Atlantic Regional Office, National Park Service, Boston.

1989   Interdisciplinary Investigations of the Boott Mills, Lowell, Massachusetts. Vol. 3, The Boarding House System as a Way of Life. Cultural Resources Management Series 21. Division of Cultural Resources, North Atlantic Regional Office, National Park Service, Boston.

Bell, Alison

1994   Widows, "Free Sisters," and "Independent Girls": Female Workers in England, 1600–1920. Paper presented at the Annual Meeting of the Society for Historical Archaeology, Vancouver, British Columbia.

Bennett, Lola M.

1990   The Company Towns of the Rockhill Iron and Coal Company: Robertsdale and Woodvale, Pennsylvania. Historic American Building Survey/Historic American Engineering Record. America's Industrial Heritage Project. National Park Service, Department of the Interior.

Blewett, Mary H.

1988   *Men, Women, and Work: Class, Gender, and Protest in the New England Shoe Industry, 1780–1910.* University of Illinois Press, Urbana.

1990   *The Last Generation: Work and Life in the Textile Mills of Lowell, Massachusetts, 1910–1960.* University of Massachusetts Press, Amherst.

Bodnar, John

1977   *Steelton: Immigration and Industrialization, 1870–1940.* University of Pittsburgh Press, Pittsburgh.

1983   *Anthracite People: Families, Unions and Work, 1900–1940.* Pennsylvania Historical and Museum Commission, Harrisburg.

1985   The European Origins of American Immigrants. In *Essays from the Lowell Conference on Industrial History 1982 and 1983*, edited by Robert Weible, pp. 259–275. Museum of American Textile History, North Andover, Massachusetts.

Bodnar, John, Roger Simon, and Michael P. Weber

1982   *Lives of Their Own: Blacks, Italians, and Poles in Pittsburgh, 1900–1960.* University of Illinois Press, Urbana.

Bomberger, Bruce, and William Sisson

1991   *Made in Pennsylvania: An Overview of the Major Historical Industries of the Commonwealth.* Pennsylvania Historical and Museum Commission, Harrisburg.

Bond, Kathleen H.

1989   The Medicine, Alcohol, and Soda Vessels from the Boott Mills. In Interdisciplinary Investigations of the Boott Mills, Lowell, Massachusetts. Vol. 3, The Boarding House System as a Way of Life, edited by Mary C. Beaudry and Stephen A. Mrozowski, pp. 121–139. Cultural Resources Management Series 21. Division of Cultural Resources, North Atlantic Regional Office, National Park Service, Boston.

Boyer, Paul

1978   *Urban Masses and Moral Order in America, 1820–1920.* Harvard University Press, Cambridge, Massachusetts.

Brady Township Bicentennial Book Committee

1976   Brady Township–Luthersburg Area Home Coming May 29th–31st, 1976. On file, Clearfield County Historical Society, Clearfield, Pennsylvania.

Bragdon, Kathleen J.

1988   The Material Culture of the Christian Indians of New England, 1650–1775. In *Documentary Archaeology in the New World*, edited by Mary C. Beaudry, pp. 126–131. Oxford University Press, Cambridge.

1997   Language and Ecology in Native Southern New England. Paper presented at the 16th Annual Meeting of the Conference on New England Archaeology, Sturbridge, Massachusetts.

Brashler, Janet G.

1991   When Daddy was a Shanty Boy: The Role of Gender in the Organization of the Logging Industry in Highland West Virginia. *Historical Archaeology* 25(4):54–68.

REFERENCES CITED

Brestensky, Dennis F., Evelyn A. Hovanec, and Albert N. Skomra
1991 *Patch/Work Voices: The Culture and Lore of a Mining People.* University of Pittsburgh Press, Pittsburgh.

Brink, Yvonne
1992 Places of Discourse and Dialogue: A Study in the Material Culture of the Cape during the Rule of the Dutch East India Company, 1652–1795. Ph.D. dissertation, Department of Archaeology, University of Cape Town.

Brooks, Allyson
1995 Anticipating Mobility: How Cognitive Processes Influenced the Historic Mining Landscape in White Pine, Nevada, and the Black Hills of South Dakota. Ph.D. dissertation, Department of Anthropology, University of Nevada, Reno.

Brown, Marley R., III
1978 The Use of Oral and Documentary Sources in Historical Archaeology: Ethnohistory at the Mott Farm. In *Historical Archaeology: A Guide to Substantive and Theoretical Contributions,* edited by Robert L. Schuyler, pp. 278–283. Baywood Publishing Co., Farmingdale, New York.

Brown, Sharon
1989 Historic Resource Study: Cambria Iron Company. America's Industrial Heritage Project. U.S. Dept. of the Interior, National Park Service.

Brunvand, Jan Harold
1978 *The Study of American Folklore: An Introduction.* 2nd ed. W. W. Norton & Co., New York.

Caldwell, J. A.
1878 *Caldwell's Illustrated Historical Combination Atlas of Clearfield County. Pennsylvania. From actual surveys by & under the directions of J. H. Newton, C.E.* J. A. Caldwell, Condit, Ohio.

Candee, Richard M.
1981 New Towns of the Early New England Textile Industry. *Perspectives in Vernacular Architecture* 1:31–51.

1985 Architecture and Corporate Planning in the Early Waltham System. In *Essays from the Lowell Conference on Industrial History 1982 and 1983,* edited by Robert Weible, pp. 17–43. Museum of American Textile History, North Andover, Massachusetts.

1992 Early New England Mill Towns of the Piscataqua River Valley. In *The Company Town: Architecture and Society in the Early Industrial Age,* edited by John S. Garner, pp. 111–138. Oxford University Press, New York.

Carter, Anthony T.
1984 Household Histories. In *Households: Comparative and Historical Studies of the Domestic Group,* edited by Robert McC. Netting, Richard R. Wilk, and Eric J. Arnould, pp. 44–83. University of California Press, Berkeley.

Cheek, Charles D., Rebecca Yamin, and Dana B. Heck
1994 Phase III Data Recovery, Mechanic Street Site (18AG206) Station Square Project, Cumberland, Maryland. Archeological Report 69. Prepared for Maryland Department of Transportation. John Milner Associates, Alexandria, Virginia.

Cohen, Lizabeth A.
1986 Embellishing a Life of Labor: An Interpretation of the Material Culture of American Working-Class Homes, 1885–1915. In *Common Places: Readings*

in American Vernacular Architecture, edited by Dell Upton and John Michael Vlach, pp. 261–278. University of Georgia Press, Athens.

Cohen, Stan
1984   *King Coal: A Pictorial History of West Virginia Coal Mining.* Pictorial Histories Publishing Co., Charleston, West Virginia.

Colorado Coalfield War Archaeology Project (CCWAP)
2000   Archaeological Investigations at the Ludlow Massacre Site (5LA1829) and Berwind (5LA2175), Las Animas County, Colorado: Report on the 1998 Season. Project #98-02-038, Product #9. Prepared for the Colorado Historical Society, State Historic Fund, Denver. Department of Anthropology, University of Denver.
2002   Archaeological Investigations at the Ludlow Massacre Site (5LA1829) and Berwind (5LA2175), Las Animás County, Colorado: Report on the 1999 Season. Project #98-P2-003, Product #7. Prepared for the Colorado Historical Society, State Historic Fund, Denver. Department of Anthropology, University of Denver.

Comaroff, John, and Jean Comaroff
1992   *Ethnography and the Historical Imagination.* Westview Press, Boulder, Colorado.

Cook, Lauren J.
1989   Tobacco-Related Material and the Construction of Working-Class Culture. In Interdisciplinary Investigations of the Boott Mills, Lowell, Massachusetts. Vol. 3, The Boarding House System as a Way of Life, edited by Mary C. Beaudry and Stephen A. Mrozowski, pp. 209–229. Cultural Resources Management Series 21. Division of Cultural Resources, North Atlantic Regional Office, National Park Service, Boston.
1995   Beyond Domination and Resistance: Gramsci, Cultural Hegemony, and the Archeological Record. Paper presented to the Radical Archeology Theory Seminar, Brown University.
1997   "Promiscuous Smoking": Interpreting Gender and Tobacco Use in the Archaeological Record. *Northeast Historical Archaeology* 26:23–38.

Cooper, Eileen Mountjoy
1982   *The Rochester & Pittsburgh Coal Company: The First One Hundred Years.* Rochester & Pittsburgh Coal Co., Indiana, Pennsylvania.

Corbin, David A.
1981   *Life, Work, and Rebellion in the Coal Fields: The Southern West Virginia Miners, 1880–1922.* University of Illinois Press, Urbana.

Costello, Julia
1998   Bread Fresh from the Oven: Memories of Italian Breadbaking in the California Mother Lode. *Historical Archaeology* 32(1):66–73.

Cotz, Jo Ann
1975   A Study of Ten Houses in Paterson's Dublin Area. *Northeast Historical Archaeology* 4(1–2):44–52.

Couvares, Francis G.
1985   The Remaking of Urban Culture in Late Nineteenth and Early Twentieth Century America. In *Essays from the Lowell Conference on Industrial History 1982 and 1983*, edited by Robert Weible, pp. 295–307. Museum of American Textile History, North Andover, Massachusetts.

Crawford, Margaret
　1995　　Building the Workingman's Paradise: The Design of American Company Towns. Verso, London.
Davis, Cullom, Kathryn Back, and Kay Maclean
　1977　　Oral History: From Tape to Type. American Library Association, Chicago.
De Cunzo, Lu Ann
　1982　　Households, Economics and Ethnicity in Paterson's Dublin, 1829–1915: The Van Houten Street Parking Lot Block. Northeast Historical Archaeology 11:9–25.
　1983　　Economics and Ethnicity: An Archaeological Perspective on Nineteenth Century Paterson, New Jersey. Ph.D. dissertation, University of Pennsylvania.
　1987　　Adapting to Factory and City: Illustrations from the Industrialization and Urbanization of Paterson, New Jersey. In Consumer Choice in Historical Archaeology, edited by Suzanne M. Spencer Wood, pp. 261–295. Plenum Press, New York.
　1996　　Introduction: People, Material Culture, Context, and Culture in Historical Archaeology. In Historical Archaeology and the Study of American Culture, edited by Lu Ann De Cunzo and Bernard L. Herman, pp. 1–17. The Henry Francis du Pont Winterthur Museum, Winterthur, Delaware.
Demarest, David P., Jr. (editor)
　1992　　"The River Ran Red": Homestead 1892. University of Pittsburgh Press, Pittsburgh.
DiCiccio, Carmen
　1996　　Coal and Coke in Pennsylvania. Pennsylvania Historical and Museum Commission, Harrisburg.
Dincauze, Dena
　1997　　Creating and Interpreting New England's Environments. Conference on New England Archaeology Newsletter 16:1–5.
Dix, Keith
　1988　　What's a Coal Miner to Do? The Mechanization of Coal Mining. University of Pittsburgh Press, Pittsburgh.
Douglas, Mary
　1982　　In the Active Voice. Routledge and Keagan Paul, London.
Douglas, Mary, and Baron Isherwood
　1979　　The World of Goods: Toward an Anthropology of Consumption. W. W. Norton and Co., New York.
Dreiser, Theodore, Lester Cohen, Anna Rochester, Melvin P. Levy, Arnold Johnson, Charles R. Walker, John Dos Passos, Adelaide Walker, Bruce Crawford, Jessie Wakefield, Boris Israel, and Sherwood Anderson
　1970　　Harlan Miners Speak: Report on Terrorism in the Kentucky Coal Fields. Prepared by Members of the National Committee for the Defense of Political Prisoners. Originally published 1932. Da Capo Press, New York.
Dublin, Thomas
　1979　　Women at Work. Columbia University Press, New York.
Dunaway, David K.
　1996　　Introduction: The Interdisciplinarity of Oral History. In Oral History: An Interdisciplinary Anthology, edited by David K. Dunaway and Willa K. Baum, pp. 7–22. 2nd ed. AltaMira Press, Walnut Creek, California.

Dunaway, David K., and Willa K. Baum (editors)

1984   *Oral History: An Interdisciplinary Anthology*. American Association for State and Local History, Nashville.

1996   *Oral History: An Interdisciplinary Anthology*. 2nd ed. AltaMira Press, Walnut Creek, CA.

Eisler, Benita (editor)

1977   *The Lowell Offering: Writings by New England Mill Women (1840–1845)*. W. W. Norton & Co., New York.

Eller, Ronald

1982   *Miners, Millhands, and Mountaineers: Industrialization of the Appalachian South, 1880–1930*. University of Tennessee Press, Knoxville.

Elston, Robert, and Donald Hardesty

1981   Archaeological Investigations on the Hopkins Land Exchange. Vol. 1. Report No. 9. U.S. Forest Service, Tahoe National Forest.

Fello, Richard N.

1969   A History of the Rochester & Pittsburgh Coal Company in Indiana County. History Seminar Paper, Graduate Course 521, Indiana University of Pennsylvania, May 17, 1969. On file, Special Collections and Archives, Indiana University of Pennsylvania, Indiana, Pennsylvania.

Ferguson, Leland

1991   Struggling with Pots in Colonial South Carolina. *The Archaeology of Inequality*, edited by Randall H. McGuire and Robert Paynter, pp. 28–39. Basil Blackwell, Oxford.

Firth, Raymond

1975   *Symbols: Public and Private*. Cornell University Press, Ithaca, New York.

Fishback, Price V.

1992   *Soft Coal, Hard Choices: The Economic Welfare of Bituminous Coal Miners, 1890–1930*. Oxford University Press, New York.

Francaviglia, Richard V.

1991   *Hard Places: Reading the Landscape of America's Historic Mining Districts*. University of Iowa Press, Iowa City.

Franzen, John G.

1992   Northern Michigan Logging Camps: Material Culture and Worker Adaptation on the Industrial Frontier. *Historical Archaeology* 26(2):74–98.

Friedlander, Peter

1996   Theory, Method, and Oral History. In *Oral History: An Interdisciplinary Anthology*, edited by David K. Dunaway and Willa K. Baum, pp. 150–160. 2nd ed. AltaMira Press, Walnut Creek, California.

Frisch, Michael

1990   *A Shared Authority: Essays on the Craft and Meaning of Oral and Public History*. State University Press of New York, Albany.

Frisch, Michael H., and Daniel J. Walkowitz

1983   Introduction. In *Working-Class America: Essays on Labor, Community, and American Society*, edited by M. H. Frisch and D. J. Walkowitz, pp. ix–xvii. University of Illinois Press, Urbana.

Gardner, A. Dudley, and Verla R. Flores

1989   *Forgotten Frontier: A History of Wyoming Coal Mining*. Westview Press, Boulder, Colorado.

Garner, John S.

1984   *The Model Company Town: Urban Design through Private Enterprise in Nineteenth-Century New England*. University of Massachusetts Press, Amherst.

Garner, John S. (editor)

1992   *The Company Town: Architecture and Society in the Early Industrial Age*. Oxford University Press, New York.

Geertz, Clifford

1973   *The Interpretation of Cultures*. Basic Books, New York.

1983   *Local Knowledge: Further Essays in Interpretive Anthropology*. Basic Books, New York.

Giesen, Carol A. B.

1995   *Coal Miners' Wives: Portraits of Endurance*. University of Kentucky Press, Lexington.

Gillespie, William B., and Mary M. Farrell

2002   Work Camp Settlement Patterns: Landscape-Scale Comparisons of Two Mining Camps in Southeastern Arizona. In Communities Defined by Work: Life in Western Work Camps, edited by Thad M. Van Bueren. *Historical Archaeology* 36(3):59–68.

Glassie, Henry

1982   *Passing the Time in Ballymenone: Culture and History of an Ulster Community*. University of Pennsylvania Press, Philadelphia.

Goodwin, Lorinda B. R.

1999   *An Archaeology of Manners: The Polite World of the Merchant Elite of Colonial Massachusetts*. Plenum Press, New York.

Gordon, Robert B., and Patrick M. Malone

1994   *The Texture of Industry: An Archaeological View of Industry in North America*. Oxford University Press, New York.

Gradwohl, David M., and Nancy M. Osborn

1984   *Exploring Buried Buxton: Archaeology of an Abandoned Iowa Coal Mining Town with a Large Black Population*. Iowa State University Press, Ames.

Grele, Ronald J.

1985   *Envelopes of Sound: The Art of Oral History*. Precedent Publishing Inc., Chicago.

1996   Directions for Oral History in the United States. In *Oral History: An Interdisciplinary Anthology*, edited by David K. Dunaway and Willa K. Baum, pp. 62–84. 2nd ed. AltaMira Press, Walnut Creek, California.

Gurcke, Karl

1987   *Bricks and Brickmaking: A Handbook for Historical Archaeology*. University of Idaho Press, Moscow.

Gutman, Herbert G.

1977   *Work, Culture, and Society in Industrializing America: Essays in American Working-Class and Social History*. Reprint. Vintage Books, New York. Originally published 1966, Alfred A. Knopf, New York.

Hall, Martin

1991   High and Low in the Townscapes of Dutch South America and South Africa: The Dialectics of Material Culture. *Social Dynamics* 17(2):41–75.

1992a   Small Things and the Mobile, Conflictual Fusion of Power, Fear, and Desire. In *The Art and Mystery of Historical Archaeology: Essays in Honor of James Deetz*, edited by Anne Elizabeth Yentsch and Mary C. Beaudry, pp. 373–399. CRC Press, Boca Raton, Florida.

1992b   People in a Changing Urban Landscape: Excavating Cape Town. Inaugural Lecture, University of Cape Town. New series, no. 169:1–27.

1994   The Secret Lives of Houses and Women, Gables and Gardens in the Eighteenth Century Cape. Seminar paper, University of California–Berkeley and University of Chicago, Jan.

Hardesty, Donald L.
1988   *The Archaeology of Mining and Miners: A View from the Silver State.* Special Publication Series No. 6, Society for Historical Archaeology.

Hareven, Tamara K.
1982   *Family Time and Industrial Time: The Relationship between the Family and Work in a New England Industrial Community.* Cambridge University Press, New York.

Hareven, Tamara K., and Randolph Langenbach
1978   *Amoskeag: Life and Work in an American Factory-City.* Pantheon Books, New York.

Harvey, Katherine A.
1969   *The Best-Dressed Miners: Life and Labor in the Maryland Coal Region, 1835–1910.* Cornell University Press, Ithaca.

Henige, David
1982   *Oral Historiography.* Longman Group, Ltd., London.

Hindle, Brooke, and Steven Lubar
1986   *Engines of Change: The American Industrial Revolution, 1790–1860.* Smithsonian Institution Press, Washington, D.C.

Hodder, Ian
1991   *Reading the Past.* 2nd ed. Cambridge University Press, Cambridge.
1995   *Theory and Practice in Archaeology.* Routledge, New York.

Hoffman, Alice
1996   Reliability and Validity in Oral History. In *Oral History: An Interdisciplinary Anthology,* edited by David K. Dunaway and Willa K. Baum, pp. 87–93. 2nd ed. AltaMira Press, Walnut Creek, California.

Hunt, Edward Eyre, F. G. Tryon, and Joseph H. Willits (editors)
1925   *What the Coal Commission Found: An Authoritative Summary by the Staff.* Foreword by John Hays Hammond. Williams & Wilkins Co., Baltimore.

Hunt, Lynn
1989   Introduction: History, Culture, and Text. In *The New Cultural History,* edited by Lynn Hunt, pp. 1–22. University of California Press, Berkeley.

Joyce, Dee Dee
1997   The Charleston Landscape on the Eve of the Civil War: Race, Class, and Ethnic Relations in Ward Five. In *Carolina's Historical Landscapes: Archaeological Perspectives,* edited by Linda F. Stine, Martha Zierden, Lesley M. Drucker, and Christopher Judge, pp. 175–185. University of Tennessee Press, Knoxville.

Kelso, William M., and Rachel Most (editors)
1990   *Earth Patterns: Essays in Landscape Archaeology.* University Press of Virginia, Charlottesville.

Kenny, Kevin
1998   *Making Sense of the Molly Maguires.* Oxford University Press, New York.

King, Julia A.

1996   "The Transient Nature of All Things Sublunary": Romanticism, History and Ruins in Nineteenth-Century Southern Maryland. In *Landscape Archaeology: Studies in Reading and Interpreting the Historical Landscape*, edited by Rebecca Yamin and Karen Bescherer Metheny, pp. 249–272. University of Tennessee Press, Knoxville.

Kirk, George

1929   *Pioneer Days in Brady Township*. Privately published. On file, DuBois Public Library, DuBois, Pennsylvania.

Korson, George

1943   *Coal Dust on the Fiddle: Songs and Stories of the Bituminous Industry*. University of Pennsylvania Press, Philadelphia.

1964   *Minstrels of the Mine Patch*. Folklore Associates, Hatboro, Pennsylvania.

Kriner, Raymond

1992   *History Notes*. Privately published.

Lalande, Jeffrey M.

1985   Sojourners in Search of Gold: Hydraulic Mining Techniques of the Chinese on the Oregon Frontier. *IA: The Journal of the Society for Industrial Archaeology* 11(1):29–52.

Lamphere, Louise

1987   *From Working Daughters to Working Mothers: Immigrant Women in a New England Industrial Community*. Cornell University Press, Ithaca.

Landon, David B.

1989   Domestic Ideology and the Economics of Boardinghouse Keeping. In Interdisciplinary Investigations of the Boott Mills, Lowell, Massachusetts. Vol. 3, The Boarding House System as a Way of Life, edited by Mary C. Beaudry and Stephen A. Mrozowski, pp. 37–47. Cultural Resources Management Series 21. Division of Cultural Resources, North Atlantic Regional Office, National Park Service, Boston.

1997   Interpreting the Social Relations of Production at Industrial Sites. Paper presented at the Annual Meeting of the Council for Northeast Historical Archaeology, Altoona, Pennsylvania.

2001   Faunal Remains from Helvetia, Pennsylvania. Unpublished report.

Lankton, Larry

1991   *From Cradle to Grave: Life, Work, and Death at the Lake Superior Copper Mines*. Oxford University Press, New York.

Laslett, Peter

1972   Introduction: The History of the Family. In *Household and Family in Past Time*, edited by Peter Laslett and Richard Wall, pp. 1–89. Cambridge University Press, New York.

Lehner, Lois

1988   *Lehner's Encyclopedia of U.S. Marks on Pottery, Porcelain, and Clay*. Collector Books, Paducah, Kentucky.

Leone, Mark P.

1988   The Georgian Order as the Order of Merchant Capitalism in Annapolis, Maryland. In *The Recovery of Meaning: Historical Archaeology in the Eastern United States*, edited by Mark P. Leone and Parker B. Potter Jr., pp. 235–261. Smithsonian Institution Press, Washington, D.C.

Leone, Mark P., Parker B. Potter Jr., and Paul A. Shackel
1987   Toward a Critical Archaeology. *Current Anthropology* 28(3):283–302.

Lewis, Ronald L.
1987   *Black Coal Miners in America: Race, Class, and Community Conflict, 1780–1980.* University Press of Kentucky, Lexington.

Long, Priscilla
1989   *Where the Sun Never Shines: A History of America's Bloody Coal Industry.* Paragon House, New York.

Magda, Matthew S.
1981   *Oral History in Pennsylvania: Summary Guide to the Oral History Collections in the Pennsylvania Historical and Museum Commission.* Pennsylvania Historical and Museum Commission, Harrisburg.

Magnusson, Leifur
1917   Employers' Housing in the United States. *Monthly Labor Review* 5:869–894. U.S. Dept. of Labor. Government Printing Office, Washington, D.C.

Markell, Ann
1992   Walls of Isolation: The Garden Fortress of Governor Willem Adraiaan van der Stel. Seminar paper for "Critical Views of the Material World." Centre for African Studies, University of Cape Town.

Markley, Richard E.
1992   An Archaeological Evaluation of Two Chinese Mining Camps on the North Yuba River, Sierra County, California. Report No. 37. USDA Forest Service, Tahoe National Forest.

Mayer, C. H.
1989   *The Continuing Struggle: Autobiography of a Labor Activist.* Pittenbruach Press, Northampton, Massachusetts.

McClymer, John F.
1986   Late Nineteenth-Century American Working-Class Living Standards. *Journal of Interdisciplinary History* 17(2):379–398.

McCreighton, I.
1938   *Memory Sketches of DuBois, Pennsylvania, 1874–1938: A History.* Gray Printing Co., DuBois, Pennsylvania.

McGuire, Randall H.
1991   Building Power in the Cultural Landscape of Broome County, New York, 1880 to 1940. In *The Archaeology of Inequality*, edited by Randall H. McGuire and Robert Paynter, pp. 102–124. Basil Blackwell, Oxford.

McKee, Larry
1996   The Archaeology of Rachel's Garden. In *Landscape Archaeology: Studies in Reading and Interpreting the Historical Landscape*, edited by Rebecca Yamin and Karen Bescherer Metheny, pp. 70–90. University of Tennessee Press, Knoxville.

Metheny, Andrew
n.d.   Metheny Family Genealogy. Unpublished manuscript in possession of the author.

Metheny, Karen Bescherer
1992   Oral Histories from the Industrial Workplace: A Look at Corporate Paternalism from the Inside. Seminar paper, AR 572, Industrial Archaeology, Department of Archaeology, Boston University.

| 1994 | Oral Histories from the Workplace: The Historical Archaeology of a Coal Company Town in Western Pennsylvania. Paper presented at the Annual Meetings of the Council for Northeast Historical Archaeology, Williamsburg, Virginia. |

1994   Oral Histories from the Workplace: The Historical Archaeology of a Coal Company Town in Western Pennsylvania. Paper presented at the Annual Meetings of the Council for Northeast Historical Archaeology, Williamsburg, Virginia.

1995   Daily Journal and Excavation Notes, Helvetia, Pennsylvania, July 10–Aug. 9.

1998   Guest lecture, Graduate Seminar AR775, Oral History and Written Records in Archaeology, Department of Archaeology, Boston University. Nov. 12.

2002   The Landscape of Industry and the Negotiation of Place: An Archaeological Study of Worker Agency in a Pennsylvania Coal Company Town, 1891–1947. Ph.D. dissertation, Department of Archaeology, Boston University. University Microfilms, Ann Arbor.

Michrina, Barry P.

1993   *Pennsylvania Mining Families: The Search for Dignity in the Coalfields.* University Press of Kentucky, Lexington.

Miller, Daniel

1987   *Material Culture and Mass Consumption.* Basil Blackwell, Oxford.

Miller, Daniel, and Christopher Tilley (editors)

1984   *Ideology, Power and Prehistory.* Cambridge University Press, Cambridge.

Miller, Donald L., and Richard E. Sharpless

1985   *The Kingdom of Coal: Work, Enterprise, and Ethnic Communities in the Mine Fields.* University of Pennsylvania Press, Philadelphia.

Montgomery Ward & Co.

1969   *Catalogue and Buyers' Guide, Spring and Summer, 1895.* Reprint. Dover Publications, New York.

Moore, Henrietta

1990   Paul Ricoeur: Action, Meaning and Text. In *Reading Material Culture,* edited by Christopher Tilley, pp. 85–120. Basil Blackwell, Oxford.

Moss, William

1996   Oral History: An Appreciation. In *Oral History: An Interdisciplinary Anthology,* edited by David K. Dunaway and Willa K. Baum, pp. 107–120. 2nd ed. AltaMira Press, Walnut Creek, California.

Mrozowski, Stephen

1991   Landscapes of Inequality. In *The Archaeology of Inequality,* edited by Randall H. McGuire and Robert Paynter, pp. 79–101. Basil Blackwell, Oxford.

Mullins, Paul R.

1992   Defining the Boundaries of Change: The Records of an Industrializing Potter. In *Text-Aided Archaeology,* edited by Barbara J. Little, pp. 179–193. CRC Press, Boca Raton, Florida.

1996   Negotiating Industrial Capitalism: Mechanisms of Change among Agrarian Potters. In *Historical Archaeology and the Study of American Culture,* edited by Lu Ann De Cunzo and Bernard L. Herman, pp. 151–184. Henry Francis du Pont Winterthur Museum, Winterthur, Delaware.

Mulrooney, Margaret M.

1989   A Legacy of Coal: The Coal Company Towns of Southwestern Pennsylvania. Historic American Buildings Survey/Historic American Engineering Record. America's Industrial Heritage Project. National Park Service, U.S. Dept. of Interior, Washington, D.C.

Murphy, Mary

1997   *Mining Cultures: Men, Women, and Leisure in Butte, 1914–41*. University of Illinois Press, Urbana.

Nichols, Janice Flood

1994   *DuBois Where and When, DuBois Now and Then*. Vol. 1. DuBois Area Historical Society, DuBois, Pennsylvania.

Oblinger, Carl

1984   *Cornwall: The People and Culture of an Industrial Camelot, 1890–1980*. Pennsylvania Historical and Museum Commission, Harrisburg.

1990   Interviewing the People of Pennsylvania: A Conceptual Guide to Oral History. Pennsylvania Historical and Museum Commission, Harrisburg.

O'Brien, Elizabeth, Joseph Balicki, Dana B. Heck, and Donna J. Seifert

1997   Detailed Background Research and Phase I Archeological Survey Maryland Route 36 in Lonaconing Streetscape Improvements, Allegany County, Maryland. Archeological Report 179. Prepared for Maryland State Highway Administration, Project Planning Division, Environmental Planning Section, Baltimore, MD. John Milner Associates, Alexandria, Virginia.

Ogundiran, Akinwumi

2000   Settlement Cycling and Regional Interactions in Central Yoruba-Land, AD 1200–1900: Archaeology and History in Ilare District, Nigeria. Ph.D. dissertation, Department of Archaeology, Boston University.

Orser, Charles E., Jr.

1996   *A Historical Archaeology of the Modern World*. Plenum Press, New York.

Paterlini de Koch, Olga

1992   Company Towns of Chile and Argentina. In *The Company Town: Architecture and Society in the Early Industrial Age*, edited by John S. Garner, pp. 207–232. Oxford University Press, New York.

Paynter, Robert

1988   Steps to an Archaeology of Capitalism: Material Change and Class Analysis. In *The Recovery of Meaning: Historical Archaeology in the Eastern United States*, edited by Mark P. Leone and Parker B. Potter Jr., pp. 407–433. Smithsonian Institution Press, Washington, D.C.

Paynter, Robert, and Randall H. McGuire

1991   The Archaeology of Inequality: Material Culture, Domination and Resistance. In *The Archaeology of Inequality*, edited by Randall H. McGuire and Robert Paynter, pp. 1–27. Basil Blackwell, Oxford.

Praetzellis, Mary, Adrian Praetzellis, and Marley R. Brown III

1988   What Happened to the Silent Majority? Research Strategies for Studying Dominant Material Culture in Late Nineteenth-Century California. In *Documentary Archaeology in the New World*, edited by Mary C. Beaudry, pp. 192–202. Cambridge University Press, Cambridge.

Prude, Jonathan

1983   *The Coming of Industrial Order: Town and Factory Life in Rural Massachusetts, 1810–1860*. Cambridge University Press, New York.

1987   The Social System of Early New England Textile Mills: A Case Study, 1812–1840. In *The New England Working Class and the New Labor History*, edited by Herbert G. Gutman and Donald. H. Bell, pp. 90–127. University of Illinois Press, Chicago.

Purser, Margaret

1992   Oral History and Historical Archaeology. In *Text-Aided Archaeology*, edited by Barbara J. Little, pp. 25–35. CRC Press, Boca Raton, Florida.

Reichler, Joseph L. (editor)

1984   *The Baseball Encyclopedia*. 7th ed. Macmillan, New York.

Richner, Jeffrey J.

1992   Archaeological Investigations at Old Munising (20AR192): A Nineteenth-Century Company Town. Occasional Studies in Anthropology No. 28. Midwest Archaeological Center, Lincoln, Nebraska.

Roberts, Ellis

1984   *The Breaker Whistle Blows: Mining Disasters and Labor Leaders in the Anthracite Region*. Anthracite Museum Press, Scranton, Pennsylvania.

Rodman, Margaret C.

1992   Empowering Place: Multilocality and Multivocality. *American Anthropologist* 94(3):640–656.

Rogers, Maria M.

1995   *In Other Words: Oral Histories of the Colorado Frontier*. Fulcrum Publishing, Golden, Colorado.

Rogers, J. Daniel, and Samuel M. Wilson

1993   *Ethnohistory and Archaeology: Approaches to Postcontact Change in the Americas*. Plenum Press, New York.

Rosaldo, Renato

1989   *Culture and Truth: The Remaking of Social Analysis*. Beacon Press, Boston.

Roth, Leland M.

1992   Company Towns in the Western United States. In *The Company Town: Architecture and Society in the Early Industrial Age*, edited by John S. Garner, pp. 173–205. Oxford University Press, New York.

Ryder, Robin L.

1988   "Why I Continue to Live Across the Tracks from Sister Sue," as Told by William Moore. *Historical Archaeology* 32(1):34–41.

Sahlins, Marshall

1981   *Historical Metaphors and Mythical Realities: Structure in the Early History of the Sandwich Islands Kingdom*. Association for Social Anthropology in Oceania Special Publications No. 1. University of Michigan Press, Ann Arbor.

1985   *Islands of History*. University of Chicago Press, Chicago.

Schmidt, Peter R.

1990   Oral Traditions, Archaeology and History: A Short Reflective History. In *A History of African Archaeology*, edited by Peter Robertshaw, pp. 252–270. James Currey, London, and Heinemann Educational Books, Portsmouth, NH.

Schmitt, Dave N., and Charles D. Zeier

1993   Not by Bones Alone: Exploring Household Composition and Socioeconomic Status in an Isolated Historic Mining Community. *Historical Archaeology* 27(4):20–38.

Schuyler, Robert L.

1978   The Spoken Word, the Written Word, Observed Behavior, and Preserved Behavior: The Contexts Available to the Archaeologist. In *Historical Archaeology: A Guide to Substantive and Theoretical Contributions*, edited by Robert L. Schuyler, pp. 269–277. Baywood Publishing Co., Farmingdale, New York.

Schwieder, Dorothy
    1983   *Black Diamonds: Life and Work in Iowa's Coal Mining Communities, 1895–1925.* Iowa State University Press, Ames.

Schwieder, Dorothy, Joseph Hraba, and Elmer Schwieder
    1987   *Buxton: Work and Racial Equality in a Coal Mining Community.* Iowa State University Press, Ames.

Scranton, Philip
    1984   Varieties of Paternalism: Industrial Structures and the Social Relations of Production in American Textiles. *American Quarterly* 36(2):235–257.

Sears, Roebuck, and Co.
    1969   *Consumers Guide, 1902, Catalogue No. 111.* Reprint. Crown Publishers, New York.
    1970   *Consumers Guide, Fall 1900, Catalogue No. 110.* Reprint. DBI Books, Northfield, Illinois.
    1983   *Consumers Guide, 1897, Catalogue No. 104.* Reprint. Chelsea House Publishers, New York.

Serrin, William
    1993   *Homestead: The Glory and Tragedy of an American Steel Town.* Vintage Books, New York.

Seymour, Harold
    1990   *Baseball: The People's Game.* Oxford University Press, New York.

Shackel, Paul A.
    1993a   Interdisciplinary Investigations of Domestic Life in Government Block B: Perspectives on Harpers Ferry's Armory and Commercial District. Occasional Report No. 6, Regional Archeology Program, National Capital Region, National Park Service, Department of the Interior.
    1993b   *Personal Discipline and Material Culture: An Archaeology of Annapolis, Maryland, 1695–1870.* University of Tennessee Press, Knoxville.
    1994   Domestic Responses to Nineteenth-Century Industrialization: An Archeology of Park Building 48, Harpers Ferry National Historic Park. Occasional Report No. 12, Regional Archeology Program, National Capital Region, National Park Service, Department of the Interior.
    1996   *Culture Change and the New Technology: An Archaeology of the Early American Industrial Era.* Plenum Press, New York.

Sheppard, Muriel Earley
    1947   *Cloud by Day: The Story of Coal and Coke and People.* University of North Carolina Press, Chapel Hill.

Shifflett, Crandall A.
    1991   *Coal Towns: Life, Work, and Culture in Company Towns of Southern Appalachia, 1880–1960.* University of Tennessee Press, Knoxville.

Shopes, Linda
    1993   Oral History in Pennsylvania: A Historiographical Overview. Special Issue: Oral History in Pennsylvania. *Pennsylvania History* 60(4):436–454.

Sisler, James D.
    1924   *Bituminous Coal Losses and Mining Methods in Pennsylvania.* Pennsylvania Geological Survey, 4th series. R. Y. Stuart, Secretary, Department of Forests and Waters for the Commonwealth of Pennsylvania.

Sitton, Thad, George L. Mehaffy, and O. L. Davis Jr.
  1983   *Oral History: A Guide for Teachers (and Others)*. University of Texas Press, Austin.

Spector, Janet
  1993   *What This Awl Means: Feminist Archaeology at a Wahpeton Dakota Village*. Minnesota Historical Society Press, St. Paul.

Starr, Louis
  1996   Oral History. In *Oral History: An Interdisciplinary Anthology*, edited by David K. Dunaway and Willa K. Baum, pp. 39–61. 2nd ed. AltaMira Press, Walnut Creek, California.

Tarbell, Ida M.
  1969   *The History of the Standard Oil Company*. 1904. Briefer version, edited by David M. Chalmers. W. W. Norton & Co., New York.

Terrell, Michelle
  2000   The Historical Archaeology of the 17th- and 18th-Century Jewish Community of Nevis, British West Indies. Ph.D. dissertation, Department of Archaeology, Boston University.

Thompson, E. P.
  1978   Eighteenth-Century English Society: Class Struggle without Class? *Social History* 3(2):133–165.

Thompson, Paul
  1978   *The Voice of the Past: Oral History*. Oxford University Press, Oxford.

Tilley, Christopher
  1990   Michel Foucault: Towards an Archaeology of Archaeology. In *Reading Material Culture: Structuralism, Hermeneutics and Post-Structuralism*, edited by Christopher Tilley, pp. 281–347. Basil Blackwell, Oxford.

Trigger, Bruce
  1989   *A History of Archaeological Thought*. Cambridge University Press, New York.

Trinder, Barrie
  1987   *The Making of the Industrial Landscape*. Alan Sutton, Gloucester, England.

Trotter, Joe William, Jr.
  1990   *Coal, Class, and Color: Blacks in Southern West Virginia, 1915–32*. University of Illinois Press, Urbana.

Turner, Arnie L.
  1982   The History and Archaeology of Fenelon, A Historic Railroad Camp. Technical Report No. 9. Contributions to the Study of Cultural Resources. Bureau of Land Management, Reno, Nevada.

Upton, Dell
  1990   Imagining the Early Virginia Landscape. In *Earth Patterns: Essays in Landscape Archaeology*, edited by William M. Kelso and Rachel Most, pp. 71–85. University Press of Virginia, Charlottesville.
  1992   The City as Material Culture. In *The Art and Mystery of Historical Archaeology: Essays in Honor of James Deetz*, edited by Anne Elizabeth Yentsch and Mary C. Beaudry, pp. 51–74. CRC Press, Boca Raton, Florida.

Van Bueren, Thad M. (editor)
  2002   Communities Defined by Work: Life in Western Work Camps. *Historical Archaeology* 36(3).

Vansina, Jan

1985   *Oral Tradition as History.* University of Wisconsin Press, Madison.

Walkowitz, Daniel J.

1978   *Worker City, Company Town: Iron and Cotton-Worker Protest in Troy and Cohoes, New York, 1855–84.* University of Illinois Press, Urbana.

Wallace, Anthony F. C.

1972   *The Death and Rebirth of the Seneca.* Vintage Books, New York.

1988   *St. Clair: A Nineteenth-Century Coal Town's Experience with a Disaster-Prone Industry.* Cornell University Press, Ithaca.

Warfel, Stephen G.

1993   *A Patch of Land Owned by the Company.* Pennsylvania Historical and Museum Commission, Harrisburg.

Wegars, Priscilla

1991   Who's Been Workin' on the Railroad? An Examination of the Construction, Distribution, and Ethnic Origins of Domed Rock Ovens on Railroad-Related Sites. *Historical Archaeology* 25(1):37–65.

Wolf, Eric R.

1982   *Europe and the People without History.* University of California Press, Berkeley.

Wood, Margaret C.

2002   "Fighting for our Homes": Archaeology and the Transformation of Women's Domestic Labor in a Working-Class, Coal Mining Community in Colorado, 1900–1930. Ph.D. dissertation, Department of Anthropology, Syracuse University.

Worrell, John, David M. Simmons, and Myron O. Stachiw

1996   Archaeology from the Ground Up. In *Historical Archaeology and the Study of American Culture,* edited by Lu Ann De Cunzo and Bernard L. Herman, pp. 35–69. Henry Francis du Pont Winterthur Museum, Winterthur, Delaware.

Wright, Gwendolyn

1981   Welfare Capitalism and the Company Town. In *Building the Dream: A Social History of Housing in America,* by Gwendolyn Wright, pp. 177–192. Pantheon Books, New York.

Wylie, Alison

1993   Invented Lands/Discovered Pasts: The Westward Expansion of Myth and History. *Historical Archaeology* 27(4):1–19.

Yamin, Rebecca (editor)

1998   Tales of Five Points: Working-Class Life in Nineteenth-Century New York. 6 vols. John Milner Associates, Philadelphia.

1999   With Hope and Labor: Everyday Life in Paterson's Dublin Neighborhood. Data Recovery on Blocks 863 and 866 within the Route 19 Connector Corridor in Paterson, New Jersey. 2 vols. John Milner Associates, Philadelphia.

2001   Becoming New York: The Five Points Neighborhood. *Historical Archaeology* 35(3).

Yamin, Rebecca, and Sarah Bridges

1996   Farmers and Gentlemen Farmers: The Nineteenth-Century Suburban Landscape. In *Landscape Archaeology: Reading and Interpreting the American Historical Landscape,* edited by Rebecca Yamin and Karen Bescherer Metheny, pp. 175–192. University of Tennessee Press, Knoxville.

Yamin, Rebecca, and Karen Bescherer Metheny (editors)

1996   *Landscape Archaeology: Reading and Interpreting the American Historical Landscape*. University of Tennessee Press, Knoxville.

Yentsch, Anne

1975   Understanding Seventeenth- and Eighteenth-Century Colonial Families: An Experiment in Historical Ethnography. Master's thesis, Department of Anthropology, Brown University.

1980   Expressions of Cultural Diversity and Social Reality in Seventeenth-Century New England. Ph.D. dissertation, Brown University.

1988   Legends, Houses, Families, and Myths: Relationships between Material Culture and American Ideology. In *Documentary Archaeology in the New World*, edited by Mary C. Beaudry, pp. 5–19. Cambridge University Press, Cambridge.

1991   The Symbolic Divisions of Pottery: Sex-Related Attributes of English and Anglo-American Household Pots. In *The Archaeology of Inequality*, edited by Randall H. McGuire and Robert Paynter, pp. 192–230. Basil Blackwell, Oxford.

1996   Close Attention to Place: Landscape Studies by Historical Archaeologists. In *Landscape Archaeology: Studies in Reading and Interpreting the Historical Landscape*, edited by Rebecca Yamin and Karen Bescherer Metheny, pp. xxiii–xliii. University of Tennessee Press, Knoxville.

Yow, Valerie Raleigh

1994   *Recording Oral History: A Practical Guide for Social Scientists*. Sage Publications, Thousand Oaks, California.

Zeier, Charles D.

1987   Historic Charcoal Production Near Eureka, Nevada: An Archaeological Perspective. *Historical Archaeology* 21(1):81–101.

Zonderman, David A.

1992   *Aspirations and Anxieties: New England Workers and the Mechanized Factory System, 1815–1850*. Oxford University Press, New York.

Index

coal company town, (cont.)
34, 36, 39, 65–67, 135, 137, 262n2; corporate hierarchy in housing, 25, 26, 30; corporate paternalism in, 37–40; ethnic diversity of, 63, 139, 239–40, 241; eviction from company housing, 32, 38, 39, 64–65, 96, 131, 233, 265n17; gardening competitions, 54, 122; gardens, 29, 128, **187**, 200, 219, **224**; housing, 25–29, **30**, 31–32, **33**, **34**, **35**, 36, **37**, 38; investment in, 27, 28, 30, 36, 55; living conditions, 27–29, 32, 36, 38–40, 205; medical care, 28, 38, 39; model coal company town, 28, 220; outbuildings, 29, 33, 36, 200; ownership of land, 27, 30, 32, 34, 40, 72; physical isolation of, 25, 27, 32, 36, 55; prejudicial treatment in, 25–27, 28, 29, 30, 36, 38, 63, 261n8, 263n8; regional housing forms, 26, 27, 29–32, 33, 34–35, 36; schools, 25, 26, 33, 34, 36, 38; standardization, 25–27, 29–32, **33**, 36, **37**; tenancy in company housing, 41, 63–65, 131, 202; town planning, 25–27, 28, 29–32, **33**, 34–36, **37**, 38; water supply, 28, 29, 32, 33
coal industry, 26, 27, 28, 29, 30, 35, 36, 38–40, 44, 53, 58, 60, 74, 75, 86, 87–88, 92, 112–14, 115, 117–18, 150, 176, 241; coercive practices, 32, 38–39, 61, 62, 143, 265n17; economic conditions, 27, 28–29, 39–40, 44, 58, 74, 117, 137; hazards, 87, 88, 99, 115–17, 156, 236, 237, 240, 263n8; paternalism in, 37, 40; practices, 37, 40, 59, 60, 61, 65, 67, 85, 112–15, 135, 177; railroad interests, 27, 28, 32, 35; recruitment of immigrant labor, 87; strikes, 28, 38, 40, 65, 117, 152, 232, 236, 260n6, 265n17, 266n13; tonnage system, 111, 112–13, 114, 115, 137, 176–77, 232, 268n10; unionization, 38, 39, 40, 58, 59, 60, 65, 117–18, 149, 160, 239, 263n9; violence in, 38–39, 61–62, 76, 117, 233, 268n16
coal miners, geographic mobility of, 36, 92, 233, 266n6; mining as a trade, 82, 84, 87, 98, 104, 105–8, 150, 234, 267n3; training of, 82, 98, 234

coal mining, methods of, 104–18
coke industry, 11, 12, 27, 35, 205, 261n9, 272n4
Colorado Fuel and Iron Company, 29, 261n8
company towns, xv, xxi, 1–23; definition, xv, 1–5, 7; churches, xv, 4, 11, 26, 33, 34, 36, 38; company-sponsored activities, 4–5, 17, 21, 22; company store, xv, 4, 9, 18; conflict in, 1–2, 5, 14, 15–17, 18, 20, 22; ethnic diversity of, 14, 22; eviction from company housing, 11, 14; expressions of ethnic prejudice, 14; function of, 1–2, 3, 13–15, 18–20; housing, xv, 10, 11, 14, 22; ideology of, 1–2, 5–7, 8–11, 12, 13–15, 17–22; link to transportation networks, 2–3, 11–13, 260n2; living conditions, 1–2, 14, 18; location, 1–3, 13; model company towns, 2, 4–5, 7, 18–20, 53, 55, 261n8; ownership, xv, 1–2, 9, 12, 13–14; population, 4; sanitation, 1, 28, 32; schools, xv, 4, 9, 11, 21; tenancy in company housing, xv, xvi, 9, 202–4; town planning, xvi, 1–2, 3–5, 7–8, 13, 18–20, 22; water supply, 1, 21, 202
controlled leisure time, 18, 22
corporate ideology, xviii–xix, xxii, xxiv, xxv, xxvi, 2, 5, 7, 12, 13, 14–15, 17, 18–20, 22, 23; opposition to, xxiv, xxvi, 41, 61, 176–77
corporate paternalism, xv, xix, xx, xxi, xxvi, xxvii, xxviii, xxix, 1–25, 260n4, 261n5; definition, 5–7, 8, 9; use in the textile industry, 8–11, 22, 25; use in other industries, 11–15, 17, 21

DuBois, Pennsylvania, 28, **43**, 44, 46, 61, 69, 71, 105, 110, 118, 129, 135, 140, 146, 221, 255, 267n3

Eckley, Pennsylvania, 32, **33**, **34**, 35–36; archaeological excavations, 32–36, 161; housing, 33, **34**, 36; oral history, 32–33

65, 118, 131, 232; recruitment of immigration labor, 45, 59, 71, 82–86, 265n16; relationship with Buffalo, Rochester and Pittsburgh Railroad, 42, 45, 263n2; schools, donation of land and funds for, 48, 49, 55, 68, 75, 90, 137, 139, 246; social and economic controls, 53–57, 58–59, 61–68, 100–102, 117–18, 131–32, 135–37, 143–49, 206, 226–27, 240, 243–47, 264n12, 269n22; tenancy, 41, 44, 68, 70, 118, 162, 171, 182, 183, 201–2, 203–4, 206, 218, 228–29, 233; tenant-landlord relationship, 63–65, 96–97, 149, 202–4, 206–16, 228–29, 231–32, 233; welfare capitalism, influence of, 41, 52–57, 118, 147, 243–47

Rochester & Pittsburgh Coal League, 57, 67, 115, 142, 143–44, **145**, 146–48, 151, 156, 226

Rockefeller, John D., Jr., 21, 29

Rock Springs, Wyoming, 261n8

St. Anthony's Church, 49, **51**, 63, 71, 100, 137, 175, 238

Slater, Samuel, 4, 9, 261n6

southwestern Pennsylvania coal towns, 29–32, 36, **37**, 86, 146, 199, 262n4, 272n4

Standard Oil Corporation, 21

Stanley, Pennsylvania, **43**, 44, 45, 46, 48, 122, 264n8, 269n28

steel industry, 12, 35, 42, 85–86, 261n8, 262n6

Sykesville, Pennsylvania, **43**, 44, 46, 120, 129, 135, 269n28

textile mills, 2–4, 6–7, 8–11, 15–17, 19, 25; paternalism in, 6–7, 8–11, 22, 25

textile workers, 6, 9, 10–11, 15–17, 18, 22

Troutville, Pennsylvania, **43**, 44, 78, 118, 120

Union Pacific Railroad, 27, 28

unions, industrial, xv, xvi, xx, 14, 16, 18, 19, 20, 22, 148

United Mine Workers of America, 60, 87, 117, 176–77, **177**, 179, 265n15, 266n16

U.S. Coal Commission, 28, 117, 266n9

Virden, Illinois, 261n8

Waltham system, 3–4, 6, 10–11

welfare capitalism, 5, 9, 18–20, 21–22, 39, 53, 260n5

Whiting, Indiana, 21

worker agency, xvi–xvii, xx–xxii, xxvi, xxix

worker housing, xxiv, 1–2, 3–4, 6, 7, 9, 10, 11, 12–15, 16–18, 22, 25–26, 169, 174, 267n18; boardinghouses, xxiv, 4, 6, 11, 16–17, 22, 34; temporary camps, 1, 2, 4, 12, 13, 249

worker responses to industrial regimen, 15, 16, 10, 20, 22, 261n8

working classes, xv, xxii, xxiv; archaeological studies of, xvi, xviii–xxi, xxiv, xxv, xxvi, 17, 32–33, 36, 104, 160–61, 168–69, 173, 174–75, 177, 207, 219, 260n6, 270n4, 271n2; disposable income, 160, 270n2; ethnic diversity of, xix, xx, xxi, xxvi, 22, 79, 86, 87–88, 102, 139, 141, 160, 174–75, 186, 219, 271n1; geographic mobility of, 7, 9, 15, 16, 174, 261n10; identity, 104, 157, 159–61, 168–69, 174, 176, 177, 179, 206, 222–23, 231, 237, 240–41, 242, 260n7, 263n9; income-earning strategies, 9, 86, 234, 235, 236; models of study, xv–xix, xxv; preferences, xxiv, 17, 168–69, 173–76, 177, 179, 195, 198–99, 206, 207, 219, 222–23, 270n2, 270nn4–5; standards of living, 160–61, 168–69, 177, 198–99; working-class culture, xvii, xviii–xxii, xxiv

FROM THE MINERS' DOUBLEHOUSE was designed and typeset on a Macintosh computer system using QuarkXPress software. The body text is set in 9.5/12.5 Goudy and display type is set in Goudy SC. This book was designed and typeset by Kelly Gray and manufactured by Thomson-Shore, Inc.